Perspectives
on Antitrust Policy

Perspectives on Antitrust Policy

EDITED BY

ALMARIN PHILLIPS

PRINCETON, NEW JERSEY
PRINCETON UNIVERSITY PRESS
1965

L. C. Card: 64-19822
Printed in the United States of America
by Murray Press

Preface

The essays collected in this volume were presented at a Seminar in Antitrust Policy at the University of Virginia during the Spring Term, 1963. The Seminar was initiated by the faculty of the Graduate School of Business Administration and was offered jointly to students of that School, the Law School, and graduate students in economics. The Seminar was supported by a grant from the McKinsey Foundation for Management Research, Inc. and by the Sponsors of the Graduate School of Business Administration, University of Virginia.

While each of the chapters is a separate essay, their arrangement is intended to provide some continuity of topics. The first three comprise a general introduction and the reader will find in them at least summary treatment of most of the issues raised in the subsequent papers. Chapters 4 through 14 present individual policy issues in depth. The concluding three chapters are again general, but reflect the particular views of corporate counsel, labor, and management.

The arrangement of topics was not intended to develop a particular, unified thesis with respect to competitive policy. On the contrary, the participants were selected not only for their expertise but also to assure that a range of opinion and analysis was presented. The participants include economists, practicing attorneys, law school professors, businessmen, labor organization representatives, and government officials. Some question the relevance of the entire effort to maintain competition; others decry what they regard as the diminishing role of competition in guiding economic decisions. Fears that current antitrust ruling impedes and restricts business management are countered with arguments that without more aggressive enforcement of the antitrust laws still more monopoly will prevail. The view that many policies protect inefficient small firms is juxtaposed with a proposal to extend *per se* rules to prohibit selected types of behavior by large firms. One author would apply antitrust principles to labor organizations and others would maintain the current exempt status of unions. In short, the entire collection is designed to illustrate the controversial aspects of competitive policy rather than to settle issues or to describe the current state of affairs.

The McKinsey Foundation, in making its grant for financial support, emphasized that the success of the program from its point of view depended largely on whether these matters could be brought to the attention of a broad segment of the public — intelligent laymen in all walks of life as well as students, professors, and practitioners of antitrust law. The Foundation and the faculty of the Graduate School of Business Administration felt that these were issues of sufficient importance in the ultimate determination of the nation's political, social, and economic organization that the widest possible audience should be reached. That was the purpose of the Seminar and, in particular, of the publication of this book.

I am deeply indebted to many persons for whatever success may have been achieved. Dean Charles C. Abbott and members of the faculty of the Graduate School of Business Administration were extraordinarily cooperative and helpful throughout the program. Professors James R. Ferguson and George R. Hall, of the Department of Economics, and Professor Laurens H. Rhinelander, of the Law School, assisted in the organization and conduct of the Seminar from its beginning. Mr. Warren M. Cannon, of the McKinsey Foundation, proffered many valuable suggestions as well as encouragement. The participants – our guests for brief intervals each week – were as congenial as they were provocative and, above all, were mindful of the demanding deadlines necessary to make a volume such as this possible.

I wish finally to give special thanks to Mrs. Nancy Dupree. She performed the onerous tasks of typing manuscripts and correspondence and of looking after the many administrative details of the Seminar with such goodwill and efficiency as to be a constant source of amazement.

Almarin Phillips

Philadelphia, May 1964

Contributors

WALTER ADAMS Professor of Economics, Michigan State University; Member, Attorney General's National Committee to Study the Antitrust Laws.

M. A. ADELMAN Professor of Economics, Massachusetts Institute of Technology; Member, Attorney General's National Committee to Study the Antitrust Laws.

H. THOMAS AUSTERN Partner, Covington and Burling; Member, Attorney General's National Committee to Study the Antitrust Laws; Chairman, Section of the Antitrust Law of the American Bar Association.

GORDON F. BLOOM President, Elm Farm Foods Company.

WARD S. BOWMAN, Jr. Professor of Economics and Law, Law School, Yale University; formerly Economic Expert and Economic Consultant, Antitrust Division, Department of Justice.

KINGMAN BREWSTER, JR. President, Yale University, formerly Professor of Law, Harvard University.

JOHN J. CORSON Partner, McKinsey & Company, Inc. and Professor of Public and International Affairs, Woodrow Wilson School, Princeton University.

DONALD J. DEWEY Associate Professor of Economics, Columbia University.

NAT GOLDFINGER Director of Research, American Federation of Labor and Congress of Industrial Organizations.

RICHARD B. HEFLEBOWER Professor of Economics, Northwestern University; formerly Member of the Senior Staff, The Brookings Institution.

RICHARD H. HOLTON Assistant Secretary of Commerce for Economic Affairs; Professor of Economics, University of California at Berkeley.

LUCILE SHEPPARD KEYES Private Consulting and Research, Washington, D.C.

JESSE W. MARKHAM Professor of Economics, Princeton University; formerly Chief Economist, Federal Trade Commission.

GEORGE W. MITCHELL Member, Board of Governors of the Federal Reserve System; formerly Vice President, Federal Reserve Bank of Chicago.

HERBERT R. NORTHRUP Professor of Industry, Wharton School of Finance and Commerce, University of Pennsylvania; formerly Employee Relations Consultant, General Electric Company.

MERTON J. PECK Professor of Economics, Yale University; formerly Member of the Senior Staff, The Brookings Institution.

LOUIS B. SCHWARTZ Professor of Law, University of Pennsylvania; Member, Attorney General's National Committee to Study the Antitrust Laws; formerly with Antitrust Division, Department of Justice.

THEODORE V. ST. ANTOINE Partner, Woll, Mayer and St. Antoine; Assistant to the General Counsel, American Federation of Labor and Congress of Industrial Organizations.

LAURENCE I. WOOD Vice President and General Counsel and Secretary, General Electric Company; Member, Attorney General's National Committee to Study the Antitrust Laws; Member, Council of the Section of the Antitrust Law, American Bar Association.

Contents

Preface v

Contributors viii

Chapter 1 3
Problems and Prospects in Antitrust Policy-I
by H. Thomas Austern

Chapter 2 32
Problems and Prospects in Antitrust Policy-II
by M. A. Adelman

Chapter 3 50
Problems and Prospects in Antitrust Policy-III
by Ward S. Bowman, Jr.

Chapter 4 62
Competitive Policy and National Goals:
The Doubtful Relevance of Antitrust
by Donald Dewey

Chapter 5 88
Conscious Parallelism and Administered Prices
by R. B. Heflebower

Chapter 6 117
Monopoly, Monopolizing, and Concentration of
Market Power: A Proposal
by Louis B. Schwartz

Chapter 7 129
The Problem of the "Good" Trust
by Lucile Sheppard Keyes

Chapter 8 164
Mergers: The Adequacy of the New Section 7
by Jesse W. Markham

Chapter 9 189
Antitrust Policy and Small Business
by Richard H. Holton

Chapter 10 225
Mergers Among Commercial Banks
by George W. Mitchell

Chapter 11 244
Competitive Policy for Transportation?
by Merton J. Peck

Chapter 12 273
Exemptions from Antitrust: Their Extent and Rationale
by Walter Adams

Chapter 13 312
Labor Unions and the Antitrust Laws: Past, Present, and Proposals
by Herbert R. Northrup and Gordon F. Bloom

Chapter 14 355
The Influence of International Factors
by Kingman Brewster, Jr.

Chapter 15 368
Antitrust Policy: A View from Corporate Counsel
by Laurence I. Wood

Chapter 16 391
A View from Labor
by Nat Goldfinger and Theodore J. St. Antoine

Chapter 17 426
The Impact of Antitrust Law on Corporate Management
by John J. Corson

Index 445

Table of Cases 451

Perspectives on Antitrust Policy

CHAPTER 1

Problems and Prospects in Antitrust Policy – I

BY H. THOMAS AUSTERN

Introduction

It is perhaps unfortunate yet singularly appropriate that this volume on antitrust policy – which through several of the next chapters is to be illuminated by so many learned economists, experienced administrators, and other profound scholars in the field of public affairs – should begin with a lawyer.

For whether we like it or not, antitrust policy in this country is manifested in Congressional enactments and judicial decision. Of course, other disciplines and diverse talents have now vastly intruded into the carrying on of government. Indeed, these newcomers are not only economists, but also biologists, statisticians, political scientists, semanticists, and even sanitary engineers. But the job of legislative drafting, advisory interpretation, and judicial persuasion and explication is still happily and rigidly fenced off for lawyers. Occasionally, law professors may be heard along with practicing lawyers.

Yet with all of their supposed channelized modes of thought and, as viewed by others, extremely narrow predicates, lawyers have an abiding sense of history. In the field of American antitrust, much of what is said and invariably the inarticulated premises of what is done, are historically derived.

H. Thomas Austern

Origins of the American Concept of Antitrust

Despite the legal patter about roots in the English Common Law and in the struggles with Crown monopolies, I believe that the concept of "antitrust" is as American as apple pie. As an article of political faith, it is a unique home product, even today only vaguely echoed in Canada and Australia and lately in the European Common Market. For its roots one probably must look to American frontier, or more precisely, middle-border, thinking and economics.

In a nation which grew by conquest of a continent, each man was free to make his own stake, usually in farming or in trade. If one felt cramped, he could always move on and take up new land. If he failed in business, there was always an opportunity to the West. No energetic man was shackled by a place, a system, or an unhappy economic circumstance. The small man, on his own and largely self-sufficient, expressed the ideal American way of life. Out of that political feeling emerged the Homestead Act of 1862,[1] passed by a Republican Congress and sponsored by President Lincoln. Offered to all who would take them were 160 acres of the public domain. Instead of the plantation aristocracy of the old South, there was the continued hope for a nation of small farmers and small manufacturers and small merchants.

But two nineteenth century developments in great measure frustrated those desires. The railroads followed the Western settlers, bringing both Eastern goods and dependence upon Eastern markets. And by 1890 the frontier had disappeared. Free or even cheap land was no longer available, and the freedom of the wide open spaces was lost. As Charles Beard has re-

1. 12 Stat. 392 (1862).

marked, American frontier life "was finally reduced to the economic laws of older societies."[2]

Yet many frontier and middle-border ideas persisted in American political thinking. Most vigorous was that of economic freedom. However phrased by lawmakers – antimonopoly, restraint of trade, or later antitrust – the underlying feeling was simply that no one should be permitted to get so big that he could overreach his neighbors and, particularly, that nonlocal ownership should not exert economic control or pressure. If either of these forms of expansion occurred, the offender should be "cut down to size." In early America, long before the necessities of mass production evolved, nobody could get "too big for his britches" in business or anything else.

The age and hardihood of that antimonopoly feeling as a slogan of political action must never be forgotten. Since almost the earliest political platform, that of 1848, an antimonopoly pledge has appeared in the political creed of *every* major political party. Indeed, in 1884, an Antimonopoly Party joined with the Greenbackers. Even Mark Hanna astutely saw to it that the Republican platform of 1900 condemned monopolies and favored remedial legislation.

In the case of the railroads, against which much of the early political ire was directed, translation of antitrust feeling into Congressional action saw the creation of the Interstate Commerce Commission in 1887, the conferring of the power to nullify discriminatory rates in 1906, the complete power to fix rates in 1910, and comprehensive control of financing, merger, and development in 1920.[3] Here the end product – where

2. Charles and Mary Beard, *The Rise of American Civilization* (New York, 1930), vol. II, p. 269.
3. See generally J. L. Sharfman, *The Interstate Commerce Commission* (New York, 1931), vol. I, pp. 1-70, 177-244.

the monopoly of an exclusive seller was inherent—was all-embracing public utility regulation which has since developed to encompass pipelines, communications, natural gas, and to a lesser extent, trucking and atomic power.[4]

Yet no small part of the antimonopoly surge which developed in the nineteenth century was directed at what were termed "corporate abuses" and business "trusts and combinations" which, to quote an 1888 platform, "rob the body of our citizens by depriving them of the benefits of natural competition."[5] The targets were the "trusts" and their practices which impinged on a free market and the economic opportunities of the little fellow. In primitive forms these included squeezing out smaller competitors by localized price-cutting, buying them out, giving and getting secret rebates, controlling production by combining all manufacturers, and fixing and holding prices.

Opportunities for new enterprises were stifled, and existing small enterprises were crushed. Added to these were the frequent quarterdeck manners of many industrial leaders which fanned political hostility. Primarily, it was believed in 1890, these activities and attitudes were made possible only by combinations among manufacturers to suppress competition or to monopolize the production and market for a particular commodity. The resulting aggregations, "the trusts," were to be destroyed by Congressional direction.

Paradoxically, the Senator who gave his name to the Sherman Antitrust Act of 1890 had very little to do with the supposed legislative panacea which was final-

4. See generally 49 U.S.C. §§ 1-124, 301-327, 1001-1022 (1958) (pipelines and trucking); 47 U.S.C. §§ 1-609 (1958) (communications); 15 U.S.C. § 717 (1958) (natural gas); 42 U.S.C. §§ 2011-2296 (1958) (atomic power).

5. Thomas H. McKee, *National Conventions and Platforms* (Baltimore, 1906), p. 235.

ly enacted. Two Draconian provisions were added to federal law. *All* combinations (and conspiracies and contracts) "in restraint of trade" were declared unlawful. "Monopolizing" or attempting to monopolize were prohibited. Violation was made a misdemeanor punishable by a fine of not more than $5,000, up to one year imprisonment, or both. Injunctions to break up combinations by court decree were authorized. More important for present-day scrutiny, the aid of the private citizen in law enforcement was sought by offering a threefold recovery of damages in a private suit by persons injured by violation.[6]

All of the then conventional legal weapons for slaying the monopoly dragon were thus forged. Any large, oppressive monopoly – whether created by contract, trust, conspiracy, or merger – could be prosecuted, the guilty punished, and the business aggregation fragmented and cut down to size.

What happened? For about twenty years, almost *nothing.* Lax and often inept enforcement combined with Supreme Court conservatism – reaching a high watermark in the 1895 *Knight*[7] decision that federal law could not control manufacturing because it was purely local and intrastate – rendered the Sherman Act a paper statute until 1911. Even more paradoxical, the period from 1895 to 1905 – when the Supreme Court backtracked to hold that two railroads could not be consolidated into the Northern Securities holding company[8] – witnessed an accelerated growth of corporate mergers, many of gigantic proportions. This period saw the birth of the original Standard Oil Company, United States Steel, American Can, International Harvester, and many other companies representing a

6. 26 Stat. 209 (1890).
7. *U.S.* v. *E. C. Knight Co.*, 156 U.S. 1 (1895).
8. *Northern Securities Co.* v. *U.S.* 193 U.S. 197 (1903).

total capitalization of $5 billion. Theodore Roosevelt remarked caustically that "antitrust legislation was as effective as a papal bull against a comet."[9]

In May 1911 the Supreme Court decreed the dissolution of the Standard Oil Company[10] and the American Tobacco Company[11] as monopolies and combinations in restraint of trade. In doing so, however, Chief Justice White announced the now famous "rule of reason." Much simplified, this read into the Sherman Act the word "unreasonable" as modifying "restraint of trade." *Every* sales contract, said the Court, monopolizes the transaction concerned, and is a restraint of trade in the particular goods bought and sold. Every act of competitive selling is therefore a minuscule monopoly and restraint. Congress could not have intended to destroy the very competition it had tried to protect. Therefore, the Sherman Act reached only "unreasonable" restraints of trade, *and left it to the courts* to say what was lawful and what was criminal.

Whether this made the Sherman Act a "charter of freedom," as Chief Justice Hughes later called it,[12] or merely made the best of bad Congressional drafting has been much fought over. But what it did beyond argument was to reawaken the clamor for more and better "antitrust laws." Response to this sensitive political nerve impulse was immediately reflected in the 1912 presidential campaign by Democrats, Republicans, and Bull Moose Progressives alike. All three beat the antimonopoly tom-tom hard. In enacting the antitrust laws of 1914 all parties joined with enthusiasm.

9. Beard, *op. cit.*, vol. II, fn. 2, p. 569.
10. *Standard Oil Co. of New Jersey* v. *U.S.*, 221 US. (1911).
11. *U.S.* v. *American Tobacco Co.* 221 U.S. 106 (1911).
12. *Appalachian Coals, Inc.* v. *U.S.*, 288 U.S. 344, 359 (1933).

To buttress the Sherman law, the Clayton Act was added.[13] Price discrimination (except to meet competition or to reflect differences in sale or delivery costs), sales or leases of goods on the promise not to deal with a competitor, interlocking directorates, and the purchase of the stock of a competing company – each of these was prohibited *where the effect "may be substantially to lessen competition or tend to create a monopoly in any line of commerce."* That qualifying phrase – making acts unlawful in terms of their probable consequences – may have reflected the desire to avoid the broad-axe drafting of the Sherman Act into which the Supreme Court had read the "rule of reason." But the change in emphasis had three important consequences which have not even today borne full fruit.

The first was that in vast measure it still left to the courts (or to the newly created Federal Trade Commission)[14] the job of deciding what particular business conduct was proper and what was unlawful. What

13. 38 Stat. 730 (1914).

14. For the story of how the Congressional arguments about the Clayton Act led to the creation of the Federal Trade Commission and the new concept of "unfair methods of competition," see H. Thomas Austern, "The Parentage and Administrative Ontogeny of the Federal Trade Commission," *Antitrust Symposiums*, New York State Bar Association, vol. 4 (1955), p. 83. Curiously, the Republicans alone in 1912 had recommended the creation of a Federal Trade Commission to take over "many of the functions now necessarily exercised by the courts" and claimed full credit for the Sherman Act of 1890 to which they pledged "the enactment of legislation supplementary to the existing antitrust act which will define as criminal offenses those specific acts that uniformly mark attempts to restrain and to monopolize trade. . . ." The Democratic platform regretted that "the Sherman antitrust law has received a judicial construction depriving it of much of its efficiency" and favored "the enactment of legislation which will restore to the statute the strength of which it has been deprived by such interpretation." The Progressives were most explicit, and promised to legislate against restriction of production, division of sales territories, exclusive dealing, and local price-cutting.

might be a *substantial* lessening of competition is still, fifty years later, not always clear. Probability of effect, at least in the hands of the Federal Trade Commission, was in 1948 judicially declared to mean "reasonable possibility" of effect.[15] As applied in determining the legality of price discrimination or the lawfulness of a merger, the differing parameters of a "mere possibility" (lawful) and a "probability" (unlawful) of lessening competition continue even today to baffle both lawyers and economists.

Not until 1929 was it ruled that "any line of commerce" included competition among customers as well as among sellers so that charging a discriminatory higher price as well as localized price-cutting was unlawful.[16] And what constitutes "meeting competition in good faith" continues in a swamp of intricate semantic argument that is as uncertain as it is removed from market reality.[17]

Another aspect of the Clayton Act was that it did very little to establish the hoped-for *certainty* as to what was lawful. The Sherman Act provisions had been sweeping; by judicial barbering they had been trimmed back to forbid only "unreasonable" restraints; but the resulting uncertainty of meaning and inefficacy appeared hardly to have been remedied by the Clay-

15. *F.T.C.* v. *Morton Salt Co.*, 334 U.S. 37, 46 (1948); *Corn Products Refining Co.* v. *F.T.C.*, 324 U.S. 726 (1945).

16. *George Van Camp & Sons Co.* v. *American Can Co.*, 278 U.S. 245 (1929), overruling, *Mennen Co.* v. *F.T.C.*, 288 Fed. 774 (2d Cir. 1923), cert. denied, 262 U.S. 759 (1923); *National Biscuit Co.* v. *F.T.C.*, 299 Fed. 733 (2d Cir. 1924), cert. denied, 266 U.S. 613 (1924), see Note, *Harvard Law Review*, vol. 42 (1929), p. 680.

17. *See F.T.C.* v. *Sun Oil Co.*, 371 U.S. 505 (1963); *Sunshine Biscuit, Inc*, F.T.C. Docket 7708 (1961), rev'd., 306 F. 2d 48 (7th Cir. 1962), and *Forster Manufacturing Co., Inc.*, F.T.C. Docket 7207 (1963).

ton Act's delusive specificity of what was now to be prohibited only when it was *likely* to have the effect of *probably* and *substantially* lessening competition.

Most important, however, was the inherent shift in 1914 in the Clayton Act away from a direct attack on monopoly – founded on combination and agreement to restrain trade – to an assault on the supposed *symptoms* of oppressive business conduct. This was not the intent, or for that matter the theory, of the framers of the Act. They believed – and said so in creating the Federal Trade Commission – that they were seeking to prohibit practices which if unchecked would flower into monopolistic corporations or illegal combinations of oppressive size and tactics. The Sherman Act had failed directly to stop this growth and was apparently then ineffectual in breaking up large aggregations illegally evolved or maintained. The remedy might well have been better legislation trained on the main target. Instead, the Congress aimed at prohibiting specific practices – price discrimination, unreasonable tying arrangements, buying of stock in competing companies – which were supposedly the indicia of monopoly and might lead to it.

This indirection of itself may have been sound as a means of curbing illegal combinations, but it has had exceedingly important and sometimes bizarre consequences to every businessman small and large. For while a particular selling or buying practice carried on by a company dominant in the market may tend unlawfully to lessen competition, the same methods pursued by a smaller concern may be both economically harmless and truly competitive.[18] American antitrust antipathy and apprehension were not originally direct-

18. On this point, see below Chapter 9, by Richard H. Holton, and Chapter 6, by Louis B. Schwartz.

ed against the little fellow. Any experienced antitrust lawyer knows and acts on this perhaps inarticulate premise in dealing with the Sherman Act. But once the statutes and decisions departed from the main road of combination, overreaching, and oppressive tactics, and talked in terms of specific business methods, the lightning of illegality might strike the little fellow as well as the industrial giants.

This dealing with symptoms, instead of the underlying disease, which began in the Clayton Act of 1914 was later carried over into the amendatory Robinson-Patman Act of 1936,[19] and is the principal source of much of the current uncertainty as to the impact of many of the recent decisions. It gathers weight from the dual enforcement structure—public and private. And although the Federal Trade Commission says that it will select for prosecution only those who are large enough to threaten competition in an important segment of the economy, in practice it goes much further. Treble damage suits may remain a threat to many who would never have been dreamed of as monopolists by those who originally framed the Clayton Act in 1914.

With the enactment of the Robinson-Patman Act in 1936, the new tendency to legislate, on the momentum of the century-old antimonopoly feeling, against particular business practices by everyone large and small, reached full tide. Here for the first time specific acts were prohibited wholly apart from their competitive consequences. The payment of "brokerage" or a discount "in lieu" of brokerage, to any buyer was made unlawful without regard to any effect on competition, as was the selective granting of advertising or sales promotional allowances. Both of these were frequently the defensive marketing device of the smaller man

19. 49 Stat. 1526 (1936).

in developing his business, as well as the aggressive buying tactics of certain chain retailers at whom the statute was primarily directed.

In the Robinson-Patman Act, the likelihood of business injury at any level of distribution — to other competitors, among resellers or those who bought for consumption, and even among those who in turn purchased from the first customer — would make a price difference illegal. Injury, moreover, did not mean actual injury, but merely the substantial likelihood of injury. Indirect as well as direct price discrimination was prohibited — a concept that is capable of indefinite expansion. Whatever else could be said of the Robinson-Patman Act, its coverage was universal. It controlled not merely what illegally contrived or monopolistic organizations could do, but what every business large and small might do. The field of potential treble damage liability was expanded to embrace all American business.

To pick up the final strand in the story, it must be recalled that the Clayton Act of 1914 and its troublesome statutory progeny in the Robinson-Patman Act of 1936 are primarily enforced by the Federal Trade Commission, the administrative agency created in 1914. It entered the arena armed not only with the weapon of the Clayton Act enforcement provisions, but with *independent power of its own* to define and to prohibit "unfair methods of competition." This vague phrase was expanded in the Wheeler-Lea Act of 1938 to include also any "unfair or deceptive act or practice in commerce."[20]

Here again much could be said about how a real purpose was distorted or futilely frittered away. The theory was that the Commission would ferret out and

20. 52 Stat. 111 (1938).

stop illegal combinations and developing monopolies in their incipiency. It would prohibit acts as "unfair methods of competition" – even though not specifically outlawed in the Clayton Act – if it believed them to be likely if unchecked to develop into full-blown violations of the Sherman Act. This at least tied into the basic antitrust objective. To a vast extent, however, the Commission originally diverted its energies and funds to lotteries, laxatives, and the foibles of free-goods advertising.

One other shift in emphasis also warrants attention. The 1914 theory was that Trade Commission action would be prophylactic, preventing monopoly in its incipiency through the use of cease and desist orders. Any developed combination or monopoly would presumably be dealt with by the sister prosecuting agency, the Department of Justice. Yet very soon, with the blessing of the Supreme Court, the Federal Trade Commission took over enforcement of the Sherman Act as well. It proceeded against conspiracies to fix prices, combinations, and other Sherman Act violations as being "unfair methods of competition" in violation of the Federal Trade Commission Act. This is roughly equivalent to saying that a murder is also a breach of the peace. Absent effective prosecution for homicide, presumably one should be put under administrative bond to insure good conduct.

The cease and desist order proved an ineffectual weapon against outright violations of the Sherman Act. Therefore in 1938 teeth were provided and failure to obey a Commission order was made punishable by a civil penalty of up to $5,000 for each violation. This applied, however, to all Commission orders, even those against penny candy lotteries. In 1959 the civil penalty was extended to embrace violation of all cease and desist orders entered by the Federal Trade Commission under the Clayton Act, including the Robinson-Patman Act of 1936.[21]

Many of these historical twistings and distortions continue, and undoubtedly will persist through the 1960's. No one can deny the current viability of the basic historical antipathy to anything that can be termed monopolistic. It serves no useful purpose to call that potent force merely political. It is political, as illustrated by the exceptions which have been carved out of the antitrust laws during the last forty years for farm cooperatives, for fishery cooperatives, for export associations, for collective action to implement national agricultural programs, for joint activities necessary for the national defense, and, cardinally, for labor organizations which in the antitrust arena have had a dynamic history of their own.[22]

What is essential perhaps is to recognize that not every proposal which marches to the political music of antimonopoly and under the banner of antitrust is truly responsive to the basic antitrust article of American political faith. A proposal entitled "Equality of Opportunity" may in reality foreclose real competition. What is called "Fair Trade" may in effect be restraint of trade. "Quality Stabilization" may be only thinly cloaked, legalized price-fixing.

Among lawyers, there are many who are concerned lest the political vigor of American antitrust lead to an invasion of fundamental due process. The desire to gratify antitrust objectives in today's dynamic econ-

21. Act of July 23, 1959, § 1, 73 Stat. 243 (1959), 15 U.S.C.A. § 21 (1963). See H. Thomas Austern, "Five Thousand Dollars a Day," *Kentucky Law Journal*, vol. 51 (1963), p. 481.

22. See the chapters by Walter Adams, Herbert R. Northrup and Gordon F. Bloom, and Nat Goldfinger and Theodore J. St. Antoine, below.

omy ought not, they insist, lead to drastic short-cuts, such as the issuance of administrative "temporary cease and desist orders" without trial, or the indiscriminate use of preliminary injunctions, both having drastic and final effect before the true facts of competition can be ascertained.

Perhaps the real lesson of history is the danger of basic antitrust policy becoming lost in newer and fancier vocabularies. It may well be that the only "good trust" would, by analogy to some frontier thinking about a good Indian, be a dead one. Conscious parallelism in pricing under the umbrella of "administered prices" may or may not amount to classical and illegal price-fixing, but developing a new label will never change the conduct being scrutinized. *Ipse dixit* denomination of a business practice as "unfair competition" does not automatically make the conduct anticompetitive any more than calling it "workable competition" should serve to inoculate it against challenge.

Even more, if one may with warrant include as historical background all of the voluminous penmanship, ventured with or without thought, on antitrust during the past forty years, the cardinal danger to guard against resides in the inescapable tendency of lawyers, economists, political scientists, politicians, and legislators and courts (none of these groups being necessarily mutually exclusive) to use the same words to mean wholly different things. As Humpty-Dumpty would say, the question more often is not what the word means, but who is Boss. It has lately become as difficult to use the term "competition" without a qualifying or confusing adjective, as it is to explain the Robinson-Patman Act without the use of both hands.

Some Current Questions of Antitrust Policy

There are three specific current problems which warrant discussion. The first is whether jail sentences should continue to be imposed for violation of the antitrust laws. The second is whether what lawyers call *per se* violations ought to be confined or whether the present efforts of the Department of Justice to expand that concept of automatic violation without full economic inquiry are in the public interest. The third is whether the turgid text and inescapable anticompetitive effects of the Robinson-Patman Act warrant a searching Congressional reexamination of that enactment.

Up to a few years ago, the sanction of a possible jail sentence for a businessman who violated the Sherman Act was a paper threat.[23] Only in isolated instances where racketeering or plainly predatory practices were present had a jail sentence ever been imposed in an antitrust prosecution, and quite often that sentence was suspended.

In February 1961 a rude awakening occurred in the cases of the electrical equipment manufacturers in Philadelphia.[24] In several of these cases, all pleas of *nolo contendere* were rejected and only guilty pleas accepted. Thirty-one jail sentences were imposed. While most of these were suspended, the court sent six

23. Only the Sherman Act authorizes criminal prosecution with possible fines and jail sentences, and necessarily only individuals, and not corporations, may be incarcerated in punishment for violation. The Clayton Act carries no criminal sanctions, but is enforceable only by administrative cease and desist order, civil injunction, and treble-damage actions where injury to business can be established. Section 3 of the Robinson-Patman Act is in terms of criminal enactment, carrying a fine of $5,000 or imprisonment for not more than one year, or both, for violation; but to date few prosecutions have been begun and no conviction has resulted in a jail sentence. Cf. *U.S.* v. *National Dairy Products Corp.*, 372 U.S. 29 (1963).

24. *U.S.* v. *General Electric, et al.*, Criminal Nos. 1496A, 1498, 1500, 1502, 1504, 1506, 1507, 1519, 1521, 1523, 1525, 1527, 1529, 1539, 1541, 1548, 1550, 1558, and 1556 (E.D. Pa., 1961).

businessmen to jail for 30-day periods. These jail sentences achieved far wider publicity than those for ninety days imposed in October 1959 on four Midwestern hand-tool manufacturers who had pleaded *nolo* to charges of price-fixing. Wide ripples of interest and, for some, of apprehension went through the business community. By and large, the general public may have been surprised, but it did not appear to be shocked. In the business world, antitrust advisers achieved an improved status. Some were even occasionally addressed as "Sir."

Yet so far as I can ascertain, there have been no further jail sentences in antitrust cases since February 1961 even though there have been numerous *nolo* and even guilty pleas. It may well be that in the absence of the blatant and cloak-and-dagger conspiratorial price-fixing found in the Philadelphia Electrical cases, the present generation of Federal judges will remain loath to jail American businessmen for Sherman Act violations. That may be responsive to the historic feeling that violation of the antitrust laws by a businessman, however reprehensible, is somehow qualitatively different from murder, embezzlement, or even repeated speeding. Moreover, the Sherman Act denominates violation as only a misdemeanor.

Whether that judicial attitude will continue in the future cannot be foretold. But what cannot be challenged is that the Philadelphia episode has awakened a new respect for the criminal sanctions of the statute, and has had a considerable degree of deterrent effect.

The more interesting question is whether the criminal sanction of not more than one year in jail is necessary or desirable for so-called hard-core Sherman Act violations. It is said to be the policy of the Antitrust Division in the Department of Justice not to seek the indictment of individuals or to ask for jail sentences except in these hard-core violations — price-fixing, boycotting, and racketeering restraints of trade — and then only where the Division is convinced that the businessmen involved were or should have been conscious of law violation.

There are many who insist that the black shadow of confinement in jail for a brief period, and the concomitant public disgrace, are necessary deterrents to obtain compliance with the antitrust laws. They urge that the evils inherent in price-fixing, collective boycotting, or predatory business conduct are as important as those underlying the prohibition of other antisocial conduct carrying jail sentences. In their view, any stigma attaching to corporate conviction is usually diffused, particularly in large companies, and individual corporate officials do not feel directly responsible. As a buttressing argument, it is suggested that in the public view there is nothing "immoral" in the crime of antitrust violation. It is therefore argued that effective enforcement of the antitrust laws warrants that a jail sentence always realistically looms as the penalty for violation and as a meaningful deterrent.

Others urge that all jail sentences for antitrust violation ought to be abolished. They argue that violation of economic rules ought to carry only economic sanctions and civil remedies. In support, it is pointed out that even in the hard-core price-fixing prosecution, there are many occasions in which businessmen are in fact not aware that what they are doing is in violation of the Act. Typically, a group of businessmen may have general discussions about prices, and there may later be price increases individually made in response to an independent initial price increase by one company. Experienced antitrust lawyers would perhaps suggest that some courts, rightly or wrongly, would hold that this sequence of events suffices for the case to go to the jury, which would then be permitted to infer the existence of an illegal conspiracy. Few would deny that it is possible in some situations for businessmen to drift into violation without any real intent or purpose. Indeed, since intent or motive is purely subjective, it is sometimes argued that the decision of a judge or jury to convict is necessarily arbitrary, and at best a moral judgment where the actors may not have had either illegal motive or purpose.

Other arguments against any jail sentences for antitrust violation are occasionally offered. Some urge that the Government decision not to prosecute criminally for all violations results in carving out indictments and jail sentences for some antitrust misconduct but not for other violations on a purely arbitrary basis. A fair argument can be developed that it is more often the officer in the smaller company who is indicted because responsibility in a large corporation is often so diffuse that it is difficult to single out a responsible officer, as contrasted with the more clearly defined responsibilities in smaller corporations whose executives, it is said, have often borne the brunt of criminal enforcement. Some believe that indictments and jail sentences are socially too Draconian a punishment for any antitrust violation.

Analytically, the justification for any criminal sanction, imprisonment, or fine, turns on whether it is a necessary and effective deterrent. That test may appear to be pragmatic, but in this field it is incredibly elusive both because of the infrequency of imprisonment and because of the availability and the use of fines. By recent amendment, the monetary fine for each count in a Sherman Act indictment may now be $50,000.[25]

25. Act of July 7, 1955, 69 Stat. 282 (1955), 15 U.S.C. §§ 1-3 (1958).

There are current proposals to increase it to $100,000.[26] But experience demonstrates that the statutory bark is far worse than its bite. Even though in the Philadelphia Electrical cases there were instances in which both fines and jail sentences (the latter usually suspended) were imposed, the maximum fines for individuals did not exceed $7,500, and more frequently ranged from $1,000 to $5,000.

That the misconduct is labeled only a misdemeanor may be small comfort for the occasional offender who is in fact jailed. If the maximum authorized fines were imposed, it might perhaps be a Hobson's choice for the individual indicted under the antitrust laws. Conviction or a guilty plea or *nolo* plea to a multiple-count indictment may potentially yield extremely heavy fines which are neither deductible from income tax[27] nor reimbursable by the employing company. For some, a few months in jail might indeed be preferable to economic devastation.

In my own view, the agitation about jail sentences for antitrust violation is largely unfounded and in any event probably futile. Throughout the law there are countless situations where the punishment asked for law-breaking rests with the prosecuting official. In almost every criminal proceeding, whether a jail sentence is to be imposed or, if imposed, is to be exacted or suspended, lies entirely with the judge. In all likelihood, Congress will not eliminate imprisonment as a possible punishment for a Sherman Act violation both

26. See S. 2252, 87th Cong., 1st Sess. (1961) (introduced by Senator Kefauver).

27. See, e.g., *Chicago R. I. & P. Ry.* v. *Commissioner*, 47 F. 2d 990 (7th Cir. 1931), cert. denied, 284 U.S. 618 (1931); *Great Northern Ry.* v. *Commissioner*, 40 F. 2d 372 (8th Cir. 1930), cert. denied, 282 U.S. 855 (1936).

because it will be persuaded that the possibility is an effective deterrent and because no legislator will vote counter to the basic American antitrust article of political faith.

My second inquiry concerns what lawyers call the *per se* doctrine. Without refined analysis, it may be defined as the type of conduct which when proved forecloses those charged from any opportunity to seek to justify their conduct as a reasonable restraint of trade or as not in fact monopolistic in purpose or effect.

Classically, price-fixing and collective boycotting are *per se* offenses. Once the government proves this type of conduct, violation is established and the defendants will not be heard as to the economic necessity or lack of anticompetitive effect or reasonableness of their conduct. The Supreme Court decision in the spring of 1963 in the *White Motor Company* case[28] may have retarded the trend by which over the years the *per se* category of antitrust offenses has been expanding. The lower court had held on summary judgment that the bare agreement between a truck manufacturer and a dealer which required the dealer to sell only to certain categories of customers located within a particular territory was illegal *per se.*[29] The Supreme Court returned the case to the lower court for trial to enable the defendant to show that the arrangements affording to each of its dealers an exclusive geographical franchise were necessary to enable the dealer effectively to compete, or that interbrand competition in the trucking field was economically more significant than intrabrand competition among local dealers, or that for some other reason the restraints concerned

28. *White Motor Co.* v. *U.S.*, 372 U.S. 253 (1963).

29. *U.S.* v. *White Motor Co.*, 194 F. Supp. 562 (N.D. Ohio, 1961).

were not unreasonable when the complete economic facts were examined.

That the *per se* approach to this type of distribution system might still be applied sometime in the future is evident from the majority opinion of Mr. Justice Douglas and the concurrence of Mr. Justice Brennan. Both emphasized that this case was the first in which a vertical, territorial restriction on dealers was involved, and that the Court did not yet know enough about the *general* economic significance of such restrictions to rule whether the reasonableness of these arrangements is to be determined *ad hoc* by examining all the economic facts surrounding their employment in particular instances or whether they are to be *per se* illegal without further inquiry. Because the use of geographically protected distributorships represents an important part of the selling pattern in many durable goods industries, whether the Supreme Court ultimately adopts one approach or the other is considered by many antitrust lawyers to be an important issue.

What seems clear is that the resolution of this issue will not be facilitated by resort to legal clichés. There are some who insist that once a man sells a product, he should not be permitted to exercise any control over what the buyer does with it. As some lawyers put it, there ought to be no equitable servitudes on any chattel. On that type of rigid approach, an agreement by a manufacturer to appoint but one distributor in a given locality would be lawful because no control would ride with the product he sells. But any agreement on the part of the purchaser to stay in his own backyard in reselling would become *per se* illegal.

On the other hand, in modern distribution, the clean-cut notion that the vendor can have no control whatever over what he sells, once it has left his hands, may be unrealistic. Much in the trademark law is inconsistent with that concept. As to product liability for injury or loss to the consumer flowing from the use of what he has sold, the original manufacturer in many fields has an almost absolute liability. For many heavily advertised products, the dealer and retailer are often mere conduits to the consumer. In measuring the required effect upon competition that renders price discrimination illegal under the Robinson-Patman Act, the ramifying effects upon retailers who purchase from the distributor to whom the manufacturer sells have been made controlling. Certainly, those who advocate Fair Trading can hardly subscribe to the argument that once a trademarked product is sold the manfacturer may properly have no concern with it.

Analytically, the concept of a *per se* violation is not so rigid as it might seem. Mr. Justice Black once phrased the rule as encompassing "agreements or practices which because of their pernicious effect on competition and lack of any redeeming virtue are conclusively presumed to be unreasonable and therefore illegal without elaborate inquiry as to be precise harm they have caused or the business excuse for their use."[30] Overall, however, if the *per se* rule is applied, it reflects far more the reluctance of judges to get into economic questions, or to make economic choices when confronted with a massive record in which the salient issues are often bogged down in a mass of complex and detailed economic data. The wide-ranging dicta in the *Madison Oil* case that any activity tampering with price is *per se* illegal,[31] and that in the famous *Trenton Potteries* opinion to the effect that courts cannot pass upon the reasonableness of agreed-upon

30. *Northern Pacific Ry.* v. *U.S.*, 356 U.S. 1, 5 (1958).
31. *U.S.* v. *Socony-Vacuum Oil Co.*, 310 U.S. 150, 218 (1940).

prices,[32] have not always been applied rigidly. Necessary trading rules for commodity exchanges, plainly reflecting overt agreement, have not fallen under the ban of automatic illegality.[33] Agreements among underwriters essential to marketing securities have likewise passed muster.[34] Bid depositories among bidders have not been called automatically illegal.[35] What emerges as *per se* violation is a number of specific patterns of conduct as to which the courts, and particularly the Supreme Court, have perhaps pragmatically determined that they will not be led into making complex economic judgments as to what is or is not a reasonable restraint. But this does not mean that the *per se* concept is rigid or ought to be expanded.[36]

The real question posed in the *White Motor* case is whether the courts should in this area of protected geographical distributorships undertake the task of determining their reasonableness in each situation, or whether there should be judicial abdication and resort to the *per se* concept of automatic illegality so as outrightly to ban every geographically protected distributorship irrespective of its actual economic effect. If we are to have a dynamic economy and if the Sherman Act is to maintain its organic flexibility, many hope that the easy judicial path will not be taken and that the *per*

32. *U.S.* v. *Trenton Potteries Co.*, 273 U.S. 392, 397 (1927).

33. *Chicago Board of Trade* v. *U.S.*, 246 U.S. 231 (1918).

34. *U.S.* v. *Morgan*, 118 F. Supp. 621 (S.D. N.Y., 1953).

35. See, e.g., *U.S.* v. *Bakersfield Associated Plumbing Contractors, Inc.*, 1958 Trade Cases, Paragraph 69,087, modified, 1959 Trade Cases, Paragraph 69,266.

36. In refreshing contrast is the recent statement of the Supreme Court that "In appraising the effects of any price cut or the corresponding response to it, both the Federal Trade Commission and the courts must make realistic appraisals of relevant competitive facts. Invocation of mechanical word formulas cannot be made to substitute for adequate probative analysis." Goldberg, J., in *F.T.C.* v. *Sun Oil Co.*, 371 U.S. 505, 527 (1963).

se approach to antitrust violation will continue to be confined rather than expanded.

Even more, there are some who insist that the application of *per se* rules to every conventional or new effort of a nondominant manufacturer to control the distribution of his product may in the long run destroy the basic competition that our antitrust laws seek to protect. If effective interbrand competition requires territorial restriction of dealers, the reservation of some categories of customers, or other forms of what is now called "dual distribution," then the manufacturer may be economically required to integrate forward into distribution. He may attempt to utilize agency-consignment arrangements which can be and are often challenged as covert resale price maintenance. Forward integration by merger is also legally vulnerable. The end result may be that only the big (short of monopoly) and financially strong companies can successfully distribute directly what they make. Intermediate distributors and retailers may disappear, and oligopoly trends in many industries may be increased. Should these fears be realized, basic antitrust policy will be disserved.

Castigating the turgid text and the vagaries of interpretation and enforcement of the Robinson-Patman Act have long been favorite pastimes of the host of caustic critics of that enactment. There are few who deny that as often applied that Act has anticompetitive effects; and that it frequently restraints price experimentation, promotes price rigidity, and places a premium on the status quo. The effort to reconcile its enforcement with basic antitrust policy, I have recently described as a process requiring mental gymnastics, both hands, and a familiarity with all schools of neo-existentialism.[37]

37. *Harvard Law Review*, vol. 76, p. 662 (book review).

Both historically and analytically, the statute is plainly backhanded legislation. It was conceived as a measure to curb, or at least to control, coercive tactics by large buyers, particularly massive chain stores in the grocery field. As enacted and applied, it controls the pricing conduct of sellers, indeed every seller large or small, in a cumbersome, inept, and uncertain manner. In most industries it would, when literally applied, make every seller of goods inescapably a law violator.

Yet at least a decade ago it was acknowledged by most that the Robinson-Patman Act is almost uniquely invulnerable to legislative revision. Fundamentally, this is due to a schizoid attitude on the part of most businessmen who as sellers of goods believe the statute helps them in resisting buyer pressure for lower prices and concessions, and who as purchasers of raw material still believe that they can with impunity somehow exact price concessions from those with whom they deal as buyers. Of course, the particular groups who have obtained a built-in domestic protective tariff for their own niche in the distributive process are always adamant against any legislative tinkering.

Nevertheless, whatever the political practicalities may be, objective scholars inevitably arrive at the conviction that it would be preferable wholly to discard the inept text of the present enactment and to begin anew. That inescapable conviction derives largely from measuring every new decision in terms of its constrictive effect upon competition. On the basic issue of the required effect upon competition that makes a price discrimination unlawful, the argument is far-ranging as to whether it is truly competition or merely a particular competitor that is being protected. Equally often, and perhaps more acutely, these anticompetitive effects are seen in the administrative and judicial handling of the justification included in the law which supposedly permits a seller in good faith to meet an equally low price of a competitor.

Originally, the Supreme Court laid down the rule that good faith could be determined by what a reasonably prudent businessman, selling in a dynamic market, would believe to be the competitive price.[38] An immediate and understandable qualification was imposed at the same time in the further rule that in delivered price selling one could not take over lock, stock, and barrel the pricing system of a competitor with the result that phantom freight was exacted. It took years of agonized litigation to overcome the Commission's insistence that what the law said about meeting competition was to be a real defense, rather than a mere procedural gimmick.[39]

Very recent decisions raise further concern. The Federal Trade Commission determined last year that a seller who sought to establish that he was meeting competition must prove that he had "reason to believe" that the lower prices of his competitor that he was meeting could be cost-justified or were otherwise lawful under any of the exceptions specified in this complicated statute.[40] Somehow he must determine, even in the competitive furnace of an active market, whether his competitor is selling at substantially different prices to purchasers who compete among themselves. Even more difficult, the seller presumably must know enough about his competitors' operations and detailed costs to make the legal-accounting judgment that no competitor could possibly have cost justification. Somehow he must also make a nice legal judg-

38. *F.T.C.* v. *A. E. Staley Mfg. Co.*, 324 U.S. 746, 759-760 (1945).

39. *Standard Oil Co.* v. *F.T.C.*, 355 U.S. 396 (1958).

40. *Tri-Valley Packing Ass'n*, Nos. 7225, 7496, F.T.C., May 10, 1962, remanded, 329 F. 2d 694 (9th Cir. 1964).

ment, at the time of each transaction, as to whether any competitor, whose prices he has to meet, is or is not in turn lawfully meeting the lower price of another competitor.

This strange notion that one may act in good faith in meeting competition only where he has adequate reason to believe that the competition he is meeting is *lawful* – or else abandon the sale – is truly fascinating. If each seller knew that much about the intimate details of his competitors' operations and costs, he might get out of the Robinson-Patman Act frying pan only to find himself in the fire of a Sherman Act price conspiracy charge. Even granting that all sales executives and salesmen are now legally literate as to the foggy text of the Robinson-Patman Act, the task of determining what is or is not lawful pricing conduct by a competitor is fairly formidable. Its correct resolution would often confound even legal experts in the field. As Fred Rowe has observed in his comprehensive text on the Act, the legality of price differentials depends upon "four jurisdictional elements and five basic prohibitions, subject to three important defensive provisos."[41] There are many who believe that if these current administrative distortions are judicially confirmed, the right to meet competition supposedly afforded by the statute will become wholly illusive.

In its own struggles with this statute, the Supreme Court sometimes employs a casual heavy hand, but more often tries to decide the issue presented as narrowly as possible. The recent *Sun Oil* decision is an interesting illustration. The Court held that where the oil company had a dealer who became embroiled in a local price war, it could not go to the aid of that dealer by giving him a price concession in order to enable him to meet the price competition of a gasoline re-

41. Frederick M. Rowe, *Price Discrimination Under the Robinson-Patman Act* (Boston, 1962), p. 36.

tailer across the road. But the Court meticulously confined its decision to the facts offered in justification by *Sun Oil.*

In his opinion Mr. Justice Goldberg went to great and repeated lengths carefully to reserve and to avoid deciding the legality of a variety of other possible situations in which a seller of gasoline might reduce his price to a particular customer in order to enable that customer to meet his local competition. In doing so, the opinion created far more ambiguities than it solved. It suggested that if the wholesaler and retailer were "integrated," a different result might be reached, but what factual contours are covered by "integrated" remains to be seen. It reiterated constantly that the Court was not deciding what the result would have been if Sun Oil had shown that the price-cutter across the road had been given aid from *his* supplier. It limited its decision only to those situations where the competing "price-cutter does not receive a 'price-break' from his own supplier."[43] What the ultimate legal rules will be, whether they will be applicable only in the context of gasoline distribution and resale, only the future may reveal.

Nevertheless, *Sun Oil* does make it clear that the Robinson-Patman Act is to be read literally to foreclose as a simple defense to a price concession the

42. For the very first time in a litigated proceeding, a divided Commission dismissed the complaint in Continental Baking Company, Docket 7630 (December 31, 1963) on the ground that the respondent had satisfied the requirements of Section 2(b) of the Robinson-Patman Act in the good faith meeting of competition. In dissenting, Commissioner MacIntyre advanced the suggestion that the Supreme Court might well review the entire concept of meeting competition and interprete the statute to permit a seller to meet competition only to combat "an unlawful" price of a competitor, but not to meet a lower price lawfully being accorded by a competitor.

43. *F.T.C.* v. *Sun Oil Co.*, 371 U.S. 505, 522 (1963). See also Lefkoe, "The Strange Case of Sun Oil," *Fortune* (August, 1963), p. 117.

meeting by a seller of the competition encountered by his customer. To that extent it constricts the right to meet competition and, in my view, confirms the general momentum of the Robinson-Patman Act toward sticky if not rigid pricing. I suggest that the judicial progeny of the *Sun Oil* decision and opinion will be numerous, that the intellectual genes will become crisscrossed to an unbelievable degree, and that the ultimate effect will become largely irreconcilable with basic antitrust policy. If I am right, there will be added reasons why this legislative monstrosity some day will require complete Congressional reexamination.

These three areas, posed as current problems warranting examination, may appear to many of you as superficial, legalistic, and perhaps even as only reflecting the not uncommon tavern laments of lawyers who have lost cases. Yet I have ventured to offer them in this opening chapter because in at least two respects they emphasize a needed approach in developing any insight into and conclusions about antitrust policy.

In the first place, it must always be remembered that antitrust policies become meaningful only through Congressional enactment and, perhaps more important, in how the generally and often only vaguely stated Congressional objectives are carried out by the enforcement agencies, and then approved, rejected, or modified by the courts. As the famous Holmes' caution goes, general propositions do not decide concrete cases.[44] Secondly, and as abundantly exemplified by the Robinson-Patman Act and decisions under it, not all that gets sponsored and enacted as antitrust contributes to the maintenance of real competition.

These elementary cautions may illuminate any inquiry into the overall problems and prospects in antitrust policy.

44. See *Lochner* v. *New York,* 198 U.S. 45, 76 (1905).

CHAPTER 2

Problems and Prospects in Antitrust Policy – II

BY M. A. ADELMAN

Introduction

As Mr. Austern has indicated, the purpose of the first three chapters is to discuss a number of live antitrust issues in some depth rather than discourse about things in general. But we would be rendering a doubtful service if we lost the forest for the trees and, hence, each chapter points out how a relatively few basic issues are invoked in many places and under many names. I shall treat three topics: mergers, administered prices, and the Common Market. In relation to each of them, the one salient issue is "economic power" – two words which cover two somewhat separate ideas. The first is economies of scale – being big enough to have lower unit costs – and the second is monopoly power – sufficient control of supply to achieve maximum profit, or at least a higher profit than if others had access to buyers.

Mergers

The current law, Section 7 of the Clayton Act, is the latest in a tradition against large business getting larger, a tradition which has been fairly successful in confusing the two meanings of "economic power" – economies of scale and monopoly. When a simple confusion lasts for at least some eighty years (for it is writ large in the discussion leading up to the Sherman Act) one can be sure that there is a potent social interest in perpetuating it. In this instance that interest is the desire of the smaller competitor to stay in business and the desire of many to keep him there because he is small. Now, if his survival is a goal, a Good Thing in itself, it is obvious that whether he is threatened by a bigger concern's *superior efficiency* (economies of scale) or power to control or foreclose markets (monopoly) is a distinction without a difference. This social goal, which I happen not to share, is a perfectly respectable one and worth the cost if you want to pay it, but there is an inhibition on stating it bluntly — something like the ban on being too explicit about the divine commandment to propagate the race. But excessive reticence can result not only in illegitimate children but illegitimate reasoning. For illustration, I turn now to the recent decision in *Brown Shoe*.[1]

In the *Brown Shoe* decision, the Supreme Court early turns to the legislative history of the amended Clayton Act to point out that Congress was concerned about a supposed rising tide of economic concentration. I have myself made some statistical studies on this subject and, statistics aside, have admired the harmonies of public discussion. For example, the Census Bureau made special tabulations of its 1954 data, which were released by Senate Committee with grave warnings about the rising tide of concentration they portrayed. In due course the warnings were repeated in Congress, the press, and other respectable places. After a while, the professors (and other fact-mongers, who may not resent being included in this generic name) pointed out that in fact there really is no evidence that

1. *Brown Shoe Co.* v. *U.S.*, 370 U.S. 294 (1962). The decision below was *U.S.* v. *Brown Shoe Co.*, 179 F. Supp. 721 (E.D. Mo., 1959), on which see "The Anti-Merger Act, 1950-1960," in *Papers and Proceedings of the Annual Meeting of the American Economic Association*, 1961.

concentration has risen at all.[2] Of course, nobody reads the professors' writings except other professors, but they seem perfectly content with this, while the wider public is not made unhappy and confused by hearing the facts. So everyone is pleased, and all is for the best.

The Clayton Act, as the Supreme Court notes, was amended in the light of an earlier Federal Trade Commission report, which was not kindly received by the academic fraternity.[3] Its authors later explained that they had really been misunderstood – they had not meant to say that concentration was on the increase, and how could anybody have thought they were? The whole controversy was very well summed up at a conference in 1952 and one can therefore say that the statistical hoax has for eleven years been dead, buried, and even mouldering in the grave, but the myth goes marching on.[4] In fact, it is reinforced. Every so often, the Federal Trade Commission announces that there were more mergers last year than the year before and then there is a great wagging of heads about inevitable trends, the grand sweep of twentieth century events, the end of individualism, and so forth. The mere number of mergers, in truth, comes close to pure, meaningless tabulation. But it would not be too difficult to do a study of the assets of the companies acquired and acquiring, which would show what effect these mergers were having on the structure of industry in general and in particular

2. See American Statistical Association, *Proceedings of the Business and Economic Section,* 1957, papers by Irving Rottenberg and M. A. Adelman; and Ralph L. Nelson, in *Journal of the American Statistical Association* (1960).

3. *The Merger Movement. A Summary Report* (1948).

4. Jesse W. Markham in *Business Concentration and Price Policy* (National Bureau of Economic Research, 1955). See also Chapter 8 below, by the same author.

branches. We can guess that the results would be imperceptible – partly by some fragmentary evidence, partly by the bland failure to request the very modest funds which would permit such a study. "Don't be a slave to the facts!"[5]

Still the myth may not be eternal. In reading *Brown Shoe*, does one see a certain disengagement from it? In the repeated phrasing that it was Congress who was concerned with the alleged rising tide, is one to sense that the Court expresses no opinion as to the fact? Perhaps a generation of exposure to law clerks drawn mostly from law review editors is beginning to have some effect; if we wait another generation or two, we may be able to tell.

At issue in the particular case was the merger of Brown's manufacturing with Kinney's retailing, and also of Brown's retailing with Kinney's. Taking the second and less interesting question first: the Court noted that the relevant markets were metropolitan areas, and in some of them the combined market share would run has high as 57 percent, though usually it was much less than that. Four reasons were given for condemning such a merger. The first was a kind of "equity" argument which I am not sure I understand and which need not be pursued here. The second and third (for the same thing is said twice), was the ability of a chain to withstand the fluctuations of business which might wreck an independent. This is simply an economy of scale. How important it is might perhaps be guessed

5. Anybody who thinks I am trying to be funny, who does not grasp the deep human resentment at having to grub around in data when we *know* the *truth* all along, cannot really understand the enforcement of any economic policy, including antitrust. But few arouse quite the reactions this one does, and that is why its study is useful, since it shows magnified what we need to study for use everywhere.

by the trend of retailing concentration—another alleged ground for the decision. Here we are confronted with two apparently inconsistent facts: that very large chains (101 retail outlets or more) increased their share of the sales of *all shoe stores* during 1948-1954, from 21 to 26 percent; while sales by all chains (eleven or more outlets) remained at a constant 20 percent of *all shoes sold*. The only way to reconcile these facts is to observe that small stores and department stores were dropping out of the trade during that time. By survival alone all survivors, large or small, would be getting a bigger share. Hence there is no logical basis for supposing that of the firms that survived through the period the larger firms were growing faster than the rest. This raises some doubt as to whether the alleged economy of scale is important or even perceptible, and the doubt is further strengthened by reflecting that the retreating department stores also typically enjoy economies of scale and financial stability. But these doubts as to the facts do not alter the importance of the Court's ground for decision. The phrase, "competitive advantages" of larger firms means nothing more nor less than "economies of scale"; it only sounds different.

If the competitive advantages of retailers who are integrated with manufacturers were important, we would expect the large manufacturers to integrate, gain the advantages, and gain business at the expense of their nonintegrated smaller rivals. A goodly number of small manufacturers were going out of business during this time, so that one would expect the larger firms to be gaining market share at least by mere survival, like the shoe chains. Yet in 1947 the largest four, eight, and fifteen manufacturers accounted for 26, 31, and 36 percent of total production, respectively; in

1954, they produced 22, 27, and 33 percent.[6] This means that the biggest firms, with their vast financial resources and allegedly decisive competitive advantages and so forth actually fell behind in the race!

But facts are dust in the balance compared with the testimony of competitors on the mounting tide of concentration, the decisive advantages, and so forth, which so impressed the District and Supreme Courts. The *unverified – and unverifiable – complaints of interested parties* become not only evidence but proof positive.[7]

So we end up with a call to end the nonexistent trend toward greater concentration in industry generally and in shoes, "particularly when these tendencies are being accelerated through giant steps striding across a hundred cities at a time." As usual, where facts are missing, rhetoric fills the gap. We are left with the real ground for decision: the *smaller retailers* and manufacturers for whose sake the competitive race toward greater efficiency is to be blunted. And yet, it is well that the Court went through the motions of seeming to analyze markets to promote competition. For it set the precedent of market analysis. Under the Tudor despotism, Parliament did little more than ratify

6. The source is not clearly stated in the decision. According to the Census, the respective shares of the largest 4, 8, and 20, were: in 1947: 28, 35, 45; in 1954: 30, 36, 45; in 1958; 27, 34, 43. Since the number of companies fell by 14 percent, mere survivorship should have raised the 1947 percentages to 33, 41, 52; hence, the largest firms were not growing as quickly as all surviving firms.

7. Here I touch on something more important than economics. It is detestable to let a man be the judge in his own case. If a judge is in the first instance a finder of facts, he has no right to hand over the job to interested parties even if they are not formally joined. That the courts let this happen is a sign perhaps of the times; I prefer to take a more hopeful view and to predict that judges will be found who treat this "evidence" with *exactly as much respect* as it deserves.

the will of the throne, yet by pretending that they had a will of their own, they established a set of precedents and arrangements that in the fullness of time and under new social conditions let them claim sovereignty and make good the claim. For the time being, it is clear that our merger policy does something to preserve competition by preventing mergers that might confer market control, and it does something also to weaken competition that might confer greater efficiency. This, at least, is what the policy does if we are to agree with the court's findings, which some of us have some trouble doing, especially since the findings do not agree with each other.

Administered Prices

The discussion of mergers indicates that it may sometimes be difficult to specify just what is meant by lesser or greater competition, and to assemble the facts bearing on these concepts. For this reason, the phrase "administered prices" is a great labor-saving invention. If we think that Industry X is monopolistic, since it is run by big businesses who all charge the same price and keep raising it, thus contributing to inflation, we evade all the awkward necessity of proof or even specifications by calling their prices "administered prices." The "Open, Sesame!" gives us the conclusion we want with no more than the labor of pronouncing the words. Not long ago, I made a rather superficial inquiry into steel prices, concluding that its price behavior could be explained only by a particular kind of monopoly control.[8] Restricted as the conclusion was, it cost me a lot of work in the assembly and appraisal of scattered and often unsatisfactory evidence, and at every point I had to admit that there might be other

8. M. A. Adelman, "Steel, Administered Prices and Inflation," *Quarterly Journal of Economics* (February, 1961).

and better ways of interpreting the data. Nonetheless, since the great bulk of wholesale prices and practically all retail prices are, in a sense, administered, something characteristic of everythihg can be distinctive of nothing. Professor Heflebower recently did a survey of the problem, and it turned out to be a most useful compendium of ideas on how to distinguish amidst the endless ebb and flow of market forces some persisting current that could not be explained by the workings of competition.[9] And in this inquiry the slogan "administered prices" is not only useless but harmful. It is harmful because, first, it insinuates knowledge when there is none; second, because it exempts as non-administered some of the most clearly monopolistic prices in the economy, chiefly farm products; third, because it magnifies form to ignore substance.

We have in Section 1 of the Sherman Act a rather stringent law which makes any communication on prices or supply, which would have the effect of influencing them, a *per se* violation of law. This does not by any means prevent all of what an economist would call collusive activity but it certainly prevents a great deal. And those who want to perpetuate the myth that big business enjoys vast political power are sweeping this accomplishment under the rug when they strike an infinitely sophisticated pose and say they know all about Section 1 – old stuff, indeed – but businessmen easily evade this by *administering* their prices.

What about collusive activity that takes place without any overt collusion? Calling it administered prices is a drag to thinking, a ball and chain we are well advised to cut off and forget, but this good riddance does not actually advance knowledge or policy. If we want

9. Richard B. Heflebower, "The Problem of Administered Prices," *Northwestern University Law Review*, (May-June, 1962). See Chapter 5 below, by the same author.

to preserve decentralized initiative, a way of life for small enterprises, etc., then of course we want to do nothing at all, but rather to temper the wind of competition to the shorn wolf, and repeal or amend Section 1 of the Sherman Act. If, however, we want to have competition, then one can go a little father along the road by prohibiting, as does Section 5 of the Federal Trade Commission Act, institutional arrangements which have a collusive effect – such as basing point systems – even when nobody could fairly urge that there was ever a conspiracy and all that can be discovered is that everyone found the pattern upon getting to a decision-making level in the business, and chose to follow it.[10]

There are, in fact, many contributing institutional factors. One could reflect that cigarette excise taxes make price competititon difficult or impossible, and therefore reduce them; or tax advertising, hence accomplishing the same result with no revenue loss.[11] More generally, when demand or cost per unit drops, and sellers are reluctant to reduce prices, as sellers always and properly are, the knowledge that no rival dares to cut prices here and there, for fear of public or of private treble-damage action under the Robinson-Patman Act, is a potent reinforcement of everyone's holding the price, in the well-founded hope that everybody else will also hold. Repeal of that law would knock out some of the props from many rigid price markets.

The general principle which I am invoking here is that noncompetitive arrangements or methods of business, absent actual collusion, are inherently frail and can last only if there is some durable institution such

10. *F.T.C.* v. *Cement Institute,* 334 U.S. 839 (1948).
11. William H. Nicholls, *Price Policies in the Cigarette Industry* (Nashville, 1952).

as a law or a concerted system to block nearly all the important avenues of competition, so that a wink and a nod can do the rest. I think the Philadelphia cases discussed by Mr. Austern in Chapter 1 supply additional proof. But an institution can be durable even when its exercise is sporadic. The celebrated case of steel is an illustration. The repeated price increases in the 1950's were largely characteristic of a group acting in concert, not of independent action in response to either higher costs or higher demand. The increase in mid-1958, with operations around 55 percent of capacity, was the most striking. I have no idea of how much of their price increases were "justified" by wage increases, since the whole impassioned subject is a pure waste of time if we are trying to understand what happened. The industry, including the union, were able to raise prices because they were able to act in concert, and they raised until they got about to the point that competition from foreign and domestic substitutes was becoming appreciable. As we say in the classroom, they had got to the neighborhood of profit maximizing, given what knowledge they had of markets. The split of the gains between companies and union is more than a detail, but it is a split of monopoly gain, not the effect of labor scarcity pushing up costs and then prices.

The April 1962 episode surely marks the end of an era. U. S. Steel put the price up and was followed, but it was plain that Bethlehem and some of the others did it reluctantly and against their better judgment, for the sake of solidarity. When Inland and Kaiser refused to follow, small though their market share was, the price rise was dead. This may seem like a "normal" result, but a little reflection will show that if a higher price would more or less clear the market (i.e. would reflect supply and demand), then Inland's reluctance would have had no result except to make a few customers happy with a little gift from Inland while the other steel companies continued to collect the higher price. It is only when an industry is keeping the price well above the cost of turning out more product and there is substantial excess capacity that relatively small producers can have a veto power – which is why I said such arrangements are inherently fragile. In any case for the first time in sixty years, Big Steel's leadership was not followed. Now, whether Inland refused to follow because of its business judgment or the pressure from the White House, I do not know. Either explanation is logical and sufficient, so we are in the uncomfortable but not unusual position in scientific work of two good hypotheses, and no way of eliminating either one.

No sooner was the April cliff-hanger finished than another great debate began as to whether or not steel deserved, or needed, higher prices in the national interest, to replace obsolescent facilities, for peace and national security, etc. To have decisions affecting the national welfare and security taken by men with a direct pocketbook interest in the decision strikes me as not the best way of running the public business. But good or bad, if the argument is to be taken seriously, it means that steel is no longer a private business at all, but public. Sooner or later, our people will take the hint and then the companies will wonder what they have done to deserve the threat of nationalization and will denounce socialistic-minded congressmen and, of course, professors. Perhaps some will recall what the New Testament says about pointing at the mote in your brother's eye.

Despite the logic of the steel executives' argument that their industry ought to be socialized, I reject the conclusion, partly on the authority of someone with experience in socialized industries, Mr. N. S. Khrushchev. In November of 1962 he complained that his planners had gone steel-happy, and had wasted Soviet resources in building too much capacity. Here is food for reflection. I have long wondered at the prevailing opinion that monopoly is a problem only in capitalist economies. It seems much more likely — at least a "rebuttable presumption," the lawyers might call it — that there would be far more monopoly in a socialist economy, if only because the State is the monopolist of all goods and services.

So long as profits are used to measure the success and to determine the salary and perquisites of managements and many of the fringe benefits of labor, the same incentives to monopoly exist even if the profits do not directly become the private income of the decision-maker (any more than they do in the U.S.!) More important, the independent appraisals of supply and demand, and of the possibilities of improvement and innovation which occur in private competition are obviously absent from the socialist scheme of things. Their mistakes are not corrected by the signal lights of a competitive market — price weakness — but go rolling up from blueprint to final construction, only to be caught when it is too late.

In the U.S., we too have wasted our substance in building too much steel capacity because the competitive mechanism was absent and oversupply did not send prices down. The steel economy has been planned by high-minded gentlemen trying to do their best by stockholders, employees, and the public. Moreover, some companies which are in whole or part much less efficient than others might now be left to mend their ways or make as graceful an exit as they can manage. It is this waste of resources that we ought to be worrying about, not whether steel prices or wages have advanced too much or too little or just about right compared with some irrelevant standard like a wholesale price index.

What can be done about these ostensibly collusive arrangements when there is no overt actual collusion? Had the Truman and Eisenhower Administrations kept out of the steel wage bargaining, a fight among producers might have come at an earlier stage, when it would have done less damage. Had it occurred, the price would not have escalated up, we would today have a smaller and more efficient industry, and we would not be bedeviled with irrelevancies about fair wages, fair prices, administered prices, and inflation. We can sometimes prevent such arrangements from lasting if sometimes we master the urge to do something – anything – and can patiently stand a while.

Would we then have any important instances of industries with a small number of sellers, able to work out noncompetitive arrangements without collusion? I do not know but that is no excuse for not facing the issue. Where nothing can be done about such an instance, either by destroying the institutional nucleus, or the law, or the promise of public intervention, around which the sellers' understandings can coalesce, then we should grin and bear it. My reason has nothing to do with economics, and everything to do with the rights of the citizen. If a company and its executives are to be held liable not for raising or lowering prices, but rather for the leadership or followership of persons over whom they have no control, that seems to me to be getting too close for comfort to guilt by association.

The European Common Market

So far as antitrust enforcement goes, the European

Common Market is hardly in existence, but the situation is interesting to the American student of antitrust in giving perspective on his own problems. The Treaty of Rome forbade "concerted practices" in Article 85, and "the abuse of a dominant market position" in Article 86.[12] The first thing that strikes one is the close parallel of these Articles with Sections 1 and 2 of the Sherman Act, and also with the British Restrictive Trade Practices Act of 1956.[13] The latter provides for the registration of what we would call price-fixing agreements and the general presumption that they are taken seriously by the Registrar and by the courts. With respect to monopolizing and mergers, the "big company" is left to the separate Monopolies Commission, with a much more vague mandate. In Europe, the Commission of the Common Market issued a demand for registration of agreements, with a deadline first in August 1963, and finally in February 1964. It is not clear how complete the registration will be (many companies contend that they have nothing to register), nor how the registered agreements will be treated, nor how the Articles will be reconciled with the diverse national laws, which vary greatly in substance and enforcement.[14] Italy, alone among the six, has no anti-

12. See Communauté Economique Européenne: Le Conseil: *Premier Règlement d'Application des Articles 85 et 86 du Traité.* Bruxelles, 7 février 1962; 69/62 (RCI) final.

13. Monopolies and Restrictive Practices (Inquiry and Control) Act, 1948; Monopolies and Restrictive Practices Commission Act, 1953; Restrictive Trade Practices Act, 1956. See contemporary summary by Grunfeld and Yamey, "Restrictive Trade Practices Act, 1956," in *Public Law* (Winter, 1956).

14. Recently a French distributor of magnetophones sued a competitor for selling appliances made by a German manufacturer who had granted them exclusive rights in France. The defendant then lodged an action with the Commission in Brussels, claiming that the contract was void as opposed to Articles 85 and 86 of the Treaty of Rome. The Commission accepted jurisdiction but the commercial court of the Seine Department asserted its own and found for the plaintiff, imposing damages and an injunction against the defend-

trust law, but one is being written by a parliamentary committee. No definite action has been taken under Article 86, the analogue to Section 2 of the Sherman Act, and none is expected soon. Indeed, corporate counsel in the Common Market area have some difficult problems.[15] It does not seem likely that the Commission would slavishly follow American precedents, and even a superficial acquaintance with the responsible personnel disposes of that motion. My own impression is of independence and intellectual vigor,[16] though the gaps in the knowledge of European industrial structure are appalling. I submit that *the double standard is inevitable,* and better faced earlier than later. The prohibition of price agreements is congenial to the legal tradition because these are overt acts being condemned. When people make agreements of this kind, they usually though not necessarily have collectively the power to control prices and output. And usually, the result will be antisocial. But for a single business, allegedly offensive because it is so big or because it is proposing an acquisition, I see no escape from the

ant. The Paris Court of appeals reversed, holding that Community Law is as binding upon national tribunals as their national law, since article 45 of the French Constitution of 1958 declared that "treaties or accords ratified or approved have . . . a force superior to that of the laws." The Court of Appeals therefore suspended the action pending decision by the Commission, "for the sake of good administration of justice" (*Le Monde,* -6 February 1963, p. 16). Aside from the substantive merits of the case, the decision of the appeals court must be welcomed, as placing squarely upon the agenda the reconcilement of Community law with the national laws.

15. Cf. Alain Murcier, "Les Professionels prennent Contact avec la Règlementation anti-trust Européenne," *Le Monde* 8-9 (July, 1962), p. 7.

16. Two excellent statements are nicely complementary in approach: academic, by Jacques Houssiaux, *Concurrence et Marché Commun*(Paris, 1960), and by a Commission member, Hans von der Groeben, "Policy on Competition in the E.E.C.," Supplement to *Bulletin* of the E.E.C. (July-August, 1961).

need for an inquiry — often elaborate — into market delimitations and market share, etc.

It remains to be seen whether in Britain and the Community the double standard will be redoubled with a rather strict prohibition against mergers. On one level of analysis, this redouble makes no sense. Why should a judgment depend on how a company got to a given stage of market control (merger) rather on that degree itself? This, however, assumes as a fact an easy and costless knowledge of the market which, as I pointed out above, does not exist but must always be won with much effort. Competent personnel are scarce, more so in Europe than in the United States. If knowledge is hard to get and usually insufficient, it follows that our judgments are often in error and we must face up to the need of dealing with the situation, much as in statistical decision theory, in which one weighs the consequence of missing a real relationship versus those of "seeing" a false one. The courts have been reluctant to break up going concerns. This is not merely judicial conservatism, but the knowledge that if they used this power freely they would not long have it. Our social policy is, implicitly but effectively, to avoid the cost of unscrambling eggs. But in merger cases, *when there has as yet been no scrambling, and when* either or both corporations are free to grow by building additions, the harm done by a wrong decision is not comparable to that done by a wrong decision ordering *dissolution of a single firm.*

The difficulty for European policy is that they do want their businesses to get bigger. In fact, that was one reason for forming the Community. They expect that with the ambit of competition enlarged over so great an area as the Six, the selective force of competition will do its work in weeding out all but the most efficient, which in many instances will mean the bigger factories and bigger firms. The Western Europeans have made a choice, the implications of which few of them clearly realize, in favor of more competition, higher production, better use of resources—and fewer and bigger firms, less and less of the "economic way of life" which the Supreme Court had to mention three times in *Brown Shoe* (370 U.S. 316, 333, 344). The Europeans have tasted the joys of that way of life, some of them to the very dregs. A great historian and martyr of the French Resistance, Marc Bloch, wrote it off after the 1940 collapse,[17] though it took World War II and then the humiliation of Suez to make the Europeans draw together.

But no decisions of this kind are ever made at one time and place; they are the cumulative result of policies and events over a span of years. It will not be clear for some time, surely, whether Europe is going down the road to greater productivity by means of wider markets and more intense competition, or whether it will slide back toward the cherished "way of life." The rejection of Great Britain is a step backward (which I expect to be reversed within a few years at most). Yet General de Gaulle, in the same press conference in which he explained his action on Great Britain, referred three separate times to the need of increasing the national income, on which rested all his and the nation's hope of a better future. But his reference to the Six as a relatively closed system seemed to assume the continuance of a relatively high rate of agricultural production among them.

The problem of agriculture throws all the issues discussed by men into so high a relief and I will best summarize my discussion by getting a little way off from the subject. Farm policy, in the U.S. and Europe,

17. Marc Bloch, *l'Etrange Défaite,* (Paris, 1957), p. 190 (actually written in 1940; Bloch was seized and killed by the Gestapo in 1944).

is indeed the outstanding example of keeping small businesses alive in order to preserve a small-business way of life. It has two purely economic features: first, it is a transfer of wealth from consumers to farmers; second, it is a waste of resources because it keeps much more labor and capital on the farms then necessary to provide food and fibers. Everybody knows that U. S. and European farm policies have some important but strangely undefined noneconomic goals. I have never seen them stated plainly and doubt that I ever will. But let us look at some of the noneconomic results. Disputes over farm programs made the British-Common Market negotiations drag on until General de Gaulle finally vetoed them, as he would not have done earlier. Dissensions over farm policy had nearly wrecked the Community just a year earlier. The U.S. Secretary of Agriculture had to fly to Brussels to issue warnings against restriction and protection which were in odd contrast to this country's practice, and the meetings degenerated into squabbles about how many American chickens would be let into Europe next year. Not only have the members of the Atlantic community become embroiled with each other, they are penalizing themselves further and earning the justified resentment of much of the underdeveloped world by restricting the exports by which they could hope to pay their way on the road to development – and incidentally, benefit us. All this economic loss and political bedevilment in order to benefit perhaps six percent of the U.S. population and perhaps double that in France. Is it worth it? Can it be that protection of this "way of life" is an economic and political dead loss? The Europeans are going to face the problem a little sooner because it conflicts with their hopes of a richer and stronger Europe. Although better off, I doubt that we do well to "sloganize" the problem away.

CHAPTER 3

Problems and Prospects in Antitrust Policy – III

BY WARD S. BOWMAN, JR.

Introduction

Public policy toward competition involves "monopoly problems" which occur in many areas of activity not encompassed by antitrust law. The antitrust laws, of course, are principally concerned with monopoly and restraints on competition in private enterprise. Although professional groups and nonprofit institutions are not specifically exempt[1] as are labor unions, the principal focus of antitrust has been, and still is, industry and commerce. Nonetheless, many types of enterprise in many industries are exempt from the proscriptions of antitrust, or are exempt with respect to certain crucial aspects of their operations.

Economic monopoly, as contrasted to illegal monopoly, properly includes supply restricting or price-fixing power and effect wherever found. The effects can occur, and do occur as much among labor groups as among enterprise groups, and as much and probably more in government than in either labor or enterprise. In short, much of the "monopoly" if indeed not most of the "monopoly" in the country is beyond the reach of the antitrust laws.

Beyond the reach of antitrust is, thus, a much broader category than *exemptions from antitrust.* For purposes of perspective in assessing public policy with

1. Medical associations and even university research institutes have, for example, been defendants in antitrust actions.

respect to competition it seems worth stressing that the "exemptions," such as resale price maintenance in the distributive trades, union wages, and that catch-all category called "regulated industries" are outranked in terms of monopoly effect by the positive activities of government such as: tariff and quota regulations; foreign trading schemes involving such commodities as sugar, coffee, tin, and Japanese textiles; crop support programs of the Department of Agriculture; the oil proration schemes of the Department of Interior and the Texas Railroad Commission; and the numerous state and local occupational licensing laws.

Fair-trading distributors, labor unions, and industries operating under rules or directives imposed by regulative bodies (these are examples, not a complete list) have been given varying degrees of exemption. Except for the one-firm "natural monopoly," the public utility, few are completely exempt from antitrust. And where the exemption is applicable, often something akin to antitrust standards are provided as an alternative form of control in lieu of antitrust law. Rules concerning secondary boycotts in our labor laws are an example. The importance and the effectiveness of these safeguards to competition under regulations, however, vary greatly.

The need, or the alleged need, for exemption under various situations varies so widely that generalization is impossible. I shall make no attempt to cover the field, but rather shall briefly touch on the exemption problem involved in resale price maintenance and in labor and then move to transportation, a regulated industry example. The resale price maintenance exemption typifies a law which stresses the importance of survival of business units. It does so by protecting dealer margins against competition. The labor exemption, as is well known, reflects a legislative determination that wage competition produces "bad" results of a sort different from the "good" results of other price competition. The regulated industries present no common pattern. The transportation exemption does involve a subject of current policy interest, even if it cannot be said to be typical of the exemption problem in regulated industries.[2]

The Resale Price Maintenance Exemption

The Miller-Tydings Act and the more recent McGuire Act permit the makers of most identifiable products to fix the prices at which these products may be resold, or below which they may not be resold. Thus the law protects dealer margins from competition of others selling the same product. This is afforded only if the original seller or the prior seller prescribes it. By no means all do. Most do not. Moreover, the exemption is limited in a number of ways. The current federal law —unlike the proposed "Quality Stabilization Act"— is only permissive and does not apply unless state statutes permit the practice. The exemption does not apply if the fair-traded goods are not "in free and open competition with goods of the same class." A seller who owns his own outlets cannot fix resale prices to resellers competing with the owned outlets. Such was the holding in *U.S.* v. *McKesson & Robbins, Inc.*[3] Agreements among competitors on the same level of distribution are not sanctioned.

Most economists have not been favorably impressed with the "fair trade" exemption. I shall not go into the weak arguments pro and the strong arguments con.

2. The chapters below by Richard H. Holton, Merton S. Peck, Walter Adams, Herbert R. Northrup and Gordon F. Bloom, and Nat Goldfinger and Theodore St. Antoine provide additional and somewhat different views on these subjects.

3. 351 U.S. 305 (1956).

Price maintenance is currently on the wane in many states and even where it is in effect it seems more honored in the breach than in the observance. Discount merchandizing waxes while fair trade wanes except on a relatively small number of items. Notable exceptions arise when price maintenance is backed by state enforcement. This is the case with liquor sales in Connecticut and in a number of other states.

The Labor Union Exemption

Agreements on wages or wage equivalents arising under collective bargaining agreements exempt employees (and employers) from what would otherwise be illegal price fixing under the Sherman Act. The exemption does not apply to "working men" who work for themselves,[4] nor does it apply to labor combinations with employer groups to achieve ends which if done by agreement among enterprises would be illegal.[5] The most recent pronouncement on these issues by the Supreme Court is in *Los Angeles Meat Provision Drivers* v. *United States.*[6] In this antitrust case, the Supreme Court held that there was an illegal combination between "business men" and a union that was not saved by the Norris-LaGuardia Act because the case was not one "involving or growing out of any labor dispute." This case involved activities of independent restaurant grease peddlers who, along with employees of the processors, collected grease. They were members in a union with employees of their customers the processors. The independent grease gatherers' earnings as middlemen consisted of the difference in price between grease purchased and grease sold to processors. The union business agent allocated territories and accounts for

4. *Columbia River Packing Assn.* v. *Hinton,* 315 U.S. 143 (1945).
5. *Allen Bradley* v. *Local Union No. 3,* 325 U.S. 797 (1945).
6. 83 Sup. Ct. 162 (1962).

both purchases and sales and protected the gatherers from nonunion competition. The plan violated the antitrust law. The relief involved evicting the independent grease peddlers from the union.

Although this case and the two aforementioned cases set limits on the antitrust exemption of labor unions, principal union monopoly power arises in the context of the wage bargain. That is, principal union power is exerted in the context of a labor dispute or a potential labor dispute. Here, labor law, unlike the antitrust law, attempts to solve the monopoly problem in terms of countervailing the power of the employers by the power of the employees. Bilateral monopoly, however, has significantly different effects than does competition, especially upon nonorganized workers and upon the consumers of final products. Collective bargaining is bilateral monopoly. Bilateral monopoly resolves the question of which side of the bargain gets the benefit from a restriction on production – labor or management. (Only under unique and unlikely circumstances will the restriction be eliminated to the benefit of third parties.) It is largely myth that countervailing power protects consumers. Wage bargains can and do raise consumer prices and these effects are receiving an increasing amount of public attention. It is becoming apparent to many that something more is needed in the public interest than is provided by existing labor law. Basically the alternatives are more regulation or more competition.

Regulated Industry Exemptions

Most of the fields of regulation are familiar. The reasons ascribed to the need or needs for regulation in these fields range from national security – the protection of an essential industry or resource, as timber or oil – to improving the "moral" standards of consumer choice – the viewing habits of television watchers, for example. Competition is often said to occasion social cost (or bad neighborhood effects) which those causing them need not bear. Professor Ronald Coase, of the University of Virginia, has seriously questioned the incompatibility of market competition with this alleged reason for regulation. His interesting work on communications regulation suggests greater use of market forces in lieu of detailed market supplanting directives.

I shall not explore these various "conflicting" policy goals, save one, economy of scale. Each of many reasons for exemption from antitrust standards would be worthy of a full-length controversial discourse. The economy of scale exemption is the least controversial. My own position is that there is neither compelling theory nor good evidence to support the proposition that effective competition is inconsistent with any of the valid goals except the goal of efficiency due to scale. "Economy of scale" may be a short phrase but it covers a great amount of ground and often masks a great deal of ignorance. It is the root of the oligopoly problem – what to do about the few firm industries – and it is no less important in the exempt than in the nonexempt areas.

The Railroad Industry

The railroad industry presents a policy dilemma of whether to foster or to replace competition. This, of course, involves a problem of the appropriateness of exemption from antitrust law. The Senate Select Committee on Interstate Commerce in a report dated January 18, 1886,[7] prior to the passage of the Interstate Commerce Act in 1887 and three years before the pas-

7. Report of the Senate Select Committee on Interstate Commerce, 29th Cong., 1st Sess., January 18, 1886, pp. 175-198.

sage of the Sherman Act, set out many causes of complaint against the railroad system. Local rates were said to be too high compared to through rates. All rates were said to be too high (partly because of monopoly in certain areas and partly because of pooling agreements). Discrimination between individuals for like service was found; discrimination between different articles and quantities existed; discrimination between localities, secret rebates and drawbacks and uncertainty of rates were all objected to. It was reported that railroads refused to be bound by contracts, that pass-granting caused privileged classes to exist; carriers rescinded obligations of their own agents and too high capitalization and bonded indebtedness existed. Carriers engaged in nontransportation activities that were extravagant and wasteful.

The original 1887 Act evidenced the same disposition toward railroads that was evidenced toward other trusts and which led to the passage of the Sherman Act. Both acts received strong Populist support. The Sherman Act was not thought to compete with but to complement the Interstate Commerce Act. The courts thought this so, too. Many of the early landmark antitrust cases involved railroads. Railroad pricing arrangements were held to be illegal under the Sherman Act in the 1890's in the *Trans-Missouri,*[8] and *Joint-Traffic*[9] cases, both of which involved rate pools. Railroad mergers were prohibited under antitrust law in *Northern Securities Co.* v. *U.S.,*[10] and in *U.S.* v. *Union Pacific Railroad Co.*[11] A combination of railroads, restraining competition in the sale of anthracite coal, was

8. *U.S.* v. *Trans-Missouri Freight Assn.,* 166 U.S. 290 (1897).
9. *U.S.* v. *Joint-Traffic Assn.,* 171 U.S. 505 (1898).
10. 193 U.S. 197 (1904).
11. 226 U.S. 61 (192).

the subject of the first *Reading* case,[12] and in *U.S.* v. *Terminal Railroad Assn.*,[13] joint boycotting of outsiders from use of an essential terminal facility was condemned. All of these railroad cases were prior to 1920. The cases were brought during a period when the Interstate Commerce Commission (under the 1887 Act) had authority over unjust and unreasonable rate charges (Section 1 of the Interstate Commerce Act), over discriminatory charges for a like and contemporaneous service (Section 2) and over undue rate or service preference to persons, organizations, locality or kind of traffic (Section 3). The I.C.C. also had power to prevent greater charges for short than long hauls over the same line (Section 4) and to prohibit pooling of freights of different and competing railroads (Section 5).

The Transportation Act of 1920 gave the Commission power over finance and security issues, allowed the Commission to establish minimum as well as maximum rates, and also gave power to the Commission over the extent of plant — power to control expansion and contraction of railroads. Problems arising from trucker competition led to the passage in 1935 of the Motor Carrier Act which gave the I.C.C. regulatory authority over motor carriers as well as railroads. The Transportation Act of 1940 gave the I.C.C. similar control over water carriage — intercoastal, coast-wise, and inland waters.

Both the Transportation Acts of 1920 and of 1940 viewed railroad consolidations as desirable means of achieving more adequate and efficient transportation service. This position has received judicial recognition under both acts.[14] Section 5 under the consolidated act

12. *U.S.* v. *Reading Co.*, 226 U.S. 224 (1912).
13. 224 U.S. 383 (1912).
14. *U.S.* v. *Lowden*, 308 U.S. 225 (1939), and *County of Marin* v. *U.S.*, 356 U.S. 412 (1958).

contains the so-called antitrust provision of the present Interstate Commerce Act. In its present form it, in effect, only admonishes the Commission in finding public interest to include in its considerations undue restraints on competition. Currently Section 5 of the Interstate Commerce Act (as amended by the Reed-Bulwinkle Act of 1948) gives railroads effective immunity from antitrust prosecution. This immunity arises only from specific approval by the Commission but approval may be given with respect to pooling, unifications, mergers, and acquisitions of control. Even though Congress has not made the antitrust laws wholly inapplicable to the transportation industry, the role of antitrust has been relegated to the minor one of adviser or intervener in I.C.C. proceedings.

The national transportation policy is the product of a long history of trial and error by Congress. Up to 1920 emphasis was directed mainly at abuses and the application of antitrust laws to preserve competition was a part of that effort. Thereafter the antitrust role waned. Emphasis since 1920 has been on "adequate transportation service" and on protecting the "inherent advantages" of each mode of transportation. This emphasis has been manifested in attempts to regulate the appropriate spheres of rail, truck, and water carriage.

But a change is in the wind. Today there is increasing awareness that all is not well with transportation policy. The Economic Report of the President transmitted to Congress in January 1963 calls for *less* supervision of rates and services and greater reliance on the market to allocate business between alternative modes of transportation. This kind of recommendation supports a previous recommendation made in the Eisenhower Administration by a Committee under the direction of former Secretary of Commerce Weeks. Independent studies by transportation experts and economists express a growing disposition to allow railroads, many of which are in dire financial condition, to attempt to improve their position through price competition with other means of carriage. The monopoly of transportation by rail, it is contended, is not what it used to be.

These newer recommendations for intercarrier competition raise interesting public policy questions. It is notable that the recommendations do not call for increased competition among railroads themselves, or among truckers, or among water carriers. Rather, only intercarrier competition is recommended. Why one form is desirable and the other not, is not evident. For long hauls and on certain products trucks may provide ineffective competiton and presumably rate regulations would continue to be applicable in such instances. Relaxation of control is not proposed for maximum rates. This may raise serious problems of survival for particular railroads. Revenues may not be sufficient for present operations. I.C.C. policy toward abandonments may need reappraisal. Also, fostering intercarrier competition is closely related to motor carrier entry requirements. Effective intercarrier competition is not solely a railroad problem. Certificates of convenience and necessity are not freely given to truckers.

Now recommendations are being made to rely more heavily upon competition in rate determination. At the same time a large number of major railroad mergers are contemplated. The applicants stress very substantial cost savings from consolidated operations. In securing Commission approval of mergers much will and much should depend upon the credibility of the detailed cost-saving estimates prepared by and for the merger applicants. It seems not at all unlikely that the railroad industry will become considerably more concentrated.

The Department of Justice has intervened to object to a number of these railroad mergers pending before the Commission. The Department's position is that the mergers would "unduly restrain competition" and be against the public interest. Undoubtedly, if the standards of Section 7 of the Clayton Act were applicable, the railroad mergers would fare badly. Under antitrust law, not only has the criterion of efficiency been minimized, it has been held to be a *detriment* to merger approval.[15] Heretical as it may sound, I.C.C. appraisal in this respect promises better performance.

As long as increased market competition in transportation is limited to intercarrier competition, merging railroads to achieve lower costs merely makes for more effective competition with trucks, or other carriers. And in the less likely case that truck mergers should promise substantial economies, presumably the railroad merger policy could be applicable to them.

If, on the other hand, increased competition among railroads is thought appropriate, railroad mergers may reduce the effectiveness of competition. For example, on long-haul traffic or on bulk carriage where truck competition is not great, it is not proposed that rate control be relaxed. But even here, even after substantial merger, is there any reason to believe that competition would be more concentrated or less effective than in the can industry, or the aluminum industry or the automotive industry?

The latter are not regulated nor are they exempt from antitrust laws. Is competition of the few in these

15. See the discussion of the *Brown Shoe* case by M. A. Adelman in Chapter 2, above, and by Jesse Markham in Chapter 8, below.

industries so slight that they should be regulated, or is it effective enough so that rate regulation is inappropriate? Few, I am sure, would recommend regulation for these nonrailroad examples, and I suspect that each is just as "special" an industry as is railroading. I am suggesting, of course, that the case for transportation regulation is unconvincing whether or not the Commission approves railroad mergers.

Exemption in General

I suspect that the case for most regulation is unconvincing. If not, consistency would seem to require that very much more of the economy deserves to be regulated. The case for exemption from antitrust typically involves a conclusion that a committee of experts can better decide than can the market who should produce how much of what and at what price. Markets are imperfect; some more than others. Many industries have relatively few sellers. Antitrust exemption is not limited to these industries. Even if exemption were so limited, my own belief is that market forces aided by the imperfect policing of the antitrust laws provides a policy solution far superior to the alternative regulation. I suggest that neither theory nor practice supports most price and output regulation. With the possible exception of the "natural monopoly" case, there is in fact no theory of regulation at all, and practice reflects no principled standards for deciding on the basis of experience what should be regulated.

CHAPTER 4

Competitive Policy and National Goals: the Doubtful Relevance of Antitrust

BY DONALD DEWEY

Preliminary Observations

In the pages which follow, I shall argue the truth of three closely related propositions. First, federal antitrust policy in its present form is largely irrelevant to the important problems of the American economy. Second, antitrust has an economic cost which may well outweigh any economic benefits that it confers. Third, the foregoing propositions being true, it follows that the case for antitrust must rest mainly upon arguments which the professional economist has no special competence to appraise.

All of the important arguments for preferring the capitalist form of market economy to the discernible alternatives have long been common currency, at least to economists and lawyers. Whether one believes or disbelieves them depends mainly upon two things—knowledge of how a price system works and the value placed upon personal liberty as against other goals, notably economic and social equality, and the type of fraternity represented by public housing, communal feeding, and the joy that comes from knowing that everyone plays some small part in the master plan of the State. It is not possible for me, in my allotted space, to write anything new about a price system. It would be an impertinence if I employed this opportunity to proselytize for my own view of the good society which, in any event, is probably very close to that of most readers of this book.

Of the arguments for preferring capitalism to the alternatives, two are important above all others. The first asserts that the free society cannot survive in an environment where the State has a monopoly on the opportunities for obtaining an income; that there must be "islands of private economic power" to which a citizen can retreat when he has offended Congress, the President, or the Attorney General. The second contends that, since capitalism makes more use of the price system than its discernible alternatives, it is bound to be more efficient.

These two arguments for capitalism have often been elaborated and supplemented. Henry Simons held that the good society depends upon maintaining consensus on fundamental values which, in turn, requires that the number of issues that arouse political passions must be kept down.[1] The best way of enforcing this restriction, according to Simons, is by leaving most economic decisions to the market. In recent years many refugees from Marxism-Leninism have chosen capitalism on less lofty grounds. Finding this variety of socialism with its limited range of standardized consumer goods unbearably dreary, they have opted for a decadent capitalism with its nightclubs, wasteful advertising, and superfluous varieties of toothpaste. Recently Professor Henry Wallich has argued that one should stick with capitalism simply because its asserted connection with personal freedom may be true. "The risk of total loss of freedom is small, but the penalty is ter-

1. Henry C. Simons, *Economic Policy for a Free Society* (Chicago, 1948), pp. 1-39.

rific if it happens."[2] Wallich does not deny the possibility of democratic socialism. He does emphasize a truth which should be obvious but apparently is not; that, as yet, the destruction of capitalism has never been followed by democratic socialism. On this point I take my stand with Wallich with one additional qualification. Even though a democratic socialist alternative to capitalism may exist, I see no way of making the transition in any reasonably advanced economy except at an unacceptable cost. A capitalist society has, so to speak, an investment in the skills of the bourgeoisie that goes down the drain with its destruction. Conceivably, Poland, if it can ever get rid of the Russians, will evolve a good society within the framework of socialist production. But by my reading of the postwar history of this unfortunate land, the cost will have been much too high. For this reason – and for others that I shall not develop – my allegiance goes to capitalism. In the language of Milton Friedman, I am prepared to act "as if" I believe that the case for capitalism is valid.

The Major Problems of American Capitalism

So much for personal philosophy. The next step is to inquire into the conditions that must be fulfilled if American capitalism is to perform in a way that merits our allegiance and to consider the role that antitrust plays in providing them. We might approach this task indirectly by identifying the threats to American capitalism that are most likely to jeopardize its health, and possibly its existence, in the foreseeable future. To state the obvious, these threats are three: possible defeat in a military contest, possible defeat in an ideological contest for the allegiance of politically influential groups, and possible defeat in some sort of output contest with

2. Henry C. Wallich, *The Cost of Freedom* (New York, 1960), p. 62.

rivals. I have nothing to say respecting the first danger except that when one contemplates nuclear war, the nature of the economic system which will emerge in the aftermath is of distinctly marginal interest.

Twenty years ago Joseph Schumpeter alerted us to the depressing possibility that capitalism will ultimately give way to some variety of socialism, not because capitalism fails by economic criteria, but rather because it succeeds too well.[3] The great Austrian scholar advanced several reasons for believing that capitalism might fall victim to its own success. He attached particular importance to the alienation of that numerous class of intellectuals whose existence is made possible by capitalist affluence. My own view is that Schumpeter was unnecessarily pessimistic on this score, at least where this country is concerned; that he greatly exaggerated the influence in the United States of that type of intellectual who is epitomized by the professor of political science who writes for the *New Republic*. Nevertheless, this type of intellectual presumably has some influence and, hence, is presumably worth influencing on behalf of capitalism. I am not sure that this task can be accomplished by any means at our disposal. I am certain that it cannot be done with antitrust litigation.

The basic difficulty is that the opposition of the *New Republic* intellectual to capitalism is not mainly the product of an erroneous view of how the system works. (His view is often erroneous but this is another matter.) His opposition is really rooted in a disdain bordering on hatred for American businessmen and the values that the American business world fosters and rewards. Nothing short of a mass program of psychoanalysis for intellectuals will rid the American scene of

3. Joseph A. Schumpeter, *Capitalism, Socialism and Democracy* (New York, 1942).

this dislike — certainly not the good news of a larger antitrust budget. In any case, I am not certain that the total conversion of intellectuals to capitalism would be a good thing. One may prefer capitalism to the discernible alternatives and still believe that the efforts of business men to convert economic power into political and cultural influence should be stoutly resisted. In any event, while intellectuals of the *New Republic* type are socialist in their economics they are, for the most part, good democrats in their politics. So long as they are not alienated to the point of subversion, I am even prepared to believe that, on balance, they do the cause of capitalism more good than harm by keeping the friends of the system from complacency.

Of course, one cannot rule out the possibility that history will prove Schumpeter correct. The fate of American capitalism may not be decided by a rational appraisal of its economic performance. But unless we are prepared to abjure politics completely, we must act on the assumption that people are capable of being persuaded by reasoned discourse and, hence, that American capitalism will get the political support that it deserves. Notwithstanding the results of the 1963 election in Italy, I submit that the decline of socialist parties in most Western countries since the Great Depression is evidence that this hope has a solid foundation.

What of the third cloud on the horizon for American capitalism — the possibility that it will be bested in some sort of output race by a rival system? Defeat could presumably result from one or both of two developments. The rate of increase in man-hour productivity in the American economy could fall below that of its major rivals for some considerable period of time. The American economy could fail to maintain a reasonably close approximation to full employment. The former possibility does not worry me; the latter worries me exceedingly.

Certain observers have been impressed by the achievement of socialist nations in raising the output of consumer goods.[4] I am not one of them. Admittedly this skepticism may be rooted in a set of preferences that runs to those goods and services that capitalism is particularly well suited to produce – variety in education, private housing, hi-fi sets, Chinese restaurants, etc. A distinguished English economist, fully cognizant of the achievements of capitalism, nevertheless condemns the system on the ground that it fails to produce the proper amounts of what, in her opinion, people need most – housing, medical care, and education.[5]

No good purpose would here be served by recapitulating the many difficulties involved in comparing the growth rates of different economic systems, in the absence of detailed information on prices and physical inputs and outputs. I will rest content with the following assertion. Given our statistical ignorance of what goes on in other countries, especially socialist countries, the productivity performance of the American economy in any decade must be measured against its own long-term trend. According to the best available evidence, we chug along at a fairly steady and predictable rate. When the measure of economic performance is annual increase in output per man-year, our annual productivity gain, by one reputable estimate, averaged 1.8 percent from 1913 through 1959.[6] In recent years we have done substantially better. From 1950 through 1959 this annual productivity gain averaged 2.2 percent.[7] So long as this pace is maintained, I decline to lose sleep over the possibility that capitalism will one day be voted out in this

4. Abram Bergson, *The Real National Income of Soviet Russia Since 1928* (Cambridge, 1961).
5. Joan Robinson, "Latter Day Capitalism," *New Left Review*, vol. 37 (July-August, 1963).
6. D. C. Paige, *et al.*, "Economic Growth: The Last Hundred Years," *National Institute Economic Review* (July, 1961).
7. *Ibid.*

country because we perceive that the inhabitants of socialist states have a dazzlingly higher standard of living.

The possible inability of the American economy to keep the wastes of unemployment within politically tolerable limits is a more serious matter. Notwithstanding the contempt for history now displayed in most of the social sciences, the castastrophic depression of the 1930's remains a terrifying fact. Volumes have been written on the achievements of the New Deal and the social import of the Roosevelt Revolution. Only a few economists recall that most of the recovery experienced by the American economy between 1933 and 1940 can be traced to a simple increase in the money supply, and that most of this increase resulted from the inflow of gold that occurred as Europe prepared for war. To put it bluntly, the recovery of the late thirties owed far more to the evil of Hitler than to the beneficence of Roosevelt. Still, one can make a good case that the Great Depression was a monumental piece of bad luck for American capitalism; that it was caused by a peculiarly perverse concatenation of circumstances at home and abroad which is not likely to be repeated in this century. Of more immediate concern is the unsatisfactory performance of the American economy in the last thirteen years. For at least half the months since January 1949 the economy has carried too much unemployment. The percentage of workers totally unemployed has been too high, the rate of labor turnover has been too low, and the work week too short. What has been holding us back?

Most economists attribute the poor economic performance to insufficient investment, and this insufficiency is traced, in turn, to the failure of the federal government (including the Federal Reserve System) to pursue those monetary and fiscal measures that would have ensured the right level of investment. This diagnosis of our recent economic malaise is correct as far as it goes. But this view of the world inherited from J. M. Keynes is distinctly superficial. If we go back to first principles, we perceive the virtually self-evident truth that unemployment exists because some labor has been priced out of the market. That is, unemployment exists because real wage rates are too high. We proceed to a truth nearly as obvious. If unemployment is to be eliminated, the real wage rate must rise less rapidly than man-hour productivity. We have three ways of achieving this result.

First, the federal government may seek to enforce a policy of wage restraint on the economy which ensures that, in time of unemployment, real wage rates rise less rapidly than man-hour productivity. As yet, this alternative has never been seriously considered in this country. Second, we can retard the rise in real wage rates by inflation. This was, of course, the solution favored by Keynes, though in a different terminology and in the context of a depression.[8] On occasions, notably in our mobilization in the early days of World War II, an inflationary policy has produced a truly spectacular rise in output. The only trouble is that such a policy presupposes that you can fool most of the people most of the time – and with the same old trick. Unhappily, there is persuasive evidence that the American wage earner is adept at devising hedges to protect himself against inflation. Labor unions insert escalator clauses into contracts that automatically tie wage increases to the consumer price index. Even a mild inflation is likely to produce political pressure that moves Congress to increase the federal minimum wage. I certainly do not object on principle to so-called Keynesian monetary and fiscal measures. I simply question whether they will suffice to achieve their objectives once the element of surprise has worn off.

8. John Maynard Keynes, *The General Theory of Employment, Interest and Money* (New York, 1936).

Which brings us to the third alternative. We can endeavor to remove the structural imperfections in the American economy that are the root cause of unemployment. The difficulties that wait us if we choose this course become apparent once we begin to list the offending imperfections – minimum wage legislation, labor unions, the so-called fair wages policies enforced by the federal government on its private contractors, and, perhaps most formidable of all, human perversity. So long as welfare payments suffice to prevent starvation, the citizens of Detroit will probably tolerate any amount of unemployment in the automobile industry. The refusal of the industry to grant an annual productivity rise will create an ugly climate of opinion. An attempt actually to cut money wages would be an invitation to civil disobedience or worse.

Here I would digress to say that the foregoing remarks should not be taken to mean that I disagree with those economists who believe that the power of labor unions over wages is grossly exaggerated by friend and foe alike. I suggest, however, that this power does not need to be very great in order to raise the unemployment figure by an average of two or three percentage points over a decade.

Can we really expect to do much about wage and price rigidities? I confess that, while I am prepared to fight the good fight, my optimism is not great. My side has taken too many bad beatings in the last thirty years. It is not merely that one must contend with vested interests and economic illiteracy. (And any country that raises the legal minimum wage in time of serious unemployment assuredly contains a high percentage of economic illiterates.) There is an additional reason for pessimism. A rich society that is yearly growing richer has too many acceptable ways of disguising unemployment. The possibilities for sugar coating are virtually unlimited; to mention only a few, the 35-hour week, retirement at age 60, junior college for everybody, and four years of graduate study before one can practice as an accountant or mortician. Once the label of *education* or *leisure* has been pinned to unemployment, any measure designed to allow the citizen more choice between work and nonwork is, by common consent, reactionary. Conceivably, the stratagems that the American economy adopts in order to disguise its inability to use human resources efficiently will eventually be hailed by everybody except a few sour economists as the visible fruits of its success.

The above remarks respecting the possibility of maintaining full employment have been rather gloomy. Let me conclude on a more optimistic note. We ought not to fall into the habit that characterizes so many members of The RAND Corporation and Central Intelligence Agency. In prognosticating about the future, they regularly assume that the enemy (increasingly difficult to identify) will do everything right while we shall do everything wrong. A perspective on economic waste is needed. I suggest that it is afforded by the reflection that every society – indeed every age – has its own particular variety of economic waste. Therefore, exceeding great care should be used in comparing the wastes of different economic systems. Admittedly, an 8 percent unemployment figure represents considerable inefficiency. But how does one compare it with the supreme economic folly of nationalizing agriculture and retail distribution? Again, when we grumble about unemployment in the 1950's, we might reflect that the movement of several million people out of agriculture during this decade represented a very considerable improvement in resource allocation. Conceivably, the arteriosclerosis of American capitalism, in the form of increasing wage rigidities, merely means that most of us will have to take our future productivity gains in the form of greater leisure. Or, in the case of professors, in released time for research. This is a bearable fate.

The Probable Irrelevance of Antitrust

We come now to the central problem of this volume. What is the present contribution of antitrust to the successful functioning of the American economy? The corpus of antitrust legislation and case law can usefully be divided into two parts. One part is technical business law and is concerned mainly with the enforceability of contracts. This type of antitrust is not peculiar to the American economy or, indeed, to a capitalist economy. (I have heard from a Yugoslav economist that, in his country, the Central Planning Commission has sometimes reprimanded state enterprises for negotiating restrictive agreements.) My concern is with the second part of antitrust activity – that which signifies a repudiation of what we commonly call laissez-faire. In retrospect, we can see that laissez-faire had two main foundations in the common law. The first was simple freedom of contract. The second was the doctrine of disinterested malevolence by which one merchant could do anything to dispose of a rival provided that he respected two restraints. He must not commit a recognized crime – arson, libel, etc. And his object in inflicting the injury must be commercial advantage and not a sadistic desire to humble an enemy.[9]

Space does not allow an examination of the circumstances and ideas that gave such a large place to laissez-faire in the common law. It will suffice to treat antitrust policy as the antithesis of laissez-faire as understood by nineteenth century lawyers and economists. The syllo-

9. The legal meaning of laissez-faire is thoroughly discussed in *Mogul Steamship Co.* v. *McGregor, Gow & Co.*, 21 Q.B.D. 544 (1888), 23 Q.B.D. 598 (1889), (1892) A.C. 25.

gism of antitrust runs as follows. Freedom of contract can be used to destroy competition; competition is more important than freedom of contract; therefore, the latter must be curbed. A merchant may manipulate prices to destroy competition; therefore he must be prevented by law from doing so. The distinctive features of American antitrust follow from this syllogism. These features are three: trust-bust in the literal sense, control of mergers, and control of commercial practices.

What, then, is the present contribution of antitrust policy to the performance of the American economy? So far as economic progress and the maintenance of full employment are concerned, the answer that I offer can have little comfort for the friends of antitrust. I shall argue that antitrust has a number of minor economic virtues that may justify its perpetuation in some form but that, so far as the two major problems of the American economy are concerned, antitrust is at best irrelevant and, at worst, a liability. Let me emphasize I do not dismiss antitrust on the ground that it "has never been tried." This position might have been tenable until the revival of antitrust in the late 1930's. But the amount of litigation in the last twenty-five years is convincing evidence of antitrust's having been tried. And I firmly believe that antitrust suits—actual and potential—have appreciably reduced the degree of ownership concentration in the American economy. I also believe that this reduction of concentration has not been without cost.

Consider first the relation—if any—of antitrust to technological progress. The main *a priori* arguments which assert that competition helps or hinders technological progress are uncomplicated and common knowledge. At one extreme, there is the Simons-Fetter view. Technological progress is traced to the efforts of small enterprises scourged by the lash of competition to survive and prosper by cutting costs and improving the product. At the other extreme, there is the Schumpeter-Galbraith view. The source of technological progress is held to be the laboratories of those large firms whose size allows them to gamble on research and development. The reasonable man may feel that these positions are not irreconcilable; that, possibly, large monopolistic firms and small competitive firms produce different kinds of economic progress. We shall not pause to examine this possibility.[10] For our purposes, it will suffice to note that, when one deals in statistical aggregates, neither of these extreme views seems to be valid. Our annual rate of increase in man-hour productivity for the years 1880 through 1960 appears to have been surprisingly constant. And when one disaggregates and attempts to correlate degree of monopoly in an industry with its productivity performance, no significant correlation emerges.[11]

Is this result really surprising? When one lists the variables that influence technological progress, would not most of us put degree of monopoly well down the list? By my ranking, it would certainly stand below expenditures on research, percentage of graduate scientists and engineeers employed, percentage of Jews and Protestants in top management, and the rate of increase in the industry's output. In short, there is, apparently, no respectable

10. Merton J. Peck explores this interesting possibility for one industry in *Competition in the Aluminum Industry, 1945-1958* (Cambridge, Mass., 1961).

11. See, for example, Jacob Schmookler, "The Changing Efficiency of the American Economy, 1869-1938," *Review of Economics and Statistics*, vol. 34 (May, 1952), or Almarin Phillips, "Concentration, Scale and Technological Change in Selected Manufacturing Industries, 1889-1939," *Journal of Industrial Economics*, vol. 4 (June, 1956). For a fragmentary statistical study whose conclusion supports the view that competition stimulates progress, see George J. Stigler, "Industrial Organization and Economic Progress," in *The State of the Social Science*, Leonard D. White, ed. (Chicago, 1956).

statistical case for or against antitrust as a source of technological progress.

Is there any reason to believe that the vigor of the antitrust effort helps to maintain full employment? If antitrust in its present form, makes any contribution at all it is assuredly small. The most troublesome cost rigidities in the American economy are wage rigidities and the antitrust agencies do not now have — and indeed, have never had — any real power to intervene in the labor market. Any contribution by antitrust to wage flexibility is indirect. The most we can say is that a policy that preserves competition among business firms may make it more difficult for unions to enforce industry-wide collective bargaining and, hence, may serve to weaken union powers to influence wage rates.

Some authorities trace some of our difficulties in maintaining full employment to the existence of "administered prices."[12] I have never been able to perceive why a monopolist should be any more loath to revise his price in the light of altered conditions of supply and demand than a perfect competitor. But, of course, the monopolist, since he must have a price policy, is likely to have a slower response. Hence, the slowness of administered prices to fall in time of recession may accelerate the rise of unemployment. If so, the elimination of administered prices by antitrust action may do some good. Unhappily, there is the other side of the coin. The object of the Robinson-Patman Act is the reduction of "price discrimination" which is merely another name for price flexibility. Moreover, any manipulation of prices that allows a large firm to penetrate rapidly the market of a small firm

12. The definitive discussion (and refutation) of this hypothesis is Richard Ruggles, "The Nature of Price Flexibility and the Determinants of Relative Price Changes in the Economy," in *Business Concentration and Price Policy*, National Bureau of Economic Research (Princeton, 1955).

is likely to be stigmatized by the antitrust agencies as unfair competition and prosecuted under one or more of the antitrust statutes.

The Traditional Case for Antitrust

So far I have managed to discuss antitrust without reference to "the monopoly problem." This, you will grant, is at least unusual. Seizing on this oversight, a cautious friend of antitrust might well offer the following admonition:

> Admittedly, antitrust has no significant contribution to make to technological progress and full employment – the really important economic problems of American capitalism. Further, I accept that, so far as the future of Parliamentary democracy is concerned, it does not greatly matter whether the 200 largest industrial firms control 20, 30, or 40 percent of the country's productive capacity. Nevertheless, there *is* a monopoly problem in the United States. Certain firms are able to enforce restrictions on the outputs of their respective industries that raise prices to consumers and "misallocate" the economy's resources. The contribution of antitrust to economic performance should be judged by its success in solving the "monopoly problem" narrowly defined.

In reply to this hypothetical remonstrance, I would begin by saying that no economist resident in New York City is allowed to forget for one day that there is a monopoly problem. It is brought home to him whenever he must deal with Consolidated Edison, hire a $25,000 taxicab to transport him a few blocks in the rain, or pay 25 cents for a quart of milk. Yet while there is a monopoly problem, it is essentially a problem of state intervention in the market – just as it was in Adam Smith's day. Antitrust policy is relevant only to that small portion of monopoly power that firms are able to create for themselves without the support of the State. Of what magnitude is this fraction? Two statistical studies that have sought to measure the costs of private monopoly have made it a very minute percentage of total output—less than one percent of national income.[13] Both of these studies were small-scale pioneering ventures and rest upon a number of debatable assumptions. Of more importance are recent developments on the analytical front that have served to raise doubts about the significance of private monopoly power.

Let us go back again to fundamentals. The traditional case for laissez-faire did not deny the existence of private monopoly. Rather it assumed first that, so long as private monopolists did not enjoy State protection, their exceptional profits would be of short duration. It assumed, secondly, that given the ineptness of State intervention, any effort to speed up the destruction of private monopoly would have an unacceptable cost. The economic case for antitrust is an assertion that these two assumptions are demonstrably wrong. More specifically, the economic case for antitrust alleges that private monopoly power can be created and perpetuated for long years by cartels, mergers, and unfair competition and that the economic cost of suppressing these monopolizing devices is low enough to make the effort worthwhile. The economic case for antitrust may be valid, but I submit that in view of recent developments in economic theory, it can no longer be taken as self-evident.

Consider the decline of the venerable doctrine of unfair competition. In the heyday of the trust problem John Bates Clark catalogued the techniques by which

13. Arnold C. Harberger, "Monopoly and Resource Allocation," *American Economic Review*, vol. 44 (March, 1954); and David Schwartzman, "The Burden of Monopoly," *Journal of Political Economy*, vol. 68 (November, 1960).

the large firm could discipline or dispatch its small rival. The rival may be producing goods cheaply; he may be the man who normally ought to survive and yet the trust may ruin him. According to Clark:

> It may make use of the "factors agreement," by which it gives a special rebate to those merchants who handle only its own goods. It may resort, secondly, to the familiar plan of cutting prices locally, – entering its rival's special territory and selling goods there below the cost of producing them, while sustaining itself by means of higher prices charged in other portions of its field. Again, the trust may depend on the cutting of the price of some one variety of goods which a rival producer makes, in order to ruin him, while it sustains itself by means of the high prices which it gets for goods of other kinds. These three things alone are enough to make the position of a competitor perilous . . . and the suppression of them would go far toward rescuing competition, protecting the public, and insuring to it a large share of the benefit that comes from economies in production.[14]

But does unfair competition as described by John Bates Clark "really" exist? Any young scholar fresh from doctoral training at Chicago will stoutly maintain that "unfair competition" is a mirage. John McGee has even rehabilitated the policies of the Standard Oil Company before 1910.[15] The argument of the Chicago people is that predatory price-cutting is not rational business behavior. It does not pay to get rid of a rival by aggressive price-cutting unless having knocked him out, you can take over his market share and hold it for some interval before a new rival is drawn in by your excess profits. But if

14. John Bates Clark, *The Control of Trusts* (New York, 1912), pp. 96-97.

15. John S. McGee, "Predatory Price Cutting: The Standard Oil (N.J.) Case," *Journal of Law and Economics*, vol. 1 (1958). See also, Wayne Leeman, "The Limitations of Local Price-Cutting as a Barrier to Entry," *Journal of Political Economy*, vol. 64 (August, 1956).

any market power once gained can be held in place for a time, rational business behavior dictates that you buy out the rival or merge with him. This way the losses imposed on both parties by price-cutting can be avoided.

One possible retort to the Chicago view of unfair competition is that it may be real enough even though it falls into the category of irrational business behavior. One has no difficulty in finding instances of mutually unprofitable price wars in American business history. Still, if unfair competition is inherently irrational, it hardly poses a serious threat to competition in important industries.

Now there is a strong presumption that certain tactics employed by professional criminals to eliminate their business rivals, notably harassment of customers, arson, physical assault, and even murder, constitute what Chicago economists would call rational behavior. They are rational in the sense that their employment costs less than the expense of buying out the business rival or purchasing his cooperation by a market share. So an interesting question is presented: do not the criminal tactics of the underworld imperceptibly shade into the unfair tactics of legitimate commerce? Cannot the threat of sales at a price below short-run marginal cost profitably be employed to intimidate a rival or potential rival?

So far as I can see, intimidation can be employed profitably only when (a) one can by an objectionable practice, inflict a loss on a rival greater than the cost of this practice to oneself and (b) the injured party is unable or unwilling to employ the same objectionable practice himself. Both conditions are often fulfilled in the commerce controlled by the underworld. Being deprived of police protection, bookies and prostitutes, for example, are the natural prey of strong arm "organizers." But it is not apparent that these conditions are present in normal commerce. Clearly, if two rivals are equally efficient and both sell at the same losing price, they should have the same rate of loss on capital employed.[16]

Actually the case for fair competition as first formulated by J. B. Clark, and subsequently incorporated into the "theology" of antitrust, would seem to rest upon the same arguments that are thought to justify tariff protection for infant industries. Both cases tacitly concede that new producers, in their first phase, are not as efficient as their established rivals. Both cases affirm that, given the chance to get organized, some new firms will ultimately prove as efficient as some old firms.

But even if these two arguments are correct, it does not follow that economic welfare is increased by a grant of protection to new firms against foreign or domestic rivals. It must be shown that the addition to economic welfare resulting from the establishment of new firms is greater than the cost of protecting them during their infancy. Given a perfectly organized capital market, no such demonstration can be made, for the losses that a firm must sustain in its first phase is presumably taken into account in the investment decision.

The case against unfair competition then does not seem to have any foundation in a body of price theory that supposes rationality, knowledge, and freedom of contract. In a world which offered no impediments to mergers or cartels, price-cutting for the purpose of dispatching a rival would be irrational conduct. And here we encounter a most curious development. Antitrust does in fact greatly limit the use of mergers and cartels and, hence, provides a *raison d'etre* for predatory price-

16. One way to avoid this conclusion is by assuming that a particularly heavy penalty loss awaits the first firm to go bankrupt. This assumption accords with reality in many trades. It also contradicts the premise that the two rivals are equally efficient. Bankruptcy imposes a cost. If a large firm can, by virtue, of its size, outlast, in a trade war or business recession, a small rival with the same operating costs, it perforce is more efficient and it pays a lower risk premium in the capital market.

cutting. The second best becomes a rational choice when the best is ruled out by law. It follows that unfair competition does exist; that it is the creation of antitrust; and that one should look for instances of it in the years since, say 1910, and not in the early history of our major corporations.[17]

From the foregoing remarks, it also follows that predatory price-cutting constitutes a minor threat to competition. If competition in any industry is precarious, it is mainly because (a) the entry of new producers is difficult and (b) the formation of a cartel or merger is easy. Cartels and mergers can be used to create private monopoly power. Cartels and mergers can also be used to improve economic efficiency. The formation of an intelligent policy toward industrial combination is complicated by the fact that, in any particular case, a cartel or merger is likely to promise simultaneously a good and bad result.

In the short run, a given output can be produced most economically in an industry only when it is distributed among member firms in quotas that keep the marginal costs of production equal in all of them.[18] If the firms sell in a purely competitive market, the condition is au-

17. Instances of price-cutting that is apparently predatory are notoriously difficult to find for recent years. This scarcity may indicate the superiority of mergers over aggressive price-cutting as means of securing market power. It may indicate the effectiveness of antitrust enforcement. Or it may mean that we are not looking in the right places; that, for example, if heavy advertising outlay is treated as a form of price-cutting, a diligent search might turn up more examples of unfair competition. Unfortunately, one would have to invest considerable energy in research and hard thinking to decide how much weight should attach to these explanations.

18. While the above rule holds in most cases, it is not universally true. In some circumstances, the total cost of a given output cannot be minimized unless one or more plants are shut down and their quotas divided among the remaining plants. On this point see, Don Patinkin, "Multi-plant Firms, Cartels, and Imperfect Competition," *Quarterly Journal of Economics*, vol. 69 (February, 1947).

tomatically satisfied. The price is the same for all producers; every one produces that output at which marginal cost equals price.

If the rival firms do not sell in a purely competitive market, production will be wasteful unless they managed to coordinate their activities so that their marginal costs are equalized. The instruments of coordination are the cartel and the merger. Of the two, the cartel is the least serviceable for "rationalizing" production, at any rate in a legal system that refuses to enforce restrictive agreements. The cartel is not likely to reduce costs appreciably unless it makes elaborate provision for profit pooling and disciplining members who exceed their assigned quotas. The elaborate cartel is difficult to negotiate, difficult to enforce, and difficult to revise as market conditions change. Except where patents are involved, the American economy now knows only those simple, furtive cartels whose main object is quite obviously the restriction of output.

The merger is the principal device for rationalizing production in imperfectly competitive markets and its regulation is the really formidable policy problem. This problem is further complicated by the fact that the vast majority of mergers have nothing to do with either monopoly or rationalization; they merely involve the transfer of assets from falling to rising firms. No doubt many—perhaps even most—of the mergers contested by the antitrust agencies over the years have threatened the creation of monopoly power that might have endured for some time. Nevertheless, I venture to assert that there was not a single one of any importance that did not also carry a discernible promise of lower costs.

Since we know so little about the economic costs and benefits of antitrust, it would be rash categorically to affirm or deny that our policy of discouraging mergers has done more harm than good. But since antitrust now has more articulate friends than articulate enemies, I will play the Devil's Advocate. My thesis is that the economic cost of enforcing the present degree of decentralization on the American economy is considerable and, possibly, excessive.

The so-called wastes of competition – advertising, a Western on every channel at 8 P.M., duplicate sales organizations, etc. – are really wastes of oligopoly. And oligopoly is, in large measure, a creation of the antitrust laws. In my opinion, no discussion of antitrust should be allowed to disregard these truths. Given freedom of contract, any promoter of average intelligence would perceive the profit to be made by combining cigarette firms and reducing their advertising budgets; or the profit to be had by rationalizing steel production through mergers so as to eliminate cross hauling. Still, a policy that preserves oligopoly by preventing mergers among the Big Four, Five, or Six does have a plausible benefit. It is conceivable that in a particular industry, an oligopoly price may be lower than a monopoly price and, as J. K. Galbraith has persuasively argued, an oligopoly market structure seems admirably calculated to foster research and development.[19] No similar benefits can be claimed for a policy that suppresses the type of small merger that figured in the *Brown Shoe* case.[20] Only visible is the cost of such a policy – a throwing away of the economies of size and vertical integration.

The Residual Case for Antitrust

I come finally to the question that, thanks to my slow rate of intellectual development, never received my se-

19. John Kenneth Galbraith, *American Capitalism* (New York, 1952), pp. 90-91.

20. *Brown Shoe Co., Inc.* v. *U.S.*, 370 U.S. 294 (1962) See also the comments by M. A. Adelman in Chapter 2, above, and by Jesse W. Markham in Chapter 8, below.

rious attention until the last few years. The question is simply: is there an economic case for antitrust? The indoctrination in the folklore of antitrust that I received with enthusiasm in my youth was so thorough that an affirmative answer was long taken for granted. The doubts expressed by a few colleagues — mostly refugee scholars from Germany — I impatiently ascribed to a faculty training in economic theory or unfamiliarity with American experience.

The answer I offer to this question is that there is an economic case for antitrust — but not a very good one. Cartels are almost always undesirable; thus the economy may have need of a vice squad whose job it is to break into hotel rooms and catch businessmen in the act of fixing prices. The urge of businessmen to avoid competition is so natural and ubiquitous, and cartels are usually so weak, that I have some reservations about the wisdom of treating price-fixing as criminal conspiracy. The harassment of cartels, however, is not the important part of antitrust.

The heart of antitrust is the resolve that oligopoly shall not give way to monopoly and that, if possible, it shall be pushed by the control of mergers, and an occasional dissolution decree, in the direction of workable competition. In particular cases this resolve can be supported by good economic arguments — as, for example, when the merger affects an industry already sheltered by a high tariff or legal restrictions on entry. But there is, so far as I can see, no general case for such a policy. The economic issues raised by merger and dissolution suits are extremely complex and a "correct" decision presumes economic analysis of the greatest sophistication and objectivity.

In view of the limitations of the adversary process for clarifying economic issues, there is, I submit, no good reason to believe that the victories of the antitrust agencies have, on balance, done the consumer interest more good than harm. One can make a case that the average price of gasoline over the last fifty years would have been a little higher had the original Standard Oil Company not been broken up in 1911. But does any one believe that his grocery bill has been lowered one whit by federal harassment of A & P and the meat packers?

The judgment I have offered on antitrust policy has been harsh. Its major goals are viewed as largely irrelevant to the problem of making a capitalist economy perform satisfactorily. Its success in reducing the minor evil of private business monopoly is purchased by sacrificing efficiency.[21] Shall we scrap the antitrust laws and surrender to the "monopoly capitalism" which, according to many authorities, is on the way unless we put more teeth in antitrust?[22] Perhaps because old allegiances die hard, I cannot go this far.

The conventional economic arguments for antitrust no longer persuade me. Nevertheless, I still count myself among the friends of antitrust. Possibly this allegiance survives for reasons that are buried somewhere in my subconscious and so are beyond my true comprehension. Nevertheless, I venture to attribute my enduring affection for antitrust to three things. The first I mention with apology. It is a discreditable sympathy with those populist causes that seek to shake the mighty in their seats

21. In this connection, the judgment of a visiting British scholar on antitrust is worth pondering. By his reading of American experience, there is nothing in the form of the basic Sherman Act prohibition or its enforcement to ensure that it operates to produce optimum economic results. On the contrary, the courts have consistently refused to take economic consequences as the criterion of antitrust right and wrong. See A. D. Neale, *The Antitrust Laws of the United States of America: A Study of Competition Enforced by Law* (Cambridge, England, 1960), p. 470.

22. See, for example, Walter Adams and Horace M Gray, *Monopoly in America: the Government as Promoter* (New York, 1955).

without putting them in any real danger of being cast down. In this category belong the crusades for free silver, banking reform, railroad regulation, federal scrutiny of the stock exchange – and antitrust. In our country, the real grievance of Everyman against the rich and powerful is not their wealth and power. Almost no one questions the usefulness of the town capitalist and town physician or begrudges them their high place on the income pyramid. Rather it is the smugness, condescension, and petty concern for their petty interests that causes us to wish them ill. To me the shadow of monopoly capitalism is an abomination because it carries the prospect that all large corporations will begin to comport themselves as public utilities. Surely one Bell Telephone Hour on television is enough. Still, the desire to express one's grievance at corporation executives through an antitrust suit maintained by hard-working, modestly paid, civil servants is nothing to be proud of.

The second ground for my continuing sympathy with antitrust is a sentimental bias in favor of smallness not uncommon among people who were born in a small Midwestern town forty years ago. I doubt that history is on the side of the small firm in most industries; but I wish that it were. In the words of Learned Hand, "It is possible, because of its indirect social or moral effect, to prefer a system of small producers, each dependent for his success upon his own skill and character, to one in which the great mass of those engaged must accept the direction of a few."[23] Incidentally, I have often wondered whether the great judge wrote this, and other often quoted passages in the *Alcoa* decision, with tongue-in-cheek. For in the modern world, the vast majority of us will be working for somebody else no matter how

23. *U.S.* v. *Aluminum Co. of America,* 148 F. 2d. 416, 427 (1945).

vigorously the antitrust laws are enforced. Their effect upon "the sociology of work" is, I submit, negligible.

Of the three reasons for continuing to support antitrust – even though I no longer share the economic theology of trust busters – the remaining one carries the greatest weight. It is that, as a citizen, I am prepared to prevent certain economic developments that I regularly act to bring about as a consumer. As a consumer I will do nothing to help Packard-Studebaker remain in business. As a citizen, I am prepared to pay something in sacrificed efficiency to keep them going. The major virtue of antitrust is that it preserves consumer choice and disperses decision-making. But, to repeat, it does so at a cost. Possibly if the magnitude of this cost were known, the remaining vestiges of my old enthusiasm for antitrust would vanish. In our present state of ignorance, however, the contribution of antitrust to preserving consumer choice and dispersing authority seems, to me, to justify the main features of the policy.

CHAPTER 5

Conscious Parallelism and Administered Prices

BY R. B. HEFLEBOWER

A series of dramas has been played during the postwar years around the common theme of the behavior of prices of manufactured goods. The first script dealt with the surge of prices to the peak of the postwar boom about 1956. Industries with few sellers and sometimes the unions were cast as villains and their victims were identified as the farmers and sometimes as the consumers. The audience, some of whom got on the stage as actors, were congressional committees and segments of the general public. A somewhat different play was put on from 1957 to 1960 when price indexes continued to move upward even after demand had slackened and excess capacity had become widespread. This led to a nondramatic but important reexamination of the accuracy of the price data and indexes and they were shown to have an upward bias, particularly in periods of slack demand.[1] Numerous analyses of price behavior, of highly variable quality, were submitted to congressional committees by economists.[2] For sheer excitement the abortive, across-the-board steel price increase of April 1962

1. "Government Price Statistics," Staff papers submitted to the Subcommittee on Economic Statistics of the Joint Economic Committee (1961).

2. "Administered Prices," *Hearings* before the Senate Subcommittee on Antitrust and Monopoly, Parts 9 and 10 (1959) and "The Relationship of Price to Economic Stability and Growth." *Compendium* of Papers of Panelists appearing before the Joint Economic Committee (1958).

wins the prize, but the quiet, selected price increases a year later attracted few viewers. What did attract a blue-ribbon audience who watched with great excitement or with shock, according to their predilections, was the scene of business executives being sent to prison for using a planned script, overt collusion, in the electric equipment industry. Noticed only by the experts, there developed after the war the doctrine of "conscious parallelism of action," or of nonovert agreement (or restraint of trade?), under which the price behavior and market practices of a number of industries were held to be in violation of the antitrust laws. Finally, worried conversations began after 1956 and continue to this date as to whether the dollar is overvalued in international trade because of the level of our industrial prices compared to those of Western Europe and Japan.

Some players in these dramas had returned to the stage after being out of public view since the thirties and they and the army of new actors caught the public's ear with both old phrases and new ones they coined. One of the former, "administered prices," is the subject of this paper and it is contrasted with "flexible prices." Added were "administered price inflation," price advances made possible because of previously "unliquidated monopoly gains,"[3] and "conscious parallelism of action," which is also a subject of this paper. Obviously not all of price behavior of manufacturing industries can be explored here, nor indeed does a large portion of it pose serious analytical or policy problems. The concern is with that large proportion of the value of manufactured goods sold in economically defined markets in which sellers are so few that price competition tends to be minimized.

Economists have not been able to develop a theory of

3. John Kenneth Galbraith, "Market Structure and Stabilization Policy," *Review of Economics and Statistics*, vol. 39 (May, 1957), p. 127.

price behavior for such markets for when sellers are few they tend to be "jointly acting oligopolists"[4] because of "conjectural interdependence"[5] among them. Each seller's behavior is restrained by his expectations as to how his rivals will react to a price-change by him. There is a circularity in sellers' reactions and there is no definitive theory of how the circle is broken except by some collusive device.

But the degree of conjectural restraint is not a function merely of the number of sellers, although a relatively few is a necessary condition for each to be so restrained.[6] In one industry there may be more conjectural restraint with ten sellers than in another with four. Clair Wilcox classified the prewar rubber tire industry as competitive even though four companies accounted for 80 percent of output while petroleum refining was classified as monopolistic[7] even though the four largest refiners provided only about 50 percent of the volume of the Gulf-East Coast regional market and much less in the Middle West. Obviously, additional attributes of each of these markets, features of the respective products, and the conditions of their production, sale, and distribution, must have influenced Wilcox' estimates. In-

4. Carl Kaysen and Donald F. Turner, *Antitrust Policy:* An Economic and Legal Analysis (Cambridge, Mass., 1959) p. 110.

5. A term suggested by Ragnar Frisch's treatment of "conjectural variation" and developed by William Fellner, *Competition Among the Few* (New York, 1949), to explore the conditions under which the few could, by this means, reach a nonovert or "quasi-agreement."

6. Kaysen and Turner, *op.cit.,* pp. 27, 32. Kaysen and Turner have estimated that of all manufactured goods produced by "national market" industries, 25 percent of the value of shipments was represented in 1954 by markets in which "recognition of interdependence by the leading firms is extremely likely" and another 40 percent in markets in which such interdepencence is possible, but could be determined only by study of individual markets.

7. Clair Wilcox, "Competition and Monopoly in American Industry," Temporary National Economic Committee *Monograph 21* (1944), pp. 48-51, 127-29.

deed the term "oligopoly," properly used, refers not to number of sellers as such but to degree of conjectural interdependence.

From conjectural interdependence we proceed to its kin but not twin brother, "conscious parallelism of action." "Conscious" refers to awareness of rivalry with particular firms and of their action, or nonaction, from which emerges "parallelism," or the advisability of doing as rivals do. More than mere conjectural interdependence, independently done—that may seem to be a confused statement—is required for parallel behavior to be deemed illegal, but more of this later.

"Conscious parallelism" and "administered prices" are in part similar concepts but also differ significantly. The latter refers ordinarily to the observed behavior of prices while the former connotes the process from which behavior emerges. But indicia of that process are also certain types of observed behavior compared to those one would expect in the absence of the process of conscious parallelism. On the other hand, administered prices can be so labelled because they reflect an "administering" process, or conscious decision-making by sellers or buyers or both, each of whom has a zone of discretion. Not all restraints on or aids to that decision-making necessarily fall under the conscious parellelism rubric, however. Both terms connote a process of price-making and kinds of price behavior that to varying degrees are in juxtaposition to those of an "open market." In the latter both buyers and sellers are numerous and each transaction is a unique event in the sense that neither the buyer's demand nor the seller's offer is conditioned by possible bearing on future transactions. An organized commodity exchange is the epitome of an open market and active buying and selling through brokers (not on an exchange) is a close approximation.

Price-making and price behavior in the economy range

over the spectrum from that of open markets to clear cases of monopoly. Within that range, conscious parallelism has meaning only in the vicinity of the monopoly pole. But administered prices as defined by the originator and publicist of the term, Gardner Means,[8] covers most of the spectrum of price behavior, but sometimes has been used by him with a conscious parallelism connotation. Some degree of administering, or failure to reexamine one's prices for each successive transaction so that the same price holds for varying lengths of time, prevails even where there is only a minor degree of imperfection of competition and for which no monopoly problem arises. Indeed, a significant amount of imperfection is a necessary condition for effective governing of most parts of a market system. Such is the gist of J. M. Clark's criticism of much of the theorizing about competitive markets.[9] It is only when administered prices take on behavioral characteristics suggestive of overt collusion or of the same results via conscious parallelism that there is public concern.

For purposes of marking out the task before us, five aspects of price behavior should be distinguished:

1. The persistent level of prices relative to costs, a crude empirical counterpart of the economists' long-run "equilibrium."
2. The degree of uniformity of prices of various sellers

8. Gardner C. Means, "The Reality of Administered Price," in his *The Corporate Revolution in America* (New York, 1962), pp. 77-96. (This was originally a confidential memorandum to the Secretary of Agriculture and was published in 1935 as Senate Document No. 13, 74th Cong., 1st Sess. under the title "Industrial Prices and Their Relative Inflexibility.")

9. J. M. Clark, "Toward A Concept of Workable Competition," *American Economic Review*, vol. 30, no. 2, Part 1 (June, 1940), pp. 241-256. A more full analysis and somewhat different conclusions will be found in the recent book by G. B. Richardson, *Information and Investment* (New York, 1960).

(or of stable differentials among them) at a given time (or on occasion, of various buyers).

3. The movement or, alternatively, the stability of these prices when there occur changes in such external conditions as the level of demand or of prices of inputs.
4. The degree to which price changes are, or are not, made at the same time and in the same amount by various sellers (or buyers).
5. The uniformity of various firms' price structures in such regards as the following, and the degree to which these elements of the price structure do or do not reflect cost differences:
   a. The structure of discounts and allowances.
   b. Geographic pattern of prices.

Attention here will focus on the fourth category, or the conditions under which prices do or do not change. At certain points comments about the other phases will fit in. Indeed, a persuasive case can be made that the price-change performance of a market is indicative of the degree to which the other aspects of price behavior are competitive or fall far short of that criterion.

There is one unequivocal meaning of competitive price behavior; each firm, without a significant degree of concern about rivals' reactions, adjusts its volume and prices so as to maximize its profits in a very short span of time. That span would be determined by imperfections which affect the speed with which buyers are able to cut back or increase their purchases as they learn of better offers. This degree of "administered prices" should not bar a market from being denoted "competitive," for where there are numerous sellers and buyers, prices will, perhaps with some delay, slide up and down an upward-rising marginal cost curve in response to significant increases or decreases of demand. In parallel fashion, prices will rise or fall with significant movement of the level of the marginal cost curve, such as occurs from changes in the prices of inputs. Because each and every seller disregards the boomerang effects of his decisions, each will put on the market the volume for which the price just covers marginal costs, and prices will respond to changes in the composite volume of the sellers. There would be no problems of uniformity, or diversity in timing and amount, of various sellers' price changes. (One could go on within this framework of analysis to comment on each of the other three aspects of price behavior sketched earlier.)

If pressed, most economists would, I believe, follow Neal's analysis, which amounts to saying that price behavior should be appraised by what happens to the unit gross margin over the relevant costs.[10] For short calendar periods average variable cost can be used as the proxy for marginal cost. Firms' prices can be expected to respond to significant changes in the level of those costs or of the demand for the product. Competitive adjustments consist chiefly of enlarging or reducing the gross margin over average variable costs as demand rises or falls relative to those costs, the criterion of unequivocal competitive price behavior.[11]

But the gross margin should be in terms of realized prices and, where multiple products are involved, for the family of items as a group. The former point covers variations from list and other forms of concessions, changes of quality, and so on. The latter, looking at what happens to a commodity line as a composite but not by a fixed weight index number, amounts to deriving something like an "implicit price index"[12] that measures the

10. Alfred C. Neal, *Industrial Concentration and Price Flexibility* (Public Affairs Institute, 1942), pp. 23-91.

11. See above, p. 93.

12. For a statement of the case for such a composite gross margin measure of short (calendar) time price behavior, see R. B. Heflebower, "Do Administered Prices Involve an Antitrust Problem," *Northwestern University Law Review*, vol. 57 (May-June, 1962), pp. 189-194.

"price" component of the firms' net sales.[13] It would take too long to explain the latter concept and its relevance but it is of major importance in my judgment. Utilizing these measures, including the one not fully explained, will show that prices nearly always move somewhat in the direction of the movements of demand regardless of what other "data" indicate. But *how promptly* and *by how much* do they move, and what behavior of prices, measured as suggested above, is socially advantageous?

In an economy in which the market system is the means of arranging the bulk of economic activities, the "best" price behavior is that which results most nearly to the optimal allocation of resources (including their use over time) and the distribution of income according to the marginal rules *in the economy as a whole.*

But the assumption that a high degree of competitive price behavior in very short periods will be the best and certain means of achieving the optimum is open to several criticisms. The theory that lies behind the case for such price behavior does not deal adequately with the problems of information of buyers and sellers and the reaction of producers, particularly to uncertainty. It is a static, full-information (or complete mobility of resources) criterion; it assumes that very short-period competitive price behavior will bring the benefits that are defined in terms of a long-run static equilibrium. Furthermore, adjustment in each market is more easily done and beneficent if it can pull resources from, or inject

13. Such an index has been developed for steel by Harleston R. Wood, "The Measurement of Employment Cost and Prices in the Steel Industry," *Review of Economics and Statistics,* vol. 41 (November, 1959), pp. 412-18. The present writer had earlier proposed a "revenue per input unit" for a composite of items as the best "price" measure for studying short term behavior in many markets. See "An Economic Appraisal of Price Measures," *Journal of the American Statistical Association,* vol. 46 (June, 1951), pp. 461-479.

unneeded resources into, other uses. But what happens when most markets want more or less resources or, for other reasons, resources are immobile for years? This is where the web of partial equilibria which forms a general equilibrium of the economy gets into trouble unless each market reacts to the impact on it of a disequilibrating force and does so with the similar speed. But this assumption is invalid and consequently particular market disequilibria can compound and the economy stagnate. That prospect is augmented by the durability of capital goods, the immobility of labor, and so on. Add the effect of sharp price reduction on the firm's cash flow and hence on their willingness to invest, even in the event of improving demand, and the prospect ot expansion becomes dim. In other words, such an analysis is distinctly non-Keynesian, and I might add, departs materially from businessmen's views of a favorable environment for investment.

Such considerations have led a number of economists to depart from what was the orthodox view of the social advantage of what could be denoted "immediate" price competition. Mason has said that he "... should support the view that the inflexibility of industrial prices tends to even out cyclical fluctuations in employment and output."[14] The reference is to price stability during a short calendar period and so is the Kaysen and Turner definition of a competitive market as one in which a few sellers do not have a "significant degree of market power for more than a very short run."[15] Stigler has defined "competition" in terms of a market in which there are no "barriers to entry and exit from an industry in the long-run normal period; that is, in the period long enough to allow substantial changes in the quantities of

14. Edward S. Mason, *Economic Concentration and the Monopoly Problem* (Cambridge, Mass., 1957), p. 176.
15. Kaysen and Turner, *op.cit.*, p. 104.

even the most durable and specialized resources."[16] Since for most industries such adjustments take several years to a decade of calendar time, Stigler appears not to disapprove of short-calendar-time price stability. Not one of these authors calls for "immediate" competitive price responses to a change in demand or, that is, that firms be solely in the role of "price takers." Administered prices considerably impervious to demand changes would be deemed socially satisfactory, and if achieving that stability required a degree of the restraining influence of conjectural interdependence, possibly buttressed to some degree by consciously parallel behavior, that would be condoned.[17]

The efficiency of a market system cannot be separated from the ways the behavior of buying and selling prices affect the efficiency with which the participants in the market perform their respective roles. That calls for a survey of influences bearing on firms' desire for and ability to provide some insulation against unfavorable market developments, and the social gain or loss from the degree of insulation they develop. Some conditions external to the individual firm, and even to all the firms in a market, must be understood in making such appraisals.

Implicit in much of the critical discussion of administered prices is a vision of a standard raw material being sold on an organized exchange or through brokers, or of a housewife choosing among cuts of meat, the re-

16. George J. Stigler, "Perfect Competition, Historically Contemplated," *Journal of Political Economy,* vol. 65 (February, 1957), p. 16. Stigler adds that in such a market and for such a period the expected returns on capital would be equal to that of other similarly structured industries.

17. Unfortunately there is not space to evaluate the current statements about excess capacity but the author is of the opinion that much of what is denoted excess capacity is not excess in the secular sense.

tailer selecting sides of beef, or a packer choosing among and predicting the hour-by-hour movement of prices of cattle brought by farmers to a large market center. Such transactions once were the bulk of all business and it was, coincidentally, the period when the theory of the competitive market system was worked out, but in the rather loose Marshallian concept of competition.

Even Marshall did not realize the seller's enormous task of arriving at, adjusting, or not changing prices, or purchaser's examining them, where thousands of items or variations thereof, are involved as in most modern industrial markets. Look at a steel price book—you will need an expert to help you interpret it—or at the catalogue of a manufacturer of mechanical rubber goods. The cost to the seller of making a study of the demand elasticity and intensity for each of these items, the usual absence of the economist's marginal cost data for each, and the cost of having other than low-rank employees operating by simple rules "work out" the prices, all impose restraints on the degree to which prices could be at the level at which marginal cost and marginal revenue are equal and could respond to changes in the prospective level of each of these variables.

Two examples will clarify the point. In a large meat packing plant most day-to-day price decisions are made by men so far down the hierarchy that they work in shirt sleeves and have no title worth quoting to their friends. Because of the perishability of the product and the irregular rates at which farmers deliver cattle, prices of cattle and of meat are almost constantly in motion. That fact is traceable primarily to the characteristics of the product and of the supplying of the raw material, not to the organization of local or regional markets. Contrast this with a mechanical rubber goods plant or one devoted to making miscellaneous metal parts that go into a variety of finished products. Numerous inquiries are made for small amounts of particular items carried in stock or to be produced either to the exact specifications of items made before or quite different specifications. No vice president will make up the price estimate. Someone at the clerical level will quote the price based on a pricing formula by summing the value of raw materials required and estimated direct labor and multiplying the total by a factor. No firm uses such a pricing formula for sizeable orders; ranking executives sharpen their pencils to meet the expected prices of rivals and to compute the effect of volume on costs.

One might respond that, without altering the relative prices of specific items, the level of prices for a group of items could be moved easily with changes in demand or input prices, and that the level would so change if the market were really competitive. But consider that the relative importance of the inputs often differs sharply among the numerous items and, more bothersome still, that the demand changes vary among them even more. It costs personnel time to obtain and analyze the relevant information, and this may involve high-level executives. It costs money to reissue price books and personnel time to explain to customers price increases or failure to reduce some items. To this must be added the "intangible costs" of buyer reaction if they are treated adversely or if they are treated differently by one firm than by the other sellers each of which had reached different conclusions "independently."

From the buyer's viewpoint there is a search cost in a market where prices are not uniform or are in motion.[18]

18. For a very important analysis of the cost of search for best price and quality and the effect thereof on buyer behavior, see George J. Stigler "The Economics of Information," *Journal of Political Economy*, vol. 69 (June, 1961), pp. 213-225.

This is unavoidable to the buyer of cattle or of meat. But in many industries such cost is zero because the buyers are certain of a "best favored nation" treatment by their respective suppliers and usually there is an implicit understanding that the seller will match better offers, even retroactively. In many markets, however, there are enough opportunities to buy at lower prices than those generally prevailing that costs can be minimized by constant search. Often business buyers are not so much concerned with the absolute level of the price of goods bought as with whether they pay more than do rivals. This was evident in the buying practices of the large tobacco companies exposed in the 1946 case[19] and explains the contentment of many manufacturers with a wage agreement that establishes a uniform change in wage rates, minimizes plant and area differentials, and assures stability of wage rates over time for the firms as a group. Certainly rubber product manufacturers have been more comfortable with stable synthetic rubber and tire cord prices than with prewar gyrations of natural rubber and cotton prices (neither capable of being fully hedged) which at times threatened the solvency of large firms. Prices paid for natural rubber and volume bought at various times were a major task of chief executives!

An aside about uniformities in price behavior is appropriate. List prices of commodities recognized as identical, particularly by expert buyers, cannot differ except very temporarily. Orders will shift to the seller with the lower price but, because of established buyer-seller relations, many buyers give the usual source an opportunity to match the better offer. This means that price-cutting, unless hidden, gains little for the initiator. Similarly, except during unusual shortages such as in a

19. *American Tobacco Co.* v. *U.S.*, 328 U.S. 802 (1946).

mobilization boom, one seller cannot successfully advance his price unless followed almost at once and in equal amount by rivals. The trade papers often report cases of unsuccessful attempts at price increase, cases in which other firms did not follow or did so by a lesser amount. There is nothing collusive or reflective of conscious parallelism of action, *per se,* in such uniformities. The real questions pertain to the degree of uniformity of actual prices, particularly when demand conditions change, to whether lists are persistently impervious to significant changes in demand or whether they rise when neither demand or input prices have advanced.

Without judging whether these various arguments are really apologia for distinctly noncompetitive behavior, the only positive case that can be made is that efficiency in transformation (or whatever the enterprise does) between material and labor purchased and products sold is affected adversely by prices that respond quickly and frequently to changes in the supply and demand conditions in the buying or selling markets. Such an argument is sometimes set forth with a supporting line of reasoning by defenders of price agreements of the "floor" sort,[20] and of comparable more or less permanent programs of agricultural price supports for staples.[21] More literature would have appeared on this subject were it not for the fact that, in a large portion of

20. Such an argument is developed by P. L. Cook, "Orderly Marketing and Competition (The Blanket Manufacturers' Agreement)," *Economic Journal,* vol. 71 (September, 1961), pp. 497-511.

21. The reference is *not* to the prolonged and expensive price support and output restrictions that have the effect of holding capacity and prices of farm products above their long-run equlibrium level. Instead the reference is to "forward pricing" schemes designed to guide farmers' choice of use of resources and perhaps to protect them from major consequences of supply errors. On this subject see D. Gale Johnson, *Forward Pricing for Agriculture* (Chicago, Ill., 1947).

quite competitive manufacturing industries, firms in fact have a low ratio of fixed to total costs, or find that raw material prices respond to changes in demand for final products.

Stating the problem more precisely, do prices that slide up and down the sellers' marginal cost curves, behaving in a clear-cut competitive fashion, adversely affect the efficiency of firms that face the following complex of conditions: (a) a highly inelastic demand, (b) a low ratio of variable costs to total costs, and (c) wide but unpredictable swings of demand? If a substantial decline of demand occurs, and with demand inelastic, cash receipts decline sharply as prices fall. The decline may not be halted until the level of average variable costs is reached. If continued for long, the reduction in the firms' cash flow will force them to be far more conservative in their behavior, including outlays for modernization, even when they are not fearing insolvency. This possibility lies back of the doubts about the economic advantage of cyclical price declines as an aid to recovery.

In many industries, however, practices of the nonconsciously parallel sort have developed that mitigate the effects of adverse movements of demand or of wide input-price movements. These include formal hedging of raw material purchases, and it is no wonder that such industries as flour milling and cotton processing, supported by producers of the corresponding raw materials, initiated a large study of the effects of support prices and the large and episodic purchases and sales by the government on the efficacy of the organized exchanges as a hedging medium. Other industries, where substantial selling risks are faced and hedging is not possible, evolve practices in timing of raw material purchases relative to orders and whether or not firms produce to stock. Such are the characteristics of the medium-priced women's dress industry[22] and of parts at least of the shoe industry.[23] Farmers plant certain crops, such as sugar beets, only when they have signed a fixed price contract. The recent surge of vertical integration and tying together by contract of poultry-feed supplying or slaughtering with production of broilers or turkeys stems in large part from the fact that larger firms have greater ability than the farmer to operate under large price risks for particular units of output.[24]

One can go on to include requirements contracts, exclusive dealing, downstream integration by crude materials manufacturers, or integration into distribution by finished goods manufacturers, including their use of exclusive dealer arrangements, as having in part the motive of avoiding or mitigating the effect of both price and nonprice competition. Need I go on to add geographic pricing systems, certain trade association activities, price leadership, and other earmarks of conscious parallelism? Only by extensive study of each case is it possible to distinguish defense against a cyclical decline of demand from attempts to avert a secular adjustment or to obtain positive monopoly profits.

In industrial markets quite far from the open-market polar type there develops — actually evolves historically — a substantial degree of what Professor Phillips

22. One can glean parts of this from the somewhat outdated exposition by Helen E. Meiklejohn, "Dresses — The Impact of Fashion on a Business," in Walton Hamilton, *Price and Price Policies* (New York, 1938) pp. 324-336, 341-384.

23. Ruth P. Mack, "Business Expectations and the Buying of Materials," in *Expectations, Uncertainty, and Business Behavior*, ed. Mary Jean Bowman, Social Science Research Council, (New York, 1955), pp. 106-118.

24. See "Contract Farming and Vertical Integration in Agriculture," United States Department of Agriculture, *Information Bulletin No. 198* (1958).

aptly terms "interfirm organization,"[25] that slows down price response to changes in demand particularly. By "organization" he means that firms come to be "arranged" vis à vis each other and vis à vis buyers. The observed "arrangement" evolves by the adaptations through time of various firms to their opportunities and to restraints imposed by rivalry with each other, and as the result of their dealings with suppliers of inputs and buyers of products.

Consequently, in what economists would designate as the market, usually each firm is conscious of being in very close rivalry with only a portion of the other firms. Ordinarily other firms are engaged in somewhat different parts of the same product line or in adjacent geographic areas. The market is segmented by degrees of product differentiation, by differences in location, by differing channels of distribution, and by other means. Within each such segment there is a very high degree of cross-elasticity of demand among sellers' products. Between the segments the cross-elasticity is lower and effective less promptly when relative prices change. After a lag, firms in the first segment are restrained by those in the second, and the latter by those in the third, and vice versa.

From this interfirm organization, compared to an auction market, one would expect sluggish price reaction to changes in the level of demand when input prices are stable. Time is required for the waves reflecting the ini-

25. Almarin Phillips, *Market Structure, Organization and Performance* (Cambridge, Mass., 1962), Chapter II. However his emphasis on differences or similarity of "values" of members of the group seems to me to be largely misnamed. Most of his points have to do with differences or similarities in the "level" of a specific "value," e.g., the profit rate, because firms have different present or prospective cost-price margins. When members of the group "agree," each presumably predicts that his profits will be higher under the "agreement" than under any alternative price upon which a consensus can be reached.

tial disturbance to spread. But with or without delay, the fact that some of the group's selling situation is more toward the open market pole than that of others becomes operative when demand changes substantially and tends, with a lag, through intergroup cross-elasticities to force additional firms' transaction prices to move.

Such developments may be delayed or averted by direct communication among rivals or by "props" that have been erected (by conscious act or evolution) on the market stage—pricing systems and price leadership are examples—or signals made by the players. The latter include publicized statements as to what ought to happen, and announcements of cutbacks in output. But where sellers are very few, and have similar costs, and the product is standardized and sold to expert buyers, such procedures are less necessary (to avert price competition), for "quasi-agreement" by conjectural interdependence alone is relatively easy. So a range of responsiveness to a disequilibrating development—a change in the level of demand with factor prices stable is the best test—can be expected. Where along this spectrum is the cutoff between desirable competitive and noncompetitive price behavior?

Compare the behavior of three types of markets under various circumstances. Type 1 is the market for a standardized material practically all of which is sold in one channel and by a handful of firms. Type 2 is an open market, the extreme opposite of the first, with many sellers and buyers and with a standardized product or with recognized grades thereof. The third type of market falls between the first two in that it has a fair degree of concentration among sellers, usually more than one channel of sale, and a variety of items in a product line. Some generalizations, from which one should expect a number of departures, can be made.

Consider the distribution of prices when demand is

high relative to capacity. In type 1 all transactions are apt to be at list price. In type 2, the open market, and taking the transactions over a day or a week during which supply and demand conditions vary only to a small degree, there is a normal distribution of prices for particular sales around the mode, and the scatter is not substantial. In type 3, or the intermediate zone market, the distribution probably is narrower than in type 2 and, if a list price is used, the distribution of transaction prices is skewed with concentration at or near the list price.

If there is a moderate decline in demand, all transactions in type 1 market probably will continue at list prices. Only if the demand falls sharply and remains low for some time will price concessions become important. With almost any decline of demand (supply conditions unchanged), the modal price in type 2, the open market, will move down and the scatter of prices increase. For the intermediate case, type 3, the modal price will also move down, but less than for the open market, and the scatter of transaction prices will become much wider. If demand does not fall more, or remain low for a longer period than one expects from a quite effective full employment policy, list prices will hold usually. But if the demand decline is more serious and prolonged, list prices will fall.

If demand rises later, any concessions in type 1 markets will disappear. Even if demand were to rise above the original level, as long as factor prices remained stable, list prices will not ordinarily rise. Average realization per output (or preferably per input) unit will increase, however, and certainly it will if demand reaches a boom level. In the open market the response to a demand increase will be the reverse of that for a decrease. In type 3, the intermediate case, transaction prices will move toward list prices and if the latter had fallen, their advance will be uncertain as to time; here is where barometric price leadership is effective. List prices will usually advance beyond the original level if demand reaches boom proportions.

Consider the interrrelated "need for and ease of agreement," *as seen by the firms* in order to minimize, given the market structure and variables governing rivalry, the effect of adverse market developments on their cash flow. The ease of agreement is a negative function of the number of sellers (assuming buyers numerous). In a market clearly short of the one or two seller pole, even firms that are relatively quite large (as well as smaller ones) are apt to act independently, particularly if fixed costs are high, and to produce the volume that individually maximizes profit without regard to the effect of doing so on the price that will prevail. Conjectural interdependence is not sufficiently strong for an effective "quasi-agreement." Turning to other influences, the ease of agreement varies directly (and possibly in a rapidly increasing degree) with the extent to which firms' costs are similar, and as a variation of that, with the degree to which they are alike in extent of vertical integration. Also important is the degree to which buyers look upon various firms' products as interchangeable. The degree of uniformity of cost structures and of vertical integration governs the size of the various firms' cost-price margins and the effect thereon of a change in factor prices or of lower selling prices. Other variables could be added of which uniformity or difference in channels of sale used and the organization of the buying side of the market are often important.

The "need for agreement" stems from the cost of disagreement. The cost is a function of the degree of inelasticity of demand and of the ratio of variable to total costs, or of how low is the variable cost floor to which prices may decline in the event of a sharp drop of demand. And there is always the possibility of a price war, with prices being forced below variable costs, as firms fight to maintain valued market connections, or even to survive.

From the "need for agreement" comes, potentially, a strengthening of the "ease of agreement." Where "need to agree" is high, rivals are certain to react to a price cut, and the loss of volume it would entail if not met. The would-be price-cutter can be certain of the penalty of being met by other firms and that all will lose because of the inelasticity of demand.

By putting together different composites of these variables, reflecting both the positive ones that facilitate agreement and the negative ones reflecting the need for agreement as seen by the firms, one can visualize an index of the probability of an agreement under varying circumstances and the properties of that agreement. Such an index could be the dependent variable in an elaborate regression equation. One could specify the independent variables, and indicate the direction of influence of some of them, but little else of their functional character. Quantifying them is another matter.

Imagining such an index facilitates estimation of how industries that lie at various points along the spectrum of market types will behave. That behavior can be noted not only when demand falls, for example, but also in some persistent practices. (Remember that this spectrum of market types reflects not merely number of sellers or degrees of concentration but also a variety of influences governing the degrees of independent versus interdependent decision-making by individual sellers.) There is a high degree of certainty at the two poles. In an open market and markets similar in character, each seller can expect that his selling price will move rapidly to the level warranted by a change in, and the elasticity of, the industry demand and supply curves. But he can expect that the price will not fall below the level of marginal variable costs as reflected in the supply curve. No seller has connections with buyers, or other longer-term considerations, that will lead him to produce and sell below marginal variable costs because of the investment value of market connections. Price wars should not occur. At the other pole – the extreme is duopolists with similar costs producing a standardized material – "agreement" is easy and can be reached without signalling devices or props. There is little reason to fear price cuts that will reduce the gross margin.

But in between those poles, particularly as the composite of variables moves toward but falls clearly short of the duopoly end of the type-of-market spectrum, the need for agreement increases sharply while the possibility of reaching it rises less than correspondingly. At least it does not do so if reliance is placed solely on interfirm "conjectural interdependence." Each firm's responsibility for what happens has not reached the critical level as viewed by it. Furthermore, it cannot count on price and output behavior by other firms that will make certain that prices will not fall or valued customers be lost. But reaction to a fall of demand probably will be sluggish. If a firm's fixed costs are a high proportion of total costs, and more so if there is a semi-open market segment into which part of output can be dumped, it is apt progressively to act so as to maximize its profits individually. As each does this via concessions, et cetera, list prices become fictitious and what have by then become "paper" list prices may break. If demand is inelastic and variable costs are a low percentage of total costs the cumulative effect of such price weakening on the firm's liquidity becomes serious. If the efforts to resist are not successful, and they rarely are for long, some firms may see a long-term investment gain from selling at prices below variable costs and a price war breaks out.

Intermediate zone markets that have the cost and demand characteristics referred to here have led to the theme that loosely defined oligopolistic markets are inherently unstable, that they oscillate between truces and wars, and that there may be alternate periods of entry and of exit via bankruptcy.[26] Were such a market to become clearly more oligopolistic – which means not merely fewer firms but also that it acquire other attributes that enhance conjectural interdependence – it would pass over this "danger" point toward an ease of agreement situation. Here is where there is a clear incentive toward oligopoly by merger, or if that is barred, a reshaping of the market structure may come by the high rate of growth of some firms and exit of others.

The observations along the roundabout route of the past several pages provide the background for considering conjectural interdependence and the extent to which it is reflected in or is buttressed by conscious parallelism and the relation of both to the market situation faced by firms. At the open-market pole, even though from the firms' viewpoint agreement might be badly "needed," the common interests of sellers cannot be implemented. Even a formal price agreement not enforceable in the courts would merely reflect the competitive price or be a piece of paper. Only when they are enforced by the allocative power of government, or by government purchases of surpluses, will such agreements work. Such is the history of attempts of farm cooperatives to hold prices above the market-clearing level for long. At the other pole, characterized by a

26. Note Joe S. Bain's category of markets where entry is "ineffectively impeded" and structure unstable, with periods of oligopolistic pricing and breakdown thereof in *Barriers to New Competition* (Cambridge, Mass., 1956), pp. 40, 41, 189, 190.

pure duopoly, agreement can be expected by conjectural interdependence unsupported by props or signaling devices. As one moves along the spectrum from the open market, attempts at nonformal "agreement" are more probable but more difficult, and "conscious parallelism" devices are apt to evolve or be established consciously. Trade association activities from which members can draw parallel inferences are the most obvious where firms are substantial in number and diverse in other qualities. Further still along the spectrum, special props and signalling devices can be more effective. Many of these initially dealt with a unique problem; e.g., block booking by film companies as a device for reducing uncertainty about viewers' reaction to the perishable investment in a film, zone pricing of durable goods with breaks in areas of sparse population so that distributors in competition with each other have the same invoice cost, delivered prices reflecting freight from a single major source of supply, and functional discounts that reflect differences in costs of doing business with different classes of buyers, adjusted for the outlays various buyers would make in reselling.

Once developed such practices tend to be institutionalized though the reasons for their origin have gone. Their longevity reflects the fact that following them is less bad than the probable alternative. Generally, they have a stabilizing influence on prices and to a less degree on market shares, and often aid in solving the "kinked" demand curve problem – the difficulty of "agreeing" on a price increase.

Since it excited attention in early postwar court decisions, the doctrine of conscious parallelism has been clarified and narrowed. Mere identity of base prices and sales provisions is not enough. Nor, apparently, is evidence that the base price does not bear a competitive relation to cost. Indeed, Professor Turner argues that if the base price reflects only what might be called "pure conjectural interdependence"—that is, where firms' behavior differs from that of a competitive market only in that each is aware of the effect of its action on price—it should not be illegal (even though there has been "quasi-agreement" via conjectural interdependence) as long as monopoly is not illegal *per se.*[27] Only if there are parallel actions to reinforce that agreement should it be illegal. But Professor Conant disagrees with the first of these points.[28] He contends that parallel behavior, whether stemming from independent action of each firm or not, should be judged as "restraint of trade" under Section 2 of the Sherman Act rather than as "implicit conspiracy" under Section 1. More detailed consideration of cases shows that a fine, but not always clear and sometimes wavering line has been drawn between illegal conscious parallelism and similarity of action taken independently. Turner would not disapprove of a base price above the competitive level that emerges from mutual awareness but holds that features of a *price structure* that do not accord with competitive behavior fall under conscious parallelism. Is it because such a price structure (not the level of prices compared to costs) is a prop or signalling device and could not exist in the absence of a consciously parallel course of action? Going on, raising prices in the presence of excess capacity (or of falling costs) appears as impossible without illegal conscious parallelism, but failing to reduce prices when demand declines seems to be approved. Identical reaction to a significant change in input prices, by itself, is not deemed con-

27. Donald F. Turner, "The Definition of Agreement Under the Sherman Act: Conscious Parallelism and Refusals to Deal" *Harvard Law Review*, vol. 75 (February, 1962), pp. 655-706.

28. Michael Conant, "Conscious Parallel Action in Restraint of Trade," *Minnesota Law Review*, vol. 38 (June, 1954), pp. 797-826, especially pp. 822-823.

scious parallelism.[29] It seems probable that a restraint of trade approach to conscious parallelism will require an economic analysis of whether a change of price reflects a change of demand or of input prices. Had the steel companies' prices fallen sharply as demand dropped after 1956-1957, the abortive attempt to advance prices in April 1962, following a small increase in wages, might not have been deemed to be conscious parallelism of action, tacit collusion, nor noncompetitive behavior as some economists asserted it was.

There seems to be general agreement that the use of indirect means of communication, persistent following of outmoded practices, price differentials that substantially exceed cost differences, and elaborate and rigid pricing systems, are beyond the limit of nonconscious parallelism. That they are methods of or results of collusion, overt or consciously parallel (or if one prefers "restraint of trade") seems obvious. The greater the difficulty of "agreeing" by independent conjectural interdependence, and the greater the firms' view of their "need" for such "agreeing", the more likely it is that there will be devices to prop the "agreement" process. Even in markets where "agreement" is relatively easy, it can be made still easier, more certain, and the provisions thereof more desirable from the point of view of the firms, by using props and signalling devices.

What seems to be evolving, therefore, is a policy that does little to weaken agreement in the easy, close-to-pure oligopoly case, but weakens the chance of "agreement" the further a market is from that pole along the spectrum of market types. Yet in the latter cases the "need," as viewed by the firms and possibly from the standpoint of the economy, for some moderation of immediate price effects of disequilibria can be more ur-

29. *Pevely Dairy Company* v. *U.S.*, 178 F. 2d 363; cert. denied, 339 U.S. 942.

gent. It is possible also that that "need" is great for industries near the open-market pole who are barred from their only feasible "softening" device, overt collusion.

In this fashion, the long-recognized inconsistency between public policy with respect to the more competitive industries facing disequilibria and of jointly acting oligopolists, not restrained under the conscious parallelism doctrine, becomes more glaring. What is approved in terms of price results for the latter is disapproved for the former. The former cannot, but the latter can, effect the desired price result by use of conjectural interdependence not deemed to be consciously parallel.

While the tone of the preceding lends support to a rule of reason in both overt collusion[30] and conscious parallelism cases, that would be a dangerous move in the present state of our knowledge. Such a policy is already being applied to conscious parallelism if one were to follow the economists' definition and include "agreement" by conjectural interdependence under that heading. I do not put the *Pevely* and similar cases un-

30. The Antitrust Division appears to be concerned about the effects of excess capacity and the prices that would result therefrom in competitive markets. This is the only rational explanation one can make for the Division's requirement, after having won a criminal action against electric manufacturing companies' executives who conspired on prices, that the companies sign a consent decree not to sell "at *unreasonably low prices* with the purpose or intent, or *where the effect is, or where there is a reasonable probability that the effect will be, substantially to injure, suppress or stifle competition or tend to create a monopoly*" (New York *Times*, June 16, 1961, p. 15, emphasis added). Left in doubt is what constitutes "unreasonably low prices" but one might presume that with the full-cost views widely held in government, the meaning is "full accounting costs." The purpose of this provision, presumably, is to avert the affect of real competitive pricing in periods of excess capacity which could force prices to the level variable costs and undermine the financial position of smaller firms, the bulk of whose volume is affected by such prices.

der this heading, for economic analysis would lead one to expect price increases of the same amount and at approximately the same time when a major input price had advanced. But there is discrimination between cases where holding prices consistently above the competitive level is easily done without use of devices that *run counter to conscious parallelism doctrine* and cases where the same results, or increase of prices after they have fallen, are not attainable easily if at all without acts that will be deemed conscious parallelism or *de facto* collusion. But I am appalled at the prospect of applying a rule of reason to all degrees of agreement — overt, tacit, conscious parallelism and conjectural interdependence.

There are several reasons for this reaction. The same devices or conduct that facilitate defense against short-term disequilibria, also can be extended to averting needed longer-term adjustments and even to exerting positive monopoly power. Separating defensive from positive conscious parallelism or more overt collusion would impose an almost impossible burden on enforcement agencies. Even defensive "agreements" are not easily identified as such; nor is the degree of their economic worth — even if the case for cyclical price (gross margin) stability is deemed to have been made — readily appraised. Furthermore, a large part of industry does not need such relief. Either their demand is fairly stable around a rising trend, or the bulk of their costs are variable, or they have developed practices of a nonconsciously parallel sort that mitigate the effects of uncertain demand. Then one must stress the gain from and need for a quite stable upward trend of GNP which means not only that general business cycle fluctuations would be small but also, as a consequence, that individual product cycles would be reduced and the required adjustments facilitated. Only in the extreme should an exception be made and that by public, not private, actions. Such an exception seems to be evolving for agriculture.

Now for some final comments on administered prices, a concept that catches the ear but has little analytical value. Its chief proponent uses it to compare frequency and degree of price change for various commodities without asking whether demand and supply conditions warrant more or less frequent price changes, or stable or widely swinging prices. Any conclusion drawn directly from frequency of change of (actual, not list) prices is a *post hoc* argument, not economic analysis. Elementary defects are the failure to relate selling price behavior to input price behavior and to consider the validity of price data. But were these errors corrected, there would be clearly a greater stability under varying demand conditions (input prices stable) in prices of much of manufactured goods made from nonagricultural raw materials than in other prices. Conjectural interdependence, and for markets where that is fairly weak, the character of interfirm organization, contribute to infrequency of price change and to moderation or delay in change of the margin between list prices (and less so, transaction prices) and variable costs. Most of this is inherent in an industrial economy and not damaging economically. Furthermore, short of a restructuring of industrial markets that will not take place, it will exist and attempts to block it will bring the inefficiencies attendant to the regulatory process.

CHAPTER 6

Monopoly, Monopolizing and Concentration of Market Power: a Proposal

BY LOUIS B. SCHWARTZ

Introduction

In thinking about national policy regarding concentration of market power, we should, whether we are for or against the antitrust laws, try to avoid dogmatism. It must be recognized that attitudes on fundamental political and economic issues often, and perhaps necessarily, reflect irrational faith as much as scientific reasoning or statistical demonstration. For one who believes in competition and dispersion of economic power, it is sobering to reflect that great industrial societies have been built on a basis of cartels and concentration, as in Germany and Japan. Similarly, one who puts his faith in political democracy must not be so dogmatic as to overlook the fact that the Greek and Renaissance societies which contributed magnificently to art, science, and the humanities, were not democracies. In our own age, the economic growth of the Soviet Union and the policies being chosen by many of the "developing" countries reflect neither competition nor democracy as we know them. The preference for wide distribution of economic as well as political power is not an obvious dictate of social science and could be regarded as the product of a culture of quite limited historical and geographical scope.

On the other hand, there is no convincing economic

basis for preferring that American industry be organized in huge units of the scale of the largest existing enterprises. The papers above by Professors Adelman and Dewey tend to portray the antitrust laws as obstacles to the achievement of optimum size. Reference is made to efficiencies of scale, sometimes as if it were an article of faith that larger units are more efficient. Yet a number of studies have provided evidence that enterprises of intermediate size may be the most efficient. The famous T.N.E.C. Monograph No. 13 supported this conclusion on the basis of a study of costs and rates of return for companies and plants classified as large, medium and small.[1] Other studies lend credence to the view that, once a minimum scale has been reached, continued increase in size produces no advantage that results in differential growth in favor of the large firms.[2] Such studies are vulnerable to hostile criticism in view of limitations in the underlying data,[3] but at least until a convincing counterdemonstration appears, one should not subscribe unreservedly to the popular belief that "the bigger, the better."

Furthermore, the concept of "efficiency" must be critically examined when people urge the proposition that very large units are the most efficient. The efficiency of a social institution cannot be measured as one would

1. On concentration beyond optimum size, see also Joe S. Bain, *Barriers to New Competition* (Cambridge, Mass., 1956), pp. 110-112, George J. Stigler, "The Economics of Scale," *Journal of Law and Economics*, vol. 1 (October, 1958) and Ward S. Bowman, "Toward Less Monopoly," *University of Pennsylvania Law Review*, vol. 101 (1953), pp. 590-607.

2. See Edward Mansfield, "Entry, Gibrat's Law, Innovation, and the Growth of Firms," *American Economic Review*, vol. 52 (December, 1962), Herbert A. Simon and Charles P. Bonini, "The Size Distribution of Business Firms," *American Economic Review*, vol. 48 (September, 1958), and P. Hart and S. Prais, "The Analysis of Business Concentration: A Statistical Approach," *Journal of the Royal Statistical Society*, Series A (1956), p. 119.

3. Richards C. Osborn, "Efficiency and Profitability in Relation to Size," *Harvard Business Review*, vol. 29 (February, 1951), p. 82.

measure the efficiency of a mechanical device. In the case of mechanical devices, one has only to relate energy input to output. The efficiency of economic organizations cannot be gauged so simply. Profitability might be one measure, but one needs to know whether the profit results from cost savings or from monopoly power to set high prices. Perhaps from a social point of view, lower profits and higher wages would be a preferable outcome of the company's operations. How do quality and diversity of product enter into appraisals of industrial efficiency? Are the major producers of moving pictures more efficient, in a socially significant sense, than independents who experiment, take greater risks, and frequently produce films that are artistically superior? Would we regard it as desirably efficient to put all national news services into a single Super-Associated-Press distributing uniform dispatches to all newspapers and broadcasting stations?

One may be skeptical also of alleged efficiency that is simply the power to overcome rivals because one's financial resources are unlimited. A small firm manufacturing a specialty product might be making a better product at lower cost than du Pont or General Motors; yet it would certainly succumb in any sharp or prolonged contest for the market, since the giants can continue for long periods to operate without profit in one of their many fields. Survival-power is not necessarily equivalent to superior efficiency.[4]

Any form of market power that is unrelated to costs and quality must be eliminated from the calculus of efficiency. The point is illustrated in the Consolidated Foods case, recently decided by the Federal Trade Commission.[5] Consolidated, a large wholesaler of

4. Mansfield, *op.cit.*, finds a much higher failure rate among smaller firms.

5. FTC Dkt. No. 7000 (November 15, 1962), *rev'd.*, 329 F. 2d 623 (7th Cir. 1964). See Jessie Markham's comments on this case in Chapter 8, below.

foods, acquired Gentry, a firm that produced dehydrated onion and garlic. Firms from which Consolidated made heavy purchases were then put under pressure to buy Gentry's products, and in some instances agreed to do so notwithstanding their objections to the quality of Gentry's products as compared with products of its competitors. Plainly the policy of reciprocal buying distorts any conclusions as to the efficiency of the large firms which are in a position to demand such reciprocity.

The efficiency gain from vertical integration seems obvious: the enterprise with assured sources of supply and assured outlets should be able to schedule operations in such a way that its plant is continuously employed and capital requirements are minimized. But two qualifying observations may be made. First, a great deal of *de facto* integration exists in the economy without formal consolidation of control. It results from voluntary stabilization of supply relationships, as where an independent fabricator regularly buys its raw materials in more or less standard proportions from several suppliers. Second, any gain which one of these suppliers achieves by purchasing control of such a fabricator-customer subjects competing suppliers to an equivalent loss of the *de facto* partial integration which existed theretofore. Integration for one firm involves disintegration for others.[6] Is there a net advantage to the community?

The foregoing remarks sufficiently warn against the too prevalent assumption that the antitrust laws obstruct the way to efficiency in seeking to control amalgamations of firms into giant units. It remains to inquire whether these laws effectively impose such restraints, and if not what kind of additional legislation might be in order.

6. Cf. *Brown Shoe Company* v. *U.S.*, 370 U.S. 294 (1962) and *U.S.* v. *Columbia Steel Co.*, 334 U.S. 495 (1948).

Monopoly and Market Power

The Inadequacy of Existing Law

Existing legal controls seem to be inadequate to prevent the achievement and maintenance of dominant concentrations of economic power. Kaysen and Turner marshalled the data showing the pervasive pattern of concentration beyond the level where workable competition may be expected.[7] They regarded concentration of one-third of sales in the eight largest sellers as *prima facie* excessive, and thought an oligopolistic response was extremely likely where the first eight firms had 50 percent or more of the business. Dozens of leading industries showed concentration ratios of 80 percent or more in the first eight firms.

Existing law cannot effectively reach these situations. The lack of price competition can be attacked under Section 1 of the Sherman Act only when an agreement or conspiracy can be proved. Section 2 of the Sherman Act prohibits only monopolization, not monopoly, and the courts have defined monopoly so as to require proof that the defendant controls as much as 50 percent or more of a market before that status is achieved. Even in that case, the monopolistic firm may escape if it lacked the purpose to monopolize, that is, if the monopolistic position was "thrust upon" it.[8] In addition to the escape afforded by the distinction between monopoly and monopolization, the courts may permit monopoly through their definition of the market. Thus, a charge that defendant was monopolizing cellophane was defeated by defining the market to in-

7. Carl Kaysen and Donald S. Turner, *Antitrust Policy: An Economic and Legal Analysis* (Cambridge, Mass., 1959), Table 1, p. 275.

8. See *U.S.* v. *Aluminum Company of America*, 148 F. 2d 416 (2d Cir. 1945) and *Union Leader Corp.* v. *Newspapers of New England, Inc.*, 284 F. 2d 582 (1st Cir. 1960).

clude all "flexible packaging materials."[9] On the other hand, the courts have sometimes defined the market narrowly so as to bring defendant's share up to the very high level required to convict. Thus in the *Alcoa* case, the market was said to include only virgin aluminum ingot notwithstanding the availability of virtually interchangeable "secondary" ingot. And a monopoly has been found in "professional world championship boxing contests," although such spectacles compete to a degree with nonchampionship bouts, and with other sports exhibitions and entertainments generally.[10] The ease with which market analysis can be manipulated is revealed in the suggestions by one able observer of American antitrust administration that each of a small group of firms collectively dominating trade in a particular product may some day be held to be monopolizing *its share* of the market.[11]

Share of the market is at best a crude indicator of defendant's economic power. In a market defined to include a variety of substitutes, a producer of one of them may keep this market share low by choosing to set a high price on his particular product. In another situation, a very high market share would not necessarily evidence real power if new products or producers were rapidly entering the field and displacing the front-runner. The Attorney General's National Committee to Study the Antitrust Law could give only equivocal support to a definition of monopoly in terms of share of a market. The percentage guides "while necessarily indefinite, are nonetheless helpful . . . power

9. *U.S.* v. *E. I. du Pont de Nemours & Co.*, 351 U.S. 377 (1956).
10. *International Boxing Club* v. *U.S.*, 358 U.S. 242 (1959).
11. A. D. Neale, *The Antitrust Laws of the United States of America: A Study of Competition Enforced by Law* (Cambridge, England, 1960), p. 183.

may also exist, as a particular matter, where the percentage of supply provided is much less."[12]

The inherent defects of the market-share test for monopoly and the visible persistence of excessive concentration have led to proposals to supplement the anti-monopoly law. Kaysen and Turner proposed to authorize divestiture where a firm possessed "unreasonable market power."[13] Market power was defined as ability to restrict output or determine prices without losing a substantial share of the market or profits. There would be a conclusive presumption of unreasonable market power where over a five-year period one firm did 50 percent or more of the trade or the four leading firms did 80 percent. I have on other occasions proposed to apply to giant industrial firms the principle of Section 11 of the Public Utility Holding Company Act of 1935. This would authorize reorganization of excessively large firms into independent units no larger than technological considerations justify. For this purpose excessively large firms would be defined, not by percentage of any particular market, but by gross assets or sales above a figure specified in the legislation or fixed from time to time by an administrative agency.

Prospects for such divestiture legislation are quite dim. There are gropings for alternative controls to apply to power concentrations which we are not ready to forbid. In Europe, there has developed the concept of restricting the freedom of "dominant" enterprises to take actions to the detriment of consumers or competitors. Thus German Law, which has no prohibition against monopoly, forbids a market-dominating enterprise to abuse its market position in respect of prices or

12. *Report of the Attorney General's National Committee to Study the Antitrust Laws* (Washington, 1955), p. 49.

13. Kaysen and Turner, *op.cit.*, pp. 266-269.

terms of doing business, or by tying agreements, and such enterprises are forbidden to engage in unjustified discrimination or restriction of other firms' business.[14] Article 86 of the Rome Treaty establishing the European Economic Community similarly prohibits an enterprise from taking improper advantage of a dominant position.

Some disposition to take a similar line in this country is shown by three extraordinary bills introduced by Congressman Celler in the 87th Congress. These bills, H.R. 11870, 11871, and 11872, defined "dominant economic power" as existing wherever four or fewer firms have 50 percent or more of the assets or capacity in any line of commerce or make more than 50 percent of the sales. H.R. 11870 would have made it unlawful for two or more of the firms sharing such dominant power "knowingly to take any similar or identical action in such line of commerce where the effect of such action may be to substantially lessen competition." H.R. 11871 would have made it unlawful to "possess or exercise dominant economic power in any line of commerce where the effect of such possession or exercise may be to substantially lessen competition." H.R. 11872 declared that no person or group of persons "shall exercise power to monopolize or to substantially lessen competition in any line of commerce."

These are crude and radical proposals. Although intended to supplement the Sherman Act in dealing with concentrated economic power, the bills do not discriminate between large and small enterprises as, for example, in a situation where the top four firms share 50 percent of the market but the top firm alone has 40 percent. Forbidding the smaller firms from taking "similar action" in response to price movements initiated by the

14. German Law Against Restraint of Competition, Sections 22 and 26.

top firm works a hardship on them while leaving the truly powerful enterprise untouched. The prohibitions against any "exercise" of dominant economic power or power substantially to lessen competition are vague to the point of unworkability. The fact that the intelligent and experienced chairman of the House Judiciary Committee sponsored such measures testifies to the strength of the impulse to do something about the problem of concentrated economic power, but more discriminating and precise legislation is required.

A Proposal

Our first legislative ventures in the direction of circumscribing the behavior of excessively powerful economic units should be confined to a clearly designated and relatively small class of "dominant" firms, identified not merely by reference to share of a particular market but more importantly by the absolute amount of their financial resources. Thus a firm might be deemed dominant if:

(1) it has total assets or annual sales in excess of a designated figure, let us say between one quarter and one half billion dollars, or

(2) it ranks first or second in any line of commerce, doing at least 10 percent of the business, and has aggregate annual sales of at least $50,000,000 including all lines of commerce in which it is engaged.

Paragraph (1) would take in between 100 and 200 of the largest industrial corporations, depending on the choice of cut-off figure.[15] Paragraph (2) is designed to take in firms that dominate a line of commerce even though they may not have the absolute size prescribed

15. See "The Fortune Directory: The 500 Largest U.S. Industrial Corporations," *Fortune* (July, 1962), p. 17.

in paragraph (1), but a minimum aggregate sales figure is also prescribed so that firms of relatively minor financial power will not be governed by the special restraints of the proposed legislation.

Dominant firms thus designated would be absolutely forbidden to:

(a) acquire any interest in another enterprise except with advance approval of the Federal Trade Commission upon a showing of compelling economic advantage to consumers or the national economy;
(b) refuse to supply on the usual terms anyone other than another dominant enterprise;
(c) restrict a customer or supplier, whether by agreement, threat of economic sanction or otherwise, in his freedom to deal with third parties;
(d) supply goods or services on terms which require or make specially advantageous the acquisition of other goods or services from the same or another supplier;
(e) discriminate or benefit from discrimination in price, service or allowance, except as the discrimination may be cost-justified;
(f) refuse to grant to anyone other than another dominant enterprise reasonable-royalty licenses under patents owned or controlled;
(g) fix the price or limit the production or marketing of a patent licensee.

It will be observed that some of these transactions—mergers, exclusive dealing, tying, and discrimination—are presently dealt with by the Clayton Act. Under that Act, however, the prohibition applies only if the effect may be substantially to lessen competition or tend to create a monopoly. The proposed legislation eliminates this qualification on the ground that the practices in question do entail a substantial anticompetitive effect when engaged in by dominant firms.

For firms which are dominant because of the absolute size defined in (1), the proposed legislation is quite definite and minimizes the occasion for courts to make difficult and inconclusive economic judgments. There would be no need to define the relevant market or to evaluate prospective competitive effects of particular transactions. Businessmen would know what was prohibited. On the other hand, some flexibility remains insofar as is necessary in construing "compelling economic advantage" to justify merger under paragraph (a), "reasonable royalty" under paragraph (f), and perhaps other phrases. The usual problems of cost justification will be inevitable under paragraph (e). Nevertheless, the *per se* aspects of the proposed legislation would go far to eliminate escapes currently available under the Sherman and Clayton Acts for behavior which plainly has a serious anticompetitive potential when engaged in by dominant firms.

With respect to the firms covered by (2), the proposed legislation would facilitate enforcement by eliminating the issue of whether a transaction within the prohibited categories has sufficient anticompetitive effect, but it would still be necessary to compute market share. As I use the phrase, "10 percent of the business," it does mean "line of commerce" as used in Sherman and Clayton Act cases. Unsatisfactory as is existing law (and economics) on this point, there appears to be no alternative to using the current doctrine.

The proposal would not directly affect existing law for firms not "dominant" according to the criteria of either (1) or (2). However, even these firms—especially as they approach the standards of dominance—would recognize that there was a national policy restricting the exercise of economic power in certain ways, and it is possible that cases under the Sherman and Clayton Acts would take on a coloration from this.

Louis B. Schwartz

What is absolutely forbidden for firms above a certain size could become indicative of what is presumptively a restraint of trade or monopolization for firms below that size. When very small firms engage in these practices, it is unlikely that harmful effects would follow.

CHAPTER 7

The Problem of the "Good" Trust

BY LUCILE SHEPPARD KEYES

Definition and Plan of Work

The subject of this chapter is the proper treatment of the "good trust" under the antitrust laws. In the discussion, the phrase "good trust" will have a denotation which I employed some years ago[1] in a study of the 1953 *Shoe Machinery* case.[2] This usage defines the good trust as an enterprise, regarded by the courts as possessing "market control,"[3] which has obtained this control without employing illegal means, and without entertaining any "specific intent" or plan to acquire such control or to use it in such a way as to exclude potential or actual competition. In the District Court's decision in this proceeding, which was later affirmed *per curiam* by the Supreme Court, it was found in effect that the United Shoe Machinery Corporation conformed to the definition as stated but had nevertheless violated the Act's prohibition of "monopolizing."

1. Lucile Sheppard Keyes, "The Shoe Machinery Case and the Problem of the Good Trust," *Quarterly Journal of Economics* (May, 1954).
2. *U.S.* v. *United Shoe Machinery Corp.*, 101 F. Supp. 295 (1953).
3. The term "market control" is used here to mean that competitive position which is regarded by the judiciary as fulfilling the nonbehavioral requirement for violation of Section 2 of the Sherman Act. This concept is also sometimes given the name "monopoly power" or "undue market power." What sort of real competitive position is thought to fit the legal category will be discussed at some length below.

The District Court did not, of course, actually employ the phrase "good trust." The phrase itself has no standing in the world of law. It is, however, intended here to be a purely legal category, in that both its key elements depend on the content of law as interpreted by the courts. Thus, what constitutes a "trust" depends on the judicial definition of "market control" (or "market power" or "monopoly power"); and what constitutes a "good" trust depends in addition on the judicial definition of legal conduct and specific intent. In short, the phrase is merely a useful means of indicating a type of enterprise which is not characterized by illegal conduct or wrongful intent but which, because of its possession of market control, *may* still be in violation of Section 2 of the Sherman Act.

According to the *Shoe Machinery* decision, it is not true that the good trust *must* be in violation of this Section. Something more is needed to complete the crime of monopolizing; and one way of completing the crime is to engage in exclusionary practices which, though regarded as legal, have some deterrent effect on the access of one's competitors to potential markets.[4] According to some other interpretations of the Act, enterprises conforming to the definition are *necessarily* in violation of Section 2, which is to say that the possession of market control, "without more," is itself illegal. These two points of view respectively indicate two different methods of dealing with the good trust: (1), to impose upon it a code of conduct more rigidly antirestrictive than that imposed upon enterprises not possessing market control; or (2), to attack the good trust with wea-

4. The exclusionary practices found relevant in the *Shoe Machinery* case were excessively long-term leases, failure to offer machines for sale as well as for lease, failure to make separate charges for repairs and other services, and lease provisions and practices that in effect penalized the substitution of machinery made by the competititors of the United Shoe Machinery Corporation, etc.

pons which go beyond any regulation of conduct – in particular, with the various modes of breaking up a single enterprise into two or more separate concerns.

From the point of view of public policy, there are at least three central questions involved in the problem of the good trust. First, is the problem being unnecessarily broadened because of an inadequate generally applicable regulation of business conduct? Second, is the market control concept, in any of its variant forms, well adapted to identifying those enterprises which, although legally blameless under the general regulation of business practices, should be subject to further corrective action under the antitrust laws? And third, if this concept is not appropriate for this purpose, is there any more promising analytical approach which might yield an acceptable criterion for the use of those additional weapons?

In the following discussion, attention will be directed primarily to the second and third of these questions. A final section will deal briefly with some aspects of the regulation of conduct.

Market Control and Related Concepts as Indicators of Need for Corrective Action

We take up first the question of the usefulness of the judicial concept of market control, and of certain related categories, suggested by economic theorists, in identifying those enterprises which, although legal in conduct and intent, should be subjected to further corrective action under the antitrust laws. Attention will be centered on the famous *Cellophane* decision[5] which provides in its majority and minority opinions convenient examples of the great range of operational def-

5. *U.S.* v. *E. I. du Pont de Nemours and Co.*, 351 U.S. 377 (1956), hereinafter referred to as *Cellophane*.

inition which can be accommodated within the judicial concept.

The concept of "reasonable interchangeability." The essential formal elements of the concept here remain the same as in previous leading decisions. Thus, in the majority opinion, Mr. Justice Reed restated the accepted formula: "Our cases," he wrote, "determine that a party has monopoly power if it has, over 'any part of the trade or commerce among the several States,' a power of controlling prices or unreasonably restricting competition."[6] As in previous cases, the precise character of the requisite price control or exclusionary ability is not clear; indeed, they appear to form two aspects of the same attribute. As Mr. Justice Reed phrased it, "Price and competition are so intimately entwined that any discussion of theory must treat them as one. It is inconceivable that price could be controlled without power over competition or vice versa."[7]

What is quite clear, however, is that not just *any* control over price, nor just *any* ability to exclude competition, is sufficient to establish the existence of monopoly power. Such control and ability must apply to a genuine "part" of interstate commerce – in other words, to a *bona fide* market in the full legal sense. It was squarely on this point of definition that the Court's exoneration of the du Pont company rested: "If cellophane is the 'market' that du Pont is found to dominate," reads the majority opinion, "it may be assumed it does have monopoly power over that 'market.'"[8] In this connection, the most notable features of the majority opinion were its relatively sophisticated approach to the question of legal market definition, and its ap-

6. *Ibid.*, p. 389: The quotation is from *Standard Oil Co.* v. *U.S.*, 221 U.S. 1, 58 (1911).
7. 351 U.S. 392.
8. *Ibid.*, p. 391.

parent recognition that the underlying policy problem had not really been solved.

The Court recognized that competition of imperfect substitutes is necessarily relevant in appraising the competitive position of any firm, and held that "reasonable interchangeability by consumers for the same purposes" is the appropriate rule for market definition:

> . . . Where there are market alternatives that buyers may readily use for their purposes, illegal monopoly does not exist merely because the product said to be monopolized differs from others. If it were not so, only physically identical products would be a part of the market. To accept the Government's argument, we would have to conclude that the manufacturers of plain as well as moistureproof cellophane were monopolistic and so with films such as Pliofilm, foil, glassine, polyethylene, and Saran, for each of these wrapping materials is distinguishable. . . . New wrappings appear, generally similar to cellophane; is each a monopoly? What is called for is an appraisal of the "cross-elasticity" of demand in the trade. . . . In considering what is the relevant market for determining the control of price and competition, no more definite rule can be declared than that commodities reasonably interchangeable by consumers for the same purposes make up that "part of the trade or commerce" monopolization of which may be illegal.[9]

Each of the packaging materials mentioned by Mr. Justice Reed, if produced by a separate firm, would definitely give rise to a monopoly in the economic-analytical meaning, both in the sense preferred by Professor Chamberlin and in the perhaps more widely used sense of any departure from infinite elasticity of the demand curve faced by the individual firm. Professor Chamberlin, of course, prefers to reserve the term to denote unified control over the supply of some product, the prod-

9. *Ibid.*, pp. 394-395.

uct definition being as broad or as narrow as is convenient in the particular context.[10]

In a related passage, the Court again emphasized that *substitutability for the same use or purpose is* the important defining characteristic of the market, and, to its further credit, recognized that price differences may affect the degree of substitutability:

> In determining the market under the Sherman Act it is the use or uses to which the commodity is put that control. The selling price between commodities with similar uses and different characteristics may vary, so that the cheaper product can drive out the more expensive. Or, the superior quality of the higher priced articles may make dominant the more desirable. Cellophane costs more than many competing products and less than a few. But whatever the price, there are various flexible wrapping materials that are bought by manufacturers for packaging their goods in their own plants or are sold to converters who shape and print them for use in the packaging of the commodities to be wrapped.[11]

10. Reasserting his adherence to the definition of monopoly as *control over supply*, Professor Chamberlin elaborates: "I do hold, however, that this traditional concept 'is meaningless without reference to the thing monopolized.'* The traditional dichotomy between competition and monopoly is dissolved, not by a new definition of monopoly, but by applying the old and familiar one with complete flexibility to cover any product whatever, no matter how broadly or narrowly defined. One can have a monopoly of Chateau d'Yquem, of all Sauternes, of all white wines from the Bordeaux region, or all Bordeaux wines, or of all white wines, of all wines, of all beverages, and so on indefinitely until we reach the limit of all economic goods. And whatever the area monopolized, the monopolist will always face competition in some degree from the wider area beyond its limits. Hence the paradoxical expresson 'monopolistic competition.'" E. H. Chamberlin, "Measuring the Degree of Monopoly and Competition," *Monopoly and Competition and their Regulation* (New York, 1954), p. 255. The quotation marked with an asterisk is from the same author's *The Theory of Monopolistic Competition* (Cambridge, Mass., 1933), p. 65.

11. 351 U.S. 395-396.

With regard to the effect of price relationships on substitutability, the price policy of a monopolist may have a very significant effect on his competitive position if this competitive position is measured in terms of cross-elasticities at going prices. Other things being equal, the higher the price he charges, the less "monopolistic" his position may appear to become, since his customers, when charged higher prices, may be more easily lured away.

Despite its realistic recognition of the importance of imperfect substitutes, its laudable refusal to adopt a rigid analytical definition of monopoly in law which would make it equivalent to the generally accepted concepts of monopoly in economics, its sense of the complexity of the determinants and results of cross-elasticities of demand, and its emphasis on substitutability as the really relevant criterion in determining the impact on any given supplier of the availability of products from independent competitors, the majority does not really offer any constructive solution for the policy problem at hand. To do so would require at least some indication of the point at which "interchangeability" ceases to be "reasonable," and "purpose" of the buyer becomes different instead of the same. As we shall see, the Court itself seems to have recognized that this crucial step in the argument had not yet been taken.

Before going on to this second main aspect of the majority opinion, however, it is appropriate here to give some consideration to the late Professor J. M. Clark's analysis of competition among different products which are fit for the same broad use or purpose – an analysis which bears directly on the problem of distinguishing "reasonable" from "unreasonable" interchangeability. Clark's view was that it is useful to distinguish between "differentiated competition," on the one hand, and "substitution" on the other.[12] In both of these subcategories, products are included which are not identical but at the same time "satisfy the same principal want," a characteristic serving to distinguish all of them from the general run of products which also in a broad sense compete for the buyer's dollar. The difference between the two subcategories is said to be this: that in "differentiated competition,... the producer is free to imitate others as closely as he wishes, using techniques that are not radically different from theirs, and differentiating his product only to the extent that it seems advantageous to him to do so, in order to appeal to some subsidiary want more effectively than other variants do, and thus fit into a gap in the array of variant products."

In "substitution," on the other hand, although the same "principal want" is appealed to, the products are "inherently and inescapably different, due either to different materials or basically different techniques." Note well the qualification "inherently and inescapably" — for it is on this particular kind of heterogeneity, rather than on heterogeneity as such, that Clark's distinction is apparently intended to rest. Though some parts of his text seem to invite interpretation to mean that "substitution" is all competition between *producers of physically different products,* rather than comprising only that competition which is between *producers who cannot produce the same product,* Clark insisted upon the crucial importance of the latter interpretation: "In the case I have called substitution, the differences between the products cannot be altered at will, and the products cannot be spaced in a continuous spectrum by the action of rival producers trying to fit their product variants into the most attractive unoccupied spaces. The differentials are persistent."[13]

12. J. M. Clark, *Competition as a Dynamic Process* (Washington, 1961), pp. 100-102.

13. *Ibid.,* pp. 101-102.

According to Professor Clark, the market results of "differentiated competition" are significantly different from those of "substitution" in two respects: first, the former but not the latter has a tendency to bring the profit level "down to a normal competitive minimum," and, second, the individual demand curve of the "differentiated competitor," as opposed to that of the "substitute competitor," though it has a slope, "tends to flatten out in a moderate time unless [the slope is] renewed."

It is essential to note that in both cases – that is, in "differentiated competition" as well as in "substitution" – the competitive process which leads to the indicated results is one which permits changes in the products offered by individual firms. The equilibrium embodying these results is in both cases a "long-run" rather than a "short-run" equilibrium: at this equilibrium point, no individual firm has open to it any unexploited opportunity for increasing its profits through entering a new line of production. It follows, then, that neither the tendency of the process nor the economic desirability of the equilibrium can be judged merely by observing the existence or persistence of physical and technical differences between competing products. If there are no long-run obstacles to entry, then those "gaps in the chain of substitutes" which persist at equilibrium must be due to the fact that any further "imitation" of the product of a competitor would be relatively unprofitable.[14] If there are such obstacles, they may or may not be manifest in physical or technical differences

14. Here "entry" must obviously be defined without reference to the pure-competition industry or to any of its vaguer modern variants, and the competing away of excess profits need not involve any "flattening" of the individual demand curves. Those who are interested in the theoretical and definitional problems connected with entry in a context of monopolistic competition may wish to consult Lucile Sheppard Keyes, *Federal Control of Entry into Air Transportation* (Cambridge, Mass., 1951) Part I.

which are more conspicuous than those observed elsewhere. In sum, it cannot be relative diversity of product which distinguishes the two types of market; the distinguishing characteristic must rather lie in their relative freedom from obstacles to entry.

Therefore, it appears that Professor Clark's analysis is not, after all, of any help in our attempt to separate reasonable from unreasonable interchangeability, and thus to delineate "markets" which are significant from an antitrust point of view. On the contrary, the analysis merely serves to reinforce the case for concentrating our efforts on eliminating unnecessary restraints on the adaptation of product and investment in response to market demand. As will be brought out later, Clark himself relied principally on a different line of analysis in developing his own judgment of the proper definition of the market under the Sherman Act.

In the other main aspect of the majority opinion with which we shall be concerned, the Court emphasized the proposition that not all interchangeability is reasonable, and apparently admitted that the central policy question has not been solved:

> Determination of the competitive market for commodities depends on how different from one another are the offered commodities in character or use, how far buyers will go to substitute one commodity for another. For example, one can think of building materials as in commodity competition but one could hardly say that brick competed with the steel or wood or cement or stone in the meaning of Sherman Act litigation; the products are too different. This is the interindustry competition emphasized by some economists.[15]
>
> The "market" which one must study to determine when a producer has monopoly power will vary with the part

15. 351 U.S. 393.

> of commerce under consideration. The tests are constant. That market is composed of products that have reasonable interchangeability for the purposes for which they are produced – price, use and qualities considered. . . . The application of the tests remains uncertain. . . .[16]

For the interesting question of why the competition between brick and wood is not to be regarded as competition "in the meaning of Sherman Act litigation," the Court's statements suggest two possible answers: (1), "the products are too different"; and (2), this competition in "interindustry" rather than "intraindustry." As to the latter suggestion, it need only be noted that the problem of defining an industry, insofar as it is relevant to the present analysis at all, is the same problem as that of defining the "competitive product group," and that the change in verbal formulation gets us nowhere. In the minority opinion, the implied distinction between interindustry and intraindustry competition is seized upon and used to attack the doctrine of "reasonable interchangeability," but this tactic also produces no progress toward the solution of the policy problem.[17] Similarly, to say that "the products are too different," even in a context which implies that the "difference" is relevant because it means a certain difficulty in the process of substitution, is to leave open the question of how "different" the legally noncompeting products have to be.

Definition of "market control" in terms of "effective competition."

On this point, Professor Clark criticizes the majority opinion as (apparently) involving "a dubious widening of the scope of the competitive market into the

16. *Ibid.*, p. 404.
17. *Ibid.*, pp. 423-424.

area . . . of inherently different substitute commodities, far from interchangeable,"[18] and offered his own formula for the proper definition of the market. "From the standpoint of the antitrust laws," he wrote, "a competitive market may be defined as an area of trading, unified control of which would deprive the customers of the benefits of effective competition."[19] "Effective competition" is a phrase which was used by Clark in a special sense, and a considerable part of his book is devoted to the elaboration of this concept. It is definitely not the same as pure competition, since it is *not* limited "to cases in which the seller merely accepts a going price, which he has no power to influence."[20] Though it is impossible to do justice to Clark's total concept in the small space which can be devoted to it here, it is not unfair to characterize the main identifying feature of "effective competition" as he defined it by the following:

> For the competition to be effective, the crucial thing seems to be that prices be independently made under conditions that give some competitors an incentive to aggressive action that others will have to meet, whenever prices are materially above the minimum necessary supply prices at which the industry would supply the amounts demanded of the various grades and types of products it produces. What profit or loss a given competitor will individually make will depend on whether he is a high-cost or a low-cost producer, and on whether the industry is shrinking or expanding.[21]

18. Clark, *op.cit.*, p. 107.
19. *Ibid.*, p. 105.
20. *Ibid.*, p. 18.
21. *Ibid.* The first sentence in this passage was also cited by Myron Watkins, in his review of Clark's work, as the "nearest approach to a definition of 'effective competition' that the reviewer encountered." *American Economic Review*, vol. 52 (December, 1962), pp. 1074-1075.

I have singled out here what I believe to be the main *causal* or *structural* characteristic of Clark's effective competition, rather than its presumed effects in terms of economic performance, which include, if I am not mistaken, dynamic progress as well as efficiency in static terms. For I believe that it would be generally agreed that if the concept of effective competition is to be useful in connection with antitrust policy, it must identify structural features to be used as guides to action, rather than leaving the administrators with the task of attempting to appraise each competitive situation by an examination of the performance of the competitors.

While Professor Clark's statement does suggest some important conditions for the existence of strong incentives to constructive effort on the part of private economic enterprises, it does not seem that this statement would be of any great help to a judge trying to decide a case or, indeed, to a legislator who is trying to draw up a new and more efficient Sherman Act. Were prices in the flexible packaging materials industry "made under conditions that [gave] some competitors an incentive to aggressive action that others [had] to meet, whenever prices [were] materially above the minimum necessary supply prices at which the industry would supply the amounts demanded of the various grades and types of product it [produced]?" In testing for the existence of the critical excess of market price above minimum supply price, is it sufficient to find that only some of the prices of competitive products within the industry fulfill this condition, or must they all do so? If not all, then how many, or which? If the profits of some firm did seem to indicate prices "materially above the minimum necessary supply price," was this condition due to ineffective competition or to the fact that the firm in question was a "low-cost producer"? What standard of comparison do we use to make a judgment as to whether the firm is a low- or a high-cost producer? And, if we find that competition is not effective, how do we know this is due to the "relative size" of du Pont's flexible packaging or cellophane output, and how many times do we slice du Pont to make sure that competition will be effective? In the end, it appears, the application of the "effective competition" criterion turns out to be fully as difficult as – if nor more difficult than – the application of direct performance standards.[22]

Definition of market control in terms of independent price policy.

Yet another standard of legal competition is suggested in the minority opinion in the *Cellophane* case. In addition to declaring that the competition among various types of flexible packaging material was of an inter- rather than an intraindustrial variety,[23] and thus presumably unworthy of notice, the minority noted that du Pont had on certain occasions "independently" chosen to change the price of cellophane, and had – at least in part as a result of the ex-

22. But Professor Clark was certainly right in insisting that widely varying types of individual firm behavior are consistent with that type of market structure which is usually termed "oligopolistic," whose major distinguishing feature is the condition that each firm acts in the knowledge that its price-output decisions can influence significantly the decisions of one or more rivals, whose decisions are in turn capable of significantly affecting the demand for the products of the first firm. Indeed, one of the best features of Clark's valuable work is its realistic and penetrating treatment of some characteristically neglected aspects of competition under these "oligopolistic" conditions. (See, for example, p. 61 and p. 15.) In relation to antitrust policy, it appears that the most important effect of this analysis is to discredit still further the sort of argument that rests on the assumption that "fewness" of competitors automatically involves "nonaggressiveness" in price policy and a tendency to an equilibrium condition with unnecessarily high costs and excess capacity.

23. 351 U.S. 424.

ercise of this culpable discretion — been able to earn substantial profits. Referring to these facts, Mr. Chief Justice Warren stated: "It is this latitude with respect to price, this broad power of choice, that the antitrust laws forbid. Du Pont's independent pricing policy," the opinion continues, "and the great profits consistently yielded by that policy leave no room for doubt that it had power to control the price of cellophane."[24] It is not the *size of the profits,* but the fact that du Pont was able "independently" to vary the price that Chief Justice used as proof of illegality.

This sort of standard has also found its recent champions in the academic world. The "latitude with respect to price" mentioned by the Chief Justice appears to be the same phenomenon as the "market power" which would be the target of attack in the trust-busting program recommended by the Professors Kaysen and Turner.[25] Unlike the "effective competition" of Professor Clark, the type of competitive situation approved by Professors Kaysen and Turner is clearly modeled after the classical ideal of pure competition:

> Where firms can persistently behave over substantial periods of time in a manner which differs from the behavior that the competitive market would impose on competitive firms facing similar cost and demand conditions, they can be identified as possessing market power. Conversely, where, on the average and viewed over long periods of time, the relations of prices, costs, outputs, capacities, and investments among a group of rivalrous firms are such as would be expected in a competitive model, then it can be

24. *Ibid.*, pp. 422-423.

25. Carl Kaysen and Donald F. Turner, *Antitrust Policy: An Economic and Legal Analysis* (Cambridge, Mass., 1959). For more complete discussion of the authors' proposals, see the review by Lucile Sheppard Keyes in *The George Washington Law Review* (October, 1960) and that by Corwin Edwards in the *American Economic Review,* vol. 50 (December, 1960).

> inferred that the market does constrain the scope of the individual firm's decisions sufficiently to be called competitive.[26]

The "relations of prices, costs, outputs, capacities, and investments" which are held to be characteristic of a competitive market are then described in terms which leave no doubt that it is the pure-competition equilibrium that is being referred to:

> In technical terms, prices should equal both long-run average costs (including normal profits) and marginal costs for each product as well as for the enterprise as a whole; capacity should be fully utilized in periods of high demand . . . and, where capacity is not fully utilized, firms should not be earning positive profits . . . output should be produced at minimum costs, in plants of efficient scale . . .[27]

For reasons which are familiar to every first-year student of economic theory, this sort of equilibrium is a logical impossibility unless the demand curve facing the individual firm is infinitely elastic, that is, unless there is pure competition.[28] The "horizontal" individual firm

26. Kaysen and Turner, *op.cit.*, p. 8.

27. *Ibid.*, pp. 12-13.

28. For the benefit of those who may have forgotten it, I present here the essential skeleton of the theoretical argument: (a) At the minimum point (or on the minimum range) of the average cost curve, where average cost is neither increasing nor decreasing, average and marginal costs are equal (MC=AC). This is the point (or range) known as "full utilization of capacity," where no further decline in average cost can be brought about by using more variable factors with the fixed elements. (b) If this output is an equilibrium one, not subject to alteration without some adverse effect on profit, then at this output marginal revenue must be equal to marginal cost (MR=MC). (c) If at this output profit is to be only "normal" – i.e., at that level which is included in the cost curve then it must be that price (or average revenue) is equal to average cost (AC=AR). From (MR=MC), (MC=AC), and (AC =AR), it follows at once that (MR=AR) that is, that AR neither decreases nor increases with a small change in output, or, in other words, that the demand curve is horizontal.

demand curve appears, then, to be the graphic equivalent of the absence of "power over price" or "market power" which is said to be the ideal state of affairs.

Though the authors aver that "the characteristic results of the competitive model define efficiency,"[29] they do not attempt a thorough justification of their anti-market power program in terms of efficient production or economic progress; therefore, they do not find it necessary to defend in detail the economic appropriateness of the pure competition ideal, given the nature of demand in the real world.

Though certain *supply* conditions – for example, the existence of a minimum self-supporting scale of a single firm – are also essential here, it seems useful to emphasize the basic nature of the *demand* conditions, since the supply conditions are already more generally treated as facts of life. Thus, those who advocate the fragmentation of markets do not ordinarily intend that this shall be done through a research campaign to develop more efficient small-scale techniques of production, but rather through a homogenization of products or an addition to the number of competitive firms for the purpose of making infinite the elasticity of the demand curves confronting each individual firm. But, given the state of techniques and factor availability, the elasticity of the firm demand curve as well as the character of the "product mix" under conditions of unrestricted entry are functions of the pattern of desired consumer spending, which must be accepted as a guidepost for economic activity rather than a condition to be manipulated for the furtherance of some superimposed objective.

As I have noted elsewhere,[30] their program is advocated because of its alleged political benefits, rather than because of its expected economic effects. In brief,

29. Kaysen and Turner, *op.cit.*, p. 12.
30. In the review cited in fn. 25, above.

the argument runs that such a program is necessary in order to preserve our "market-organized society" against what would otherwise be an irresistible public demand that "economic decisions [with respect to prices and outputs] be made or supervised by politically responsible authorities."[31] Since the political aspects of antitrust are not included in the subject matter of the present study, no lengthy consideration of this argument will be undertaken here. It may be appropriate to suggest, however, that a change from private to public ownership of any given enterprise would seem to broaden rather than to narrow the range of discretionary choice open to those who decide on that enterprise's price-output policy, if only because under private ownership there is usually a real necessity for making ends meet in the long run.[32]

At any rate, no political argument can make the pure competition model any more defensible from the economic point of view. In the words of Professor Chamberlin, "the welfare ideal itself (as well as the description of reality) involves a blend of monopoly and competition and is therefore correctly described as one of monopolistic competition."[33] The existence of some

31. Kaysen and Turner, *op.cit.*, pp. 48-49.

32. On this point, and also for some considerations which are relevant to the "political responsibility" of the price-makers under government ownership, see Lucile Sheppard Keyes, "Some Controversial Aspects of the Public Corporation," *Political Science Quarterly*, vol. 70 (March, 1955).

33. E. H. Chamberlin, "Product Heterogeneity and Public Policy," *American Economic Review*, vol. 40 (May, 1950), p. 86. The point is here further elaborated as follows: "Let us proceed at once to the proposition that monopoly is necessarily a part of the welfare norm. In abstract terms it seems to follow very directly from the recognition that human beings are individuals, diverse in their tastes and desires, and moreover widely dispersed spatially. Insofar as demand has any force as a guide to production, one would expect entrepreneurs to appeal to them in diverse ways, and thus to render the output of the economy correspondingly heteroge-

"blend of monopoly and competition" does not arise simply from exploitative propensities on the part of the bourgeois entrepreneur or from undue inertia on the part of the Antitrust Division of the Justice Department, but is inherent in the structure of market demand, the efficient satisfaction of which must be one fundamental element in any acceptable economic ideal.

We have now considered two judicial conceptions of market control, one suggested by the majority and one by the minority opinion in the *Cellophane* case, and have in each case considered also what might be termed an academic opposite number. In addition, we have given some attention to Professor Clark's proposed standard of "effective competition," upon which his own major market control concept is based. The conclusion with respect to all of these conceptions is the same: they do not offer any sound basis for the identification of situations which require corrective antitrust action beyond the general regulation of conduct.[34]

neous, using this term in its broadest sense to embrace not only the qualitative aspects of the product itself, but also the conditions surrounding its sale, including spatial location. And since what people want – an elaborate system of consumers' preferences – is the starting point in welfare economics, their wants for a heterogeneous product would seem to be as fundamental as anything could be. Heterogeneity as between producers is synonymous with the presence of monopoly; therefore monopoly is necessarily a part of the welfare ideal."

34. A similar conclusion holds with respect to the treatment in *Cellophane* of the narrower question of legal "market share." Though the minority spokesman (p. 425) gives unequivocal support to the doctrine that whoever has the "lion's share" of a *bona fide* market "must have monopoly power," and also to the proposition that 75 per cent is enough to constitute the requisite "lion's share," this assertion is not supported by any new reasoning designed to supply the still missing link in the argument: namely the connection between market share and economic performance.

Lucile Sheppard Keyes

An Alternative Approach

Is there any more promising line of analysis by means of which the economist may hope to provide guidance in the shaping of antitrust policy where conduct is not in itself illegal? To escape the shortcomings of the analyses just discussed, such an approach would have to single out some structural feature of the market which reliably exhibits an adverse effect on economic performance, and at the same time is practically identifiable in each particular case and also capable of successful modification by antitrust weapons other than the generally applicable regulation of conduct. As we have seen, the analysis based on the traditional "industry" concept cannot be said to fulfill any of these requirements: an ambiguously stated hypothesis (as to economic performance) cannot be proved or disproved, and an unidentifiable characteristic cannot be held to be modified in any definite way.[35] A more promising *conceptual* starting point appears to be at hand when attention is concentrated on the market environment of the individual firm, since it is surely true that the beneficial effects of competition must be brought about through its stimulating and disciplining effect on the decision-making centers within individual firms. In other words, "in the light of such universally accepted policy objectives as the provision of stimulus to management and the protection of the consumer from exploitation, . . . the 'market' with the control of which we are concerned is that confronting the individual firm, and . . . the 'control' that may be obnoxious

35. Thus, it still seems to me to be a good idea, in this context, to disregard "the 'industry' concept, which has definite analytical significance only in connection with pure competition, and which has tended to center attention on the number of firms in an ill-defined group and the percentage of sales of an ill-defined product." Keyes, "The Shoe Machinery Case and the Problem of the Good Trust," *op.cit.*, p. 300.

...may be identified with the protection enjoyed by such a market from the inroads of competitors."[36]

Probably it would be well to refer to such a protected position as "market security" instead of "market control" in order to distinguish it from categories defined in terms of conventional market shares or price-elasticity of demand. If "profit" is defined as the excess of average costs at maximum efficiency for a given firm's actual output (*not* necessarily that at the minimum point of the cost curve), then the idea of market security *can perhaps be interpreted as a sort of* "profit-elasticity" of demand at super-normal profit levels. However, it seems more convenient and less confusing to regard shelter from competition as a matter of the *persistence of the existing firm demand curve* in the face of super-normal profits or unduly high costs. This formulation emphasizes the fact that the effect of new competition may be expected to be manifest throughout the entire individual demand function rather than being concentrated on sales at certain price levels. The formulation thus appears to make it easier to bring into the analytical picture the fact that new competition may make the individual demand function less price-elastic rather than more so.

Having thus focused attention on a structural feature which has a plausible causal connection with stimulus to producers and protection to consumers, can we proceed to develop any useful policy implications? Before attempting to deal with this question in detail, it may be well to indicate what appears to be the answer in general terms: As far as I have been able to determine, the analysis is not capable of yielding guides for antitrust action which goes beyond the general regulation of conduct, although it does suggest a rationale for investigating the possible desirability of action along lines

36. *Ibid.*

which are not a part of traditional antitrust policy. In spite of this lack of positive result, however, it does seem useful to consider here two lines of approach to policy questions which are suggested by the market security analysis, and this for two reasons: first, the discussion may suggest to others some way out of the difficulties which I have not been able to surmount; second, if these difficulties are indeed insuperable, the discussion may serve to put an end to an inevitably fruitless and wasteful search.

Both lines of approach are centered on the problem of finding criteria for the employment of dissolution, divorcement, or divestiture to improve the functioning of markets. When we speak of antitrust action beyond the general regulation of conduct, it is after all this specific type of weapon with which we must be concerned. The only other possibility here seems to be that suggested by Judge Wyzanski: that is, the proposed application of a special, more strict regulation of conduct to large or somehow "powerful" enterprises.[37] And the argument for this proposal appears to have a basic defect. While a good case can apparently be made for subjecting large enterprises to a broader range of prohibitions against exclusionary practices than that which is currently in force, there does not seem to be any good reason why such a stricter code should not be applied to small enterprises as well. If it is desired to give special preferential treatment to small business, other means can be found which are cheaper, fairer and less dangerous as precedents than selective exemption from proper antitrust regulation.

The first line of approach, which is similar to a sug-

37. A similar proposal is made by Professor Schwartz in Chapter 6, above.

gestion that I made some years ago,[38] is an attempt to develop "numbers" or "relative size" criteria on the basis of a factual investigation of the correlation of these factors with the market security enjoyed by various firms in the past. Although, as we have seen, market theory provides no formula for delimiting the boundaries of areas of significant competition and for setting maximum permissible "shares" within these limits, the theory itself does not, on the other hand, rule out the actual existence of such areas. If factual investigation should reveal, for example, that an unusual degree of market security had been strongly associated with market shares of over 50 percent of the output of groups of firms between which cross-elasticity of demand averaged more than 30 percent, this finding would provide at least a *prima facie* case for action with respect to existing markets. For purposes of such an investigation, various more or less arbitrary boundaries (defined in terms of minimum cross-elasticities) theoretically might be used to delimit the "market" – or area in which relative share is calculated, provided only that the principle of delimitation was in every case sufficiently definite and objectively applicable to be capable of generalization to other similar situations.

I use the word "theoretically" with *emphasis*. It should have been obvious to me at the outset, as it was

38. The earlier suggestion was for an investigation which would have included the correlation between economic performance and market vulnerability as well as the correlation between vulnerability and recognizable causal factors (e.g., number of firms producing "similar" products, on various chosen definitions of similarity). "The Shoe Machinery Case and the Problem of the Good Trust," *op.cit.*, p. 304. If we can assume a positive correlation between performance and vulnerability, as it seems to me reasonable to do, then we can at least avoid some of the problems involved in measuring performance, and concentrate attention on the causal factors.

no doubt obvious to anyone else who happened to take note of this suggestion, that the key elements in the proposed factual study (i.e., market security and the various hypothetical market boundaries) were not in fact capable of measurement. Major stumbling blocks would have been the calculation of cross-elasticities, without which no meaningful boundaries could have been defined, and the correction of profit figures to allow for departures from minimum efficient costs. (Since firm demand curves cannot be observed directly, their persistence would have had to be inferred from data on prices and costs.)

The second suggested line of approach is to proceed directly to consider the effect of the deliberate creation of a new competitor on the security of the market of an existing firm, with a view to discovering, if possible, some objectively identifiable circumstances in which such deliberate action could be confidently expected to result in a net economic benefit. As will be seen, the following argument is by no means new. If there is anything at all unusual here, it is the avoidance of the analytical use of the industry concept.

In general, the existence of competition, whether actual or potential, homogeneous or differentiated, subjects the individual firm to a price "ceiling," or series of price "ceilings," above which all or some of its business is lost to other sellers. In the traditional theory of pure competition, there is but one long-run price ceiling for each firm, and it is for every firm in the industry equal to the minimum average costs of the marginal firm. At any price above this level, all the business of the firm will be lost: its rivals can always accommodate all of its customers without any delay, for their combined purchases are negligibly small compared to the total capacity of all the competitors; there are not customers who are willing to pay a higher price for the product of one firm than for that of another (since the product is homogeneous); and other firms are not deterred from invading any given firm's market by fear of provoking warfare (because no firm is in a position individually to affect appreciably the sales of any other).

Where existing competitors are not so many as to be individually negligible, the level of the "ceiling" fixed by competition is no longer necessarily determined at a definite cost figure and may be "graduated" – that is, different for different quantities of output – rather than "flat." Even where the product of every firm is homogeneous from the point of view of all buyers, rivals may be unable to accommodate all of a given firm's business without time-lag and may refrain from or limit invasion of a given firm's market because of fear of retaliation.

In the latter situation, it is possible to argue that the larger the number of close competitors, the closer to the "ceiling" will be held the minimum supply price necessary to enable the firm to stay in business. This is because the policies of the various firms in question will probably be coordinated by agreement or quasi-agreement;[39] because the stability of the agreement may reasonably be supposed to vary inversely with the strength of the incentive to individual firms to breach the agreement by price-cutting; and because individual members of *large* groups would have a stronger incentive to do so than members of *small* groups, since the former can presumably make relatively larger short-run gains at the expense of rivals without affecting any other individual rival's sales enough to provoke countermeasures. Thus, the larger the group, the more likely the individual firms would be to undermine any "agreed" price level high enough to offer substantial

39. The underlying analysis of "small group" behavior is due to William Fellner, *Competition Among the Few* (New York, 1949).

profit opportunities to a solitary price-cutter. (Here the "group" is defined in terms of business behavior—if the reactions of firm A are taken into account in the policy-determinations of firm B, then he is in the "group" which is relevant in the analysis of B's competitive position. No particular values for the actual degrees of substitutability or cross-elasticity need be postulated in defining the group.)

Under certain favorable conditions, then, it is possible that the deliberate addition of a new competitor might make some consumers better off, through decreasing the security of each existing firm's market. Unfortunately, however, the demonstration of such a possibility apparently cannot be developed into a useful rationale for the use of the dissolution weapon, because it is as a practical matter not feasible to identify the situations in which the favorable conditions are in fact fulfilled.

In the first place, the effect of an increase in numbers on the stability of the quasi-agreement depends entirely on management appraisals of the opportunities confronting their firms. These opportunities, and the attitudes which determine their development into programs of action, vary not only from group to group but from firm to firm within a group. For example, it is quite conceivable that in some circumstances each member firm in a large group would be more careful to avoid the appearance of raiding the markets of others than would each member of a smaller group, if only because the former would typically have relatively smaller resources to sustain it in the event that retaliatory price-cutting should take place.

Moreover, instead of "shaking up" an unsatisfactory oligopolistic situation so that a new equilibrium would be established at lower prices and/or costs, it is quite conceivable that the addition of the new firm might result in its peaceful absorption into the "group," and that the new equilibrium might be at a higher price and/or cost level than the old. It is at least doubtful that there are many situations in which the addition of only one or two new competitors would have a significant destabilizing effect on the operative quasi-agreement. On the other hand, the redistribution of demand among a larger number of firms may result in higher costs as the average scale of operation declines. Indeed, if there were no significant diseconomies of small scale, and no special obstacles to entry, there would be more reason to expect that any excess returns or unduly high costs would be eroded without the necessity for government action, since new entrants would not be deterred by the prospect of cost disadvantages in their initial stages of operation. Here the market security of the incumbent firms would be relatively low, regardless of their number, and this fact would undoubtedly be reflected in the going level of prices and costs.

Finally, in estimating whether or not the addition of a new firm will in any given instance have a favorable net effect, account must also be taken of the administrative and transitional costs of applying this remedy, which may be far from insignificant. In short, there seems to be no hope of ever being able to predict in any particular case whether or not the possible resulting economic benefits will exceed these costs.

So far, then, it appears that no practical guide has been found for the use of the dissolution remedy as a direct means of improving economic performance. It seems evident, however, that this weapon can be fruitfully employed as an added deterrent in the prevention of restrictive conduct. The particular use which immediately commends itself in this connection is the breaking up of combinations that have been formed by mergers which were themselves illegal, as exemplified in the 1957 du Pont – General Motors decision.[40] If the original Clayton Act had been applicable to acquisitions of assets as well as of stock, the present scope for action along this line would presumably be much broader than it actually is; since, however, no *ex post facto* law will be enacted to correct this essentially unjustified limitation, it will have to be lived with.

As to the positive suggestions which can be derived from the market security type of approach, and which do not obviously relate to traditional antitrust policy, I shall merely indicate their general character by mentioning two corollaries to be drawn from the proposition that there is a significant negative correlation between market security and economic performance. First, the assurance of a high "background level" of potential competition, through the maintenance of "many" independent sources of productive factors and new enterprise, is evidently one way of promoting good performance on the part of existing firms. Second, the absolute size of certain firms may be a drag on their performance by making them relatively secure from competitive inroads.[41] These considerations have an obvious bearing on the as yet relatively neglected policy problems connected with the powerful trade union and the "conglomerate merger."[42]

40. *U.S.* v. *E. I. du Pont de Nemours and Co., et al.*, 353 U.S. 586 (1957), hereinafter referred to as *du Pont – G.M.*

41. On the special shelter which may accompany bigness, see Corwin Edwards, "Conglomerate Bigness as a Source of Power," *Business Concentration and Price Policy* (Princeton, 1955).

42. According to a recent staff report of the House Select Committee on Small Business, the new Section 7 of the Clayton Act applies to conglomerate as well as to vertical and horizontal mergers. *Mergers and Superconcentration* (Washington, U.S.G.P.O., 1962), pp. 15-16.

Some Thoughts on the Regulation of Conduct

In conclusion, I should like to offer a few comments which are relevant to the third major question which presents itself in connection with the policy problem of the good trust: that is, is the problem being unnecessarily broadened by an inadequate generally applicable regulation of restrictive conduct? Generally speaking, it appears that the Celler-Kefauver Amendment of Section 7 of the Clayton Act represented an extremely important advance in bringing about an adequate regulation of conduct. It may be that the acceptance by the Supreme Court in the *du Pont-G.M.* case of the view that the old Section 7 applied to vertical as well as horizontal combinations[43] will also turn out to be a big step forward, though, as suggested above, its significance will inevitably be limited by the fact that this legislation did not apply to acquisitions of assets.[44]

But these overall appraisals are inevitably subject to an important qualification: like that of Section 2 of the Sherman Act, the operational meaning of Section 7 of the Clayton Act depends crucially on the specific, *ad hoc*, judicial interpretation of what is meant by the relevant market, and in the latter instance the situation has been recently aggravated by the introduction of further legal criteria whose relative weight is uncertain. Recent cases seem to reemphasize both the great practical significance and the essential ambiguity of the judicial market concept. Thus, in the *du Pont-G.M.* case,

43. 353 U.S. 590-593.

44. As a part of the general regulation of conduct, the rationale for merger regulation is "based on the general economic case against practices restricting the choices open to sellers or buyers." See Lucile Sheppard Keyes, "The Bethlehem-Youngstown Case and the Market Share Criterion," *American Economic Review*, vol. 51 (September, 1961), p. 653.

one of the main factual issues in determing whether or not the law had been violated was whether the legally relevant market was in fact "the automotive market for finishes and fabrics," or "the total industrial market for these products,"[45] the majority holding that "automobile finishes and fabrics have sufficient peculiar characteristics and uses to constitute them products sufficiently distinct from all other finishes and fabrics to make them a 'line of commerce' within the meaning of the Clayton Act."[46] The orthodox view on market definition is restated in this decision as follows:

> determination of the relevant market is a necessary predicate to a finding of a violation of the Clayton Act because the threatened monopoly must be one which will substantially lessen competition "within the area of effective competition." Substantiality can be determined only in terms of the market affected.[47]

In the more recent decision in *Brown Shoe,*[48] the Chief Justice cited the above passage and gave renewed emphasis to the idea that not only *bona fide* markets but also *bona fide sub*markets could be significant in antitrust proceedings:

> The outer boundaries of a product market are determined by the reasonable interchangeability of use or the cross-elasticity of demand between the product itself and substitutes for it. However, within this broad market, well-defined submarkets may exist which, in themselves, constitute product markets for antitrust purposes. *United States* v. *E. I. du Pont de Nemours and Co.*, 353 U.S. 586,

45. 353 U.S. 649.
46. *Ibid.*, pp. 593-594.
47. *Ibid.*, p. 593.
48. *Brown Shoe Co.* v. *U.S.*, 370 U.S. 294 (1962), hereinafter referred to as *Brown Shoe.* See also the discussion of this case in the chapters by M. A. Adelman and Jesse Markham.

> 593-595. The boundaries of such a submarket may be determined by examining such practical indicia as industry or public recognition of the submarket as a separate economic entity, the product's peculiar characteristics and uses, unique production facilities, distinct customers, distinct prices, sensitivity to price changes, and specialized vendors. Because §7 of the Clayton Act prohibits any merger which may substantially lessen competition "in *any* line of commerce" (emphasis supplied), it is necessary to examine the effects of a merger in each such economically significant submarket to determine if there is a reasonable probability that the merger will substantially lessen competition. If such a probability is found to exist, the merger is proscribed.[49]

Perhaps this passage may be interpreted as an attempt to distinguish between the "product markets" which may be considered relevant under the Sherman Act and the "submarkets" which are considered relevant under the Clayton Act in the computation of market share. Like the similar distinction which was made by Judge Weinfeld in the *Bethlehem-Youngstown* decision,[50] this distinction does not suggest a definition of the smaller category which is any more objectively determinate than that suggested for the larger category under the Sherman Act; moreover, it cannot be successfully argued that the economic significance of the competition of imperfect substitutes is necessarily diminished in Clayton Act cases.[51]

49. *Ibid.*, p. 325.

50. *U.S.* v. *Bethlehem Steel Corporation and The Youngstown Sheet and Tube Company,* 168 F. Supp. 576 (1958).

51. On this point, see Keyes, "The Bethlehem-Youngstown Case and the Market Share Criterion," *op.cit.*, p. 646: "The suggestion that competition among imperfect substitutes can always be ignored under Section 7 must, of course, be rejected. A merger involving two producers of imperfect substitutes obviously could have as much anticompetitive impact, in depriving buyers of alternative independent sources of effective substitutes, as a merger

In connection with the horizontal aspects of the Brown-Kinney merger, the treatment of market share itself does not appear necessarily to involve any essential departure from accepted doctrine;[52] but further ambiguities of interpretation are introduced by the recital of other factors which are apparently considered important but which are of uncertain weight in determining the actual decision.[53] First, it is noted; "In an industry as fragmented as shoe retailing... a merger achieving 5 per cent control" might further the "oligopoly Congress sought to avoid" through making it necessary for the Court "to approve future merger efforts by Brown's competitors seeking similar market shares." (A similar remark is made in connection with the vertical aspects of the merger, and will be commented on below.) Second, it is pointed out that a small share of a particular market, "held by a large national chain," would represent a threat to the "fragmented" competitors, since "a strong, national chain of stores can insulate selected outlets from the vagaries of competition in particular locations and... can set and alter styles in footwear to an extent that renders the independents unable to maintain competitive inventories." Third, it is held to be significant that the economies brought about by the integration of shoe manufacturing with "a large national chain" of retail outlets would enable it to sell at lower prices than the small independents, contrary to the desire of Congress "to promote competition

between producers of perfect substitutes. And if it is admitted that imperfect competition between the participants must be considered in determining their premerger competitive relations, then it must also be admitted that imperfect competition between the participants, on the one hand, and the firms remaining outside on the other, must be considered in assessing the expected competitive status of the proposed combination."

52. 370 U.S. 339-343.

53. *Ibid.*, pp. 343-346.

through the protection of viable, small, locally owned businesses." No adequately general principle is, however, enunciated for the guidance of government officials charged with maintaining high prices through enforcing the antitrust laws: is protectionism henceforth always to come before economic efficiency in the order or priority of antitrust objectives? At the very least, something more should have been said to indicate the intended significance of the word "occasional" in the Court's explanatory statement:

> Congress appreciated that occasional higher costs and prices might result from the maintenance of fragmented industries and markets. It resolved these competing considerations in favor of decentralization.

Fourth, the Court stated that "other factors . . . lend additional support to the District Courts' conclusion that *this merger may substantially* lessen competition" and specified one such factor – that is, "the history of tendency toward concentration in the *industry*."

In connection with the vertical aspects of the merger, the majority asserted that "the size of the share of the market foreclosed," though an "important consideration," would "seldom be determinative,"[54] and the shares of the legally relevant markets which were foreclosed in this particular case indeed appear to be small.[55] The majority also indicated that the critical share under the Clayton Act would in any case be less than that under the Sherman Act.[56] But whatever might have been gained in predictability, as a result of this de-emphasis on market share, was more than lost in the ensuing discussion, which implied, among other things, that legality of vertical merger under the new

54. *Ibid.*, p. 328.
55. *Ibid.*, pp. 303, 369.
56. *Ibid.*, pp. 328-329.

Section 7 could also turn on "the trend toward concentration in the industry,"[57] and "its probable effects upon the economic way of life sought to be preserved by Congress."[58]

This last aspect of the *Brown Shoe* decision may be contrasted with the corresponding feature of *Bethlehem-Youngstown*: while the former merger was considered especially suspect because it occurred in an "industry . . . composed of numerous independent units,"[59] the latter was especially to be condemned because it was in an industry which was "already highly concentrated."[60]

As in connection with Section 2 of the Sherman Act, the objection to the use of the market share criterion here is not merely that it is ambiguous, but that it does not efficiently serve a justifiable purpose. The evident result of the criterion is to allow some mergers with anticompetitive effects to proceed unhindered, and the justification for it must therefore be found in the expectation that the constructive effects of these mergers are expected to outweigh the harm done by the extinction of some amount of competition. But in fact the harm done by any merger does not obviously correlate with its effect on judicially defined market share, and the expected benefits may well be nonexistent even though the effect on legal market share is very small. In other words, if a *per se* prohibition is not to be applied to anticompetitive mergers, a more suitable "rule of reason," or screening criterion, should be formulated which would give better guidance to the judiciary in applying Section 7.

In general, it would seem that a "rule of reason" ap-

57. *Ibid.*, p. 332.
58. *Ibid.*, p. 333.
59. *Ibid.*
60. 168 F. Supp. 604-605.

proach is appropriate to the regulation of restrictive practices only under certain quite limited circumstances. First, it must be established that the practice may in some instances be indispensable for the achievement of otherwise unobtainable economic benefits; and, second, it must be possible to formulate a general screening rule which will enable the judiciary fairly consistently and efficiently to separate the sheep from the goats. In some instances, it may be desirable to forego an attempt at perfect separation and settle for good results on the average (i.e., most of the sheep admitted; and most of the goats excluded). Some of these screening rules may be capable of separating with a fair degree of reliability those particular instances of a given practice whose net result is an economic benefit from those whose result is a loss; in other cases – and this appears to be true with respect to mergers – the only available rule serves merely to distinguish those instances which can be credited with some otherwise unobtainable benefits from those which are, in effect, purely restrictive.[61] Where the two stated conditions do not hold, it would seem wiser to apply a *per se* rule in the courts and leave the exceptions, if any, up to Congress. This condition may occur, for example, when the "benefits" attributable to the particular restrictive practice in question are such things as stable incomes for a relatively needy group of persons, where a proper consideration of the policy problem involved necessitates a broad scrutiny of other governmental actions capable of achieving these benefits, and an informed choice among the available means.

61. See Keyes, "The Bethlehem-Youngstown Case and the Market Share Criterion," *op.cit.*, p. 655.

CHAPTER 8

The Effectiveness of Clayton Act Section 7

BY JESSE W. MARKHAM

Introduction

The effectiveness of any instrument of public policy must be assessed in terms of how closely the results directly attributable to the policy conform to those it clearly seeks to achieve. When both the objectives and the results can be quantitatively defined such assessment can be conclusive. The federal government's minimum wage and social security policies, for example, illustrate quantifiable objectives and results. The present minimum wage legislation makes it unlawful to pay employees covered by the law's provisions less than $1.25 per hour. If a survey of wage rates revealed that out of every 100 employees that would have been paid less than $1.25 in the absence of minimum wage legislation, 99 actually received the minimum wage or more, the policy can be rated as 99 percent effective.

Antitrust policy generally, and Clayton Act Section 7 (as amended) particularly, are patently not assessable in such quantitative terms. The objective of Section 7 as set forth in its text is to prohibit intercorporate stock and asset acquisitions "where in any line of commerce in any section of the country, the effect . . . may be substantially to lessen competition, or to tend to create a monopoly."[1] The standards the law erects can scarcely be viewed as comprising a set of objective

1. Public Law 899, Sec. 7, 38 Stat. 731, as amended; 15 U.S.C. 18.

tests by which unlawful mergers can be defined. The term "may" was interpreted from the beginning to mean "reasonably probable," but even a merger that, to the reasonable mind, probably lessens competition substantially is not readily identifiable, at least not on the basis of its measurable dimensions. A cursory examination of the expressed views on the subject reveals that even among the less passionate students of industrial organization a merger that would probably have serious anticompetitive consequences to some would be just the merger needed to stimulate competition to others.

But while neither the objectives nor the results of recent antimerger policy can be measured quantitatively, assessment of the policy's effectiveness must rely heavily on quantitative indicia relating to its administration. In this connection, the following tests should provide a basis for certain qualitative conclusions concerning the effectiveness of the Act (as amended):

1. Has the amended statute led to a greater number of merger prosecutions, and especially to a greater number of more successful prosecutions than the initial 1914 statute? To be sure, data that measure the overall intensity or vigor with which the statute is being exercised require careful interpretation: changes in the volume of cases may simply reflect the difference between zealous and lethargic antitrust agency staffs. Although the effectiveness of any public policy depends heavily on those who administer it, a distinction must be made between the results attributed to administrative personnel and those attributable to changes in the law itself. To paraphrase that famous dicta the court enunciated in *Trenton Potteries*, "the zealous antitrust agency today may be the lethargic antitrust agency tomorrow." The number of *successful* merger litigations rather than the total number of merger proceedings may there-

fore more accurately indicate the effectiveness of Section 7. The law is ultimately what the courts say it is, and in the dispassionate calm of the courtroom the antitrust agency's passion, or lack of passion, for its cause theoretically exerts at most a modest effect on the final decision. But interpretation of successes is also subject to ambiguity. A zealous agency may prepare its cases more thoroughly and argue them more persuasively than a lethargic agency, and in antitrust matters thoroughness and persuasion cannot be written off as unimportant.

2. Has the amended statute halted concentration-increasing mergers which would not have been arrested under legal doctrines prevailing prior to 1950? This is probably the most relevant test of the effectiveness of Section 7. Whatever else Congress may have had in mind when it amended the statute, it is clear from the Senate and House reports on the bill that one of its purposes was to check the rise of market concentration before it attained Sherman Act proportions. It was designed, to use the language of its legislative architects, to arrest the market power attending high levels of industry concentration in its incipiency. Accordingly, if present antimerger policy has substantially reduced the legal level of concentration in specific markets attainable through merger it has effectively fulfilled at least one important legislative objective.

3. Finally, it is relevant to inquire into the effect Section 7 has had on the volume of mergers it presumably was designed to prohibit. In any society governed by law it is generally expected that the law's principal effect is to be found in its observance rather than its breach.

While these three tests may indicate the approximate effectiveness of recent antimerger policy, a large portion of the data they require are not readily available.

Mergers and the New Section 7

In recent years the Federal Trade Commission has reported slightly over 1,000 mergers and acquisitions per year. Only a small fraction of this total is involved in formal proceedings, where the important economic facts are developed and made a part of the public record. Hence, conclusions drawn on the basis of such tests apply only to those relatively few mergers challenged by one of the antitrust agencies. The validity is therefore significantly affected by the capabilities, capacities, and competence of the agencies themselves. It can probably be assumed that the agency staffs try to select the most promising cases to challenge, and that those eliminated in the screening process raise no serious question of legality. But it must be emphasized that the results obtained from an analysis of litigated cases indicate the effectiveness of antimerger policy only to the extent agency staffs successfully follow this procedure.

The Volume of Merger Cases Before and After the 1950 Celler-Kefauver Amendment

If judged from the extent to which Section 7 has been exercised, the Celler-Kefauver Amendment has unquestionably enhanced the effectiveness of public policy toward mergers. In the entire 37-year period 1914-1950, the Department of Justice and the Federal Trade Commission challenged a total of 79 mergers and stock acquisitions (Table 1). In 15 of the 20 cases indicted by the Department of Justice violation of Section 7 was added as a supplemental charge to an alleged Sherman Act violation and therefore comprised only a secondary aspect of the 15 cases. All but one of the Federal Trade Commission's 59 cases were pure Section 7 cases; in one case the Commission alleged violation of both Section 7 of the Clayton Act and Section 5 of the Federal Trade Commission Act. The 79 cases represent-

TABLE 1

The Volume and Disposition of Merger Cases Initiated by the Department of Justice and the Federal Trade Commission, 1914-1950 and 1951-1964

	Department of Justice		Federal Trade Commission	
	1914-1950	1951-1962[a]	1914-1950	1951-1964[a]
Total Cases Initiated	20[b]	73	59	50
Dismissed	10	17[d]	48	9[e]
Dismissals Appealed	—	6	—	—
Reversed	—	2[f]	—	—
Confirmed	—	0	—	—
Pending	—	4	—	—
Orders of Divestiture	10[c]	28[f]	11	4
Divestiture Orders Appealed	—	4	8	31[f]
Affirmed	—	3	2	10
Reversed, Modified, or Set Aside	—	—	6	2
Appeal Pending	—	1	—	4
Initial Decision Pending	—	28	—	10

NOTES:

a To April 7, 1964, all figures reflect status of cases up to that date.

b In fifteen of the twenty cases Section 7 charges supplemented charges under the Sherman Act or other antitrust statutes.

c Eight by consent decree; two by court order after trial.

d Six on motion of the Department of Justice.

e Four are Hearing Examiner dismissals still pending before the Commission.

f Thirty-six of the sixty-one divestitures were obtained through consent orders or decrees, twenty-one by the Department of Justice and fifteen by the Federal Trade Commission.

SOURCE:

Neither the Federal Trade Commission nor the Department of Justice publishes periodic tabulations of antitrust cases and their status before the Commission and the Courts. I am indebted to Dr. Betty Bock of the National Industrial Conference Board for data making this tabulation possible. Dr. Bock's sources were the mimeographed copies of complaints issued by the Justice Department and the Federal Trade Commission, and the Commerce Clearing House Trade Regulation Reporter. While these data are not official, they are believed to be up to date and reasonably complete and accurate.

ed about one case per year for each of the two agencies and one out of every 125 firm disappearances by merger recorded by the Federal Trade Commission.[2]

Only 15 of the 79 merger cases ultimately resulted in dissolution, and frequently the dissolution required fell short of that sought in the initial complaint or civil action. The record built by the Federal Trade Commission during this period was especially unimpressive. Of the 59 Section 7 complaints the Commission issued, 48 were dismissed and 11 resulted in a cease and desist order requiring divestiture. However, eight of the Commission's orders were appealed, and either the Circuit Court of Appeals or the Supreme Court reversed, set aside, or significantly modified six of them. Altogether, the Commission succeeded in bringing about only five dissolutions and one modified dissolution in the entire 37-year period.[3] The Department of Justice compiled a higher percentage of victories, but in part only because it employed Section 7 much more sparingly and willingly accepted, through the instrument of consent decrees, less in the way of divestiture than it had initially sought. Ten of the twenty Section 7 cases the Department initiated resulted in some form of stock divestiture, eight by consent and two by court decisions. The big court victory was of course the *du Pont-General Motors* decision, and the Supreme Court's opinion in this case apparently was greatly influenced by the 1950 amendment.

The statistics on merger proceedings under the 1950 revised statute are much more impressive. Between the

2. The Federal Trade Commission series is confined to Manufacturing and Mining. It reported a total of 9,410 firm disappearances in the period 1919-1950, and Ralph Nelson reported 493 for the period 1914-1918. See his *Merger Movements in American Industry* (Princeton, 1959), p. 37.

3. Information obtained from Federal Trade Commission records and Commerce Clearing House Trade Regulation Reporting Service.

Pillsbury Complaint of 1952 and April 1964, the Department of Justice and the Federal Trade Commission initiated a total of 123 cases.[4] Of these, Justice initiated 73 and the Federal Trade Commission, 50. Accordingly, in the relatively short period of thirteen years the antitrust agencies have challenged more mergers and acquisitions than they had in the entire previous history of the Clayton Act. The annual rate of about one merger action per year for each of the agencies has been stepped up to about five, and the pre-1950 challenge rate of only one out of every 200 firm disappearances has been increased to approximately one out of every 95. Since four out of every five of the post-1951 merger proceedings have involved asset acqusitions, it can be reasonably concluded that a larger proportion of the cases initiated in the recent period is attributable to the clause relating to asset acquisitions incorporated in the revised statute.

In all but a small fraction of the challenged mergers in which at least an initial decision has been reached, the government has successfully sustained its case. As of April 1, 1964, initial decisions on 38 of the 123 cases were pending; an initial or final decision had issued on 85. In 61 of the 85 decided cases the government was granted at least a portion, in some cases all, of the divestiture it sought. However, 36 of the 61 divestitures were obtained through consent orders or decrees and five of the 25 adjudicated dissolutions are either on appeal or have been remanded to the Commission, a Commission hearing examiner, or court for consideration of additional issues or facts.

In those cases that have gone before the Supreme

4. For information on merger actions taken up to October 1, 1962, see *Mergers and Superconcentration*, Staff Report of the Select Committee on Small Business, House of Representatives, 87th Cong. (Washington, 1962), p. 272. See also Betty Bock, *Mergers and Markets: A Guide to Economic Analysis of Case Law*, 2d ed. (New York: National Industrial Conference Board, 1962).

Court the government has compiled an unblemished record of victory. As of April 7, 1964, parties to eleven cases arising under amended Section 7 had petitioned the Supreme Court for review. In four of these cases the Court upheld a lower court's order of divestiture; in two it reversed the district court's decision to deny divestiture; and in one the Court denied certiorari, thereby permitting the lower court's order of divestiture to stand. The remaining four appeals are still pending.

Numbers standing alone are at best a fatuous measure of a policy's effectiveness. Nevertheless, an important indicator of the effectiveness of any piece of legislation is the frequency with which it is used to curb the activity it is designed to curb. In the past twelve years Section 7 was employed with considerably greater frequency and, at least in terms of initial decisions, halted far more mergers, than it had in any preceding period in history. Moreover, the Supreme Court has sustained the government in all the cases that have reached it on appeal. The amended Section 7 is therefore arresting far more mergers than its parent statute, and the arresting process has thus far met the tests of final judicial review.

The New Standards of Illegality: A Study of Specific Cases

Horizontal Merger Decisions. In view of the obvious causal relationship between horizontal merger and the level of market concentration, it is not surprising that antitrust agencies launched their initial cases, and won their initial signal victories, against firms acquiring other firms in the same line of commerce (Table 2). Of the 29 cases initiated by the Department of Justice and Federal Trade Commission between 1952 and the end of 1956, all involved some aspect of horizontality. By April 7, 1964, the Government had obtained complete or partial divestiture in 25 of the 30 cases. To be sure, in some cases the traditional understanding of horizontality had been stretched, and the government's victory limited. In Scott Paper's acquisition of three geographically dispersed pulp and paper mills the complaint alleged horizontal effects on the grounds that Scott, the largest producer of sanitary paper products, in fact acquired sanitary paper plant sites on which it could easily erect sanitary paper capacity. And in Continental Can's acquisition of Hazel-Atlas, the civil action alleged that a tin and plastic container manufacturer, in acquiring a glass container manufacturer, in fact acquired the equivalent of another tin container manufacturer. The District Court dismissed the Continental Can case and the government has appealed the case to the Supreme Court. The Scott case has been remanded to the Federal Trade Commission for reconsideration of its initial divestiture order in the light of additional market facts. But where the antitrust agencies adhered to clearer cut cases of horizontal merger they succeeded in establishing new and pertinent tests for their adjudication.[5]

Generalizations on markets that range all the way from safety pins (*Scovill*), through frozen citrus juices (*Minute Maid*) to blast furnace products (*Bethlehem*) and kitchen sinks (*American Radiator*) admittedly must plead the indulgence of a tolerant audience. With few exceptions, however, the first thirty cases involved markets susceptible to reasonably unambiguous definition and one or more of the following important considerations:

1. The merger gave the acquiring firm 20 percent or more

5. For an earlier and more detailed assessment of these tests see the author's "Merger Policy Under the New Section 7; A Six-Year Appraisal," *Virginia Law Review*, vol. 43, no. 4 (1957), pp. 489-528.

TABLE 2
Cases Initiated Under Amended Section 7 of the Clayton Act
(June 1952-December 1956)

Date Case Initiated	Acquiring Firm	Acquired Firm	Alleged Market Share Involved
*June 16, 1952	Pillsbury Mills	Ballard & Ballard Duff's Baking	8%-45%
January 19, 1954	Luria Bros., Inc.	7 iron and steel scrap dealers	-----
*February 15, 1954	Crown Zellerbach	St. Helens	70% (regional market)
*February 14, 1955	Schenley Industries	Park & Tilford	17%-26%
*March 29, 1955	General Shoe	Delman, Inc.	-----
*April 27, 1955	Hilton Hotels	Statler Hotels	-----
*June 30, 1955	Farm Journal	Better Farming	24%
*June 30, 1955	Union Bag	Hawkins Container	-----
*September 7, 1955	Minute Maid	Snow Crop	25%-35%
*November 28, 1955	Brown Shoe	G. R. Kinney	3.5% (national) 25% (certain cities)
*December 8, 1955	A. G. Spaulding	Rawlings Mfg. Co.	-----

(table continues)

TABLE 2 — *Cases Initiated Under Amended Section 7 (contd.)*

Date Case Initiated	Acquired Firm	Acquiring Firm	Alleged Market Share Involved
*January 17, 1956	Foremost Dairies	30 dairy companies	3.4% (national)
*March 12, 1956	Scovill Mfg. Co.	De Long Hook and Eye	-----
*March 30, 1956	American Radiator	Mullins Mfg. Co.	27%-30%
*May 22, 1956	Brillo Mfg. Co.	Williams Co.	30%-50%
*June 1, 1956	Scott Paper Co.	3 pulp and paper cos.	16%-36%
August 17, 1956	Fruehauf Trailer	5 trailer cos.	47%-49%
September 10, 1956	Continental Can	Robert Gair Co.	-----
*October 11, 1956	The Vendo Co.	Vendolator Mfg. Co.	50%
October 16, 1956	National Dairy	39 dairy cos.	-----
October 16, 1956	Beatrice Foods	131 dairy cos.	-----
October 16, 1956	The Borden Co.	80 dairy cos.	-----
October 30, 1956	Continental Can	Hazel-Atlas	9%-82%
October 30, 1956	Erie Sand and Gravel	Sandusky	92%
*November 6, 1956	International Paper	Long-Bell Lumber	25%-50%
*November 21, 1956	Maryland and Virginia Milk Producers Assoc.	Green Springs Milk Co. and Milk, Inc.	92%
December 4, 1956	Owens-Illinois	National Container	-----
*December 12, 1956	Bethlehem Steel	Youngstown	20%-21%
*December 13, 1956	Gulf Oil Co.	Warren Petroleum	-----

*indicates cases in which government had obtained at least an initial order of divestiture by April 7, 1964 of the relevant market as defined in the complaint or civil action.

2. The merger enhanced the market position of a firm already listed among the largest five, frequently among the largest three, in terms of its relevant market share.
3. Mergers in the recent past had substantially increased the level of concentration and reduced the number of independent firms in the industry, and in most cases successive mergers by the defendant had contributed to this trend.

There can be little doubt that through application of these standards the new Section 7 arrested several dozen mergers that would easily have passed muster prior to 1950. This point was emphasized by the Federal Trade Commission in its *Pillsbury*[6] opinion, the Commission's first interpretation of amended Section 7 in the context of a specific merger case. In declaring Pillsbury's two acquisitions, Ballard and Ballard & Duff, in contravention of Section 7 the Commission sought to clarify the standards it employed. In doing so it observed that the merger in *U.S.* v. *Columbia Steel Co.*,[7] which safely passed the Sherman Act tests of legality two years before Section 7 was amended, would probably have been declared illegal under the tests laid down in *Pillsbury*.

It was generally conceded by the antitrust fraternity, however, that the biting strength of the amended statute's new teeth would not have been fully demonstrated until it outlawed a steel merger. The Bethlehem-Youngstown merger was therefore proclaimed the "Big Case."[8] But the significance of Bethlehem went beyond the mere fact that the defendants were steel companies. Bethlehem and Youngstown accounted respec-

6. 50 FTC 555.
7. 334 U.S. 495 (1948).
8. *U.S.* v. *Bethlehem Steel Corp.*, 168 F. Supp. 576 (S.D. N.Y., 1958).

tively for 16.3 percent and 4.6 percent of the nation's ingot capacity. Their combined shares of 21 percent fell close to the lower limit of the range of market shares given significant weight in previous decisions upholding the government.[9] For over a half-century the steel industry had been singled out as a signal example of dominant firm price leadership, with the colossus of Pittsburgh, U.S. Steel, in control of steel prices. Expert witnesses, including some prominent economists, testified that the more balanced oligopoly resulting from the merger would reduce U.S. Steel's dominance and hold out prospects for more competitive steel prices. The contention was not entirely lacking in logical appeal. Finally, the combined market shares of the two participants, standing alone, overstated the merger's impact on concentration in specific geographical markets. Defendants offered factual evidence showing that the market overlap between Bethlehem and Youngstown was relatively small. Bethlehem sold primarily in the eastern area of the United States. Youngstown's shipments into this area, with the single exception of buttweld pipe, accounted for an insignificant 0.04 percent to 1.4 percent of the total of such shipments. Youngstown sold primarily in the mid-continent area. Bethlehem's shipments into this area ranged from 0.6 percent to 6.5 percent of the total of such shipments.

The court took judicial notice of these arguments supporting the merger but found the counterarguments more persuasive. In finding the proposed merger of Bethlehem and Youngstown violative of Section 7 it laid heavy stress on the following actual and probable

9. For example:

Case	Market Share
Pillsbury Mills	8% - 45%
Schenley Industries	17% - 26%
Farm Journal	24%
Minute Maid	25% - 35%
International Paper	25% - 50%
Crown Zellerbach	70%

efforts of the merger on competition:

1. While the merger would make Bethlehem's size more comparable to that of U.S. Steel, it would also widen the size gap between the two largest steel producers and the remaining firms. The merger would therefore increase the level of concentration, already high, and thereby reduce rather than increase the possibility of more effective price competition in steel.
2. Approval of the merger on the grounds that the industry contains larger firms than that the merger would create clearly runs counter to the Congressional intent of Section 7. In the steel industry, as in many other industries, public policy would be resigned to a diminution of firms until ultimately such industries contained only three or four large rivals. Congress had fashioned Section 7 to halt tendencies toward concentration rather than foster them.
3. The merger would eliminate a substantial independent competitive factor from a vital industry, and the industry's past history left little reason to believe that Youngstown's capacity would be made up by the entry of new and independent firms.

The Bethlehem decision brought the new antimerger policy on horizontal merger full circle. In the *Columbia Steel* case the courts had permitted U.S. Steel, then in control of about 32 percent of total steel output, to acquire a West Coast steel plant on the grounds that the antitrust laws could not prohibit U.S. Steel from accomplishing through acquisition something it could legally accomplish by internal expansion. This decision more than any other single event had sparked the vigorous drive in Congress for a more effective legal curb on mergers that culminated in the Celler-Kefauver Amendment of 1950. In the *Bethlehem* case the courts — on the same industrial scene — made it clear that that amendment imposed a special constraint on growth by the merger route. Bethlehem's expansion pattern to gain access to the mid-continent area since its acquisition of Youngstown was denied serves to emphasize the sharp difference in legal status between merger and internal growth. It has since entered the area by constructing a large steel plant near Chicago, an event that is not likely to be challenged under the antitrust laws.

Not only has Section 7 been administered with greater effectiveness against horizontal mergers in areas for which the statute was thought to be primarily, if not exclusively, designed, it has been extended to economic sectors long considered beyond its jurisdiction. In the *Philadelphia National Bank* case[10] the Supreme Court, contrary to the views then prevailing in Congress, the Justice Department, the Federal Trade Commission, lower courts, the private bar, and the banking industry,[11] held that Section 7 was applicable to bank mergers. The court went on to declare the consolidation of the Philadelphia National Bank and Girard Trust Corn Exchange Bank, bringing together over 30 percent of the commercial banking business in Philadelphia and the four-county area in which defendants' offices were located, in contravention of the statute. The Court also rejected the argument that the legality of a merger should be judged in terms of its *net* competitive effects. Defendants argued that the consolidation would stimulate competition in commercial banking in the United States as a whole and result in economic and social benefits to the Philadelphia community. Judgment on this issue, according to the Court, was beyond judicial competence and, in any event, had been removed from judicial decision by Congress when it amended Section 7 proscribing all anticompetitive mergers. The stronger national policy against horizon-

10. *U.S.* v. *Philadelphia National Bank,* 83 S. Ct. 1715 (1963).
11. Richard E. Day, *Developments in Antitrust During the Past Year,* Antitrust Law Section of the American Bar Association, 1963.

tal mergers also became an important consideration in a 1963 Civil Aeronautics Board decision denying a proposed merger between American Airlines and Eastern Airlines. The Hearing Examiner's Recommended Decision approved by the Board devoted considerable space to evidence showing that the proposed merger would clearly contravene Section 7 of the Clayton Act were that statute directly applicable to airline mergers.[12]

The visible evidence therefore makes a persuasive case that amended Section 7 has effectively arrested tendencies toward concentration in specific industries directly traceable to horizontal merger. In the process the standards established have clearly made merger a hazardous road to greater market occupancy, especially for any one of the top half-dozen firms in an industry already moderately—though not necessarily highly—concentrated. These same standards have no doubt produced considerable *invisible* evidence that, if revealed, would support this conclusion. Many merger plans have unquestionably been dropped to avoid prosecution and the high probability of a diverstiture decision. In short, the Celler-Kefauver Act has now become the principal factor in determining corporate growth policy.

Vertical and Conglomerate Merger Decisions. When Congress amended Clayton Act Section 7 it was made clear that the revised statute applied to vertical and conglomerate as well as horizontal mergers. This explicit extension of the compass of Section 7 is, at least politically, understandable. While some who supported the amendment were against mergers that enhanced market power, it is fairly evident that others were simply opposed to mergers by big business. Big business can grow bigger by merging in any direction. The Fed-

12. Civil Aeronautics Board, "American-Eastern Merger," Docket 13355, Recommended Decision of Ralph L. Wiser, Hearing Examiner, November, 1962 (mimeographed).

eral Trade Commission's Report on *The Merger Movement* in 1948 had revealed that 38 percent of all the mergers and acquisitions consummated in the period 1940-1947 had been of the vertical or conglomerate variety. If the new law was to check mergers for growth as well as those for growth of market power, its jurisdiction could not be limited to barely more than 60 percent of all mergers.

There probably are logical reasons for imposing legal limits on vertical and conglomerate acquisitions, but if they exist economists have been extraordinarily unsuccessful in discovering them. Elsewhere, I have suggested that the principal objection to vertical mergers, aside from the extension of horizontal market power they may entail, is that they reduce the possible number of market channels through which final prices may be determined. As for the term "conglomerate," Corwin Edwards has pointed out that it has been used negatively in economics—applied to a void customarily neglected by economic thinking.[13] Negative description of neglected voids can scarcely be expected to provide operable criteria for public policy.

This lack of an analytical framework for assessing the competitive effects of vertical and conglomerate mergers has injected into the adjudication process a phenomenon which, for the lack of a more elegant term, may aptly be described as the "ping-pong" effect. The Federal Trade Commission's case against Scott Paper was among the first vertical acquisitions challenged. The initial Hearing Examiner's decision dismissed the complaint on the grounds that the Commission's staff supporting the complaint had not proved Scott's "dominance" in the field of sanitary paper products, the concept on which the staff had built its case. On appeal, the Commission remanded the case back

13. Corwin D. Edwards, "Conglomerate Bigness as a Source of Power," *Business Concentration and Price Policy* (Princeton, 1955), p. 331.

to the Examiner, ruling that proof of dominance did not require a showing of absence of competition. On the second go round the Hearing Examiner ruled against Scott, and the Commission subsequently upheld the Examiner's decision. Scott then appealed, and the Circuit Court in March 1962 remanded the case to the Federal Trade Commission for additional market share evidence, which the Commission supplied in 1963. As of April 1964 the case was still pending before the Circuit Court of Appeals. Procter & Gamble Company's acquisition of Clorox, one of the Commission's first conglomerate cases, appears to be in store for a similar fate. The Hearing Examiner's initial decision ordered divestiture on the grounds of what has been called the "deep-pocket" principle—the large resources of Procter & Gamble, when put behind Clorox, can work to the serious disadvantage of smaller liquid bleach manufacturers. On review, the Commission remanded the case to the Hearing Examiner for clarification of how the merger tended substantially to lessen competition. The case went back before the Commission, which decided in late 1963 that divestiture should be ordered. Following this, the case was appealed to the Circuit Court.

Parallel to, and possibly because of, the difficulties encountered in clear-cut bases for the trial and adjudication of vertical and conglomerate acquisitions, there has developed a much simpler standard—the substitution of "injury to competitors" for "injury to competition." With this shift in standards has apparently come a shift in objectives: Section 7, designed and once administered to check tendencies toward monopoly in their incipiency, has in the recent past been directed toward the protection of small business.

The most far-reaching of the decisions under this new standard is, of course, *Brown Shoe*,[14] if for no other reason than that it has been confirmed in a unani-

14. *U S.* v. *Brown Shoe Co.*, 179 F. Supp. 721 (E.D. Mo., 1959); *Affirmed*, *Brown Shoe Co.* v. *U.S.*, 370 U.S. 294 (1962).

mous 9-0 Supreme Court decision. Four of the earlier chapters in this volume have devoted some attention to this case,[15] but some of the salient features bear repeating. The statistics of the Brown-Kinney merger were unimpressive. Brown, the fourth largest shoe manufacturer, accounted for only 4 percent of total shoe production. Kinney, the acquired shoe retailing chain, although the largest of such chains, accounted for only 1.6 percent of total shoe sales. At the horizontal level the merger brought together only 2.3 percent of the nation's retail outlets, although in certain cities outlets of the acquiring and the acquired companies together accounted for as much as 20 percent of women's shoe sales.

The trial court ruled the merger in violation of Section 7 almost entirely on the basis of its vertical aspects. The trial judge, while avowing his rejection of the substantiality doctrine urged on him by the Department of Justice attorneys, in substance accepted it. In the final analysis his decision rested on (1) a trend toward vertical integration that was drying up outlets available to unintegrated shoe producers; (2) acceptance of the argument that the Brown-Kinney merger would foreclose a substantial additional amount of business from the unintegrated producers – a finding that rested on Brown's past practice of using retail outlets it acquired for distributing its own shoes; and (3) acceptance of the idea that the cost savings resulting from the merger could be passed on as price reductions, thereby inflicting a further disadvantage on unintegrated shoe producers.

The Supreme Court in fact rendered two decisions on appeal. One is a scholarly treatment of the merger issue deserving the applause of the most judicious and analytical of the antitrust fraternity; possibly even the

15. See the chapters above by M. A. Adelman, Donald Dewey, Louis B. Schwartz, and Lucile Sheppard Keyes.

applause of those gifted in *belles-lettres.* The Court argued in simple and straight-forward language that market shares were the beginning but not the end of its inquiry, that the effect of the merger must be "on competition generally in an economically significant market," that "the percentage of the market foreclosed cannot itself be decisive," and that markets must be defined for antitrust purposes genererally — they cannot be defined differently for Section 7 of the Clayton Act and Section 2 of the Sherman Act.

The second decision is virtually an unqualified acceptance of what, in one decision, the Court explicitly rejected. When, as in every case, the Court eventually had to state the specific reasons for confirming the trial court's decision, it fell back on the substantiality doctrine the Justice Department had urged on the trial court in the first place. In declaring the vertical aspects *of the case illegal the Court said:*

> "We reach this conclusion [of illegality] because the trend toward vertical integration in the shoe industry, when combined with Brown's avowed policy of forcing its own shoes upon its retail subsidiaries, may foreclose competition from a substantial share of the markets for men's, women's, and children's shoes, without producing any countervailing competitive, economic, or social advantages."[15a]

With this, the high-level judicial reasoning became irrelevant prologue, and cost reductions enabling consumer price reductions became the enemy of small business rather than an economic and social benefit. The only purpose served by the term "countervailing" apparently was to show that at least one justice was familiar with books written by Professor John Kenneth Galbraith.

Since *Brown Shoe,* the initial decisions on three addi-

15a. 370 U.S. 334.

tional cases have relied on the "injury to competitors" standard, although the avowed standards were introduced in more bizarre language. The vertical acquisition by Reynolds Metals Company of Arrow Brands[16] gave rise to the "deep-pocket" doctrine. Reynolds, the largest of ten United States aluminum foil producers, accounted for 40.5 percent of total aluminum foil output. In 1956 Reynolds acquired Arrow Brands, one of 200 foil converters that buy "jumbo" rolls, convert foil into a wide variety of specialized types, and sell to customers requiring smaller lots than the minimum quantity sold by foil producers in a single order. Arrow accounted for 5.2 percent of a line of commerce known in the trade as decorative foil, and for about one-third of a much narrow submarket known as decorative aluminum foil for the florist trade. While the narrowly defined markets made Arrow loom large, the Commission condemned the acquisition on much more subjective grounds:

> "The converter's assimilation into the producers enormous capital structure and resources gave the converter an immediate advantage over its competitors. The power of the 'deep pocket' or 'rich parent' for one coverter in an industry where previously no company was very large and all were relatively small opened up the possibility and power to sell at prices approximately cost or below, thereby enabling it to undercut and ravage the less affluent competitors."[17]

The Court of Appeals upheld the Commission's order of divestiture, but modified it to permit Reynolds to retain a foil converting plant it had constructed with its own funds after acquiring Arrow.

The Federal Trade Commission's order of divestiture

16. *Reynolds Metals Company* v. *F.T.C.*, 309 F. 2d. 223 (C.A D.C., 1962).
17. *Ibid.*

in *Foremost Dairies*[18] was also based on the "injury to competitors" standard—in this case injury to very small local dairies. However, in its April 1962 *Consolidated Foods*[19] opinion the Commission extended the standard to new limits, and under a somewhat novel banner. In antitrust circles this case is more often referred to as "The Saga of the Dehydrated Onion: Or What Happened to Business Reciprocity in Gentry's Dehydrated Garlic Business?" The complaint was issued against Consolidated Foods' acquisition of Gentry, a manufacturer of assorted capsicum spices and dehydrated onion and garlic. The Commission's theory of the case was simple and clear: Consolidated bought large quantities of prepared foods from suppliers who in turn used substantial quantities of capsicum spices and dehydrated onion and garlic. Accordingly, when Consolidated acquired Gentry it acquired a weapon for carrying out a program of "business reciprocity"—it would insist that its suppliers buy their spice, garlic, and onion requirements from its Gentry Division. The Commission's decision apparently was not to be confused by the facts. In the course of the trial evidence was placed on the record showing that Consolidated tried to practice reciprocity but apparently met with little success. Between 1951, when it acquired Gentry, and 1958 its share of the dehydrated onion market rose from 28 percent to 35 percent, but its share of the dehydrated garlic market declined from 51 percent to 39 percent. Reciprocity, it appears, has a stronger affinity for onion then for garlic.

These four decisions add up to significant steps in the direction of an "injury to competitors" standard for Clayton Act Section 7. The directional movement may

18. *Federal Trade Commission in the Matter of Foremost Dairies, Inc.*, Opinion of the Commission, Docket No. 6495 (April 30, 1962).

19. *Opinion of the Federal Trade Commission in the Matter of Consolidated Foods Corp.*, Docket No. 7000 (November 15, 1962).

possibly have been arrested in the 1963 *Aluminum Company of America-Rome Cable* decision,[20] but this depends on the Supreme Court, where the case is now on appeal. Alcoa's acquisition of Rome Cable was primarily a vertical merger, but all the industrial trends playing such a prominent role in the four cases cited above were in the opposite direction: The level of concentration in the production of aluminum ingot and various classes of cable, conduit, rods, wire, and related products was on the decline; in most product lines the number of independent producers was increasing; the cost of entry into most of the fabricated lines involved was low, and there was no evidence of a substantial merger trend in the industry. In view of these facts Judge Brennan concluded that the market impact of the acquisition was *de minimis* and not violative of Section 7. But it is significant that the Judge addressed himself to the issue of the impact of the acquisition on competitors, and took note of the testimony of competing firms:

> "No competing manufacturer of aluminum conductor wire and cable products has complained that this acquisition has or may adversely affect his competitive position. On the contrary, representatives of ------ wire and cable manufacturers stated that in the three years since the acquisition there had been no adverse effect. No manufac turer-witness testified that he foresaw any future adverse effect, as a result of this acquisition."[21]

Summary: *The Adequacy of Clayton Act Section* 7

There is now little doubt that the 1950 amendment to the Clayton Act has been much more effective in ar-

20. *U.S.* v. *Aluminim Company of America and Rome Cable Corp.*, civil no. 8030 (N.D. N.Y., 1963).
21. *Ibid.*, Findings, of Fact., p. 12.

resting mergers than its statutory predecessor. In the first five years of its existence there emerged a standard whereby mergers leading to control of approximately 20 percent or more of a relevant market were generally presumed to be illegal. Few economists would seriously quarrel with this standard, or with the way it has been applied, unless they are prepared to quarrel also with virtually all that their fellow economists have written on the broad subjects of oligopoly and workable competition over the past three and one-half decades. In general, *ceteris paribus,* economic theory argues persuasively that competition is more effective with a dozen or so sellers than with four or five. For over seventy years public policy has sought an effective instrument for curbing mergers that unreasonably enhance market power. This instrument seems finally to have been found.

More recently, however, Section 7 seems to have been bent to serve the ends normally served by small business legislation, and the standard of "injury to competitors" has emerged as a companion, if not the ranking partner, to the standard of "substantial injury to competition." The more recent standard has thus far been applied to, largely because it evolved from, vertical and conglomerate mergers. Economists, having had little to say on the competitive effects of such mergers, can only identify the preservation of small business as a broad social and political issue and urge that it not be confused with the issue of maintaining reasonably effective competition. An inevitable consequence of a move by one firm to better its competitive position, if successfully carried out, is that competing firms will be disadvantaged, temporarily or permanently. It is equally inevitable that some of the disadvantaged firms will be smaller than the firm initiating the move. But action and counteraction have historically been viewed as indispensible ingredients of vigorous and effective competition, whether the action be a new process, a new product, a new advertising campaign, or the acquisition of an especially promising fabricator in Franconia.

Moreover, the historical data on small business suggest that the preservation of small business in specific industries may be purchased at a high price to society in terms of economic growth and efficiency in resource allocation. Small business has demonstrated a remarkable capacity to shift from industry to industry in response to economic incentives. For example, it was once the dominant form of enterprise in iron and steel, later in automobiles, and recently in certain branches of the electronics industry. This demonstrated mobility contributes importantly to efficient resource allocation and business growth. The recent preoccupation of antitrust agencies and the courts with preserving the competitive position of small business in their present occupations may, if intensified and continued, restrict this healthy process of adjustment that has given the American Economy much of its dynamism. Similarly, the recently developed "deep pocket" and "rich parent" doctrines, by limiting the entry of large corporations into the traditional dominions of small business, tends to impair further the adjustment process. While no one would seriously contend that the handful of recent Section 7 decisions giving birth to the "protection of small competitors" and "deep pocket" doctrines have already perceptibly weakened the dynamic processes of an economy comprising nearly eight million private business firms outside of agriculture, it would be unfortunate if Section 7 were used eventually to dull the incentives of the competitive process in the name of preserving a *status quo ante* reasonably competitive structure.

CHAPTER 9

Antitrust Policy and Small Business

BY RICHARD H. HOLTON[1]

Introduction

The ambiguous position of small business in our antitrust laws continues to trouble those who would like this body of legislation to lay down clear guides to business behavior. The Sherman Act rather precisely prohibits conspiracy, collusion, and monopolizing and would seem to call for "hard" competition of the devil-take-the-hindmost variety. On the other hand, parts of the Clayton Act, as amended by Robinson-Patman and interpreted by the courts, serve to protect the small businessman from at least some of the competition he might otherwise face. Certainly resale price maintenance legislation also attempts to shield the independent retailer from the chill winds of vigorous competition.

The arguments against any special protection for small business are persuasive. Small business perhaps can be charged with wasting capital, because of the many unwise investment decisions of the owners of these capital resources. Small business may be wasting

1. The author is Assistant Secretary for Economic Affairs in the U.S. Department of Commerce and Professor of Business Administration (on leave), University of California, Berkeley. The views expressed in this paper are not necessarily official views of the Department of Commerce. The author is indebted to Professor Delbert J. Duncan, of the University of California, Berkeley, with whom he worked in developing much of the material below dealing with the gasoline price war problem.

manpower in that the proprietors and employees in the small firms might in most cases be earning higher incomes in other firms or industries. In some industries, where entry is easy, the existence of too many small enterprises in an industry may prevent any one firm from achieving the economies of scale which might be possible if the small firms were to step aside: and no single firm may have the capital required to finance a long competitive struggle which would eventually force the smaller competitors out. It might even be argued that too much small business in an economy makes for a misallocation of resources because larger firms, with their greater expenditures for market research, are better able to make good decisions about what the market wants and what it does not want.

On the other hand, perhaps small business should be encouraged even at some short-term cost to society. The supply of entrepreneurial talent in the longer run may be greater if we go out of our way to maintain small business as a breeding ground for such talent. The probability that new ideas will be tried out might be greater if small business is encouraged, assuming (as some observers would) that larger firms tend to be too conservative in this regard. Perhaps society should pay some premium for the sake of a lively fringe of small concerns in most industries so that the threat of really significant competition from this source would serve to keep the dominant firms more alert.

On the noneconomic side of the picture, more small business means more small businessmen, and we are told that the psychic income from owning one's own business is substantial. (I have always suspected that this psychic income is closely correlated with the money income from the business.) A society of more small businessmen may well be, in some sense, a healthier society.

It is clear that we have a great deal of this latter view embodied in our antitrust laws. Consequently there is continual debate about how far one should go in designing the antitrust laws explicitly to exempt or encourage small business and in applying the antitrust laws in such a way that small firms are implicitly exempt. In this paper I do not pretend to offer an exhaustive review of small business and the antitrust laws. Instead I will concentrate, after a brief initial look at the merger problem and the gradually shrinking role of small business in the economy, on the distributive trades, which spawn so many of the anti-trust cases involving small business. The case of gasoline distribution is used as a vehicle for exploring the economic interrelationships in distribution which lead to antitrust problems. This approach at least puts the dilemma of antitrust as applied to distribution in a different light from that one generally finds but, unfortunately, it does not go far toward providing new antitrust standards. It might, however, be a step in the right direction.

Small Business and Mergers

The view that the economy is rapidly coming under the control of a few large corporations and that small business is dying out is a common one. In his letter of transmittal accompanying the Staff Report of the Select Committee on Small Business, *Mergers and Superconcentration*, Congressman Patman said:

> "The Congress has repeatedly paid allegiance to a competitive enterprise system. Such allegiance has been expressed in the passage of our various key antitrust statutes. . . . Both the Senate and the House have Small Business Committees, and small business has a voice in the executive branch in the Small Business Administration.
>
> "Yet despite these noble efforts designed to preserve

opportunity for small, local enterprise, big business has grown apace. Loopholes have appeared in our antitrust laws, and big business has fashioned new techniques of controlling markets and enhancing its power.

"It is most appropriate that this report be entitled *Mergers and Superconcentration,* for all appearances suggest that we are moving into a new phase of industrial and financial domination and control of American industry. Merger movements have fed this cancerous growth. The United States is rapidly becoming a nation of clerks and hired hands. Opportunities for independent small business are eroding."[2]

It is exaggerating things a bit to say that we are "rapidly" becoming a nation of hired hands; the reference to erosion in the last sentence quoted is probably more nearly appropriate. The staff report notes that according to the most recent data shows that the share of value added by manufacture accounted for by the 100 largest manufacturing companies rose from 23 to 30 percent between 1947 and 1958 while the share of the largest 200 such firms rose from 30 to 38 percent.[3] But the Collins-Preston data are also cited in the *Mergers and Superconcentration* report (p. 13); these show that the share of *total assets* accounted for by the 100 largest firms in manufacturing, mining, and distribution increased more slowly, from 26.7 percent in 1948 to 29.8 in 1958. While recognizing that the ratio of value added to assets might possibly have risen more for the larger firms than for the average, it would seem more likely that the modest increase in the concentration

2. *Mergers and Superconcentration,* Staff Report of the Select Committee on Small Business, House of Representatives, 87th Cong, November 8, 1962, p. iii.

3. The staff report cites the report prepared by the Bureau of the Census for the Antitrust and Monopoly Subcommittee of the Senate Judiciary Committee, "Concentration Ratios in Manufacturing Industry, 1958," Part I, p. 8.

ratio by the asset measures for the manufacturing, mining, and distribution data reflects a smaller increase in the concentration ratios outside manufacturing as contrasted with the concentration ratios inside manufacturing.

The 1948-1958 comparison, however, may give a distorted view of the rate of increase in concentration since the 1948 concentration ratio (the Collins-Preston version) was unusually low when cast up against the long run trend. Compared with the 29.8 percent figure for 1958 and 26.7 percent for 1948, the 1935 figure was 28.0 and in 1929, 25.5 percent.

Although one cannot use the 1958 company statistics in comparison with the 1954 company statistics to get as good a measure of industrial concentration as one would like, nonetheless it is reasonably clear that the percentage of employment accounted for by the larger firms probably increased a bit even between 1954 and 1958 if we include all companies covered in the Census. The 1954-1958 company statistics comparisons definitely show an increase in the percentage of employment accounted for by multi-unit firms, for all industries except the minerals.[4] For all nonagricultural industries combined, the percentage of employment accounted for by multi-unit companies rose from 52.0 percent in 1954 to 53.8 percent in 1958. Thus the evidence does seem to support the argument that we are moving toward greater concentration in industry in the United States. But it is easy to exaggerate the rate at which this is happening.

As we view the movement toward larger firms, we can ask how small business is being treated under the antitrust laws first as a firm competing with firms about to merge and second, as a firm which itself wants to

4. U.S. Bureau of the Census, *Enterprise Statistics:* 1958, Part I (Washington, 1963), p. 33

merge. With regard to the first matter, I think antitrust specialists would generally agree that the Antitrust Division and the FTC are now quite tough on mergers.[5] And it may well be now that the courts will be freer with preliminary injunctions against mergers. Various cases suggest that the courts are prepared to analyze the economic effect of the proposed merger in terms of a relevant market area which is small enough and in terms of a definition of "substantiality" sufficiently narrow to give the small businessman about as much protection from mergers as he can probably expect.[6]

Although the small business community might be encouraged by the degree of protection currently provided by the relatively tough enforcement policy regarding mergers, some minority of small businessmen are surely having second thoughts. I am thinking of the small manufacturer who builds up an enterprise of considerable substance only to find that, when he wants to retire, he has no obvious successor or independent purchaser of the company; and the most obvious prospective buyers are the giants of the industry, who may argue that they cannot purchase the company because the Antitrust Division would challenge the merger. Thus a more limited market for the sale of small companies is a price small business perhaps must pay for a tough merger policy.

On balance, it is probably accurate to say that, generally speaking, markets are being defined narrowly enough, and the substantiality test is being applied with sufficient rigor to slow the merger movement at least as much as it should be slowed. We may be sacrificing

5. See, for example, the *Wall Street Journal* article, "New 'High Fashions' Seen in Enforcement of Antitrust Laws," (March 8, 1963).

6. See *U.S.* v. *Bethlehem Steel Corporation,* 168 F. Supp. 576 (D.C. S.D. N.Y., 1958) and *Brown Shoe Company* v. *U.S.* 370 U.S. 294 (1962).

some economic efficiency in the system at any one point in time in order to give the small business firm the protection which it now has. Hopefully over the longer pull this policy will provide the economy with a more vigorous competition and more long-run efficiency than we would otherwise have.

Small Business and Big in Distribution Channels

The merger question aside, small business probably comes in contact with antitrust policy more in the field of distribution than in any other, simply because of the predominance of small business in the distributive trades. Certainly in recent years many of the prominent cases have dealt with distribution problems. I would like first to make some general observations about the forces which are at work to shape the structure and practices in distribution channels. I will then use the problem of the gasoline price war as a framework within which to examine at least some of the contrasting characteristics of distribution channels, characteristics which should color the application of our antitrust laws to the distributive sector.

The simple graph of the supply and demand functions from the elementary economics course leads us to consider, as a first approximation to reality, manufacturers as selling a single product into a market consisting of highly competitive buyers. The realities of the case are of course far more complicated. The manufacturer in most cases is not interested in selling a given product, but rather a line of products with the attendant services. The "product," defined to include the services that go with it, is not given, but is a variable. The manufacturer can consider innumerable combinations of tactics by which he can earn a profit. He can vary the quality and design of the physical product; he can vary the product line; he can employ a whole host of promotional devices; he can market through a number of alternative distribution channels; he can vary the price and the structure of prices, not only by setting different prices for different products but also by setting quantity discounts, cash discounts, and functional discounts.

Consider the alternatives open to the manufacturer of consumer goods. He faces in essence a very complicated production function. The textbook example of the production function gives units of output as a function of the inputs of labor and capital; labor and capital can be substituted for each other. In practice, this idea of substitution can be extended to cover many other variables besides labor and capital. The manufacturer selling direct to retailers who follow the manufacturer's recommended retail price (either because of a resale price maintenance agreement or because of the terms of an exclusive franchise) can consider reducing the retailer's margin and increasing advertising expenditures, while holding the retail price constant. This would be substituting advertising input for the input of the retailer's services, if we assume that the retailer gives the item less attention when the margin is reduced. For some goods, demand may be sensitive not so much to price changes as to changes in advertising outlays or to availability; i.e., to the proportion of all retail outlets offering the product in question. In such instances one is likely to find a relatively high retail price, with the retailer's margin high enough to persuade many retailers to stock the product. In other cases, advertising might be so successful in creating demand that retailers would feel compelled to stock the item in order to satisfy requests for the product, even though the margin is low. For these items the elasticity of demand with respect to accessibility or convenience may dictate a very intensive type of distribution with many retailers handling the product. No individual retailer, therefore, has any significant degree of monopoly on the brand in question.

By contrast, manufacturers of certain other kinds of goods may consider sales to be particularly elastic with respect to explanation and to other services provided at the point of sale. In this case the manufacturer may choose to gain the retailer's full cooperation by giving him a local monopoly for the brand, thereby extending to the retailer some of the monopoly power enjoyed by the manufacturer himself.

To empahsize the many ways in which the manufacturer can design and use distribution channels is not to overlook the fact that in many cases the manufacturer is not really free to call the tune as he might like. The retail chain stores are such a factor that manufacturers often fight for their trade. Here the power of the retailer may be dominant and the manufacturer may have little or no discretion over the detailed distribution policies that are used.

As soon as we recognize that the manufacturer's sales are sensitive to much more than the quality of the product and the price at which he sells the product to the first handler, it becomes apparent that the manufacturer would like to have a great deal of control over *all* the terms of the retailer's offer of the product. Ideally he would like to dictate not only the price the retailer charges for the item but also the size of inventory of the item held by the retailer, the credit terms offered the consumer by the retailer, the location of the item in the store's whole display (if not the location of the retail store itself), and he often would like to dictate whether competing brands will be offered by the retailer; he would even like to have control of the retail clerk's smile and haircut, if he could manage it.

This desire for control leads in some cases to full

vertical integration, with the manufacturer or wholesaler owning and operating the retail stores. However, various means of quasi-integration are also available. Resale price maintenance is one of these. Under this arrangement the manufacturer has the degree of control over resale prices which he would have if he were to own and operate the retail establishment himself, assuming that he is successful in policing his resale price maintenance agreements. Exclusive franchises can also be used to give the manufacturer a substantial amount of control over the manner in which his goods are handled and priced at the retail level.

Now consider the retailer's position. He, like the manufacturer, presumably wants to select a combination of policies which will maximize his profits or at least generate a satisfactory level of profits. He can vary his product lines, the depth and breadth of his stocks, his advertising, his pricing and promotion policies, his credit policies, and other services. The competitive strategy of the retailer may be to offer a combination of policies which is very similar to the combination offered by competing retailers in the hope that the total demand for that particular combination is great enough to yield satisfactory if not maximum profits. Alternatively, and this may be the more common case, the retailer can offer a combination of policies which differentiate him from his competition and which therefore give him some degree of monopoly power.

Economists have generally restricted their theoretical discussions of monopoly in retailing to the question of spatial monopoly. However, in the case of shopping goods a firm does not necessarily want a spatial monopoly; but a spatial monopoly of convenience goods is very desirable indeed. Shopping goods can be defined as those goods for which the consumer feels that the probable gains from price and quality comparisons are high relative to the cost of making those comparisons, "cost" here meaning costs in terms of time and effort as well as in terms of money. Convenience goods are those goods for which the probable gains from price and quality comparisons are low relative to cost of making the comparison. It can be shown that the total market demand for a given shopping good is likely to be higher if the firms offering that good are clustered, but the total market demand for a given convenience good is likely to be greater if the stores are scattered so that they do enjoy a spatial monopoly. This is why one finds an "automobile row" in so many cities but never a "drug-store row" or a "grocery row." So the spatial monopoly idea is of limited usefulness. The retailer of shopping goods typically is more interested in achieving some monopoly power by other means. In particular, he is likely to be interested in having an exclusive franchise for a manufacturer who is himself enjoying some monopoly power. Thus the automobile dealer who has no competition from other dealers handling the same brand is in a particularly strong position if his supplier is one of the stronger automobile manufacturers.

To summarize to this point, the manufacturer of consumer goods is vitally interested in his distribution system since it obviously influences his ability to compete. He would like to have considerable control over the performance of that system. The manufacturer may be able to achieve this control through outright ownership and operation of the retail outlets. Alternatively he may use various types of quasi-integration, such as exclusive franchises or resale price maintenance, to reach the same ends.

Meanwhile the retailer wants to have maximum freedom to determine his product line, the prices he will charge, the depth and breadth of inventory he will carry, and the whole range of services he will offer. The particular strategy he would choose of his own volition might not be wholly consistent with the strategy the manufacturer of any particular good would have him choose. Consequently one often finds conflicts between the retailers or wholesalers, on the one hand, and the manufacturer on the other. If the retailers do follow the dictates of the manufacturer, however, competition among the retailers may be illegally restrained. Therefore the manufacturer may be severely restricted in his efforts to reach down through the distribution channel to affect competition at the retail level.

Small Business and the Big Supplier: The Gasoline Price War Problem

One of the most dramatic and troublesome examples of big business-small business relationships from the antitrust point of view is found in the plaguing problem in gasoline distribution, namely, the gasoline price war. By examining this extreme case of supplier-dealer (big business-small business) relationships with some care and contrasting its distinguishing characteristics with other cases in distribution, one can at least clarify some of the antitrust policy issues in the distributive trades.

One has the impression that the price war is much more common in the case of gasoline than in the case of other goods. Although this impression may be accurate, the frequency of gasoline price wars is probably exaggerated. Price competition in other consumer goods may also be intense, but gasoline price competition may attract particular attention because: (1), gasoline prices during a price war are so apparent to motorists in the affected area; (2) gasoline is bought so frequently by so many people that the public is more aware of price competition in this good than in most others; (3) price reductions below "normal" are often so great, percentagewise, and (4), in general the public thinks of gasoline as usually having a relatively stable price in all areas except those characterized by chronic price wars.[7]

Every product no doubt moves through a distribution network, even though it may be a simple one, with some unique characteristics. In the case of gasoline, characteristics of the markets in question can be reviewed to show not only why price wars are more common and more apparent in gasoline distribution than in the distribution of other goods, but also why the antitrust problems involved are so difficult. The gasoline price war illustration will serve to highlight certain features of the distribution process which lead to antitrust problems in the case of other goods as well.

The Product Characteristics. Judging from the available studies, there are apparently only minor differences in the product characteristics of major and of minor brands of gasoline.[8] For most automobile owners, any differences in quality are difficult to ascertain. Gasoline is not evaluated by any of the five senses unless it can be said that one "feels" the difference in performance in one's car when different grades or brands of gasoline are used. And even in the technical

7. The term "price war" itself implies abnormality and suggests that "price peace" is the usual state of affairs. Hence for those goods for which prices are more variable over time with the change in competitive pressures, and in the case of gasoline in areas of chronic price war, the mere term "price war" may have no significance because of the absence of any periods of "price peace."

8. See Joe S. Bain, *The Economics of the Pacific Coast Petroleum Industry, Part I: Market Structure* (Berkeley and Los Angeles, 1944), pp. 119-123; Ralph Cassady, Jr. and Wylie L. Jones, *The Nature of Competition in Gasoline Distribution at the Retail Level* (Berkeley and Los Angeles, 1951), pp. 62-66; and *Consumer Bulletin* (May, 1958), p. 23.

sense, the product qualities apparently vary among brands only within rather narrow ranges. Therefore many brands, perhaps most brands, are very nearly perfect substitutes for each other, at least in the eyes of a substantial body of consumers.

Thus the price elasticity of demand for any given brand of gasoline or any given service station is widely granted to be very high. Yet the market demand for gasoline, at least in the short run, is considered to be very low, since it has virtually no substitutes and the alternatives to travel by any means other than the automobile are apparently not considered generally attractive by most Americans.[9]

The Consumer of Gasoline. Perhaps the most important characteristics of the consumer of gasoline insofar as the present problem is concerned is that he is geographically mobile. It is especially easy for him to begin buying from a dealer other than his usual dealer if the latter chooses not to join in a wave of price reductions. However, the fact that the motorist is in his car when he is looking for a place to buy gasoline does not mean that he will necessarily buy in the station with the lowest prices in the neighborhood, even if he is interested in price alone and not quality. After all, there is a cost involved in seeking out the lowest priced dealer. On the average purchase of gasoline the buyer saves something less than a dime by patronizing a station where the price is one cent a gallon below the price which he would otherwise pay. If the motorist gives any thought whatsoever to his own time and to the cost of operating his automobile during the search, he will not wander far in order to save one or even two cents per

9. See Harry E. McAllister, *The Elasticity of Demand for Gasoline in the State of Washington,* Bulletin No. 29, Bureau of Economic and Business Research, State College of Washington (February, 1956), especially Chapter 6.

gallon. Therefore gasoline price wars sometimes are "spotty" even within a single metropolitan area and are often concentrated along major traffic arteries and at the busier intersections.

The mobility of the consumer takes on special significance when it is remembered that typicallly he is not especially loyal to a given brand.[10] Some motorists are intensely loyal to given brands, others care nothing of the brand and buy the cheapest gasoline available. The remaining majority are the consumers over whom the marketers fight.[11] Among the many buyers who lie between the two extremes it seems that several factors other than brand or price determine the station at which the gasoline will be purchased. One careful study has shown that the location of the station, the quality of the service, and the personality of the dealer, all outrank brand as the main attraction of the favored station.[12]

Finally it is important to point out that when the motorist stops at a service station to buy gasoline he is generally interested in buying only gasoline. True, the motorist may have the tank filled when he has taken the

10. A 1957 survey by du Pont revealed that major brands of gasoline are "all alike" to 76 percent of the motorists. See "New du Pont Survey Tells What Makes Motorists Tick: Buying Patterns at Service Stations," *National Petroleum News* (September, 1957), pp. 134-137. A 1952 survey sponsored by du Pont indicated that only 12 percent of the motorists in the western part of the country buy at their favorite station because of the brands of products sold there; 43 percent patronized their favorite station because they liked the service; 32 percent because its location was convenient. See E. I. du Pont and Co., Inc., *The Service Station and the Motorist* (Wilmington, Delaware: n.d.).

11. It has been reported secondhand that the purchasers of the minor brands are more price conscious with respect to goods in general than are the people who buy major brands. S. Morris Livingston and Theodore Levitt, "Competition and Retail Gasoline Prices *Review of Economics and Statistics*, vol. 41 (May, 1959), pp. 119-132.

12. E. I. du Pont and Co., Inc., *op.cit.*

car to the service station for lubrication, but *usually* when he buys gasoline he is buying nothing else from the dealer. This feature of gasoline consumption is of particular importance to the competitive strategy of the gasoline retailer and his suppliers, whose roles in the channel we will now summarize.

The Retailer and His Supplier. The gasoline retailer is unique among the various kinds of retail business in that he is very nearly a single-product firm. Typically, from two-thirds to three-fourths of his total sales revenue is from gasoline.[13] Furthermore, he sells (with rare exception) but one brand and only two or, at the most, three grades of that brand. It must be mentioned again that different types of dealers show differing percentages of sales originating from gasoline. The minor brand, multi-pump station which operates from a large physical layout in a heavily traveled route is likely to rely almost exclusively on gasoline sales for revenue. The neighborhood dealer, by contrast, puts more emphasis on lubrication and minor garage work and is likely to pump considerably less gallonage than many minor brand dealers. This is not to deny, of course, that there are numerous instances of small, minor brand stations which do a considerable amount of servicing and which pump less than 20,000 gallons per month. And there are many examples of multi-pump stations selling major brands and relying almost completely on gasoline sales for revenue.

The stations can be divided into three basic groups, namely the company-owned stations, the company-leased stations, and the open account stations. Company-owned stations might be operated by the company or they may be leased to and operated by dealers. Simi-

13. This proportion is based on examination of accounting records of a number of dealers and on conversations with oil company executives in close contact with retail operations.

larly the stations leased by the companies from third parties might be either operated by company personnel or leased to and operated by dealers. The dealer-operated stations, whether owned by the company or leased by the company from a third party, might also be operated by the dealer on consignment. In the case of the open account, the property is either owned by the dealer operating it or is owned by a third party who leases it directly to the dealer. These different types of dealers have slightly different financial arrangements with their suppliers. For company-owned stations, of course, supplier and dealer are one. Dealers who lease from the supplier may pay a flat monthly rental, or a flat rental plus a fixed amount per gallon of gasoline sold.

In the case of the open accounts, the dealer obviously pays no rent to the supplier since he owns his own station or else rents it from some third party. He typically pays the tank-wagon price for his gasoline, less what is often called a "competitive allowance" of one to two cents or more per gallon, depending on the account. The competitive allowance has developed largely because of the competition among suppliers for the open account dealers. If a dealer is approached by a supplier other than that dealer's current supplier and is offered gasoline at, say, one cent off the prevailing tank-wagon price, the dealer of course is likely to inform his present supplier of the offer. The present supplier can, under the Robinson-Patman Act, meet this offer without violating the law.[14] Open account dealers can be expected to see to it that they receive this competitive allowance.

14. One can ask whether the competing offer is always a legitimate one, particularly in view of the fact that the competing supplier would be violating the restrictions on price discrimination himself if he in fact were to begin supplying the account in question at a price lower than that offered to his other customers.

During a price war, the dealer handling a major brand may be given some form of "dealer aid," generally a discount off the announced tank-wagon price based on the difference between the market price of gasoline at retail and the "normal" price. The supplier may have instead a policy of outright reduction of the tank-wagon price to the affected retailers. On at least some occasions in the past, certain companies have adjusted rents as a means of aiding particular dealers, but this practice seems to be disappearing.

Suppliers have attempted to cope with price wars not only through the dealer aid device, but also by putting dealers on a temporary consignment basis. This permits the supplier to hold title to the gasoline until it is bought by the motorist, so the supplier has complete control over the retail price.

With these various characteristics of gasoline marketing in mind, we can now examine the various major hypotheses concerning the causes of gasoline price wars.

The Inception of the Price War: The Hypotheses. According to the excess gasoline hypothesis, the gasoline price war is triggered by above-normal gasoline stocks; that oversupply causes price reductions in gasoline just as in a market which more nearly meets the requirements of the perfectly competitive market. Excess stocks might develop because total market demand fails to meet expectations or because individual refiners overestimate the rate at which they are likely to expand their individual markets.[15] These excesses may be pushed onto the market by the independent refiner, who cuts his price to move the gasoline, or by the major

15. This hypothesis is suggested in *Gasoline Price War in New Jersey*, Hearings before a Subcommittee of the Select Committee on Small Business U.S. Senate, 85th Cong., 1st Sess. (hereafter referred to as the Humphrey Hearings), at pp. 3ff., 27, 284, 335.

refiner who sells it to rebranders at reduced prices.[16]

Unfortunately, the available price and quantity data for the retail gasoline market are not sufficiently detailed or reliable to test this hypothesis satisfactorily, although the anecdotal evidence one hears in the industry strikes me as quite persuasive. The excess gasoline hypothesis can draw some support from the rather common observation that the price wars are much more prevalent in refining centers and in areas around transportation terminals than elsewhere. New Jersey, Los Angeles, and Philadelphia are refining centers which have had more or less perpetual price wars. Hartford, Connecticut is a barge terminal; Boston and Providence have both refineries and terminal plants. And the Piedmont Belt in North Carolina is reported to be a trouble spot because the Plantation pipeline ends at Greensboro. Gasoline stocks are readily available at the refineries and at the terminals, and rebranders may tend to cluster around such ready sources of supply. When the supplies become excessive, these rebranders are able to take advantage of the refiner or terminal operator with pressure on his storage capacity and buy at a reduced price and perhaps pass on the reduction to the consumer. And thus a price war may get under way.

The outstanding exception to this latter bit of evidence is the Texas Gulf Coast Area. The largest refining area in the country is not known to be a chronic price war trouble spot. Only one possible explanation

16. For specific cases of major brand refiners selling to rebranders, see statements by R. H. Scholl of Esso Standard Oil Co. and J. W. Liddell of Continental Oil Co., *Distribution Practices in the Petroleum Industry,* Hearings before Subcommittee No. 5 of the Select Committee on Small Business, U.S. House of Representatives, 85th Cong. 1st Sess. (hereafter referred to as the Roosevelt Hearings), Part I, p. 392, and Part II, p. 75.

comes to mind. The Texas Gulf market is primarily a bulk cargo market. If a refiner has excess gasoline, he may choose to sell it off in cargo lots for shipment elsewhere in the country rather than to reduce his local tank-wagon price or his price to local rebranders who buy in less than bulk cargo lots. Cutting the price on the bulk cargo in effect exports the price cut to other areas. This explanation would be consistent with the argument that price wars tend to cluster around terminal points in the product transportation system in the country.

In their study, *Integration and Competition in the Petroleum Industry*, de Chazeau and Kahn suggest "dynamic imbalance" is one reason for price instability in the industry.[17] This dynamic imbalance is one possible version of the excess supply hypothesis. According to the authors, the "lumpiness" of capital investment at various stages in the petroleum industry causes some stages within any one firm's organization to become larger in capacity than the "downstream" stages in the same organization, necessitating sales to outside buyers. For example, a refinery must be of some minimum size in order to be efficient. Yet this size may produce more gasoline than the refiner's outlets in the area can handle, or the refiner may choose to sell his excess product to competing firms. The authors might have added that this problem is minimized through exchange agreements. Under such agreements, a firm with an excess of refining capacity relative to its marketing capacity in Market A will give product to a firm in that same area, a firm whose marketing capacity exceeds its refining capacity. In exchange, the latter company in Market B will give the equivalent volume of product to the former company. These exchange agreements thus help to minimize the excess capacity problem.

17. M. G. de Chazeau and A. E. Kahn, *Integration and Competition in the Petroleum Industry* (New Haven, 1959), p. 456.

On balance, the excess gasoline hypothesis seems to be reasonable. But there is little doubt that there are price wars brought on by conditions not associated with excess gasoline stocks. In some markets new firms have entered by purchasing old locations or building on new ones and then fighting to win a tolerable share of the market by cutting prices. This might be called the "new entrant" hypothesis. Price wars of this variety can occur in the absence of collusion or excess gasoline stocks.[18]

The excess retailing capacity hypothesis can be treated very briefly. One of the reasons for the prolonged gasoline price war in New Jersey was the relocation of a substantial amount of the automobile traffic through the state because of the development of expressways.[19] Established stations found that their volume was seriously reduced and so some operators were tempted to cut prices as a means of regaining their old position in terms of total monthly income. In certain other areas the excess retail capacity may have been brought about by the decline in income of the area and the concomitant decline in the gasoline volume. Because relatively few metropolitan areas are in this position, the applicability of this hypothesis may be rather limited.

Some of the oil company marketing executives argue for the "eager dealer" hypothesis as a commonly observed case. According to this hypothesis, frequently price wars are started by the dealer who thinks that he can *increase his volume substantially if* he cuts his price. He must assume, of course, that his volume will rise sufficiently to yield a larger gross margin (in dol-

18. Good illustrative cases are found in the testimony of Willard W. Wright, Humphrey Hearings, pp. 358ff., in which the entry of the California Oil Company into New Jersey is discussed and in the Roosevelt Hearings, pp. 2-13. The latter concerns a small refiner whose customers suddenly switched to other suppliers, causing the refiner to find new outlets by building very low-cost stations through which he sold at exceptionally low prices.

19. See Humphrey Hearings, especially the statement of Governor Robert Meyner.

lars per month) despite the lower margin per gallon sold. This is particularly likely to happen in the case of the dealer who is aggressive and eager to improve his position permanently. Stations which are located on high traffic locations are most suited for this type of policy.[20] The individual dealer may also become particularly eager for volume if he is on a "minimum requirements" contract with his supplier and his volume is falling short of the minimum he has agreed to purchase. Under some supplier-dealer contracts, the dealer cannot sign a contract on favorable terms for a given time period unless during the previous time period he actually bought all he had been expected to buy. So if such a dealer sees the end of his contract period looming up while his total gallonage for the period promises to fall short of his commitment, he may be eager to cut his price to increase his gallonage so that he can meet his quota.

Finally, we must take note of the collusion hypothesis. The argument, that gasoline price wars are sometimes the result of collusion among the major companies, must be based on circumstantial evidence alone. Direct evidence is not available either because the hypothesis is incorrect, or because the evidence is assiduously concealed. The counterargument can only draw on equally indirect and unsatisfactory evidence. The core of the case for the collusion hypothesis is that the major companies in the market are motivated and have the power to keep the market shares of the smaller companies at a minimum level.[21] The major companies are in a particularly strong position to do battle with the

20. See Humphrey Hearings at pp. 302, 391, 398, 426. The "aggressive price competitors" are discussed by R. Cassady, Jr. and W. L. Jones, *op.cit.*, pp. 95-97.

21. The collusion hypothesis is apparent in the Amended Complaint, *U.S.* v. *Standard Oil Company of California et al.*, especially pp. 31-32.

independents, generally speaking. First of all, the large, integrated company derives its earnings not only from the marketing of the product, but also from refining and from crude oil production and transportation. The independent marketer is less likely to be fully integrated; he must earn a profit on the distribution of petroleum products or he will fail. The larger, integrated company, by contrast, can survive for an extended period with a low or even a negative profit on its marketing operations because of its profitable operation of the other segments of its business.

Secondly, the major company is likely to market in many areas where independents are unimportant. In such areas, the argument runs, the majors can make a profit in distribution rather easily because of less competition from the minor brands. Being larger than the minor company both in terms of the degree of vertical integration and in terms of geographical coverage, the large firm can tolerate losses on its operations in some areas. The major companies, according to this argument, can be virtually assured of outlasting the independent in a price war.

The argument for the collusion hypothesis can accommodate the widely recognized fact that price wars are started at times by price cuts at independent, rather than major brand, stations. Some majors supply a good many rebranders from their own refineries. If a major wishes to start a price war while avoiding the appearance of having started it he has only to sell at a reduced price to an independent marketer, thereby encouraging the latter to cut his price at retail and so start a wave of price reductions. Considering that the majors account for the greater part of the refining capacity in most refining areas, they are clearly in a position to overproduce and to force prices in the rebrand market downward if they choose to do so.

The case against this hypothesis, though its proponents must grant that the majors in most markets do have the requisite power to outlast their smaller rivals in a price war, nevertheless argues that the motivation to start price wars is lacking. True, an extended price war might result in the collapse or at least the containment of the independent brands. But a price war is costly to the major companies not only because of the consequent reduction in net price to the refinery, but also because price wars erode dealer morale.[22] Typically the dealers must absorb some portion of the price reduction before the supplier begins to pay any dealer aid. But the companies cannot require that the dealer post the retail price the supplier prefers without running afoul of the Sherman Act unless the gasoline is fair traded.

Many if not most dealers realize this and resent any pressure from the supplier. Furthermore, the dealers resent the companies' setting the dealer aid for what they (the companies) consider to be the affected trading areas. Frequently a dealer learns that a nearby dealer for the same brand is being given more dealer aid than he is, and he complains about it. Considering that it is virtually impossible for a supplying company (or anyone else) to delineate clearly definable and defensible trading areas in gasoline retailing, complaints from dealers just outside the trading area in which dealer aid is being given are almost inevitable. One firm has attempted to avoid this problem by using a special plan. Under this arrangement each dealer's competitive position is evaluated individually and dealer aid is computed accordingly. This approach circumvents the difficulties inherent in delineating trade areas.

The spokesman for one of the major oil companies

22. Ample evidence of this appears in the testimony of almost every witness in both the Humphrey and Roosevelt Hearings.

summarized the conflict effectively during one of the hearings:

> "The paradox of these (competitive allowances) is that if the supplier refuses to extend price assistance to its dealers, they would surely be out of business promptly and bitterly resent the refusal to help them; if the supplier limits price allowances to a locality, the dealers outside of such a locality claim discrimination; if the allowance is given in too wide an area, the dealers complain that the supplier is causing and spreading a price war; if the allowance is statewide, dealers in adjoining states claim discrimination and ruinous price practices by the supplier; and last but not least, where the price becomes uniformly the same in a wide area, legislators call for investigation and claim the public is being highjacked by big corporations. Gentlemen, you can see some of our problems resulting from price wars."[23]

Price wars undoubtedly raise the dealer turnover rate, which is already 20 percent and higher for some companies.[24] The operating expenses incurred because of dealer turnover – namely credit losses, dealer training expenses, additional salesmen's time, and closed stations – are undoubtedly large.

The price war, then, upsets the normal relationship between the supplier and the dealer and gives rise to troublesome conflicts and costs which both parties would prefer to avoid. The major companies profess to be especially eager to maintain good relations with dealers. Good dealers are continually being sought out by the major companies and, in attracting these dealers, the company wishes to have as part of its bargaining power the reputation of treating its dealers fairly. A company has a better opportunity of winning such a

23. Humphrey Hearings, statement of Charles J. Guzzo, Gulf Oil Corporation, p. 289.

24. See Humphrey Hearings, p. 301.

reputation if it can maintain stable relations, free of conflict with its dealers.

Other portions of the argument against the collusion hypothesis are worth noting. The independent marketer is virtually certain to remain a factor in the gasoline market as long as there are independent refiners, or as long as any of the major refiners produce more gasoline than they can sell through their own outlets. Therefore, the large company cannot foresee an end of competition from the fringe, even if price wars were to be employed by the majors as a tactical device from time to time. If a major company is interested in expanding its market share, rather than start a price war the company may generally find it simpler to follow the policy of acquiring good locations and setting up attractive, well-staffed stations, an almost routine means of expanding market share. Starting a price war is "messy"; it is not easily controlled, and attendant uncertainties are considerably greater than those surrounding the establishment of new outlets.

In seeking evidence for one side of this case or the other, one is forcibly struck by the fact that no witnesses in either the Humphrey Hearings or the Roosevelt Hearings suggested the collusion hypothesis.[25] They stressed instead that suppliers often treated competing dealers inequitably, urging them to price as the suppliers wished, or demanding that they carry only the suppliers' TBA brands. Furthermore, the major companies are aware that the dealers, being an important segment of small business, can readily bring about Congressional

25. In the Humphrey Hearings a dealer did note that the majors' tank-wagon prices moved up and down together, but he did not extend this to suggest collusion to squeeze out the independent refiners or marketers (p. 50). Another dealer indicated that he thought the oil companies were attempting to drive out the independent dealers *handling the suppliers' brand* so they (the companies) could acquire the property themselves (p. 155). But this is quite different from the collusion hypothesis.

hearings on their problems. Collusion or any other type of activity alienating dealers and bringing about unfavorable publicity and its hidden costs is something the major companies may wish to avoid.

The dealers appearing before the Humphrey committee quite obviously saw that the alignments were not between the major refiners on the one hand and the independent refiners and marketers on the other. They saw instead that the supplying companies were opposing the interests of the dealers, with the dealers struggling constantly for a "fair shake" from the companies, expecially during price wars. The companies time after time in the hearings were referred to as the generals, safe behind the lines, in contrast with privates, i.e., the dealers, who do the dirty work and get hurt during price wars. Said one dealer of the New Jersey price war resulting from the entry of Standard Oil Company of California: "The generals on each side were the Standard Oil Company of California; and on the other side were the majors who were firmly entrenched in the New Jersey market, Esso, Sun, Texaco, Tydol and Gulf, the principal ones. They held our coats while we fought it out."[26]

Finally, the collusion hypothesis may be inconsistent with the fact that economic concentration in petroleum refining has been gradually declining. The percentage of the value of shipments accounted for by the four largest refining companies fell from 38 percent in 1935 and 37 percent in 1947 to 32 percent in 1958. The percentage of the market held by the eight largest declined from 58 and 59 percent in 1935 and 1947 to 55 percent in 1958.[27] Industry sources would argue that

26. Humphrey Hearings, p. 49.

27. *Concentration Ratios in Manufacturing Industry, 1958*, Report prepared by the Bureau of the Census for the Subcommittee on Antitrust and Monopoly of the Committee on the Judiciary, U.S. Senate, 1962, Part I, p. 26.

these percentages have been falling much more rapidly in those metropolitan and regional markets in which the independents have made a major effort to expand their operations. This evidence on market share says only that if there is collusion among the majors, it has not been successful in protecting the majors' market from erosion.

To say that the available information seems inconsistent with the collusion hypothesis is not to say that major companies never start price wars. Any single major company may of course be active in initiating a price war if it finds its market share slipping below some tolerable minimum. Other majors may then follow suit in self-protection, thus giving the appearance of collusive action.

The Suppliers' Pricing Policies During Price Wars. Regardless of the cause of the price war, the suppliers must adopt a strategy to deal with, even if it is a policy of inaction. The most common policy appears to be the offer of some form of "dealer aid." This aid typically takes the form of what is in effect a discount off the tank-wagon price. The discount in a large percentage of the cases is the difference between the "named" price and the price actually charged by the dealer, with the dealer being guaranteed some minimum absolute margin so he will be protected if the price drops well below normal. Some suppliers have offered dealer aid to all dealers in the affected area, however that might be defined, in order to avoid charges of price discrimination.[28] Others have offered dealer aid on an individual dealer basis, holding that this was price discrimination in good faith to meet competition.[29] In offering the

28. It is widely granted that the boundaries of a "trading area" are subject to debate. Humphrey Hearings, pp. 207, 288, 343, 404.

29. For an excellent discussion of the legal problems of price wars, see Amzy B. Steed, "Antitrust Problems under Price War Condition," *Proceedings of the* 1958 *Institute on Antitrust Laws* (New York, 1958), pp. 77-103.

dealer aid, however, the supplier cannot legally stipulate the price to be posted by the dealer, since this would be price-fixing and therefore illegal *per se*. This disadvantage has led other companies to put their affected dealers on a consignment basis so that the supplier can dictate the retail price on a station-by-station basis.

Presumably resale price maintenance does not recommend itself for use in gasoline distribution because of the difficulty the supplier would face in holding to a single price in an area in which competing brands were beginning to fall in price. The minor brands can apparently cut into the majors' market if the price differential between major and minor brands is greater than two cents. Therefore, any single minor brand can cause trouble even if all the other suppliers in a market are operating under resale price maintenance agreements. This is not to say that "fair trading" in gasoline is impossible, but only that it is likely to be more tenuous than in the case of goods characterized by greater product differentiation among brands.

Quasi-Integration. I have developed this discussion of the gasoline price war because it illustrates one extreme set of supplier-retailer relationships. In this particular case, the major refiners as suppliers recognize: (1), that a high proportion of consumers consider the major brands to be very nearly perfect substitutes for each other; (2) that the motorist is so mobile that he can easily switch his gasoline purchases from one station to another; (3), that the motorist typically buys only (or at least primarily) gasoline at the service station and therefore cannot readily be persuaded to pay more for gasoline than at competitive stations on the grounds that the other goods cost less; and (4), that for all these reasons motorists are ready to switch brands and stations even if small price differences develop. The supplier, therefore, is especially interested in seeing to it that the retailer keeps his price competitive. With competitive prices the refiner's success depends largely on the nonprice features of the retailer's operations—the location, quality of service, and the appearance of the station. Therefore, it is little wonder that the supplier wants to control *all* of the terms of the retailer's offer, these "terms of the offer" being defined to include not only the price and the quality of the gasoline itself but also such features as the location and appearance of the station, the quality of the personnel, and the other services available at the station.

Under these circumstances, why doesn't the supplier own and operate his own station so that he can have complete control over the retailer's offer? Although some companies do use company-owned and operated stations in some areas, most of them rely on independent dealers. The usual reason cited is that only in the high volume stations can the wages of company personnel be covered. The independent dealer is allegedly more efficient than the salaried operator, although there is some evidence that the former may typically earn less than a going wage and that the latter simply earns more money. There is even doubt in the trade that the company-operated stations in existence are really profitable. Some are kept only for training and market research purposes and so are not expected to be profitable.

Because the supplier typically finds full integration unattractive, and because he is so interested in the terms of the retailer's offer, he often uses various means of quasi-integration. By owning the station property and leasing it to the dealer, he can influence the location and the appearance of the station. By selling on consignment he can control the price. By offering dealer aid he may be able to influence, though not control the dealer's price.

In the distribution of other goods as well one often finds suppliers reluctant to integrate forward by owning and operating retail and wholesale outlets, but since the supplier wants some degree of control over his distribution channel he may use various means of quasi-integration. The manufacturer-supplier may be reluctant to integrate forward into retailing because of inadequate capital; because he considers independent retail store owners to be more efficient than salaried retail store managers which the manufacturer might hire; or because his item is typically bought by stores handling many other items so integration forward would involve retailing mostly other manufacturer's goods.[30] But since the manufacturer wants to control at least certain features of the terms of the retailer's offer, he often employs one of the following devices or some combination of them.

(1) *Resale Price Maintenance:* This prevents the manufacturer's retail customers from competing with each other on a price basis and assures that the manufacturer's product will be carried in many stores because of the attractive margin which he can guarantee, assuming the resale price maintenance agreement is adequately policed. The manufacturer selling direct to retailers can enforce an informal resale price maintenance agreement by refusing to supply retailers who depart from the manufacturers' suggested retail prices.

(2) *Consignment Selling:* This again prevents price competition among dealers. This is especially useful if the consumer demand for the product is particularly sensitive to the availability of the product and if retailers otherwise would tend to use the item as a loss leader.

(3) *Exclusive Territorial Franchises*: This gives the retailer a territorial monopoly and thus removes the

30. Some firms have nevertheless integrated forward into retailing despite this obstacle.

necessity for price competition with the other retailers handling the same brand.

(4) *Exclusive Buying Contracts*: This gives the supplier the assurance that no competing goods will be handled by the retailer.

Our antitrust legislation as enforced by the Department of Justice and the FTC and as interpreted by the courts suggests that full integration forward into retailing is quite legal, given no conspiracy or attempt to monopolize. Quasi-integration, however, is suspect. Resale price maintenance obviously is in deep trouble and recently the FTC challenged consignment sales in gasoline distribution.[31] Exclusive franchises have also been under attack, although Justice Douglas indicated in the Supreme Court decision in the *White Motor* case that vertical territorial restrictions may be the only practicable means for a small company to break into or to remain in business.[32]

How much control over the retailer's policies, and under what circumstances, should be considered in restraint of trade? If the manufacturer is fully integrated into retailing, owning, and operating his own retail outlets, he can set the retail prices charged on his own brands. And he can in effect give each of his own retail outlets an exclusive territory. All this is apparently legal if there is no attempt to monopolize. A large scale retailer can develop his own brands by buying out his suppliers or by special contracts with them, and can follow the same policies as the manufacturer who is full integrated forward.

The nonintegrated manufacturer interested in achieving some degree of control over the retailing or wholesaling of his product often attempts some type of quasi-

31. *In the matter of Sun Oil Co.*, FTC Docket 6934, issued May 15, 1963; and *The Atlantic Refining Co.*, FTC Docket 7471, issued May 16, 1963.

32. *White Motor Co.* v. *U.S.*, 372 U.S. 253 (1963).

integration. Such quasi-integration often leads to charges of price-fixing among retailers, of price discrimination and of unequal treatment in violation of Section 2(d) of the Robinson-Patman Act, or of attempts to restrain trade or to create a monopoly. Such cases of quasi-integration are among the more common instances of small business involvement with the antitrust laws.

Conclusion

Should quasi-integration be permitted, as long as there is no attempt to monopolize and if competition is not substantially lessened, just as full integration is permitted if there is no attempt to monopolize and if competition is not substantially lessened? Since the reasons why the supplier should be permitted to employ the various methods of quasi-integration are familiar, I will only summarize them here. First, the manufacturer of a branded product in a sense has a property right in that product even after the retailer has bought it and taken title to it. In order to protect the name of the product and the name of the manufacturer, the manufacturer should be permitted to dictate to the retailer the terms of sale to the final consumer. If the item becomes a "loss leader," the manufacturer is definitely hurt since the public comes to doubt the quality of the product or the public considers the manufacturer to be a "chiseler" because of the difference in prices in different stores.

Second, quasi-integration should be permitted to the independent manufacturer because he can then compete on common grounds with his integrated rivals. For some kinds of goods, however (e.g., many food products), the manufacturer may have little interest in any of the forms of quasi-integration. But where quasi-integration is important, the small manufacturer is likely to be in a stronger position. If the manufacturer wishes to set up exclusive franchises and to set prices as well as the other terms of sale of his retailer, perhaps he should be so permitted. According to this view, one "looks through" the retailer, back to the manufacturer and sees the manufacturer in competition with other manufacturers using the retailer in effect as his competitive agent.

Third, permitting quasi-integration may encourage the survival of the independent retailer since in the absence of exclusive franchises, resale price maintenance and such devices, retail competition would be more intense.

Fourth, under quasi-integration there is still plenty of room for competition since even if retail prices are fixed by the manufacturer the retailers would still compete on the basis of location, services offered, the depth and breadth of inventory, and other aspects of the total package of products and services offered by the retailer.

Fifth, permitting this kind of quasi-integration does not restrict the retailer unduly in his relation with suppliers. It is true that he cannot set his own terms of sale on the product, but he can accept or reject the whole package of terms offered by the manufacturer who is willing to let the retailer handle the product. In this sense, the retailer has some freedom in dealing with his supplier. The manufacturer must make his terms sufficiently attractive so that his retailers do not desert him for other suppliers.

The arguments on the other side of the case are also compelling. First, the good in question really does belong to the retailer and he can price it as he wishes or display it as he wishes. Once the retailer has bought the item, the manufacturer is no longer in control. The manufacturer need not worry about a price reduction destroying the image of quality; countless branded items are available in different outlets at different times at different prices (automobiles, coffee, and cigarettes are obvious answers) with no visible effect on the public's view of the quality of the product.

Second, the retailers should be permitted to experiment as much as they wish with the price as well as with the other terms of sales. It is such experimentation that led to the discount house and which revealed to the retailers of hard goods that their margins were quite out of date.

Third, with manufacturers dictating the terms, retail margins are almost certain to be higher than they would be otherwise (as manufacturers would seek widespread distribution) with consequent excess capacity in retailing.

Fourth, high margins on individual products would not necessarily mean that retailers would be better off; retailers are misleading themselves when they equate high margins with high profits. With high margins, retailers will compete for customers either by offering more services or more low-priced merchandise and more retailers will spring up to compete the volume per store down to the point where only normal profits are earned. Thus high margins might lead to more retailers but not necessarily to stronger ones.

Finally, to say that the retailers to whom the terms of sale are being dictated by the manufacturer can accept or reject the whole package of terms suggests that the retailer has a satisfactory number of competing suppliers to turn to. This may or may not be true.

The basic problem in many of the antitrust cases involving distribution stems from the desire to maintain competition at each of two levels in the distribution process. Full and unfettered competition on the offer terms for all products handled at the retail level would call for no quasi-integration whatsoever. Yet under such circumstances the competition among the manufacturers selling to these retailers (omitting for the time being the problem of the wholesaling level) might be hampered by the large size of some of the manufacturers. In order to survive, the smaller manufacturer may wish very much to use various forms of quasi-integration. Yet if one takes the view that the manufacturer not integrated into retailing should be permitted to use quasi-integration in order to compete on equal terms with the integrated manufacturer, one is left with more limited competition among retailers.

Perhaps we should consider the application of a rule of reason to these quasi-integration problems. Under such a rule, the manufacturer could use various means of quasi-integration as long as this is clearly not an attempt to monopolize. If a manufacturer has a small share of the market, this is *prima facie* evidence that quasi-integration by the manufacturer is not an an attempt to monopolize. Thus, if the manufacturer's market share is small, as in the *White Motor* case, quasi-integration would be permitted. Sun Oil, if its market share in the area in question is substantial, would not be permitted to engage in quasi-integration at least to the point of fixing retail prices by means of dealer aid. Competition among retailers would thus be restrained in the case of goods marketed through independent retailers by manufacturers with small market shares who choose to practice quasi-integration, but manufacturers with a large share of the market would not be permitted to impose restrictions on their retailers. Such an approach obviously would involve troublesome ambiguities because it involves a double standard, one for firms with a large market share and one for firms will small market shares. But since the antitrust laws as formulated and enforced already involve a double standard (as in the case of the "substantiality" test), applying the double standard as suggested would not be such a striking innovation.

CHAPTER 10

Mergers Among Commercial Banks

BY GEORGE W. MITCHELL[1]

Introduction

Recent developments in the structure of banking markets have caused concern in Congress, in the several agencies responsible in one way or another for the regulation and supervision of banks, and—belatedly—in the academic community. The concern of the 1930's, centered primarily in the ambiguous notion of an "overbanked" economy and in the inadequate safeguards to the safety and liquidity of the banking system, have shifted in the past decade to concern over growing concentration, a lessening of competition and—in some quarters, at least—a fear that regulation is too encompassingly confining to permit banks adequately to respond to changing requirements of a growing economy.

The view of banks as *sui generis* implicit in the policies designed to regulate and supervise them fails to recognize the change and rapid growth of highly competitive financial markets and alternative financing de-

1. It is perhaps unnecessary to point out that the views expressed herein are my own and that they do not necessarily accord with those of any of my colleagues on the Board of Governors. In addition, my remarks are generalizations about what, in my opinion, policy *should* be. Translating these generalizations into a consistent position on actual cases within the context of existing statutes is, I can testify, a most difficult task. I am very much indebted to Mr. Myron A. Grove for the development of many of the views expressed in this paper.

vices that have occurred in recent years and, hence, creates the impression of a body of policy rather badly out of step with the times. In the multi-stage and institutionally specialized financial markets of today, commercial banking is an important element but not the unique element it was in earlier times. This increasingly competitive environment has caused bankers to become more like the managers of any other profit-seeking enterprise.

It is my view that despite superficial differences between banking markets and those for other goods and services the market mechanism and the decisions made in the market place ordinarily can and should be relied upon to protect the interests and needs of individual communities and the general welfare of the country. Historic worries about bank safety and liquidity—which often ignore the vital distinction between safety and liquidity for depositors as contrasted with that of stockowners—and the chronic fears of "overbanking" have, I think, led to an overzealous regulation, overly restrictive policies on the entry of new banks, and inescapably to monopolistic and collusive practices. These practices have brought on too much suspicion of size, and too little faith in the integrity of the profit motives in assessing the benefits of mergers[2] among banks. In short, it seems to me that what might be described as "procompetitive" policy toward banking would produce more, better, and cheaper banking services for the public than a policy of shelter and sanctuary.

The Characteristics of Banking Markets

Many students of industrial organization regard com-

2. Except where otherwise clear from the context, I use the term "merger" to include holding company acquisitions as well as other types of consolidation.

mercial banking as an example of a "regulated industry." The role of competition is minimized and only in exceptional cases is the ordinary theory of the firm employed in explaining the behavior of banks. There clearly are reasons for this in addition to the fact of comprehensive regulation. The concept as well as the measurement of production by banks is illusive, and certainly not established practice, e.g., there are no census product classifications for banks. And the banker – perhaps more because of the prototype of romantic Americana than because of accord with reality – is viewed differently from other businessmen.

The result is that the analogues which banks have with other businesses are obscured. Banks, as other firms, buy factors of production, utilize these factors to convert units of input to units of output, and sell this output in multi-product forms. Land, labor, and money capital come from a variety of markets, but there is no basic reason to suppose that the supply of or demand for these productive agents is based on principles other than those applicable to other kinds of businesses. The demand and supply schedules for the several products of banks have as much operational validity as do those of other goods and services.

The industry concept is as vague for commercial banking as it is for other groups of firms. Inter- as well as intra-industry competitive forces operate in the markets because of substitute products being offered by nonbank competitors. Estimation of the degree of substitutability among products and the delineation of markets is difficult, but hardly more so than is true of, say, cellophane and other flexible packaging materials. In its purchases and sales of Government and private securities, even the largest of banks is small in relation to the national market of many buyers and sellers. The individual bank cannot perceptibly affect prices by its decisions in this market. Similarly, banks are typically a small part of both the residential and commercial mortgage loan markets. In some respects, banks often sell a product here which is inferior from the point of view of the buyer to that sold by savings and loan associations and insurance companies. For personal loans, the products of commercial banks compete with those of finance companies, small loan companies, credit unions, and with many evolving systems of trade account credits.

The market for business loans is really a complex structure of segmented submarkets.[3] The number of alternatives available to business borrowers depends more on borrower characteristics than on the structure of bank and nonbank financial institutions. Large and reasonably well known corporations can appeal to many banks in several financial centers for lines of credit. They may, in addition, place term loans with insurance companies and, in most instances, have recourse to alternative longer plans of financing through security markets.[4] At the other extreme, however, small businesses, while relying heavily on commercial bank credit,[5] have few available alternatives. The small, local firm, whether or not incorporated, may have borrowing sources which include only those banks in its immediate environs, trade account credit from its suppliers, and credit from personal loans made by individuals in the community.

3. See David A. Alhadeff, *Monopoly and Competition in Banking* (Berkeley, 1954).

4. See R. R. Moss, "Financing of Large Corporations," *Federal Reserve Bulletin* (June, 1956) and Herman I. Liebling, "Financing the Expansion of Business," *Survey of Current Business* (September, 1957).

5. See George W. Mitchell, "Review of Survey Findings," *Financing Small Business*, Report to the Committees on Banking and Currency and the Select Committees on Small Business, U. S. Congress (Washington, April 11, 1958).

In the deposit market, commercial bank savings-type deposits appear to be close substitutes for share accounts in savings and loan associations and deposits in mutual savings banks and with credit unions. Commercial bank corporate time deposits compete with a variety of money market instruments well known to corporate treasurers. But there is no close substitute for the general use made of commercial bank demand deposits, unless it is currency. And currency is hardly a substitute for large or distant money settlements. Some depositors minimize the cost of their demand deposit by converting interest-bearing deposits to money as needed, but this is, at best, a quite imperfect substitute for the convenience of regular demand deposit service.

Before turning to questions of why banks merge, a comment or two on the problem of the existence of economies of scale in banking seems in order. Evidence on the existence of scale economies have been presented by several commentators.[6] This evidence, however, is sketchy and rather speculative and rests on the assumption that *accounting* costs are an adequate proxy for the relevant *economic* costs. This assumption, as Professor Friedman points out,[7] is not a good one and can be rather badly misleading.

Even if one were to assume, *arguendo,* that scale economies exist, I am not convinced that these are so pronounced as to preclude a banking system of "many banks" and to make such a structure incompatible with

6. Alhadeff, *op.cit.;* L. E. Gramley, "Scale Economies in Banking," *Federal Reserve Bank of Kansas City Review* (1962); Paul Horvitz, "Economics of Scale in Banking," an unpublished paper for the Committee on Money and Credit.

7. Comment on Caleb Smith, "Survey on the Empirical Evidence on Economies of Scale," in *Business Concentration and Price Policy* (New York, National Bureau of Economic Research, 1955), pp. 230-238.

efficiency. It should be remembered that over half the banks in this country are small and operate in one- and two-bank towns. For these, it is the extent of the deposit market, not scale economies, which dictates size and the efficiency question reduces to whether a *small* branch or a *small* unit bank is most efficient or whether the town's banking services are provided by the nearest larger town or city. I would be surprised if there were not substantial economies of scale up to, say, banks of $5 million of deposits. But the suggested reappearance of economies among large banks[8] – those beyond $50 million or $100 million of deposits – is, I suspect, associated with a different type of banking business and a very different economic environment, as much if not more with scale economies *per se*. Virtually nothing is known concerning economies associated with scale of unit banks versus growth through branching and holding companies, but my view is that the advantage of the latter is not so pronounced that the policies I shall advocate below spell the demise of unit banking.

The Reasons for Bank Mergers

The analyst interested in undertaking a serious attack on the problems of mergers and competition in banking would, I think, be concerned with extending and deepening the analogies sketched above between banks and other firms. A good deal of the existing discussion of the reasons banks merge treats banks as a special kind of firm with special kinds of problems. Reasons having fairly wide currency are that banks merge because: (1) one of them has a management problem; (2) they wish to obtain capital more readily; (3) they wish to increase their loan limits; (4) they wish to offer a more complete range of banking services; (5) there are inevitable imperfections in the mar-

8. Alhadeff, *op.cit.*

ket for the stocks of small banks which causes both undervaluation and lack of liquidity; or (6) there is social prestige and political power associated with "bigness." I do not wish to imply that analysts who interpret bank motives for mergers in these terms are committing grievous error. They are needlessly complicating matters and taking the long way round to a rather simple proposition: banks merge because they find it profitable to do so.

I would suggest that if the tendency of banks to seek profits is examined closely enough, we shall have come a long way toward understanding the forces that lead to bank mergers. Detailed analyses of the implications of the profit motive for mergers have been presented by George Stigler and Edith Penrose.[9] It is an interesting and, I think, revealing exercise to apply their analyses to the case of banks.

Both Stigler and Penrose argue that an important reason why merger is a natural consequence of profit-seeking is that the dominant form of business organization in the economy is the corporation. This means that capital, market position, and good will once created are durable in time and separable from any particular set of owners. It means that there is a choice between purchasing what already exists or building anew. The choice between these alternatives will depend on which course for expansion is the more profitable. A bank can build new facilities and/or develop new markets on its own or it can acquire the facilities and markets of already existing banks.[10] If a planned expansion is considered profitable regardless of the com-

9. George J. Stigler, "Monopoly and Oligopoly by Merger," *American Economic Review*, vol. 40, no. 2 (May, 1950); Edith Penrose, *The Theory of the Growth of the Firm* (New York, 1960).

10. Expansion may be of the form of branching into other areas, increasing present on-site facilities, or extension of the "loan product line."

petitive implications for existing position of other banks or for the distribution of control over existing bank assets, then the bank will expand through acquisition only if acquisition is cheaper than doing so *de novo*. But if the change sought is in the market position of existing banks – through, say, a reduction in competition or a change in control over existing assets (the legal charter and established deposit relationships) – then merger may be the *only* way of achieving these objectives. In either case, acquisition will occur only if there are banks willing to part with their assets, including good will, and all other parts of their "establishment" that command a price, at a price equal to or less than their value to potential buyers. For an acquisition to occur, that is, there must be a buyer *and* a seller, both of whom expect to gain by the transaction. There must be a negotiable difference between "bid and asked."

I can provide only a general sketch of the way the profit motive, for both the buying and selling bank, tends to encourage mergers rather than *de novo* branching and internal expansion. In a reasonably perfect market, it should be noted, the purchase price of existing banks should correspond closely to the outlay necessary to build and develop a new bank, including in the latter the cost of forming the depositor good will, loan channels, and knowledge of the market which the existing bank stands ready to sell with its physical and financial assets.

One source of market imperfection which encourages acquisition of existing banks is the differential uncertainties involved. The intangible assets of existing banks can be accurately valued compared with the very uncertain cost of creating the same assets for a *de novo* branch. The reduction of uncertainty involved in acquisition would, by itself, cause the buying bank to offer what might appear to be an excessive premium over book or market valuation of the selling bank. In such circumstances, the buyer is paying what amounts to a risk insurance premium and the seller is receiving a larger discounted present value of future income from the sale than would be received from continued operations. Each is profit-maximizing.

Another reason for the existence of a negotiable difference between bid and ask might be thought of as a "management problem," but it is again a form of individual gain-seeking. It cannot be assumed that all bank owners view the future in the same way. That is, allowance must be made for different utility-risk-income-effort preferences among alternative prospective owners of the bank that would lead them to value the bank's assets in different ways. An example would be the case in which the owners of a bank in a rapidly growing new area find the problems of growth of the bank overwhelming. In order to meet its potential, the owners may have to install formal management techniques and deal with complexities such as an elaborate personnel training and development program and electronic customer accounting. In sum, life may become too complicated for and require too much effort from the present owners simply to maintain current income. A premium on the book value and market value of their shares may seem quite attractive, permitting the retention of income and a reduction of responsibility, time, and effort.

A *negotiable difference* in the valuation of the bank by its current and prospective owners may arise because of what might be called "differential loan capacities." The notion of a bank's loan capacity might be stated informally[11] as follows: A bank operates under three constraints in its efforts to maximize net earnings.

11. The formal statement of the theory is contained in David Chambers and Abraham Charnes, "Intertemporal Analysis and the Optimization of Bank Portfolios," *The Technical Institute of Northwestern University,* O.N.R. Memorandum No. 27.

Two of these constraints are precisely defined. They consist of the balance sheet requirement (assets must equal liabilities plus capital) and the reserve requirement (a given percentage of deposits must be held as reserves). The third constraint is a complicated and informal limitation on the extent to which a bank may "lever" its portfolio.[12] The constraint consists of a classification scheme which orders assets according to their quality and liabilities by their exposure to withdrawal. The upper limit on the leverage of the balance sheet becomes progressively more stringent as assets become more risky and liabilities more exposed.

If the capital and deposit position of the bank is given, then an upper bound on the set of proportions of a bank's portfolio in loans and investments is given. This upper bound is the bank's loan capacity. If yield rates on loans and investments can be forecast, then the bank can compute the addition to earnings an increase in capital (or deposits) can produce. A bank will find it profitable to expand if the addition to earnings from an increment to capital exceeds the cost of the increment to capital.

A bank's loan capacity, it must be emphasized, cannot be defined so precisely in practice. The leverage limit is not a formal constraint which imposes penalties for infraction but is at most a "guideline of prevailing practice." Most bank managements have independent judgment about capital adequacy, shaped by their own understanding about the stability of their deposit structure and modified by the investment alternatives that appear most attractive. The loan capacity of a bank operating in the "real world" is not a single boundary but a flexing band.

Differential loan capacities among banks may afford

12. See the Federal Reserve System's "Form for Analyzing Bank Capital."

opportunities for joint profits which are larger than the sum of the independent profits before merger. If one bank, call it A, has "excess loan capacity" because it has specialized in loans (e.g., business loans) the demand for which has declined relative to other types of loans (e.g., consumer loans), it will be anxious to increase its earnings by developing a new line of loans. Bank A then has the choice of, say, branching into an area in which these types of loans are important, or purchasing a bank making such loans which it may develop. A negotiable difference between bid and ask will exist because banks already in the area must revise downward their estimates of the loans and deposits they can command should A decide to enter *de novo*. And Bank A will be willing to purchase other banks if they are cheaper than developing a new location.[13]

Two banks, each of which has excess loan capacity, may be confronted with a local market in which the expansion of either would be at the expense of the other. If either or both attempt to expand, the profitability of both may be jeopardized by competitive effects on loan rates and costs. A joint venture in the form of a merger could be profitable to both sets of owners — though it should be noted that this type of profit-seeking through merger is at the expense of a reduction in competition.

It is also true that two banks, neither of which has excess loan capacity, may increase combined profits through a merger, even without a reduction in capital costs, an increase in yields on particular loans and investments, or economies of overhead in combined operations, if the ratio of incremental costs of placing particular loans and investments to the incremental

13. A somewhat similar rationale for merger has been discussed by D. A. and C. P. Alhadeff, "Recent Bank Mergers," *Quarterly Journal of Economics,* vol. 69 (November, 1955).

revenue gained by these loans and investments is different between the two banks. The increase in profit which results from merger in these conditions is a rather peculiar case of gains from specialization.

I repeat that the above is no more than suggestive of an analysis of mergers through use of the profit motive. But, limited as it is, it appears to me to have more analytic promise than continued dependence on general assertions that banks merge because of management problems, imperfect capital markets, increased loan limits, et cetera. So long as emphasis on the profit motive is stressed, banks seem much less like a special kind of firm and seem amenable to conventional economic analysis.

The Need and Requirements for Competition in Banking

An economic and political case for a procompetitive policy in banking, like the case against sin, is an easy one to make. But thinking through the full implications of such a policy is another matter.

Competition is important in banking for precisely the same reasons it is important in other industries. On the technical level, competition is the regulator that assures that each bank will combine resources in the "best" proportion to produce the "best" output. It will assure that monetary rewards reflect relative efficiencies and not positions in a power hierarchy. On a less abstract level competition in banking is a desideratum because it is *the* policy among feasible policies most likely to exploit differences of opinion among bankers on what is "an adequate return" and what constitutes "a maximum of risk." Without such differences of opinion, the banking system is much more likely to avoid than accommodate the marginal and innovative undertakings which become brilliant successes in service and profit. What is worse, the dead hand of monopoly administering credit is an exceedingly strong bulwark for the status quo in business organization and an exceedingly strong agent for those who would "keep competition within reasonable bounds" in other industries.

Only two basic objections can be raised against making competition the appropriate policy goal for our monetary system. The first is that economies of scale are such that competitive results are impossible to achieve. I have already indicated that I do not believe the facts support this argument. The second is that banking, because of the need for safety and liquidity in the monetary system, must be supplemented by such extensive regulation that competition cannot operate even though the structure of the industry is conducive to competition. Put another way, the argument is that competition in the absence of regulation would cause extensive bank failures and seriously damage the public interest.

In the guise of protecting the public interest, many policies inconsistent with competition have arisen. Chief among these are barriers to entry—restrictions on the chartering of new banks and restrictions on *de novo* branching and branching by merger. The rationale is that without such barriers an "overbanked" situation would degenerate into a rash of bank failures.

It is difficult to give overbanking an operational meaning. Counting the number of banks in an area is an imperfect guide to whether the area is overbanked. For one thing, not all banks do the same kind of business. This is analogous to deciding that a city contains "too many" restaurants without checking to see which of these are lunch counters and which night clubs. Then too, a city with 10 banks can be seriously underbanked if these 10 banks are operating as a perfect cartel. A more workable index of overbanking may be bank earnings. If a group of banks in an area are earning less than a given percentage on capital, one might conclude that the area is overbanked. If these banks are earning more than a prescribed percentage on capital, one might conclude that the area is underbanked. The troublesome problem with such a measure is deciding whether low earnings are a result of too much competition or too little competence and aggressiveness.

It is important, I think, to be very clear about the nature of the conflict between a procompetitive policy and bank safety. If we mean by bank safety the safeguarding of the stockholders' equity then this conflict is present. Competition among banks, like competition among drug stores and lumber mills, does risk stockholders' equity. This, however, is the essence of an enterprise system where the entrepreneur is literally a "risker of capital." If, on the other hand, we take bank safety to mean *depositor safety*, then competition is *not* inconsistent with bank safety. The depositor can be, and in most circumstances is, insulated from bank failure through the capital cushion and insurance.

I am not saying that I seek a system that might lead to more bank failures. I do not think that anyone does. I am saying that we ought to have a hard second look at the basis for the conflict between competition and sound banking. The logical distinction of bank safety and depositor safety is part of such an appraisal.

Barriers to entry certainly do keep down the number of banks but it is not clear that they do much to help the bank lead a monastic existence. Banks face a variety of aggressive, expanding nonbank competitors in major components of their loan product lines. Entry barriers do little or nothing to insulate banks from competition for Government securities or tax exempt obligations; except in geographically isolated pockets of limited extent they are ineffective against the nonbank competition for mortgages and consumer credit. These barriers can, however, contribute very significantly to keeping down the number of alternatives small business possesses. It is indeed questionable whether such an effect is a desirable one.[14] Barriers to entry also strictly limit the alternatives of demand deposit account holders and the users of a variety of miscellaneous services conveniently packaged by banks – all in all vital services to the public.

It is difficult to avoid the conclusion that entry restrictions and other regulations have created opportunities for the growth of other financial intermediaries and that these have made substantial inroads on markets formerly served by banks. There is much to be said for an easier policy that would do more to allow banks to judge what is and what is not an overbanked area on the basis of what they think bank customers need and what they think they can earn. It is time, I think, for a stronger procompetitive stance on the part of the banking regulatory bodies.

A Procompetitive Policy for Bank Mergers

Statutory authority is given to the banking agencies to approve or disapprove of merger and holding company cases in the Bank Holding Company Act of 1956 and the Bank Merger Act of 1960. The Supreme Court, in the recent *Philadelphia National Bank* case,[15] construed the Clayton Act to cover bank merger cases. The impact of the latter is, at best, uncertain but it is clear that under the Clayton Act the standard used is a com-

14. See David A. Alhadeff, "A Reconsideration of Restrictions on Bank Entry," *Quarterly Journal of Economics,* vol. 76 (May, 1962) and "Bank Mergers: Competition Versus Banking Factors," *Southern Economic Journal,* vol. 29 (January, 1963).

15. *U.S.* v. *The Philadelphia National Bank,* 374 U.S. 321 (1963).

petitive one – the determination of whether there is likely to be a substantial lessening of competition in any line of commerce in any relevant market.

The acts under which the banking agencies operate do not limit consideration to the competitive factor. On the contrary, the agencies must consider a *list* of factors, *one* of which is competition. The agencies are directed to examine the "banking factors" – character of management, financial history, prospects – and "the competitive factor." Congressional sponsors explicitly stated that neither of these factors would control decisions and "each must be considered in relation to the other."[16] Congress clearly had in mind that the agencies should attend to a "weighted sum" of banking and competitive implications of a merger and that it may be necessary to substitute among them in particular instances.[17]

This is a difficult assignment since both the interpretation of and weight given to each of the factors will vary from individual to individual. A procompetitive policy, however, would clarify some of the issues. Under such a policy, there would be a deliberate refusal by the regulatory agencies to collect and sift evidence which it can use to weigh motives. Mergers among banks, as we have seen earlier can occur for a variety of reasons – most of them ultimately traceable to the profit motive. Banks do good but they are not "do-gooders." Moreover, motives are modified by changing circumstances. Banks may merge in an attempt to establish monopolistic dominance. They may merge to get out of business or quickly to reach into new lending activities or to follow a shift in the location of de-

16. Remarks of Senator A. Willis Robertson, *Congressional Record*, vol. 105 (1959), p. 8075.

17. *Ibid.* See also Senate Report No. 196, 86th Cong., 1st Sess. (1959), especially pp. 16ff.

posits. I do not know how one could go about untangling these motives, nor do I think that much in the way of a principle – or even a rule of thumb – could be developed to do so. Even if it could, good motives should hardly excuse a merger if monopolistic effects are present.

It suffices to assume the motive to merger is profit. In fact, if we really take the enterprise system seriously, we *must* assume that it is the profit motive that assembles resources to meet needs and that it is ordinarily an efficient and workable apparatus for this purpose. If this is accepted, regulating agencies need not enter into vastly complicated deliberations on whether the motives for a given merger are in the "public interest." If the regulatory body cannot demonstrate a significant reduction or potential reduction in competition – a significant reduction in the alternatives of bank customers – it should conclude that the merger is not repugnant to the public interest. Such an approach would have the virtue of avoiding *ex cathedra* judgments on whether the profit motive ought or ought not to be allowed scope in particular merger cases. It also has the virtue of assuming that banks are best able to judge their stockholders' interests.

But what of the interests, convenience, and needs of the public? Will these also be served by this posture? In large part the answer to this question is implicit in the answer to the question "Do banks pay attention to their community's demand for bank services?" I think they do. A successful bank will be one which is able to determine or forecast its community's needs and shape the array of its service offerings to the pattern of demand. An unsuccessful bank will be one which does not attempt to determine or continually fails to forecast demand. A bank that persists in error or stubbornly refuses to adapt its service line, will experience declining earnings (customers will go elsewhere) and will become a failing rather than a going or growing concern. If other banks feel that this bank is not realizing the earnings potential of the area, they will have reason to consider the bank as a valuable piece of property and bid for it or attempt to enter the area *de novo*. In short, if the banking system is competitive, and if regulation is not misguided, a community's convenience and needs are not long unserved. This is the same as saying that earnings result from satisfying demand, not from not satisfying it. If there is a rule of thumb to be observed, it might be stated as follows: allow banks the judgment of their own best interest; the public's interest will best be served by vigorously promoting and maintaining competition.

The key to promoting and maintaining competition is a merger policy which explicitly recognizes the nature of the bank as a multiple-product, multiple-market firm. As I have emphasized above, banks do not sell *a* product in *a* market but rather sell a range of products in a series of markets to borrowers having differential borrowing mobilities. The effect of mergers among banks must, thus, be judged in terms of the merger's impact on the structures of the multiple markets in which the banks participate – a judgment which, so far as I can see, reduces in the typical case to an assessment of the impact of the merger on the alternatives of the consumer and small business seeking demand deposit services and small loan accommodations. In any event, a sound merger policy must await empirical researches attempting to specify workable product and market concepts. Remarkably little energy has been spent in this direction.

Some feel that the regulatory agencies are incapable of a proper assessment of the problems in bank competition and merger. Perhaps they are right. I am, however, more optimistic because I believe that the considerations irrelevant to merger questions will largely vanish on proper exposure and that the durable consideration of competition can become the core of a consistent merger policy.

CHAPTER 11

Competitive Policy for Transportation?[1]

BY MERTON J. PECK

Introduction

The question mark added to the title reflects the fact that the central question in transportation is the extent to which competition should be substituted for the existing forms of direct regulation. Elsewhere in the economy, apart from the special case of public utilities, it is a settled question that competition should be the dominant public policy, although as the other papers in this volume demonstrate, such agreement on the first principle leaves economists and lawyers a delightful margin of dispute over the meaning of competition and how to achieve it.

In transportation, public policy took the quite different form of extensive direct regulation. The Interstate Commerce Commission now controls rates, entry, and service of interstate rail, water, and motor carriers.[2] These controls represent the culmination of a 75-year history in which each major piece of transportation legislation since the Interstate Commerce Commission Act of 1887 has increased the regulatory authority of the ICC.

1. I wish to acknowledge the valued suggestions of my Brookings Institution colleagues, Edward Denison and Joseph Pechman.

2. The Civil Aeronautics Board exercises similar controls over aviation. In addition, state commissions exercise controls over intrastate traffic. Since truck, rail, and water transportation are often close substitutes in freight carriage, I have concentrated upon these sectors of the transportation industries.

Competitive Policy for Transportation

The Transportation Message of April 5, 1962, by the late President Kennedy, was widely hailed as a reversal of this historical trend of increasing regulation. It called for "greater reliance on the forces of competition and less reliance on the restraints of regulation." More specifically the Message proposes the elimination of all minimum rate regulation for bulk commodities where substantial nonregulated transportation now exists. The Congressional Commerce Committees held hearings in the summer of 1962 on the specific legislation implementing the Message, but adjourned before filing their reports. These hearings clearly identified the warring parties; the proponents being the railroads and the executive branch, the opponents being the water carriers, the truckers, and the majority of the Interstate Commerce Commission.

This paper examines, first, the economic costs of the present regulatory policy; second, the specific Presidential proposals for deregulation; and third, some further solutions to the organization of transportation.[3]

The Failures of Regulation

The general tone of the Presidential Message was a vote of no confidence in the regulatory process – delivered with perhaps undue cruelty on the seventy-fifth birthday of the ICC. Since the Message also proposed that "practices by carriers freed of minimum

3. The Transportation Message is a comprehensive statement of transportation policy, including sections on taxation, passenger traffic, urban mass transportation, and international transportation. Since these topics are not central to competitive policy, I cheerfully leave their discussion to others. The Presidential Message has a fairly substantial discussion of railroad and airline mergers – matters of obvious central importance to competitive policy. But the discussion really says no more than that there are good and bad mergers and it is difficult to tell one from another. I shall follow this precedent on this topic and forego a substantive discussion of the current enthusiasm for transportation mergers.

rate regulations would be covered by existing laws against monopoly and predatory trade practices," the implied long-run objective is to reduce the uniqueness of transportation policy and to bring public policy here in line with that for the rest of the economy.

Such a direction of change is not, I think, prompted by an abstract desire for policy uniformity or consistency. The Kennedy administrative style exhibited a New England pragmatism and Irish concreteness rather than a search for intellectual tidiness. I read the Message as reflecting two assumptions: first, that the transportation sector today represents a singularly inefficient allocation of resources — capital and labor; and, second, that competition rather than regulation is the best way of improving the allocation of transportation resourccs.

Inefficient allocation of transportation resources is defined here as an allocation that falls substantially short of meeting the transportation needs of the economy with a minimum total expenditure of resources. More concretely, rails carry a great deal of short haul and small lot traffic that could more cheaply move by truck, and trucks carry long haul and bulk traffic that could more cheaply move by rail. The overall extent of such a misallocation cannot be completely quantified with present data. Using only partial information, a study of relative costs of transportation in which I collaborated indicated a substantial degree of misallocation.[4] With more complete data, my guess would be

4. John R. Meyer, Merton J. Peck, John Stenason, and Charles Zwick, *The Economics of Competition in the Transportation Industries* (Cambridge, Mass., 1959). Much of this paper draws from ideas in that work, although I must take sole responsibility for the interpretation. Some ideas are also borrowed from my "Transportation in the American Economy" in *American Economic History*, Seymour Harris, ed. (New York, 1961), pp. 340-365.

that the "price" of the present misallocation would turn out to be several billion dollars per year.

A major source of the misallocation is, I would argue, the high degree of economic price discrimination in transportation rates. Economists generally define price discrimination as price differences that do not reflect cost differences. Price discrimination so defined is a long-standing characteristic of railroad rates, though it is better known as value-of-service rate-making. In 1956 railroad rates ranged from a low of 15 percent to a high of 566 percent of fully distributed costs.[5] The elaborate detail of railroad price discrimination explains the existence of 75,000 tariffs, including a distinction between horses for slaughter and draft horses, sand for glass manufacture and sand for cement, and lime for industrial use and lime for agriculture.[6] Table 1 indicates the general direction of the price discrimination. Manufactures and miscellaneous traffic bear a substantially higher mark-up over out-of-pocket rail costs than commodities of lower value such as minerals or agricultural products. Although such discrimination is of long standing, it has narrowed since 1939.

Through the 1920's the railroads, at least collectively, had the monopoly that extensive price discrimination requires.[7] Not only could railroads practice price discrimination, but most distinguished economists of that day argued that they should. The argument for price discrimination or value-of-service rate-making was that

5. U.S. Interstate Commerce Commission, Bureau of Accounts, "Cost Finding and Valuation, Distribution of the Rail Revenues by Commodity Groups, 1956."

6. D. Phillip Locklin, *Economics of Transportation* (Homewood, 1954), p. 455.

7. This discussion ignores the problem of competition between railroads and water carriers, important for some locations and commodities even in the 1920's. In addition there was intrarail competition which was moderated by the introduction of the ICC.

TABLE 1

Ratio of Rail Carload Revenues to Out-of-Pocket Costs

	1939	1949	1959
Agricultural Products	135%	142%	122%
Animal and Animal Products	125	128	109
Products of Mines	178	129	113
Products of Forests	153	135	122
Manufactures and Miscellaneous	203	192	159
ALL TRAFFIC	172	157	135

SOURCE: 1939 and 1949: ICC Bureau of Accounts and Cost Finding, *Distribution of the Rail Revenue Contribution by Commodity Groups – 1952,* (1955), pp. 8-9; 1959: *Distribution . . . by Commodity Groups – 1960* (1962), p. 11.

low rates on commodities that would not move otherwise (high elasticity of demand) and that covered the additional costs of their carriage would make some contribution to railroad fixed costs. Thus, such traffic would ease the burden on the higher price traffic and make fuller use of society's heavy investment in railroad roadbeds. Value-of-service rate-making would also add to railroad profits. Consequently, it was argued that with differential rates everyone would be gainers and no one would be a loser – the welfare economists' ideal.

The appearance of competitive alternatives to the railroads, beginning in the 1930's with large-scale trucking, the revival of the waterways, and the construction of pipelines eliminated the monopoly required by this kind of pricing. This fact – the relative decline of the railroads and rise of their competitors – is clear from the changing distribution of traffic shown in Table 2. The major factor in the shift of traffic was the technological changes that made it possible for these newer forms of transportation to develop. Yet the value-of-service railroad rates played a contributing role, particularly in connection with the growth of trucking. The truckers, naturally enough, concentrated their traffic-gathering activities on the high-profit traffic of the railroads, that is, as Table 1 indicates, on the *manufactures and miscellaneous traffic.* Here the motor carriers could successfully compete even though both their average and marginal costs were higher than the railroads, for it was on such traffic that the railroads recouped a major portion of their overhead. The consequences were obvious; traffic was shifted from the low-cost to the high-cost carrier, and the resulting loss for the railroads of their overhead-contributing traffic had a major impact on their financial fortunes.[8]

We should be careful, however, not to overrate resource misallocation associated with the rise of trucking. For a considerable volume of traffic, trucks were, in fact, the low-cost carrier when allowance was made for the inventory and warehouse savings of the shipper made possible by the quicker and small shipment characteristics of truck transportation. But there were enough shifts from the low-cost to the high-cost mode of transportation, as measured in the sum of shipper

8. These consequences were clearly seen at the time. The ICC Annual Report for 1938 states that since value-of-service rate-making had "resulted in rates disproportionately high from a cost standpoint, it has provided opportunities for competitors that might not have otherwise existed. Where rail freight rates have been considerably higher than the cost of service would justify . . . trucks and waterlines have not been slow in availing themselves of the opportunity to compete." Quoted in Henry J. Friendly, *The Federal Administrative Agencies* (Cambridge, Mass., 1962), Chapter VI, p. 111. But this foresight was not matched with effective action.

TABLE 2

Percent Distribution of Intercity Ton-Miles by Form of Transportation

	1930	1935	1940	1945	1950	1955	1960
Railroads	74%	68%	61%	67%	57%	49%	44%
Truck, Private, and For-Hire	4	6	10	7	16	18	22
Pipelines	5	10	10	12	12	16	17
Waterways	17	16	19	14	15	17	17
Rivers and Canals	n.a.	n.a.	(4)	(3)	(5)	(8)	(9)
Great Lakes	n.a.	n.a.	(15)	(11)	(10)	(9)	(8)
	100%	100%	100%	100%	100%	100%	100%

SOURCE: *ICC Seventy-Sixth Annual Report* (1962), p. 16, and James C. Nelson, *Railroad Transportation and Public Policy* (Washington, 1959).

and carrier costs, to produce the misallocation of transportation resources that now confronts us.[9]

In response to the growth of intercity trucking ICC regulation was extended to the motor carriers, thus permitting regulatory policy to maintain value-of-service rate-making. In administering rail and truck rates, the ICC held to the general view that rail rate reductions to meet truck competition should be limited to those necessary "to regain or to retain a fair share of the traffic."[10] In practice this meant parity between truck and rail rates, so that the division of traffic turned

9. Business logistics, the newest wrinkle in traffic research, places great premium on formally analyzing the overall costs of distribution, although shippers have obviously always done so on a more informal basis. For a discussion of business logistics, see E. Grosvenor Plowman, "For Good or Ill, Users Influence Transportation," *The Annals of the American Academy of Political and Social Science* (January, 1963), pp. 6-13.

10. For a lucid discussion of the founderings of the ICC in minimum rate regulation, see Henry J. Friendly, *op.cit.*

largely on service competition in which the trucks had an inherent advantage.[11] Thus, the ICC's rate policy (1) denied the shipper the advantages of the lower-cost transportation by rail, (2) diverted resources toward the high cost carrier, (3) added capacity to the nonrailroad sectors of transportation at a time when the railroads had substantial excess capacity, and (4) encouraged the growth of private truckers as a way for a shipper of higher rate commodities to escape the consequences of value-of-service rate-making. Surely this is almost a *prima facie* case of resource misallocation.

It would, however, be an obvious oversimplification to make value-of-service rate-making the sole culprit in the misallocation of transportation resources. A balanced view would recognize the effects of the maintenance of uneconomical rail service, the public provision of transportation facilities without adequate user's charges, the resistance of unions to cost-reducing technical changes, the possible failings of carrier management, and the unwise specifics of regulatory administration. But since the focus here is on prices and competition, there is no need to examine all of these factors. Indeed, since prices and competition are the crux of the present transportation difficulties, this parochialism may well be an asset.

11. On occasion the ICC did allow the railroads to charge lower than truck rates to offset their service disadvantages. One of the difficulties in generalizing in this field is that ICC decisions are like the Bible; textual support can be found for any position. I rely on Professor Williams' summary of his study of 900 truck-rail decisions as follows: "The attitude of the Commission has not been fixed and certain. In some cases it has ignored service differences and insisted upon rate parity, or at least disapproved rail reductions below the motor carrier basis. In other instances it has permitted differentials. And in a number of cases, it has permitted rates below motor rates by the amount of the proved added costs to the shipper of using rail reserves." Ernest W. Williams, Jr., *The Regulation of Rail-Motor Rate Competition* (New York, 1958), p. 44.

The Prospects for Competition

The preceding harsh words about economic consequences of regulation do not prove the case for deregulation, unless one emulates Professor Stigler's king, who in judging between two singers, heard only the first before awarding the prize to the second. Relying on competition also has problems which can best be examined in the context of the specific propoasls for deregulation.

The Proposals for Deregulation. The President's proposals for deregulation were limited to removing minimum rate regulation for traffic in bulk and agricultural commodities. The ICC would retain its other regulatory powers on such traffic, including control of maximum rates and the right to disallow rates granting undue preference. No changes were proposed for the regulation of other traffic.

Yet the two commodity classes proposed for deregulation account for 44 percent of rail revenue and 70 percent of rail tonnage, 47 percent of ICC regulated water carrier revenue and 84 percent of the tonnage, and 22 percent of ICC regulated truck revenue and 55 percent of truck tonnage.[12] The discrepancy between revenue and tonnage is explained by the fact that bulk and agricultural commodities both have shorter hauls and carry lower rates than other traffic.[13] And as discussed subsequently, minimum rate regulation may be the most economically significant form of regulatory control.

12. *Transportation Act Amendments — 1962,* Hearings before the House Committee on Interstate and Foreign Commerce, 87th Cong., 2d Sess. (1962), p. 161. Hence forth cited as *House Hearings.*

13. These data omit the unregulated carriers. On the waterways about 90 percent of the traffic is now exempt from regulation. Data are not available on the bulk and agricultural commodity traffic of exempt and private motor carriers.

Bulk and agricultural commodities were selected for deregulation in part because unregulated carriers now compete for such traffic. Water transport of bulk commodities was exempted from regulation by the 1940 Transportation Act, which otherwise extended regulation to water traffic, because such traffic was not considered competitive with the regulated rail and motor carriers. During and immediately after the war, however, technological advances in tug design and in handling of large tows widened the range of bulk commodities that could be competitively carried on the Mississippi River system. (As indicated in Table 2, the share of river traffic in all traffic rose from 4 percent in 1940 to 9 percent in 1960.) Motor transport of agricultural commodities was exempted from regulation by the 1935 Motor Carrier Act, which otherwise extended regulation to motor carriers, on the grounds that farmers and small carriers serving the farm-to-market trade were not competitive with regulated transportation. Once more technological change, this time in the form of the large trailer truck, made the exemption economically significant, with exempt carriers hauling agricultural commodities hundreds of miles.[14]

The opponents of the provisions of the message rest their case largely on four predictions as to effects of re-

14. While comprehensive data on the growth of exempt traffic are lacking, the following truck receipts at Chicago as a percentage of total receipts illustrate the trend.

	1939	*1949*	*1955*
Two dairy products	52%	73%	89%
Seven fruits and vegetables	15	26	28
Four livestock groups	37	70	90
Four poultry and egg groups	66	86	98

SOURCE: Department of Agriculture, Agricultural Marketing Service, *The Marketing and Transportation Situation* (1956) p. 17, as quoted in James C. Nelson, *Railroad Transportation and Public Policy* (Washington, 1959), p. 61.

moving minimum rate regulations: (1) geographic price discrimination will become pervasive; (2) the railroads will engage in rate wars that will drive the truckers and water carriers out of business: (3) the competition among railroads will be ruinous; and (4) the final outcome will not improve the financial position of the railroads. The opponents of deregulation offer an alternative proposal—to place the regulated and unregulated carriers on a parity by extending regulation to the presently unregulated bulk water carriers and agricultural motor carriers.

The Brief Economics of Competition in the Transportation Industries.[15] To consider these objections to deregulation requires a brief economic profile of the rail, water, and motor carrier industries, including the staples of competitive analysis—concentration of sellers, economies of scale, and the relative costs of the different modes of transportation.

The railroads are, of course, the highly concentrated sector of transportation. Although there are over one hundred Class I railroads, the major cities are connected by one to five railroads, with the smaller communities seldom served by more than one. Most of the longer-haul traffic passes over major routes which have more than one but never more than six railroads.

Common carrier trucking represents the other extreme—one of the most atomistic industries in the economy. The hundred largest firms realize about half the common carrier revenues, the next 2,000 firms a quarter, and the 14,000 smallest firms account for the rest. Of course, the numbers are considerably fewer on individual routes, but the higher volume routes have as many as sixty carriers. Inland water carriers are likewise a highly unconcentrated industry of about

15. See Meyer, *et al.*, for a fuller discussion, *op.cit.*, particularly Chapter VII.

1,000 firms in total, with numerous carriers operating on the high volume routes.

These differences in market structure are easily explainable by obvious differences in technology. The trailer-truck and the tug-barge are highly divisible units of capital and so available equally to large and small firms. The railroad is a relatively indivisible and capital-intensive collection of roadbed, switching yards, and terminals, all of which preclude small firms. The differing technologies not only create differences in economies of scale; they also create differences in the relative importance of fixed and variable costs. With capital highly divisible and easily transferred from one route to another, costs in trucking and waterways are variable with changes in traffic, whereas the indivisibilities and immobility of capital in railroads create a substantial proportion of fixed costs, at least in the short run. Exactly what proportion of rail costs are fixed depends on the time period selected, but for the purposes of this discussion it may suffice to regard about a third of rail costs at today's traffic volume as fixed, allowing about a decade for adjustment to changed traffic volumes.

Costs vary not only by type of carrier but also by type of shipment and other characteristics of the haul. The "cost" of each type of carrier is a nonsense number, for relative cost rankings vary with type of traffic, volume, terminal facilities at the origin and destination points, length of haul, availability of return traffic, and the time period for adjustment of capacity to traffic. Yet this analysis requires some notion of relative long-run cost standing of the different modes of transport (where "long-run" means a sufficient time period, say a decade, to adjust capacity to volume). For traffic ideally suited to river barges (large volumes, little value placed on early delivery, both origin and destination on the water so transshipment is not required, and so forth), the water carriers have at least a 50 percent long-run cost advantage over the railroads. Similarly for traffic clearly suited to railroads (private siding at both ends, long hauls, and so forth), the railroads have at least a 50 percent advantage over the trucks.[16] Trucks, on the other hand, have a cost advantage for shorter hauls, for small shipments, and along routes with low traffic volumes. But a good deal of traffic does not fall into these "ideal" cases, so that there is a volume of traffic where the identity of the low-cost carrier is not clearly apparent.

Thus, the various types of carriers in direct competition with one another are strikingly dissimilar in firm size, market structure, and cost characteristics. Such differences account for the difficulties of forecasting the outcome of competition in transportation and, indeed, of devising a workable public policy.

Geographic Price Discrimination. Geographic price discrimination, involving the first of the four objections to deregulation, means geographic rate differences unrelated to cost differences. Existing rail rates are characterized by a considerable degree of geographic price discrimination – the most extreme and obvious examples being the "long and short haul" cases where traffic carried the greater distance is charged a rate less than traffic carried a shorter distance over the same route.[17] The marked instances of geographic price discrimination are associated with the prevalence of water competition, where historically the railroads cut rates to meet water competition while leaving inland rates unchanged. While the ICC largely accepted the

16. Under other assumptions the difference is four to one. See Meyer, *et al.*, *ibid.*, Chapter VI.

17. Specific ICC approval, however, is now and would be required for this particular kind of geographic discrimination, although not for less obvious cases.

geographically discriminatory rate structure it inherited, the effect of its regulation has been to moderate the railroad efforts to reduce rates to meet water competition. The opponents of deregulation predict that with the removal of minimum rate regulation, the railroads will reduce rates even further to meet water competition, thus adding to the degree of geographic discrimination.[18]

The objections to a greater degree of geographic price discrimination center, first, on the possibility that railroads would raise their rates on inland traffic to offset the rate reductions on water-competitive traffic. The difficulty with this argument is that if the railroads can raise rates on inland points, why have they not already done so? Railroad mangement is certainly under considerable pressure to increase prices, in view of a 1960 return on railroad stockholders' equity of 2.21 percent.[19] Nor is regulation a limiting factor. The ICC has repeatedly voiced its concern over low rail earnings and has not to any major extent prevented rate increases. From the 173,248 rail, motor, and water tariffs filed with the ICC in 1962, the Suspension Board of the ICC considered only 5,170, the others becoming effective without formal regulatory review. Of these 5,170 rates, about 95 percent were rate decreases so that, as noted previously, the intervention of the ICC in rate-making is directed largely at preventing rate reductions rather than rate increases.[20] I would submit the reason inland rates are not now increased is that intracarrier competition, the railroads' concern with the competi-

18. Railroad witnesses argue that the reduced rates to meet water competition tend to spread to inland points. While evidence indicates there is this diffusion effect, the present existence of substantial geographic price discrimination would indicate it is by no means an automatic result.

19. ICC, *Seventy-Sixth Annual Report* (1962), p. 214.

20. Of the 5,170 rates, 4,712 were decreases, 212 increases, and 173 both increases and decreases, *ibid.*, p. 42.

tive standing of its shippers, intercarrier competition, and political prudence hold inland rail rates down. Lower rail rates on water-competitive traffic would not remove these restraints on inland rail rates.

A second argument against more geographic discrimination is more compelling. The water-located towns, of course, have an inherent advantge over inland towns, which only the most rigid kind of regulation could alter. The removal of rate regulation would intensify their advantage, for the railroads could cut rates and the barge lines could meet the competition, thus further adding to the inherent advantage of river and lake towns over inland cities. But surely the question that ought to be asked is how large such an additional advantage would be.

The revitalization of inland waterways has been the significant factor in the river location of such transportation-intensive operations as large coal-fired electric power plants serving aluminum reduction plants on the Ohio River. Yet deregulation will have little effect on such operations, for here the advantages of water transportation are so decisive that the railroads cannot compete. Rather, deregulation would affect traffic on the margin between rail and water. I estimate such marginal traffic to be about 10 percent of the current revenue of the inland waterways or $140 million.[21] Rate reductions that affect traffic volume of this magnitude, even if the reductions spread to other traffic, will hardly induce a large-scale relocation of industry. Yet the uncertainties, particularly in a system where political representation is on a geographic basis, damp-

21. I base the percentage estimate upon the type of tonnage carried by water carriers. The sources of the estimate of revenue are given in Table 3. The distressing feature of the extensive Congressional testimony is the lack of quantitative estimates of the effect of deregulation. This omission is rightly bothering Congressmen. See *House Hearings*, *op.cit.*, p. 419.

ens Congressional interest in deregulation. The problem, however, can be kept within manageable bounds because the ICC will retain the power to prevent undue preference on specific rail rates, and thus the Commission can limit the extent of geographic discrimination. Nonetheless, some increase in the extent of geographic discrimination may be reckoned as a cost of deregulation.

Intramodal Competition. The hypothetical computations of the preceding paragraph raise the second objection to deregulation – that the railroads will cut rates and eliminate their truck and water competitors, and then raise rates to monopoly levels.

The costs of the water carriers are a quarter to a half that of the railroads for much of their traffic. Indeed, for this traffic the bulk water rates, now unregulated, are largely determined by competition among water carriers and the latent opportunity for private water carriage by big shippers.[22] Thus, even though 85 percent of water traffic is bulk commodities for which rail minimum rate regulation would be removed, the cost advantages of water, as noted above, would protect this traffic from rail competition. Traffic on the margin between water and rail is estimated in the preceding section as about 10 percent of current water traffic. The transfer of such volumes of traffic would leave a viable water carrier industry.

The rail-motor cost comparison favors the railroads by about the same two-to-four factor that exists between rail and water. About 24 percent of the regulated motor carrier revenue is realized in bulk and agricultural commodities. I would hazard a guess that no more than half this traffic can be regained by the rails,

22. The importance of competition between water carriers would explain the long-standing sentiment in favor of regulation for themselves by executives of the common carrier barge lines.

which would reduce truck industry revenues again by 10 percent. Again, a traffic shift of this magnitude would leave a viable trucking industry.

Thus, I would argue that the kind of competition involved would shift no more than 10 percent or so of their present revenues from the trucks and water carriers. Both of these are variable cost industries and could economically adjust in a relatively short time to a lower volume, though they can hardly be happy at such a reduction in their sales. Indeed, extrapolating the postwar growth trends of trucking and river water traffic shows that a 10 percent shift of traffic would be more than recovered by the trucking industry in two years and by the inland waterways in three years.[23]

Intrarailroad Competition. Another argument against removing minimum rate regulation is that, without such controls, rate wars between railroads will jeopardize their financial stability. This argument assumes that railroads differ from other small numbers markets like steel or automobiles where, if I read the records of the late Senator Kefauver's hearings on administered prices correctly, violent price-cutting has not been a major problem. To be sure, the railroads prior to their regulation had a history of rate wars, but it is often forgotten that the rate wars were the exception and rate stability the rule.[24]

23. From 1939 to 1959, excluding four war years, the annual growth in ton-miles for all common carriers averaged 4 percent, with the following distribution between transportation sectors: 9 percent for unregulated motor carriers, 8.6 percent for regulated carriers, 38 percent for pipelines, 3.5 percent for inland waterways, and 2 percent for railroads. Data from Arthur P. Hurter, "A Summary of a Theory of Private Carriage and Its Empirical Testing" (paper presented at the Conference on Private and Unregulated Transportation, Northwestern University, October 29-30, 1962).

24. Professor Troxel states: "References to rate wars are common in historical writings on transportation. Perhaps this follows from the business mind that sees even an occasional extremity in

We should note, however, that the likelihood of rate wars is increased by the fact that the bill providing for deregulation also removes the antitrust exemption of railroad rate conferences for other than joint or through rates. Railroad men will no longer be able legally to discuss rates with one another. While it is true that railroad rates are more complex than other prices, the public filing of rates combined with a 30-day notice and the illegality of off-list pricing should strengthen the oligopolistic discipline of a small numbers market. Thus, the elimination of rate bureaus would probably have little effect. There may be somewhat more rate innovation, since the practice of full discussion of rates with competitors and near unanimity for rate bureau decisions may dampen experimentation.[25] The railroads, of course, have always had the option of filing rates independently of the rate bureaus.[26]

The Effects on the Railroads. A final contention is that deregulation would not improve the financial position of the railroads. While the Presidential proposals ought not to be viewed as a rescue operation for one industry, the persistent low profits of the railroad

price competition as a terrifying event. Or perhaps it follows from habitual concern for person-to-person struggles. In any event, for every rate war we can count many more, possibly thousands or tens of thousands of days, of no rate wars. There were some spectacular rate pricing conflicts in the earlier days of railroad; e.g., a few battles for Chicago to New York traffic were notable. Yet order was soon restored in each instance and most buyers throughout the country had infrequent experience with competitive bargains in railroad rates." Emery Troxel, *Economics of Transport* (New York, 1955), p. 428.

25. The rate bureaus have also provided a forum for shippers to state their views on rate changes, which is considered by some to be beneficial. A railroad could still discuss rate changes with its customers.

26. There seems to be more independent pricing by railroads in recent years. See the testimony of Jervis Langdon, President of the Baltimore and Ohio, *House Hearings*, p. 297.

industry surely acted as a catalyst for a change in transportation policy. Therefore, a crude estimate of how deregulation might affect the profits of the railroad industry is in order.

I emphasize the adjective "crude," for such a calculation requires arbitrary assumptions and the use of considerably less than ideal data. In Table 3 it is estimated that deregulation might double rail profits. Suppose these estimates are correct. Railroad profits before taxes would then be at about their 1956 levels, a year in which the railroads were hardly considered financially prosperous. Only if these estimates understate the effect on railroad profits by a factor of two would railroad profits be above the postwar peak of 1952. If on the other hand, as I think likely, the estimate in Table 3 is 50 percent too high, the effect would be to restore rail profits to about their 1957 level. The preceding remarks about 1956 apply with more emphasis to 1957.[27]

The calculations show, then, that deregulation is likely to turn the clock back to recent years of better, although absolutely not very good, railroad profits. Thus, I would argue that deregulation falls considerably short of a cure for the ills of the railroads. I find unpersuasive, however, the view that deregulation would make the railroads worse off, which is based on either a proposition that rate reductions will not shift traffic from one carrier to another (which is unsupported by the evidence in numerous rate hearings),[28] or that the railroads will conduct ruinous rate wars, a point discussed above. My conclusion that deregulation will make the railroads better off is confirmed by the vigor

27. Profit data from Department of Commerce, *Survey of Current Business* (July, 1962), and *U.S. Income and Output* (Washington, 1958), Table VI-17.

28. Nelson, *op.cit.*, Chapters 3, 10.

TABLE 3

Estimated Effect of Deregulation on Railroad Profits
(millions of dollars)
(three-year average – 1957, 1958, and 1959)

I. Assumed Existing Revenue Diversions to the Railroads by Deregulation	
1. 10% of for-hire truck revenue other than agriculture	$670
2. 25% of agricultural commodity carriers revenues	475
3. 5% of the private trucking traffic	390
4. 10% of the bulk water carrier revenues	140
TOTAL	1675
II. Allowance for Change in Rail Rates to Divert Traffic	–460
Net railroad gain	1215
III. Rail Out-of-Pocket Cost to Serve the Additional Traffic (2/3 the gain in revenue)	–805
IV. Addition to Profits Before Tax	410
V. 1957-1959 Rail Profits Before Tax	+483
VI. Recomputed Profits	$893

NOTES:

The methods underlying Table 3 are extremely straightforward; Item I provides an estimate of the percentage of existing revenues that might be diverted to railroads, II adjusts these revenues downward to reflect the reduction in rail rates to shift the traffic from other modes of transportation, III deducts the rail out-of-pocket costs to serve the additional traffic, IV provides the addition to gross profits before income taxes, V simply indicates 1959 profits, and VI provides the resulting gross profits. Data are a three-year average for 1957, 1958, and 1959, the last three years for which data were available. The three-year averages minimize the unique economic circumstances of any one year.

SOURCE OF THE ESTIMATES:

I. Total intercity motor carrier revenue – common, contract, private, exempt, and intrastate was derived by adding the reported revenue for ICC Class I, II, and III motor carriers and the imputed revenue for other carriers, computed as the product of the ton-miles for such carriers (from Bureau of Public Road Surveys) times the intercity revenue per ton-mile of contract carriers. This assumed that private and exempt carrier revenues are more like those of contract than common carriers. (Contract carriers charging has fewer value-of-service elements.) The total revenue series on this basis was available only through 1955 (Department of Commerce, *Modern Transport Policy,* 1956, pp. 73-74). Projections for 1957, 1958, and 1959 assumed total carrier revenue increased by the same percentage from 1955 as corporate highway traffic and warehousing sales in the national income tables (i.e., 19 percent, Department of Commerce, *Survey of Current Business,* July 1962, Table 49, p. 27). The justification for such procedure was the proportional division of ton-miles between private and common carriers has been relatively stable since 1939. Following these methods, average annual total truck revenues for 1957-1959 were estimated as $16.4 billion.

The total motor revenues of $16.4 billion were than allocated as follows: $6.7 billion to ICC motor carriers (ICC estimate, Supplement to ICC *Annual Report.* 1962, p. 144), leaving $9.7 billion for other carriers. This $9.7 billion was in turn divided between agricultural ($1.9) and private ($7.8) carriers in proportion to the relative ICC vehicle registrations of each.

Ten percent of the revenue of motor common carriers was assumed to be subject to rail diversion, as discussed in the text. All the present agricultural carrier traffic would be subject to deregulated rail competition. I interpret the papers presented at the Conference on Private and Unregulated Transportation, Northwestern University, October 29-30, 1962, as indicating that trucks have a substantial service advantage in agricultural commodities and much of the traffic is still under 100 miles. Therefore, 25 percent of the revenue of agricultural carriers was assumed to be subject to rail diversion. Finally, the conference material indicated that private carrier taffic was even more short-haul and service-oriented than agricultural carriers. Furthermore, much of this traffic was manufactures and miscellaneous commodities, which were not subject to deregulation. Therefore, 5 percent, half the percentage for common carriers, was assumed to be subject to rail diversion.

The revenue for water carriers was computed from the annual average of 1957-1959 corporate sales of water transportation ($2.75 billion, *Survey of Current Business,* July 1962, p. 27) by subtracting estimated ocean carrier sales. This figure, of course, includes exempt carriers. I have made no allowance for private water carriage, since most such traffic is on the margin between common and private water carriage, not rail and water. The 10 percent estimate for diversion is discussed previously in the text.

II. Estimates in Meyer *et al., op.cit.,* Appendix D, indicate rail rates must be about 20 percent below those of truck to offset the service advantages of truck. In addition, allowance must be made for (1) the possibility that trucks will in turn reduce their rates to meet rail reduction, thus requiring further rail reductions and (2) with which railroad executives argue for deregulation.[29]

Extending Regulation to the Nonregulated Carriers. The opponents of deregulation offer an alternative – extend regulation to the presently nonregulated water carriers of bulk commodities and restrict the scope of the agricultural commodity exemption. These two unregulated sectors of transportation are doing extraordinarily well; they show a marked growth in traffic, both have a good record of cost-reducing technological change, and both the majority of shippers and the carriers (apart from the common carrier barge lines) appear content with their unregulated status. Thus, regulation would be extended largely to protect other sectors of the transportation industry.

the rate reductions given to existing rail traffic which falls into the same general category as the traffic shifted from the trucks. (The second item reflects the fact that the railroad cannot entirely seal off existing traffic from the competitive reductions made to attract new traffic.) These two secondary effects are estimated to amount to another 10 percent of the revenues diverted from the trucks. Thus, revenues of traffic shifted from truck to rail are reduced by 30 percent in order to indicate the revenue gain of the railroads.

The diversion of traffic from water to rail is the converse case in that here the railroads have the service advantage. Hence, the railroads should be able to shift traffic from the water carriers at rates higher than existing water rates. These higher rates are assumed to offset the two secondary effects discussed in the preceding paragraph. Thus, the $140 million in revenues diverted from water to rail is assumed to be transferred to the railroads on an equal dollar basis.

III. Short-run out-of-pocket costs appear to be about two-thirds of rail revenues.

V. 1957-1959 rail profits before income taxes from the *Survey of Current Business,* July 1962, Table 56.

29. Their belief in deregulation may also reflect the fervor of a convert. Until recently, the dominant view of railroad management was that regulation should be extended to the nonregulated carriers rather than removing regulation from the presently regulated.

Would such a change improve the allocation of transportation resources? Presumably its purpose and effect would be to raise rates in these unregulated sectors. Yet both are relatively susceptible to competition from private carriage so that higher rates here would add further to the overcapacity in the transportation industry and to the cost of transportation.

The Public Gains from Deregulation. The preceding examination of deregulation has been in economic terms. The Administration witnesses at the hearings tended to refute the possibility of predatory competition, price discrimination, and ruinous interrailroad competition by arguing that such behavior would be checked by the antitrust laws which would now apply to transportation. This leads to the conclusion, as Senator Monroney pointed out to Mr. Loevinger, then Assistant Attorney General in charge of the Antitrust Division, that "It would appear to me from your testimony that all we are asking for is transference of regulation which we now have from the ICC to the Courts."[30] But if our economic analysis is correct, competition can be largely self-maintaining, with the proviso that antitrust laws may be needed here, as in other industries, to treat pathological extremes.

Yet if deregulation will not result in major increases in geographic price-discriminating, destructive rail competition against water and motor carriers, or ruinous competition among railroads, and is of some aid to the hard-pressed railroads, there remains the question of what are the public benefits from this change in policy. They are, I would submit, lower transportation

30. *Proposed Amendments to Federal Transportation Laws*, Hearings before the Senate Committee on Commerce, 87th Cong., 2d sess. (1962), p. 84. Henceforth cited as *Senate Hearings.*

rates,[31] associated with some reduction in excess capacity in transportation by higher utilization of the railroad plant, matched by some withdrawal of capital in water carriage and trucking (or more likely a slower rate of growth in these sectors), and the transfer of some traffic by higher-cost trucking to lower-cost railroads. By the definition and analysis in the first part of this paper, these are changes in the direction toward a better allocation of transport resources.

Yet we ought not to expect too much. The adjustment will be via relatively small changes at the margins of the various sectors of transportation. Still, such marginal changes are the substance of economic analysis and even limited Washington experience creates an appreciation for small shifts in public policy in what one considers the right direction. There is, of course, the possibility that deregulation will sufficiently alter the entrepreneurial climate in the transportation industry sufficiently to trigger both marketing and technical innovations. In this way, the gains from deregulation would be much greater than estimated here. Even so, the specific Presidential proposals leave many questions of transportation policy untouched.

Longer-Run Solutions to the Organization of Transportation

In an academic environment, there is the duty to go beyond the present policy proposals and to consider more broadly and boldly what should be the overall

31. By the analysis in Table 3, the rate reductions would reduce the transportation cost by $460 million (item II), a not too impressive amount compared to the $20 billion expended in 1961 for purchased freight transportation. On the other hand, the difference between an efficient and inefficient economy is such differences in each industry which amount in aggregate to considerable.

direction of American transportation policy. Past experience suggests that the transportation problem will still be here, whatever the outcome of the specific proposals now being considered by Congress. After all, Mr. Childe, a transportation expert of fifty years' standing, began his Congressional testimony by noting, "During my lifetime there has always been a railroad problem serious enough to command the attention of Congress."[32]

Specifically I would suggest that the further changes in transportation policy ought to include fairly complete removal of direct Commission regulation of transportation, combined with the massive simplification of railroad rate structures. The final result would be a public policy for transportation that differs little from that for the rest of the economy.[33]

The Further Reduction of Regulation. If the proposals of the late President Kennedy become law, the ICC will retain (1) minimum rate regulation over all

32. *Senate Hearings, op.cit.*, p. 339.

33. These two measures are most directly related to competitive policy. I would rank as of equal importance in an overall transportation policy (1) considerable railroad disinvestment in branch lines, private sidings, and low density routes that can be more cheaply served by trucks, combined with investment in railroad modernization; (2) increased reliance on intermodal transportation such as truck-trailers or flat cars; and (3) freer entry into trucking. The rationale for these measures is discussed in Meyer, *et al.*, *op.cit.*, Chapter IX. I attach much less importance than most to a proper system of user taxes on water carriers and trucking, for I find the advantages of government-furnished public ways not too significant in the allocation of traffic between carriers. Water carriers now pay nothing, but these carriers have such significant cost advantage over the railroads for much of their traffic that user taxes would make little difference. Trucks now pay substantial user taxes and they ought to pay more, but again, even doubling user taxes would change truck costs by little. Thus, the case for user taxes is a matter of good government housekeeping, and it is on these grounds I support them. I exclude labor relations on the grounds of ignorance.

traffic other than bulk and agricultural commodities (2) maximum rate regulation for all traffic, and (3) the control of undue preference or discrimination between rates on all traffic.[34] In each case, however, ICC jurisdiction excludes the water carriage bulk commodities and private carriage, traffic now and always exempt from regulation. All the arguments for deregulation for bulk and agricultural commodities apply also to manufactured miscellaneous traffic, and for the latter there are additional arguments that reinforce the case for the removal of minimum rate regulation. Such traffic has traditionally been the high profit traffic of the railroads, so that, as Table 1 indicates, rates depart the most from rail costs. Thus, with the development of trucking, this kind of traffic has been the most subject to shifts from the low- to the high-cost carriers and hence a sector with considerable resource misallocation. Second, competition between truck and rail does not raise the problem of geographic price discrimination, since for-hire truck competition is widespread and private carriage is available to shippers. Third, rates are a much smaller proportion of the delivered price of the individual commodities in this group, so that shipper adjustments to rate changes introduced by competition is of lesser significance.

The political wisdom of excluding this traffic from the first step in deregulation is also clear. This traffic is not now subject to direct competition from for-hire, unregulated carriers, so that the competitive equality argument does not apply. An even more potent political reality is that this traffic is the life-blood of the trucking industry. Therefore, prudence suggests that deregu-

34. The ICC will also continue to control entry into all sectors of interstate surface for-hire transportation except, again, motor carriage of agricultural commodities and water carriage of bulk commodities.

lation be applied first to the bulk and agricultural commodities. But there seems no reason on economic grounds to distinguish between this traffic and that for which the removal of minimum rate regulation has already been proposed, except that the adjustment problem will be more severe for the trucking industry. Even here the service advantage of trucking would ensure the survival of a substantial long haul, for-hire trucking industry.

Maximum rate regulation was initially devised as a protection against excessive railroad profits. With the inadequate earnings problem, this function has disappeared along with the steam locomotive. Maximum rate regulation can still provide useful consumer protection against excessive rates on specific traffic that is not subject to intercarrier competition. As so applied, this control becomes indistinguishable from the third kind of control—the prevention of undue preference or discrimination between rates.

This regulatory control, I think, must remain. Competition in all parts of the economy is notoriously uneven, but outside of transportation it is difficult as a practical matter to separate out the various buyers, so that competition-induced, selective price reductions are eventually extended to most buyers. In transportation the fact that the purchase is consumed on the seller's property permits a high degree of discrimination, as the first section of this paper indicates. Furthermore, tradition by now allows considerable price discrimination in transportation rates. It is not only that high value commodities are generally charged more, but about 85 percent of rail traffic moves on "commodity" rates —that is, separate prices devised for individual commodities for specific origins and destinations. Such tailor-made pricing offers possibilities for the bargaining power of large shippers, management arbitrariness, and sheer inertia to create inequities between consumers of transportation.

Rate Simplification. One way out of this problem may be a massive simplification of the transportation rate structure to replace the present complex rate structure. A new rate structure could be based on such simple and objective phenomena as distance, special cost of handling a particular commodity, and so forth. The ICC might well take the lead in the simplification of the rate structure. A rate structure composed of a limited number of commodity classes would automatically reduce the unevenness of competition by forcing transportation companies, like manufacturing companies, to make price reductions on broad classes of products rather than to devise more special rates to meet specific competitive situations.[35] But such a rate simplification carries with it a danger that it might impose a new orthodoxy and rigidity upon the transportation system.

A Concluding Comment

I have indicated my view that a competitive policy is not only possible but desirable in transportation. To be sure, there will be problems, but they will be no more vexatious in transportation than in steel or the automobile industries. What is more decisive, the results of competition in transportation should be superior to what regulation is now achieving in terms of economic efficiency. Indeed, the failings of regulation provide an interesting insight into achievements of competition. As my collaborators and I wrote in 1958:

35. The President's Transportation Message states that Congress should "Direct the regulatory agencies to sanction experimental freight rates, modifications, and variations in systems of classification documentation, and new kinds or combinations of service." The context of the Message does not indicate whether the objective would be the kind of rate simplification I have discussed.

Merton J. Peck

"Thus in a very real sense, the American experience with transportation regulation stands as an eloquent, though negative, testimonial to the great strength of free enterprise: an ability to adapt quickly and efficiently to change in the economic environment."[36]

36. Meyer, *et al., op.cit.*, p. 272.

CHAPTER 12

Business Exemptions from the Antitrust Laws: their Extent and Rationale

BY WALTER ADAMS

Introduction

"The statesman, who should attempt to direct private people in what manner they ought to employ their capitals," Adam Smith wrote, "would not only load himself with a most unnecessary attention, but assume an authority which could safely be trusted to no council and senate whatever, and which would nowhere be so dangerous as in the hands of a man who had folly and presumption enough to fancy himself fit to exercise it."[1] Not the state, but the free play of market forces should determine the kinds of goods to be produced, the factors of production to be employed, and the division of distributive shares. Individual economic activity should be coordinated through an autonomous and impartial planning mechanism – one that is external to human control, manipulation, or perversion. Competition should serve the dual function of harnessing the individual to social ends, while depriving him of power so great that, if abused, it would result in harm to his fellows.

This is still the official credo of American free enterprise. It is the ideological façade of N.A.M. slogans –

1. *The Wealth of Nations* (New York, Modern Library ed., 1937), p. 423.

the ritual cant invoked on behalf of "rugged individualism," "rigorous competition," and "undiluted laissez-faire." It is the catechrestic catechism nurtured at home and the redemptive formula promoted abroad. It is, as Galbraith notes, the medicine which American businessmen would not think of taking themselves but which they unhesitatingly prescribe to others — especially to foreigners.[2]

Like other religious beliefs, the free enterprise dogma is no guarantee of behaviorial purity. The doctrine need not be translated into concrete action. Thus, American businessmen can embrace the official position articulated by spokesmen like Henry Ford II. They can proudly proclaim: "We believe that monopolies cause stagnation. We believe that our country could not prosper as it has without the benefit of sound antitrust legislation which has helped to keep us competitive over the past half-century. Though American businessmen may sometimes complain about the interpretation or administration of those laws, we know that — like spinach — they are good for us."[3] This is the official version of the creed. It accepts the regulatory mechanism of competition and the legal framework of antitrust. While tolerant of the government as umpire, it still holds that the government which governs least, governs best. It abhors socialistic interference and abjures the protection of the welfare state — at least, in theory.

The practice is quite different and, as the old proverb tells us, "it ain't what you pray for that counts, it's what you bet on." Despite its ideological precepts, American business seems to follow a course of compromise and pragmatism. It opposes governmental in-

2. *The East and West Must Meet: A Symposium* (East Lansing, 1959), p. 103.

3. Address by Henry Ford II to a group of German industrialists and government officials in Cologne, Germany, June 25, 1954.

tervention only when such intervention is clearly for someone else's benefit. It seems to have no qualms about accepting "socialistic" favors, privileges, and subsidies. (Apparently, it has no fears that governmental largesse will weaken *its* moral fibre.) Indeed, American business actively seeks particular forms of government interference. Its richly endowed lobbies wage a constant battle to manipulate the rules of the competitive game, to gain special advantages and immunities, and to secure protective shelter from the impersonal cruelties of competition. There is no frontal attack on the citadel of competition. The strategy is simply one of erosion, attrition, and subversion.

If I am correct, the study of antitrust policy and enforcement represents an unduly restricted approach to the public control problem. Covering an ever-narrowing sector of American industry, it leaves out of account the proliferation of exemptions and exceptions which tend to undermine the core of competitive philosophy and policy. In our preoccupation with antitrust, we may well be straining at a gnat while swallowing the camel.

The extent to which we have forsaken competition as a national policy is most dramatically illustrated by the simple listing of the statutory exemptions from the antitrust laws which appears in the Appendix to this paper. Some of these exemptions are partial, others complete. Some apply to particular industries or organizations, others immunize specific activities and practices. Some were originally installed in periods of depression, others in periods of war or defense mobilization. *All* were secured by the political influence of special interest groups which succeeded in persuading Congress to accord them private commercial advantage—ostensibly to promote some legitimate public purpose.

Obviously, these exemptions are piecemeal responses

to particular pressures and circumstances. They do not constitute integral parts of a master plan. Nor can they be easily reconciled or synthesized with the pattern of antitrust control. Their thrust, however, is unmistakable—reflecting a judgment by Congress that competition is not a paramount economic, social, or political objective. The pervasiveness of such exemptions, as Justice Frankfurter observed, indicates that competition is at best a coordinate, not paramount, goal of national policy. "That there is a national policy favoring competition cannot be maintained today without careful qualification. It is only in a blunt, undiscriminating sense that we speak of competition as an ultimate good. Certainly, even in those areas of economic activity where the play of private forces has been subjected only to the negative prohibitions of the Sherman Law, this Court has not held that competition is an absolute." In the exempt industries, this would be even more difficult. "To do so would disregard not only those areas of economic activity . . . in which active regulation has been found necessary to compensate for the inability of competition to provide adequate regulation. It would most strikingly disregard areas where policy has shifted from one of prohibiting restraints on competition to one of providing relief from the rigors of competition. . . ." Therefore, Justice Frankfurter concluded, "it is for us to recognize that encouragement of competition as such has not been considered the single or controlling reliance for safeguarding the public interest."[4]

In the pages which follow, I propose to discuss two major phenomena: exemption by regulation and exemption by administrative preemption.

4. *Federal Communications Commission* v. *RCA Communications, Inc.*, 346 U.S. 86 (1953), pp. 91-96.

Exemption by Regulation

The creation of independent regulatory commissions, exercising a potpourri of legislative, administrative, and judicial powers, and armed with the doctrine of primary jurisdiction, today constitutes the single most important explicit antitrust exemption. In creating this headless fourth branch of government, Congress did not intend to underwrite a total abandonment of competition. It did not make the antitrust laws wholly inapplicable to the regulated industries, nor did it authorize the commissions to ignore their policy. At the very least, Congress commanded the commissions, as an administrative matter, to take antitrust considerations into account. But the legislative mandate was so broad as to make commission discretion virtually unlimited.

Originally, Congress had hoped that the commissions would be staffed by men "bred to the facts" and imbued with a dispassionate professional expertise. The commissions, it was thought, would curb the power of the "economic royalists" by substituting rational planning, promotion, and policing for an ineffectual and anachronistic market mechanism. They would make the economic well-being of entire industries their bailiwick, and formulate policies directed "toward broad imaginative ends, conceived in terms of management rather than police."[5] This was the justification for extending the public utility concept from local, "natural" monopolies to nationwide industrial empires in transportation, communications, and energy. "This was the ultimate view that enthralled the New Dealer," says Professor Jaffe. "This was the torrid specter that terrified the world of private industry."[6]

5. James B. Landis, *The Administrative Process* (New Haven, 1938), pp. 13, 16 ff.

6. Louis L. Jaffe, "The Scandal in TV Licensing," *Harpers*, vol. 215 (September, 1957), p. 77.

In practice, neither the hopes nor the fears of the 1930's were realized. The independent regulatory commissions turned out to be a disastrous experiment in economic statecraft and an abomination of administrative law. They have been neither administratively independent nor politically responsible.[7] Their vaunted expertise has become a euphemism for red tape, ritualism, and harassment.[8] Canons of judicial

7. Marver H. Bernstein, *Regulating Business by Independent Commission* (Princeton, 1955).

8. Louis B. Schwartz, "Legal Restriction of Competition in the Regulated Industries: An Abdication of Judicial Responsibility," *Harvard Law Review*, vol. 67 (January, 1954), esp. pp. 471ff. The low repute which commission expertise enjoys in some judicial quarters is illustrated by Judge Frank's review of an I.C.C. valuation decision:

> If, however, the Commission is sustained in this case, and, accordingly, behaves similarly in future cases, then its conduct will indeed be a mystery. Its so-called valuations will then be acceptable, no matter how contrived. In that event, it would be desirable to abandon the word 'valuation' – since that word misleadingly connotes some moderately rational judgment — and to substitute some neutral term, devoid of misleading associations, such as 'aluation,' or, perhaps better still, 'woosh-woosh.' The pertinent doctrine would then be this: 'When the ICC has ceremonially woosh-wooshed, judicial scrutiny is barred.' It would then be desirable to dispense, too, with the Commission's present ritualistic formula, 'Taking into consideration, etc.' replacing it with patently meaningless words – perhaps the same words spelled backward, i.e., 'Gnikat otni noitaredisnoc, etc.,' Then no one would be foolish enough to believe that the figures in a Commission plan necessarily have anything to do with deliberation, but everyone would know that the figures might well have been the product of omphalic inspiration, or ornithomancy, or haruspication, or aleatory devices, and that the conclu-

ethics have been violated, and commission integrity shaken by periodic scandals.[9] Regulatory policy has been negative, unimaginative, wasteful, and restrictionist – characterized by undue limitation of entry, benign tolerance of mergers, sanction for anticompetitive rate and service agreements, erosion of interindustry rivalry, and outright suppression of yardstick competition.[10] In short, the commissions turned out to be handmaidens of the regulatees rather than protectors of the public – using their quasi-legislative, quasi-administrative, and quasi-judicial powers to build a never-never land of quasi-solutions.[11]

Two aspects of commission regulation deserve particular emphasis: the proclivity to neo-mercantilist protectionism and the related tedency toward euthanasia of competitive interlopers. Both have been accomplished under the guise of regulating entry, rates, and such business practices as collusive agreements and mergers. In the motor carrier industry, for example, the I.C.C. has repeatedly held that where existing carriers "have expended their money and energy in developing facilities to handle all available traffic, they are entitled to protection against the establishment of what would be tantamount to a new service in compe-

sions of the ICC might well be but the conjurations of mystagogues. – *Old Colony Bondholders et al.* v. *New York, New Haven & Hartford R. R.*, 161 F. 2d 413 (1947).

9. Bernard Schwartz, *The Professor and the Commissions* (New York, 1959).

10. Walter Adams, "The Role of Competition in the Regulated Industries," *American Economic Review*, Papers and Proceedings, vol. 48 (May, 1958), pp. 527-43.

11. Address by Newton N. Minow, then chairman of the Federal Communications Commission, to the National Association of Broadcasters, Chicago, April 2, 1963.

tition with them."[12] As long as such carriers had the *physical* capacity to perform a given service, the Commission would deny the entry bid of newcomers who, in the opinion of shippers, could perform the service faster, better, and cheaper. In one, not atypical, case the Commission denied a small trucking company (operating 6 tractors, 9 semi-trailers, and 3 pick-up trucks) the right to expand into two towns with a combined population of 8,115 inhabitants—on the ground that this might injure competing colossi like the Southern Railroad.[13] In exercising its minimum rate powers, as the Brownell Committee found, the Commission apparently made it its duty "both to protect the railroads from motor carrier competition as well as to safeguard the motor carrier industry from 'descructive' competition in its own ranks. Indeed, from the inception of motor carrier regulation to the present day, the power to fix minimum rates has been more significant than the authority to fix maximum charges."[14]

Other commissions have shown a similar addiction to protecting the status quo. "In every instance," says a former C.A.B. chairman "in which the Board has found that additional and competing passenger trunkline services on high density segments are required by the public convenience and necessity, it has concluded that the

12. See e.g. Willers, Inc. — Purchase (Portion) — Everson, 10 Fed. Carr. Cas. 222 (1953). See also Walter Adams and James B. Hendry, "Trucking Mergers, Concentration, and Small Business; An Analysis of Interstate Commerce Commission Policy, 1950-56," Hearings before the Senate Small Business Committee, *Trucking Mergers and Concentration,* 85th Cong., 1st Sess. (1957), pp. 213-384.

13. Hearings before the Senate Samll Business Committee, *Administration of the Motor Carrier Act by the Interstate Commerce Commission as it Affects Small Truckers and Shippers,* 84th Cong., 1st Sess. (1955), pp. 93-94.

14. *Report of the Attorney General's National Committee to Study the Antitrust Laws* (Washington, 1955), p. 265.

objectives of the act would be better served by the award of the route to a carrier already holding certificate authority than to a new company."[15] Thus, despite an increase in demand of truly fantastic proportions, amounting to more than 4,000 percent between 1938 and 1956 alone, the Board has not allowed a single new passenger trunkline carrier to enter the industry. The Federal Maritime Board's administration of the operating differential subsidy and dual rate contracts has also resulted in undue entry limitation. So has the F.C.C.'s refusal to order A.T. & T. to interconnect Western Union's microwave system with its long-distance telephone lines.

Such protectionism sometimes manifests itself in regulatory apathy and nonfeasance. Thus, the Federal Power Commission has expended more energy in persuading the courts that it lacks the power to regulate field prices of natural gas than in protecting consumers against possible extortion. The C.A.B. and F.M.B. have shown little inclination to examine discriminatory practices or unfair competition in their respective industries. The F.C.C. has never investigated international telephone rates, nor exercised any direct control over television networks. Indeed, speaking through its former chairman, the commission has defended two-network domination of the industry: "Somebody has to be dominant," Mr. Doerfer told a Congressional Committee. "Somebody is big . . . [D]ominance is just the natural result of the ebb and flow of business relations from day to day . . . [W]hen you are talking about dominance, there is always somebody that is domi-

15. Address by Judge Ross Rizley before the Chamber of Commerce, Enid, Oklahoma, November 18, 1955, quoted in *The Airlines,* H. R. Rep. No. 1328, 85th Cong., 1st Sess. (1958), pp. 102-103.

nant."[16] The I.C.C. has shown the same tolerance for trucking concentration, proceeding on the assumption, candidly stated by former chairman Clark, that "there hasn't been enough concentration in the industry."[17] The Controller of the Currency, entrusted with enforcement of the Bank Merger Act, has eschewed interference with giant mergers — the recommendations of the Attorney General and the Federal Reserve Board to the contrary notwithstanding.[18] In so doing, the regulators have transmuted the meaning of regulation; not only was it to be an exemption from competition, but a protective device against meaningful surveillance.

The "undue shift of emphasis from public convenience and necessity to the seeking and protection of private carrier rights"[19] is perhaps best illustrated by the commissions' treatment of competitive "interlopers." So persistent and ruthless has been the attempt of some commissions to eliminate the fringes of unregulated competition, that the Albigensian crusades appear like missions of mercy by comparison. The suppression of the infidels has been executed with monolithic single-mindedness and unparalleled bureaucratic

16. Quoted in Bernard Schwartz, "Antitrust and the FCC: The Problem of Network Dominance," *U. of Pennsylvania Law Review*, vol. 107 (1959), p. 763.

17. Hearings before the Senate Small Business Committee, *loc. cit.*, fn. 12, above, p. 111.

18. See e.g. *U.S.* v. *Philadelphia National Bank et al*, 374 U.S. 321 (1963) and *U.S.* v. *Continental Illinois National Bank et al.*, Civil Action No. 61-C-1441, U.S. District Court, Northern District of Illinois, filed August 29, 1961. Between November 16, 1961 and April 19, 1963, the Comptroller approved 144 bank mergers, consolidations and purchases — 39 of which the Attorney General considered to have substantially adverse effects on competition. For additional data, see *Annual Report of the Comptroller of the Currency* (1961), pp. 65 and 79ff. and Hearings before the House Committee on Banking and Currency, *Conflict of Federal and State Banking Laws*, 88th Con., 1st Sess. (1963), pp. 403, 482, and 500ff.

19. Ross Rizley, *op.cit.*, fn. 15, above.

efficiency. In the airline industry, the "non-skeds," despite their innovative progressiveness and the value of their promotional competition, have been subjected to "strangulation by regulation." In trucking, the haulers of agricultural commodities – and, to a lesser extent, private and contract carriers – have been victimized by systematic persecution, carried out with algorismic precision. In ocean shipping, such independents as Isbrandtsen have been forced, first by administrative harassment and eventually by legislative mandate, to submit to a government-sponsored, compulsory cartel. In industry after industry, regulatory rule-making and adjudication, operating within a broad delegation of discretion and reinforced by Congressional tolerance or support, have resulted in the elimination of both actual and potential competition.

In a sense, this was almost inevitable. Regulation breeds regulation. Competition, even at the margin, is a source of disturbance, annoyance, and embarrassment to the bureaucracy. By providing a yardstick for performance, an outlet for innovation, and a laboratory for experiment, competition subverts the orthodox conformity prescribed by the regulatory establishment. It undermines the static, conservative, and unimaginative scheme of bureaucratic controls, and erodes the artificial values created by protective restrictionism. From the regulator's point of view, therefore, competition must be suppressed wherever it may arise.

What starts as regulation almost inevitably winds up as protection.[20] The power to license becomes the power to exclude; the regulation of rates, a system of price supports; the surveillance of mergers, an instrument of

20. For a discussion of the regulatory protectionism practiced by state and local governments under the aegis of their licensing power, see Walter Gellhorn, *Individual Freedom and Governmental Restraints* (Baton Rouge, 1956), pp. 106ff.

concentration; and the supervision of business practices, a pretext for harassing the weak, unorganized, and politically underprivileged. Given the power of the commissions to dispense and protect privilege, there is little hope for competition. To suggest that commissions follow a libertarian policy of entry control, rate regulation, and yardstick competition, is like asking East Germany to tear down the Berlin Wall.

Exemption by Administrative Preemption

Another instrument of privilege creation, more recent in vintage than regulation, but equally significant, insidious, and virulent, and operating without the benefit of explicit antitrust exemptions, is the unimaginative, short-sighted, discriminatory, or corrupt use of the government's executive power. It constitutes a (perhaps unwitting) promotion of monopoly by the government itself, and represents a major deviation from our national commitment to the preservation of competition.[21] For want of a better term, this phenomenon may be called "exemption through administrative preemption."

In an age of Big Government, born in response to the needs of a Garrison State, the "conjunction of an immense military establishment and a large arms industry" not only affects "the very structure of our society," but poses the very real danger "of unwarranted influence, whether sought or unsought, by the military-industrial complex."[22] In defense, space, and atomic energy, governmental creation of privilege can damage competition more seriously and more quickly than all other specifically authorized antitrust exemptions

21. Walter Adams and Horace M. Gray, *Monopoly in America: The Government as Promoter* (New York, 1955).

22. Farewell Address by President Dwight D. Eisenhower, January, 1961.

combined. It can create by administrative decision – by the stroke of a pen – what the antitrust laws are designed to prevent.

Patents on Government-financed Research. The allocation of government research and development expenditures (R&D), and the patent policy governing the distribution of proprietary benefits therefrom, is a prime case in point. The importance of federal policy in this area derives from a number of characteristics of federally financed research:[23]

(1) Since World War II, the government has generally paid for roughly 65 percent of the nation's research and development, but performed only about 15 percent of the work. Industry, by contrast, has paid for about 33 percent and performed 75 percent of the R&D activity. In other words, the government has financed over half of industry's R&D effort.

(2) Two agencies, the Department of Defense (DOD) and the National Aeronautics and Space Agency (NASA), account for about 80 percent of the government's R&D outlays. In fiscal year 1964, this will amount to almost $12 billion.

(3) The lion's share of these expenditures is concentrated in a few industries – notably the aircraft and parts industry and the electrical and communications industry. The former receives 85 percent, the lat-

23. The following data are based primarily on Robert F. Lanzillotti, Hearings before the Senate Small Business Committee, *Economic Aspects of Government Patent Policies,* 88th Con., 1st Sess. (1963), pp. 117-143, hereafter cited as *Long Committee Patent Hearings,* and Richard J. Barber, *Long Committee Patent Hearings,* pp. 47-91, and Hearings before the Joint Economic Committee, *State of the Economy and Policies for Full Employment,* 87th Cong., 2d Sess. (1962), pp. 858-65. For a comprehensive examination of the impact of government patent policies, see the hearings and reports issued by Senator Russell B. Long's Monopoly Subcommittee of the Senate Small Business Committee, 1959-1963.

ter 70 percent of its R&D financing from the government.

(4) The concentration of R&D contracts is even greater than that of procurement contracts. Thus, small business tends to get about 17 percent of the DOD's procurement business, but only about 3.5 percent of the military R&D. In fact, as Table 1 indicates, federal R&D bounties accentuate the concentration pattern in privately financed research and development work.

(5) There is a high correlation between companies receiving R&D contracts and those receiving defense production orders. (See Table 1.) In fiscal year 1962, General Dynamics, Lockheed, and Boeing headed the list of DOD research contractors, and also captured the top three spots on the DOD list of prime procurement awards. Production orders seem to follow R&D contracts as night follows day.

(6) The benefits of military R&D tend to spill over into civilian markets. The development of nuclear power, blood plasma, drugs, new high-temperature alloys, and a variety of plastics during World War II, and the more recent development of Boeing's 707 jet and North American's Sabreliner are merely suggestions of the strong link between military research and civilian use. "More than 90 Sabreliners," says North American in a recent Fortune ad, "have already proved themselves in military service. Now this remarkable twin-jet aircraft is available for purchase."

In the light of this situation, it is not surprising that the Department of Justice has consistently attempted to countervail the anticompetitive effects of federal R&D policies. It has repeatedly recommended against granting private patents on inventions developed at public expense: "Where patentable inventions are made in the course of performing a Government-financed

TABLE 1

Rank of Principal Contractors in Research and Procurement for DOD, Fiscal 1962

Company	Rank Among DOD Research Contractors	Rank Among DOD Prime Contractors	Rank Among Fortune's 500 Largest U.S. Industrial Corporations For 1962
General Dynamics	1	2	13
Lockheed	2	1	28
Boeing	3	3	19
North American	4	4	29
General Electric	5	5	4
Martin Marietta	6	6	32
Western Electric	7	8[a]	9[b]
Aerojet-General	8	12	55
Douglas	9	13	56
Sperry Rand	10	9	34

NOTES:
a. Included with American Telephone & Telegraph Co.
b. Rank given is for Western Electric alone. Western Electric is a subsidiary of AT&T, the largest utility.

SOURCE: Based on Hearings before the U.S. Senate Small Business Committee, *Economic Aspects of Government Patent Policies*, 88th Cong., 1st Sess. (1963), p. 57.

contract for research and development, the public interest requires that all rights to such inventions be assigned to the Government and not left to the private ownership of the contractor. Public control will assure free and equal availability of the inventions to American industry and science; will eliminate any competitive advantage to the contractor chosen to perform the research work; will avoid undue concentration in the hands of a few large corporations; will tend to increase and diversify available research facilities within the United States to the advantage of the Government and of the national economy; and will thus strengthen our American system of free, competitive enterprise."[24] Despite this policy pronouncement, however, some government departments—notably Defense—have made it a practice to grant patent rights along with their R&D contracts, as if an extra bonus were required to make a giant bonanza acceptable.

The typical R&D contract, it should be noted, is a riskless cost-plus-fixed-fee venture. It usually protects the contractor against increases in labor and materials costs; it provides him with working capital in the form of periodic progress payments; it allows him to use government plant and equipment; in addition, it guarantees him a fee up to 15 percent of the estimated cost. Nevertheless, some contractors demand additional incentives. With the arrogance characteristic of all privilege recipients, they want to extend and compound such privilege. "We recognize," says the Vice President of the Electronics Industries Association, a prime beneficiary of government-financed R&D, "that the ownership of a patent is a valuable property right entitled to protection against seizure by the Government without just compensation."[25] In this view, the patent is a right, not a privilege voluntarily bestowed by the govern-

24. U.S. Department of Justice, *Investigation of Government Patent Practices and Policies*, Final Report, vol. 1 (Washington, 1947), p. 4.

25. *Long Committee Patent Hearings*, p. 132.

ment to effectuate a public purpose. Instead of being recognized for what it is—an alienation of the public domain—the patent is assumed to be a vested right belonging to private interests, even where it is paid for with public funds. By a curious perversion of logic, it becomes a vested privilege to which the private recipient feels entitled and of which he is not supposed to be deprived without just compensation.

In the United States, patents have traditionally been held out as an incentive "to promote the progress of science and the useful arts"—an incentive to private persons, willing to assume the necessary risks to earn the stipulated reward. They were never conceived to be property rights inherently vested in private hands. Nor were they ever intended to reward persons who performed research at someone else's expense as part of a riskless venture. To allow contractors to retain patents on research financed by and performed for the government, therefore, "is no more reasonable or economically sound than to bestow on contractors, who build a road financed by public funds, the right to collect tolls from cars that will eventually use it"[26]—or the right to close down the road altogether. It would be tantamount to socializing the financial support for research, while permitting private monopolization of its benefits.

Yet this is the current practice of the Defense Department. If, as is proposed, NASA is allowed to adopt the same patent policy, the two agencies accounting for 80 percent of the government's R&D outlays, in effect, would be sanctioning the erection of private toll booths on public access routes to scientific and technical advance. The bulk of the government's R&D expenditures would forge a chain of privilege protection, and

26. Wassily W. Leontief, *Long Committee Patent Hearings*, p. 234.

privilege subsidization. It would solidify an implicit (but crucial) antitrust exemption produced by simple administration fiat.

Procurement and Power. The DOD procurement of weapons systems further illustrates the anticompetitive effects of administrative discretion, wrought without explicit exemption from the antitrust laws. Here, too, the public grant becomes a "haven of refuge for all aspiring monopolists who [may find] it too difficult, too costly, or too precarious to secure and maintain monopoly by private action alone. Their future prosperity would be assured if only they could induce government to grant them monopoly power and protect them against interlopers, provided always of course, that government did not exact too high a price for its favors in the form of restrictive regulation."[27] The steps in the process are deceptively simple: government dismantles its facilities for serving a public need, and turns the job over to a chosen instrument; as the government's dependence increases, so does the arrogance of its instrument; the government becomes vulnerable to blackmail; to get the job done, it is forced to pay extortionate profits and subsidies; stripped of its bargaining power, and lacking competitive alternatives, it cannot break the self-imposed stranglehold. Thus, it winds up not as the master but the servant of its own chosen instrument. It becomes an accomplice in the stifling and suppression of competition.

The development of the NIKE missile illustrates the process. Early in 1945, having dismantled its in-house R&D capability, the Army asked Western Electric to conduct a preliminary feasibility study on a guided

27. Horace M. Gray, "The Passing of the Public Utility Concept," *Journal of Land and Public Utility Economics*, vol. 16 (February, 1940), p. 11. Gray's observation, originally made with reference to public utility franchises, is equally applicable to all governmental grants of privilege.

missile system for defense against supersonic aircraft. A CPFF contract for $181,450 was signed on May 30, 1945, marking the kick-off of the NIKE program. In September 1945, Western got its first R&D contract, amounting to $4.9 million. By 1961, Western's R&D and service contracts for the NIKE totaled $956 million.[28]

In 1950, the first production contract on the new missile was let — and, to no one's surprise, it went to Western Electric. The eventual total of NIKE production contracts was $1,545 million — with Western collecting a 31.3 percent mark-up on an in-house effort of $359.3 million. By using subcontractors for roughly three-quarters of the work and retaining responsibility for overall "system compatibility," Western was able to play what Robert Lanzillotti has called the "game of piggy-back profits" — complete with piggy-back refills. Table 2 shows the profit pyramiding which took place.

Each subcontractor collected not only his in-house cost of production (including overhead costs for general and administrative expenses) plus a profit, but also a profit on the work done by other subcontractors further down the line. Thus Douglas Aircraft, a second-tier subcontractor, was allowed a $8.3 million markup on its in-house costs (including G&A) of $103 million, in addition to profits of $3.7 million on the work of Fruehauf, $10.4 million on the work of Consolidated Western, and $23.2 million on the work of other subcontractors for a total of $37.3 million. This represented a return of 44.3 percent on the total of work done in its own plants.[29] Similarly, Western Electric collect-

28. Hearings before the Senate Permanent Subcommittee on Investigations, *Pyramiding of Profits and Costs in the Missile Procurement Program*, 87th Cong., 2d Sess. (1962), part 2, pp. 344-345, 416.

29. For other examples of profit pyramiding by Douglas, see *Ibid.*, part 1, pp. 207-228.

TABLE 2

Pyramiding Profits Through Top Three Tiers Nike Production
(in millions)

	In-House Costs of Producer	In-House Mark-up of Producer	Douglas Mark-up on Subcontracts & Purchases	Western Electric Mark-up on Subcontracts & Purchases
3d Tier				
Fruehauf Trailer Co.	$ 49.3	$ 4.5	$ 3.7	$ 3.3
Consolidated Western	146.2	9.3	10.4	9.9
Misc. 3d Tier Subcontractors to Douglas	286.6	*	23.2	16.3
2d Tier				
Douglas In-House Cost Including G & A	103.0	8.3		5.9
Misc. 2d Tier Subcontractors to Western Electric	428.8	*		42.0
1st Tier				
Western Electric In-House Cost Including G & A	359.3	35.2	—	—
Total Production Costs	$1,373.2			
Total Mark-up by Producers		$57.3		
Total Douglas Mark-up on Subcontracts & Purchases			$37.3	
Total Western Electric Mark-up on Subcontracts & Purchases				$77.3
Total Cost to Army				$1,545.1

NOTE:
*Undetermined Profits Included in Costs.

SOURCE: Hearings before the U.S. Senate Permanent Subcommittee on Investigations, *Pyramiding of Profits and Costs in the Missile Procurement Program*, Part 2, 87th Cong., 2d Sess. (1962) p. 427.

ed an in-house mark-up of $35.2 million, as well as $77.3 million profit on the work of all the subcontractors, giving it total profits of $112.6 million on an in-house effort of $359.3 million – or 31.3 percent.[30]

The McClellan Committee Hearings which unearthed these revealing statistics did not produce the far more interesting figures on profits as a percentage return on investment. Hence, we can only speculate about the astronomic proportions involved. Such speculation, however, is somewhat concretized by Table 3 which shows a comparison of profit rates as a percentage of net worth, invested capital, and sales for 12 aircraft companies during the year 1955. The staggering rates on invested capital, including 102.7 percent for Boeing, 127.3 for Douglas, 151.9 percent for Lockheed, and 1038.0 percent for North American, indicate that "modest" mark-ups on sales can be translated into fantastic returns on invested capital – especially by companies which typically receive sizable portions of their fixed and working capital from the government. Western Electric, for example, paid a rental of $3.075 million for the use of certain government plants; the company was then reimbursed in full for this expenditure and, in addition, allowed to charge the government a profit of $209,000 as a mark-up on this cost item.[31]

Why, then, does the government not procure certain items directly instead of assigning a procurement package to the prime contractor who employs several tiers of subcontractors and then pyramids the profits charged to the government? Why, in DOD parlance, does the government not "break out" certain parts of the procurement package for competitive bidding? The answer, as the NIKE history demonstrates, is the re-

30. For similar examples of profit pyramiding by Boeing, see *Ibid.*, part 4, p. 706.
31. *Ibid.*, part 2, p. 482.

TABLE 3

1955 Profit Rates for Twelve Aircraft Companies

	Profit Rate on		
	Net Worth	Invested Capital	Sales
1. Boeing	51.6	102.7	7.3
2. Chance Vought	39.1	58.9	7.0
3. Convair[a]	29.9	70.9	4.7
4. Douglas	29.9	127.3	5.2
5. Fairchild	25.5	63.0	5.9
6. Grumman	47.5	120.7	10.0
7. Lockheed	44.8	151.9	6.5
8. Martin	40.5	74.1	7.8
9. McDonnell	52.3	316.1	7.4
10. North American Aviation	71.8	1038.0	8.3
11. Northrop	92.0	386.7	9.1
12. Republic	71.0	198.9	5.7

NOTE:
a. For 1953.

SOURCE:
Committee on Armed Services, House, *Report on Aircraft Production Costs and Profits*, 84th Congress, 2d Sess., July 13, 1956, pp. 3105-3109. Reproduced in Frederick T. Moore, *Military Procurement and Contracting: An Economic Analysis*, Memorandum RM-2948-PR, The RAND Corporation (June 1962), p. 107.

fusal of the prime contractor to permit such a breakout. Despite repeated efforts to effect cost-savings by buying parts of the NIKE directly from their manufacturer — efforts initiated by Redstone Arsenal, the

New York Ordnance District, or G-4 of the Army – Western Electric was able to exercise a virtual veto. On one occasion the Army asked Western to screen a list of 13,000 items that might be procured directly and then give its approval for the break-out of some of these items. Western delayed long enough, so that the Army was forced to continue its sole-source procurement through Western.[32] On other occasíons, Western refused to give the Army production drawings – developed at Government expense – so that certain replacement parts components could be broken out for competitive bidding.[33] In 1954, Redstone Arsenal wanted to break out the missile's thrust structure and miscellaneous parts of the booster, but Western replied that it could not concur in the purchase of these items from any other source than itself. This, despite the fact that the thrust structures were connected with the booster, which was government-furnished, and which was in a sense separate from the rocket itself.[34] On each occasion, Western Electric threatened to decline responsibility for system compatibility and to discontinue performance of the management function. Knowing that the Army had substantilly dismantled its in-house engineering capability, and that the Army was in effect its captive, Western repeatedly and consistently refused to give its permission for direct procurement of NIKE components. With the exceptions of certain automotive components, as well as minor items, Western for 17 years (1945-1962) successfully resisted the break-out of the NIKE missile – until Senator McClellan started his investigation. Thereafter Western acted with dispatch. The investigation started in the middle of May 1961. Two weeks later, Western suggest-

32. *Ibid.*, part 2, pp. 338-340.
33. *Ibid.*, part 2, pp. 349-353.
34. *Ibid.*, part 2, pp. 357-359.

ed to the Army that the NIKE be broken out for direct procurement.[35]

In his appearance before the McClellan Committee, Paul R. Ignatius, Assistant Secretary of the Army, stated: "I am convinced that only through competition can we be assured of receiving the maximum amount of defense for the dollars which we in the Army have to spend. I am well aware that in some instances sole-source procurement may be necessary. However, I am also convinced that in many instances . . . we have found ourselves in a sole-source position not as a result of a careful assessment of the situation leading to a deliberate decision, but by default. In these cases, we have had no alternative other than to buy from a single company."[36] The testimony – at least, in the case of the NIKE missile – showed that "the government was almost helpless in this case, that the government was almost a captive of Western Electric because every time they would want to break out Western Electric would say, 'We will not assume responsibility for the system.' "[37]

The moral is clear: The government favors a private corporation with an R&D contract. It makes no provision for protecting itself against future dependence on this corporation as a sole-source supplier. By getting in on the ground floor, the corporation is able to preempt the future – more so than through similar activity in the free market sector. Whether or not it receives patent rights on its inventions developed at government expense, the corporation has achieved preminence without meeting any market test. It has been successful in obtaining government favor – perhaps through manipulation of administrative discretion – and this

35. *Ibid.*, part 2, p. 405.
36. *Ibid.*, part 2, pp. 509, 508
37. *Ibid.*, part 2, p. 359.

initial success then breeds further advantages. The production contract almost inevitably goes to it because of its R&D lead. It becomes the prime contractor for an entire weapons system – an entire procurement package. Not only can it pyramid profits – i.e., accumulate piggy-back rewards for work done by others – together with piggy-back refills on replacement orders – but also prevent the government from breaking out portions of the contract for competitive procurement. It thus is in the enviable position of benefitting from government subsidies, while insulating itself from competition. It becomes a chosen instrument which dictates to its master. Having reduced the government to a position of abject dependence, it can effectively blackmail the government out of any effort to terminate such dependence. And blackmail leads to extortion and further dependence. No explicit exemption from antitrust is necessary. Competition is foreclosed by administrative discretion. Concentration results not from technological or economic imperatives, but from governmental action. "Everything," as Jane Austen said, "nourishes what is strong already."[38]

Conclusion

Our concern here, of course, is not with the exploitation of the public purse by greedy courtiers. But when public subsidy for riskless ventures becomes the underpinning for a system of privilege creation and privilege protection – when the government promotes what the antitrust laws forbid – and when all this is accom-

38. Long ago, Alfred Marshall warned of "the danger that in the trade which had got a bounty and in other trades which hoped to get one, people would divert their energies from managing their own businesses to managing those persons who control the bounties." *Principles*, p. 473. Not only does this warning apply to all forms of governmental privilege creation and protection, but *a fortiori* to an economy in which the state plays a preeminent role.

plished without explicit exemptions from the national commitment to competition, then there is need for redefining the problem. We must recognize that both the dimensions and the context of the problem of promoting competition is no longer the same as in 1890. When Government is as big as it is today—when it dispenses favors and privilege on a gargantuan scale—"decisions will not be on the lofty and abstract grounds which are somewhat naively assumed by many economists who favor pervasive and far-reaching economic controls." Instead, as Senator Douglas so sagely observed, "the crucial decisions will commonly be made in an atmosphere of pressure, influence, favoritism, improper deals, and corruption."[39] To suppose that these decisions will promote competition by favoring the outsider, the newcomer, the unorganized, or the disadvantaged is to engage in catatonic self-deception. Concentrated power in the hands of government is not likely to be a source of countervailance but coalescence—not compensatory but reinforcing.

The real issue in preserving competition, therefore, is not so much a vigorous enforcement of the antitrust laws—important though that may be—but rather an end to explicit exemptions which erode the competitive sector of the economy, and a reversal of government policies which wittingly or otherwise undermine the competitive fabric of our society.

Policy toward that end should follow the central guideline of diffusing economic power to the maximum degree feasible and confining bureaucratic discretion within the narrowest practicable limits. This means *inter alia* the implementation of the following recommendations:

(1) Total deregulation of those industries where the regulatory scheme protects an industry from competi-

39. Paul H. Douglas, *Ethics in Government* (Cambridge, Mass., 1954), p. 33.

tion rather than the public from monopolistic extortion. In trucking, for example, where competition is both technically and economically workable, where entry in the absence of regulation would be easy, and where economies of scale are virtually nonexistent, why not let the market decide who shall transport what commodities over what routes at what rates? Why not consider the deregulation of the entire surface transportation industry – subjecting that industry to the general prohibitory restraints of antitrust, while maintaining a strict proscription against the erosion of intermode competition either by merger or internal expansion? There is no longer the same need for government regulation as in the days of the railroad monopoly.[40]

(2) In other regulated industries, where unrestricted competition is not workable for technical or economic reasons, and where total deregulation is therefore not feasible, Congress should specifically direct the regulatory agency "to promote competition to the maximum extent practicable," to deny entry to an applicant only where such entry can be shown to be inconsistent with the public convenience and necessity, and to permit structural or behavioral arrangements contrary to the antitrust laws only where "the regulatory need therefore is clear."[41] Under such a mandate, in TV for example, there would be no reason to tolerate network ownership of television stations, multiple ownership of stations, erosion of intermedia competition, and such restrictive practices as "must buy" and "option time."

(3) In those industries where competition is not allowed to have full sway, yardstick competition should be encouraged from whatever source it may spring. This implies promotion (instead of the current harass-

40. See Chapter 11 above, by Merton J. Peck.

41. See recommendations of the Attorney General's National Committee, *loc. cit.* fn. 14, above, pp. 269-270.

ment) of airline "non-skeds" and charters, educational and pay television, independents in ocean shipping, and federal, state, municipal, and cooperative organizations in electric or atomic power. In necessarily concentrated industries, institutional competition, even though it is only marginal, should be allowed to supplement regulation and thus serve as an antidote to bureaucratic conservatism and protectionism.

(4) The antitrust philosophy should be built into the decision-making structure of the federal government, so that government does not act as a creator and protector of privilege. There is no justification for protecting concentrated, administered price industries through tariffs or antidumping statutes. Nor is there a public purpose to be served by giving R&D contractors patent rights on inventions growing out of government-financed research. Nor is there sound reason for dismantling in-house capabilities of the Defense Department as a prelude to making the government a dependent vassal of industrial barons. In short, where the government, by force of circumstance must become a participant in the nation's economic life, it should participate to a sufficient extent to prevent concentration in the private sector resulting from a proliferation of restraints by its chosen instruments.

Above all, the government must not be captured by private interests and made subservient to them. If it is to play its proper role, it must intervene in the economy only as a public shield, never as a mask for privilege.

Enough has already been said to sketch the outlines of the work to be done. There are cases where words are superfluous. The government now knows what to do. As somebody once said, "The milk-wagon horse knows where to stop."[42]

42. Herbert Block, *Herblock's Special for Today* (New York, 1958), p. 246.

APPENDIX

STATUTORY EXEMPTIONS FROM THE OPERATION OF THE FEDERAL "ANTITRUST (OR ANTIMONOPOLY)" AND CERTAIN TRADE REGULATORY LAWS[43]

A. Exemptions and Immunities Under the Principal Antimonopoly Statutes

1. Sherman Antitrust Act (as amended by the Miller-Tydings Act):
   (a) A general exemption for vertical minimum resale price maintenance agreements on identified commodities in free and open competition, when lawful as applied to intrastate transactions under the law of the place of resale (sec. 1, 26 Stat. 209, as amended Aug. 17, 1937, 50 Stat. 693, U.S.C. 15:1).
2. Federal Trade Commission Act (as amended by the Wheeler-Lea Act):
   (a) Same as 1 (a), supra:
3. Clayton Act (as amended by Robinson-Patman Act):
   (a) Price differentials making only due allowance for differences in the cost of manufacturer, sale, or delivery resulting from differing methods or quantities of sale or delivery; bona fide selection of customers; price changes due to changing conditions affecting the market for or marketability of the goods concerned, such as but not limited to actual or imminent deterioration of perishable goods, obsolescence of seasonal goods, distress sales under court process, or sales in good faith in discontinuance of business in the goods concerned (sec. 2 (a), 38 Stat. 730, as amended, 49 Stat. 1526, U.S.C. 15: 13 (a)).
   (b) Discrimination made in good faith to meet an equally low price of a competitor, or the services or facilities furnished by a competitor (sec. 2 (b), 38 Stat. 730, as amended, 49 Stat. 1526, U.S.C. 15: 13 (b)).

43. House Small Business Committee, *A Report on the History of Congressional Action in the Antitrust Field since 1900*, 84th Cong., 2d Sess. (1956), pp. 33-41.

(c) Return of net earnings or surplus by cooperatives to their members – exempt from section 2 of Clayton Act (relating to price discrimination) (sec. 4, Robinson-Patman Act, June 19, 1936, 49 Stat. 1528, U.S.C. 15: 13b).

(d) Purchases of supplies for their own use by schools, colleges, universities, public libraries, churches, hospitals, and charitable institutions not operated for profit – exempt from Section 2 of Clayton Act, (relating to price discrimination) (amendment to Robinson-Patman Act, May 26, 1938, 52 Stat. 446, U.S.C. 15: 13c).

(e) Legitimate activities of labor, agricultural or horticultural organizations – exempt from operation of the antitrust laws (sec. 6, 38 Stat. 731, U.S.C. 15: 17).

Section 6 of the Clayton Act reads as follows: "The labor of a human being is not a commodity or article of commerce. Nothing contained in the antitrust laws shall be construed to forbid the existence and operation of labor, agricultural, or horticultural organizations, organized for the purposes of mutual help and not having capital stock or conducted for profit, or to forbid or restrain individual members of such organizations from lawfully carrying out the legitimate objects thereof; nor shall such organizations, or the membership thereof, be held or construed to be illegal combinations or conspiracies in restraint of trade, under the antitrust laws."

(f) Acquisition of stock solely for investment and not using the same by voting or otherwise to bring about, or attempt to bring about the substantial lessening of competition, formation of subsidiary corporations for the actual carrying-on of their immediate lawful business, or the natural and legitimate branches or extensions thereof, or the owning and holding all or a part of the stock of such subsidiary corporations, when the effect of such formation is not to substantially lessen competition; common carriers acquiring branch lines or extending its lines through the medium of stock acquisition or otherwise of any other common carrier where there is no substantial competition between the company extending its lines or acquiring branch lines and the company whose stock property or interest is so acquired – exempt from Section 7 of the Clayton Act (relating to the acquisition by one corporation of the stock of another) (sec. 7, 38 Stat. 731, U.S.C. 15: 18).

(g) Certain specified banks and directors – exempt from section 8 of the Clayton Act (relating to interlocking directorates and officers) (sec. 8, 38 Stat. 732, as amended, May 15, 1916, 39 Stat. 121; May 26, 1920, 41 Stat. 626; March 9, 1928, 45 Stat. 253; March 2, 1929, 45 Stat. 1536; August 23, 1935, 49 Stat. 717, U.S.C. 15: 19).

(h) Open bidding agreements of common carriers with corporations having the same directors – exempt from section 10 of the Clayton Act, (relating to purchases by common carriers in case of interlocking directorates) (sec. 10, 38 Stat. 734, U.S.C. 15: 20).

(i) Common carriers subject to the regulation, supervision, or other jurisdiction of the Interstate Commerce Commission are exempt from private injunctive relief under section 16 of the Clayton Act (sec. 16, 38 Stat. 737, U.S.C. 15:26).

(j) Labor Union activities – exempt in certain cases from injunctive relief (cf. secs. 4 and 5 of the Norris-La Guardia Act, 47 Stat. 70, U.S.C. 29: 104, 105) (sec. 20, 38 Stat. 738, U.S.C. 29: 52). (But cf. secs. 10 (h), 208 (b), and 302 (e) of the Taft-Hartley Act. 62 Stat. 136, U.S.C., Supp. II 29: 160 (h), 178 (b), 186 (e).).

For discussion of the scope of the exemption of labor union activities from the antitrust laws see *Allen Bradley Co. v. Local Union No. 3, International Brotherhood of Electrical Workers* ((1945) 325 U.S. 797) and *United Brotherhood of Carpenters and Joiners v. U.S.* ((1947) 330 U.S. 395.)

(k) Transactions duly consummated pursuant to authority given by the Civil Aeronautics Board, Federal Communications Commission, Federal Power Commission, Interstate Commerce Commission, the Securities and Exchange Commission in the exercise of its jurisdiction under section 10 of the Public Utility Holding Company Act of 1935, the United States Maritime Commission, or the Secretary of Agriculture under any statutory provision vesting such power in such Commission, Secretary, or Board (Public Law 899, 81st Cong.).

B. Exemptions Under Supplemental Antitrust Statutes, Other Special Statutes, or Specific Statutory Provisions
   1. Agriculture:
      (a) Capper-Volstead Act:
         (1) Declaration of legality of agricultural or horticultural cooperatives (sec. 1, 42 Stat. 388, U.S.C. 7: 291).
      (b) Cooperative Marketing Act, 1926:
         (1) Cooperative marketing associations are permitted to disseminate past, present, and prospective crop, market, statistical, etc., information (sec. 5, July 2, 1926, 44 Stat. 803, U.S.C. 7: 455).
      (c) Anti-Hog-Cholera Serum and Hog-Cholera Virus Act:
         (1) Anti-hog cholera serum and virus marketing agreements with handlers made with the Secretary of Agriculture are exempt from the operation of the antitrust laws and are declared to be lawful (sec. 57, August 24, 1935, 49 Stat. 781, U.S.C. 7: 852).
      (d) Provisions of Agricultural Adjustment Act, 1933:
         (1) Marketing agreements made with the Secretary of Agriculture are exempt from the operation of the antitrust laws, and are declared lawful (sec. 8b, May 12, 1933, 48 Stat. 34, as amended April 7, 1934, 48 Stat. 528; August 24, 1935, 49 Stat. 753, June 3, 1937, 50 Stat. 246; June 30, 1947, 61 Stat. 208, U.S.C. 7: 608b).
      (e) Agricultural Marketing Agreement Act, 1937:
         (1) Arbitration awards for milk made by Secretary of Agriculture after prescribed meetings are exempt from operation of the antitrust laws (sec. 3, June 3, 1937, 50 Stat. 248, U.S.C. 7: 671).
      (f) State Tobacco Compacts Act:

(1) Grants congressional consent to compacts between States for regulation and control of production and marketing of tobacco (but not compacts for the purpose of fixing prices or creating or perpetuating monopoly) in order to enable growers to receive a fair price for tobacco (49 Stat. 1239, U.S.C. 7: 515).

2. Banks:

Bank Holding Company Act of 1956:

(a) Prohibitions against a bank holding company having interests in nonbanking organizations shall *not* apply—

(1) to shares owned or acquired by a bank holding company in any company engaged solely in holding or operating properties used wholly or substantially by any bank with respect to which it is a bank holding company in its operations or acquired for such future use or engaged solely in conducting a safe deposit business, or solely in the business of furnishing services to or performing services for such holding company and banks with respect to which it is a bank holding company, or in liquidating assets acquired from such bank holding company and such banks;

(2) to shares acquired by a bank holding company which is a bank, or by any banking subsidiary of a bank holding company, in satisfaction of a debt previously contracted in good faith, but such bank holding company or such subsidiaries shall dispose of such shares within a period of 2 years from the date of enactment of this act, whichever is later;

(3) to shares acquired by a bank holding company from any of its subsidiaries which subsidiary has been requested to dispose of such shares by any Federal or State authority having statutory power to examine such subsidiary, but such bank holding company shall dispose of such shares within a period of 2 years from the date on which they were acquired or from the date of enactment of this act, whichever is later;

(4) to shares which are held or acquired by a

bank holding company which is a bank or by any banking subsidiary of a bank holding company, in good faith in a fiduciary capacity, except where such shares are held for the benefit of the shareholders of such bank holding company or any of its subsidiaries, or to shares which are of the kinds and amounts eligible for investment by national banking associations under the provisions of section 5136 of the Revised Statutes, or to shares lawfully acquired and owned prior to the date of enactment of this act by a bank which is a bank holding company, or by any of its wholly owned subsidiaries;

(5) to shares of any company which are held or acquired by a bank holding company which do not include more than 5 percent of the outstanding voting securities of such company, and do not have a value greater than 5 percent of the value of the total assets of the bank holding company, or to the ownership by a bank holding company of shares, securities, or obligations of an investment company which is not a bank holding company and which is not engaged in any business other than investing in securities, which securities do not include more than 5 percent of the outstanding voting securities of any company and do not include any single asset having a value greater than 5 percent of the total assets of the bank holding company;

(6) to shares of any company all the activities of which are of a financial, fiduciary, or insurance nature and which the Board after due notice and hearing, and on the basis of the record made at such

4. District of Columbia Cooperatives:

(a) District of Columbia Cooperative Association Act:

(1) Declaration of legality of District of Columbia Cooperative Associations (54 Stat. 490, D.C.C. 29: 840 ff.). For other cooperatives see under headings Agriculture and Fishing; also

see exemption of cooperatives under the Clayton Act and Robinson-Patman Act, supra.

5. Fishing:
   (a) Fisheries Cooperative Marketing Act:
      (1) Declaration of legality of fishing cooperatives (see. 1, 48 Stat. 1213, U.S.C. 15: 521).
6. Fabrics:
   (a) Flammable Fabrics Act:
      (1) Exempts from the act any common carrier, contract carrier, or freight forwarder in respect of fabrics shipped in commerce in the ordinary course of business (Public Law 88, 83rd Cong., sec. 11).
7. Foreign Trade:
   (a) Webb-Pomerene Export Trade Act:
      (1) Blanket exemption for qualifying (i.e., those not in restraint of domestic trade or the export trade of a domestic competitor, etc.) export associations from the Sherman Antitrust Act (sec. 2, 40 Stat. 517, U.S.C. 15: 62).
      (2) Special exemption for qualifying export associations from section 7 of the Clayton Act (relating to the acquisition by one corporation of the stock of another) (sec. 3, 40 Stat. 517, U.S.C. 15: 63).
8. Fur:
   (a) Fur Products Labeling Act:
      (1) Exempts from the misbranding, false advertising, and invoice provisions of the act any common carrier, contract carrier, or freight forwarder in respect of furs shipped in commerce in the ordinary course of business (Public Law 110, 82nd Cong., sec. 3 (f)).
9. Insurance:
   (a) McCarran-Walter Act (Insurance Antitrust Moratorium Act):
      (1) Declares that the continued regulation and taxation of the business of insurance by the several States is in the public interest. Suspends the application of the Sherman, Clayton, Federal Trade Commission, and Robinson-Patman Acts from March 9, 1945, to January 1, 1948 (extended to June 30, 1948, 61

Stat. 448) but provides that after that date they were to become applicable to the business of insurance to the extent that it was not regulated by State law. (This statute was enacted as a result of the decision of the Supreme Court in *U.S. v. Southeastern Underwriters Association, et al.* (1944) (332 U.S. 533) which held that a fire insurance company conducting a substantial part of its business across State lines is engaged in interstate commerce and that Congress did not intend to exempt insurance from the prohibitions of the Sherman Act.)

10. Registered Securities Associations:
    (a) Maloney Act:
        (1) Permits the rules of a registered securities association to provide that no member shall deal with any nonmember broker or dealer except at the same prices, for the same commissions or fees and on the same terms and conditions as are by such member accorded to the general public (sec. 15A, 52 Stat. 1070, U.S.C. 15: 780-3, adding sec. 15A to the Securities Exchange Act of 1934).
11. Rubber:
    (a) Rubber Producing Facilities Disposal Act:
        (1) Generally exempts alcohol-butadiene facilities from the restrictive provisions of the act (Public Law 205 83rd Con., sec. 8 (a)).
    (b) Amendment to the Rubber Producing Facilities Disposal Act:
        (1) Adds section providing for disposal of Plancor No. 877 at Baytown, Tex. Makes amendment inapplicable to disposal of any other Government-owned rubber-producing facility (Public Law 19, 84th Cong.).
        (2) Same as above except that it is for Plancor No. 980 at Institute, W. Va. (Public Law 336, 84th Cong.).
12. Shipping:
    (a) Sections 15 and 16 of the Shipping Act, 1916:
        (1) All agreements approved by the Maritime Commission – exempt from the Sherman An-

titrust Act (sec. 15, 39 Stat. 728, as amended, June 29, 1936, 49 Stat. 1987, 2016, U.S.C. 46: 814).

(b) Section 29 of Merchant Marine Act of 1920:

(1) Associations for insurance business entered into by marine insurance companies are exempt from the antitrust laws (sec. 29 (b), June 5, 1920, 41 Stat. 1000, U.S.C. 468: 85 (b)).

13. Transportation:

(a) Section 5 of Interstate Commerce Act:

(1) Common carriers who are parties to consolidation, merger, etc., agreements approved by the Interstate Commerce Commission (after a finding by the Commission that the national transportation policy would be furthered thereby) are relieved from the operation of the antitrust laws (sec. 5 (*11*), 24 Stat. 379, as amended, September 8, 1940, 54 Stat. 905, June 17, 1948, 62 Stat. 472, U.S.C. 49: 5b).

(b) Reed-Bulwinkle Act:

(1) Suspends the antitrust laws respecting certain agreements between common carriers and to freight forwarders subject to the Interstate Commerce Act concerning transportation services, charges, etc., on a finding by the Interstate Commerce Commission that such suspension will further the national transportation policy. Such agreements must assure to each partly the free and unrestrained right to independent action (June 17, 1948, 62 Stat. 472, U.S.C. 49: 5 (b)).

(c) Sections 408, 409, 411, 412, and 414 of the Civil Aeronautics Act, 1938:

(1) Persons who are parties to agreements approved by the Civil Aeronautics Board under sections 408, 409, 412 of the Civil Aeronautics Act 1938, are relieved from the operation of the antitrust laws (sec. 414, 52 Stat. 793, U.S.C. 49: 494).

(d) Interstate Commerce Act:

(1) Amends the Interstate Commerce Act, with respect to the authority of the Interstate Com-

merce Commission to regulate the use by motor carriers (under leases, contracts, or other arrangements) of motor vehicles not owned by them, in the furnishing of transportation of property but specifically provides that the Commission may not under this act regulate leases where the motor vehicle is used by a carrier in a single movement in the general direction in which such vehicle is based (Public Law 957, 84th Cong.).

14. Defense production:
    (a) Defense Production Act:
        (1) Under section 708 (a) the President is authorized to consult with representatives of industry, business, financing, agriculture, labor, and other interests, with a view to encouraging the making by such persons with the approval by the President of voluntary agreements and programs to further the objectives of this act. And under section 708 (b) it is provided that no act or omission to act pursuant to this act which occurs while this act is in effect, if requested by the President pursuant to a voluntary agreement or program approved under subsection (a) and found by the President to be in the public interest as contributing to the national defense shall be construed to be within the prohibitions of the antitrust laws or the Federal Trade Commission Act of the United States (Public Law 774, 81st Cong., 64 Stat. 798).
    (b) Defense Production Act Amendments of 1955:
        (1) Limits exemption under the Defense Production Act from the prohibitions of the antitrust laws and the Federal Trade Commission Act of the United States to acts and omissions to act requested by the President or his duly authorized delegate pursuant to duly approved voluntary agreements or programs relating solely to the exchange between actual or prospective contractors of technical or other information, production techniques, and patents or patent rights, relating to equipment

used primarily by or for the military which is being procured by the Department of Defense or any department thereof, and the exchange of materials, equipment, and personnel to be used in the production, of such equipment; and (2) acts and omissions to act requested by the President or his duly authorized delegate pursuant to voluntary agreements or programs which were duly approved under this section before the enactment of the Defense Production Act Amendments of 1955 (Public Law 295, 84th Cong., sec. 6).

CHAPTER 13

Labor Unions and the Antitrust Laws: Past, Present, and Proposals[1]

BY HERBERT R. NORTHRUP
AND GORDON F. BLOOM

Introduction

Antitrust policy, according to Thurman Arnold,[2] can be considered a logical development resulting from the contradiction of American mythology with the needs of American economic development. Certainly, the contrasts between the belief that the products of industry stem largely from many little happy business concerns and individuals and the reality of a United States Steel, General Motors, or General Electric is as great as the ambivalence of those who believe that bigness is a curse but enjoy the low prices resulting from the economies of large scale; or as hypocritical as the politicians who attack "big business" on the one hand, seek its favors on the other, and all the while realize the extent to which all Western civilization is today dependent upon the capacity of the large corporation to research, engineer, develop, and produce goods, services, and defense material.

Although business managements are usually on the receiving end of this confusion between economic reality and American mythology, their yearning to place

1. Most of the material herein is based upon Herbert R. Northrup and Gordon F. Bloom, *Government and Labor: The Role of Government in Union-Management Relations* (Homewood, 1963), by permission of the publisher.

2. Thurman Arnold, *The Folklore of Capitalism* (New Haven, 1937), p. 210.

labor "in an equal position" is on an emotional footing with most popular thinking in the antitrust field. How this came about and why it is so can best be examined by a brief review of past judicial applications of antitrust legislation to unions; then by an examination of reversal of the earlier decisions; third, an analysis of the Norris-La Guardia Act and the consequent judicial reversal of the earlier decisions; third, an analysis of the "labor monopoly" issue and the proposals to legislate in that area; and finally, what the writers believe are some practical measures of dealing effectively with the question of union monopoly power.

The Early Application of the Antitrust Laws to Organized Labor

For some years after the Sherman Act was passed, there was speculation as to whether or not it applied to labor. Finally, in 1908, in the case of *Loewe* v. *Lawlor*,[3] commonly known as the Danbury Hatters case, the United States Supreme Court ruled that a nationwide boycott organized by the union to persuade wholesalers and retailers to refrain from buying the company's products was an illegal restraint on commerce. The Court interpreted the statutory phrase, "restraint of trade or commerce," to apply to interference by a union with the interstate shipment of goods. The Court ordered the union to pay treble damages amounting to over half a million dollars, and individual members of the union were held responsible for their share of such damages.

Labor leaders were justifiably concerned about this result and immediately commenced pressure for exemption of labor from the antitrust laws. This drive culminated in the passage of the Clayton Act. Section 6 of that Act declared:

3. 208 U.S. 274 (1908).

> ... nothing contained in the antitrust laws shall be construed to forbid the existence and operation of labor ... organizations, instituted for the purposes of mutual help, and not having capital stock or conducted for profits, or to forbid or restrain individual members of such organizations from lawfully carrying out the legitimate objects thereof; nor shall such organizations, or the members thereof, be held or construed to be illegal combinations or conspiracies in restraint of trade under the antitrust laws.

Section 20 of the Clayton Act barred issuance of federal injunctions prohibiting activities such as strikes, boycotts, or picketing "in any case between an employer and employees, or between employers and employees, or between employees, or between persons employed and persons seeking employment, involving or growing out of, a dispute concerning terms or conditions of employment."

Section 20 concludes with a broad statement that none of the acts specified in this paragraph shall be considered violations "of any law of the United States."

Despite this broad language, the Supreme Court in 1921, in the case of *Duplex Printing Company* v. *Deering*,[4] held that the Clayton Act did not give labor unions a complete exemption from the antitrust laws. In that case the union sought to organize the Duplex plant and succeeded in getting members of other unions to refuse to handle the products of that company. In holding that such action was an illegal restraint of trade and a violation of the antitrust laws, the Court ruled that Section 20 of the Clayton Act applied only in cases where the relationship of employment existed between the company and the union members involved. Furthermore, the Court stated that the Clayton Act did not exempt unions "from accountability where it or they depart from ... normal and legitimate objects

4. 254 U.S. 433 (1921).

and engage in an actual combination or conspiracy in restraint of trade."[5]

By this decision the Supreme Court nullified what appears to have been the clear purpose of Congress and set up the judiciary as the judge of what actions by unions were "normal" and "legitimate." It is hard to believe that Congress, by use of the phrase "in any case between an employer and employees," meant to *limit* the protection of the statute to concerted action by labor only when it was carried out by employees of the employer involved in the dispute, for this would obviously make organization of a nonunion plant almost impossible. Nevertheless, the Supreme Court adopted a *narrow construction* of the statutory language which boiled down to saying that the only activities of organized labor that were protected by the Clayton Act were those that had been lawful before its enactment! As a result of this decision, employers stepped up their use of the injunction as a weapon to curb labor's organizing efforts.

The Norris-La Guardia Act

In 1932, when the membership of the American Federation of Labor was the *lowest in twenty years*, the AFL achieved its greatest legislative triumph to date. After almost fifty years of sustained effort the AFL succeeded in making the federal judiciary "neutral" in labor disputes. The law which accomplished this result was the Norris-La Guardia Anti-injunction Act passed by a Democratic-controlled House of Representatives and a Republican Senate, and signed by the then Republican President, Herbert Hoover.

We have seen how labor had been frustrated in its aim to secure passage of legislation which would effectively make lawful the use of union tactics deemed

5. 254 U.S. 443, 469.

necessary by labor for its survival and successful growth. The Norris-La Guardia Act represented a new approach to this problem. It did not legalize union action; it simply deprived the federal courts of jurisdiction in most situations involving labor disputes. It reflected essentially a laissez-faire philosophy: The law should intervene only to prevent damage to tangible property and to preserve public order; otherwise, the disputants should be left to their own resources to work out their problems. Both labor and business would now be free to promote their own interests in the field of labor policy through self-help without interference of the courts. The Act thus represented a reaction to judicial policy-making which had produced the anomalous result of the same action being enjoinable in one state and not in another. Henceforth, all federal courts were barred from passing judgment as to the lawfulness or unlawfulness of the objectives of labor's actions. This same principle was soon extended to many state courts, for the federal act was immediately copied by a dozen or more state legislatures.

The Norris-La Guardia Act commences with a statement of public policy which affirms the right of workers to engage in collective bargaining through unions of their own choosing. Yellow-dog contracts are declared to be against this public policy, and the federal courts are instructed not to enforce such contracts. Then Section 4 of the Act establishes the following rules for the courts:

> No court of the United States shall have jurisdiction to issue any restraining order or temporary or permanent injunction in any case involving or growing out of any labor dispute to prohibit any persons participating or interested in such dispute (as these terms are herein defined) from doing, whether singly or in concert, any of the following acts:

a) Ceasing or refusing to perform any work or to remain in any relation of employment; . . .

. . .

e) Giving publicity to the existence of, or the facts involved in, any labor dispute, whether by advertising, speaking, patrolling, or by any other method not involving fraud or violence.

f) Assembling peaceably to act or to organize to act in promotion of their interests in a labor dispute;

g) Advising or notifying any person of an intention to do any of the acts heretofore specified;

h) Agreeing with other persons to do or not to do any of the acts heretofore specified; and

i) Advising, urging, or otherwise causing or inducing without fraud or violence the acts heretofore specified. . . .

The Norris-La Guardia Act has been aptly called "the last monument to the spirit of complete free enterprise for unions."[6] It left unions pretty much free to use their tactical weapons without judicial interference. As we shall see, a "liberalized" Supreme Court interpreted the statute broadly so as to confer almost complete immunity on labor leaders in labor disputes. As long as violence was not used, unions could resort to threats, coercion, boycotts, picketing, strikes, and so on without fear of federal court action. Some labor critics say that the Act went too far in this direction and that the problems we face today in terms of abuse of union tactics would not have resulted had the Norris-La Guardia Act attempted to make a distinction between lawful and unlawful union objectives, as did the Clayton Act. This is a debatable issue which we shall better understand after discussing the Norris-La Guardia Act and its aftermath.

The Act defines "labor dispute" in the broadest pos-

6. Charles O. Gregory, *Labor and the Law,* 2d rev. ed. (New York, 1961), p. 197.

sible way so as to preclude judicial constructions, such as occurred in the Clayton Act, which whittled away the effect of the latter law: "The term 'labor dispute' includes any controversy concerning terms or conditions of employment, or concerning the association or representation of persons in negotiating, fixing, maintaining, changing or seeking to arrange terms or conditions of employment, regardless of whether or not the disputants stand in the proximate relation of employer and employee." It will be observed that Congress specifically took account of the fact that organized labor had a valid interest in conditions of employment even where it did not represent a single employee and that although such a situation did not involve a dispute technically between "an employer" and its "employees," nevertheless the protection afforded by the Norris-La Guardia Act was applicable.

The Act, in effect, outlawed injunctions in labor disputes except where violence is involved. Even in such cases the granting of injunctions is severely restricted. The Act provides that except for a five-day restraining order, no injunction may be granted restraining unlawful activities of a union in labor disputes cases except on a full hearing in open court. Furthermore, before the court can issue an injunction, it must find that unlawful acts have been and will be committed unless restrained; that the plaintiff will suffer substantial and irreparable injury; that as to each item of relief sought, greater injury will be inflicted upon the plaintiff by the denial of relief than will be inflicted upon the defendants by granting it; that the plaintiff has no adequate remedy at law; and that the police officers of the community are unwilling or unable to furnish adequate protection. Moreover, even if the above findings are made, the Act provides that no relief shall be granted a plaintiff who has failed to comply with any obligation imposed by law involved in the labor dispute, or who has failed to make every reasonable effort to settle the dispute by negotiation or any available governmental machinery of mediation or voluntary arbitration. It is understandable after reading this long catalogue of conditions that union attorneys are generally able to frustrate the attempts of management attorneys to secure injunctions even in cases where the union may have engaged in violence, intimidation, and other unlawful acts which were not intended to be protected by the Act.

With a single piece of legislation, Congress thus repealed a century of judicial interpretation and created laissez faire, or economic free enterprise, for organized labor as well as for business. Henceforth, the courts were not to interfere with strikes, boycotts, and picketing which were conducted peacefully and otherwise within the law. Moreover, by defining "labor dispute" in a broad fashion, Congress ensured labor's right to engage in sympathy strikes, secondary boycotts, stranger picketing, and other activities in which nonemployees of a concern come to the aid of the concern's employees in labor disputes directly or by applying pressure upon third parties.

Despite the clarity of its language, the Norris-La Guardia Act might either have been misconstrued or declared unconstitutional by the courts if the attitude of the courts had not altered fundamentally on labor matters by the time litigation arising out of the Act reached the Supreme Court. Between the dates when the Act was passed by Congress and reviewed by the highest Court, the New Deal of Franklin D. Roosevelt had intervened, and the thinking of the highest Court had been altered. As a result, the Norris-La Guardia

Act and similar state laws were interpreted to preclude injunctive relief in peacefully conducted labor disputes.[7]

Reversal of Sherman Act Decisions

The combined effect of the Norris-La Guardia Act and the liberalized view of labor disputes which the Supreme Court took after 1937 resulted in a revision of precedents on the application of the Sherman Act to labor. In 1940 the Supreme Court, in the case of *Apex Hosiery Co.* v. *Leader,*[8] handed down the first of a group of landmark decisions which delineate the present legal status of unions under the antitrust laws. In that case the union, in the course of an organizational strike against a hosiery company, seized the company's plant, engaged in a sit-down strike on company property, and refused to let the company make a shipment of hosiery, most of which was destined to out-of-state customers. Despite the fact that there was clear evidence of a restraint in interstate shipment of goods similar to that involved in the Danbury Hatters case, the Court held that such action did not violate the antitrust laws. The Court reasoned that the Sherman Act was aimed at restraints upon commercial competition in the marketing of goods or services, whereas the union's purpose was not restraint upon commerce, but only to compel the employer to accede to its demands.

According to the majority opinion, "in order to render a labor combination effective it must eliminate

7. The Supreme Court has held, however, that the Norris–La Guardia Act does not bar the United States government from obtaining an injunction in a labor dispute in which it technically is the employer. In 1947, in the case of *U.S.* v. *United Mine Workers*, 330 U.S. 258, the Supreme Court held that an injunction could validly be issued by a federal court at the request of the United States government to prevent the Mine Workers from continuing to strike after the government had seized the coal mines.

8. 310 U.S. 469 (1940).

competition from nonunion made goods, ... an elimination of price competition based upon difference in labor standards is the objective of any national labor organization. But this effect on competition has not been considered to be of the kind of curtailment of price competition prohibited by the Sherman Act." This decision is generally interpreted to mean that trade unions do not violate the Sherman Act if their activities do not actually result in price-fixing or restraint on competition unless this was the primary intention of their activities. While the Court attempted to reconcile earlier decisions, in effect it overruled them by making it clear that mere interference with interstate commerce was not sufficient to make such union action unlawful.

The effect of the next decision by the Supreme Court was to grant an even more sweeping immunity to labor organizations. In the case of *United States* v. *Hutcheson*,[9] decided in 1941, the court had before it a national boycott of the products of the Anheuser-Busch Brewing Company instituted by the carpenters' union be cause the company had contracted with machinists to dismantle certain equipment. Here was a boycott similar to those organized and held unlawful in the *Danbury* and *Duplex* cases. How could this new "liberal" Court hold such action lawful without overruling those early cases?

The Court accomplished this objective through a feat of circuitous reasoning. The conduct in question was held lawful because it fell within the general language of Section 20 of the Clayton Act which, after describing various union activities, concludes with the statement that none of such acts shall be considered violations of "any law of the United States." Recognizing that the Supreme Court in the *Duplex* case had re-

9. 312 U.S. 219 (1941).

fused to apply this same language to legalize similar union action, the Court now ruled that Congress, by enacting the Norris–La Guardia Act, had breathed new life into this exemption! Since the action in question could not have been enjoined in federal court under the terms of that Act, the Court argued that it should not therefore be held unlawful under the Sherman Act. Labor union conduct of the type described in Section 4 of the Norris–La Guardia Act was henceforth not only nonenjoinable, but lawful for all purposes under federal law.

Justice Frankfurter, in speaking for the majority of the Court, did suggest one exception to this sweeping exemption: "So long as a union acts in its self-interest, and does not combine with non-labor groups, the licit and the illicit under Section 20 [of the Clayton Act] are not to be distinguished by any judgment regarding the wisdom or unwisdom, the rightness or wrongness, the selfishness or unselfishness of the end of which the particular union activities are the means." In this dictum, he suggested that if unions conspired with employers to control the supply and price of commodities for their mutual benefit and thus departed from legitimate union objectives, they might still be liable under the Sherman Act.

The third major case in this series, *Allen-Bradley Co. v. Local 3, International Brotherhood of Electrical Workers,*[10] was decided by the Supreme Court in 1945. In this case a union of electrical workers in the New York area agreed with contractors to purchase equipment only from local manufacturers who had closed shop agreements with Local 3. It also obtained agreement from manufacturers to confine their New York sales to contractors employing Local 3 members. The Supreme Court found that the contracts were "but one

10. 325 U.S. 797 (1945)

element in which contractors and manufacturers united . . . *to monopolize all the* business in New York City." The Court therefore held that the union and the employers were both guilty of violating the antitrust laws.

The extended immunity granted to labor from the antitrust laws and the injunction was followed to its logical conclusion in other decisions further elaborating the laissez-faire attitude. The American Federation of Musicians was permitted to maintain a nationwide boycott of recordings by refusing to have its members make such recordings;[11] a hod carriers' union was permitted to prevent usage within its jurisdiction of a low-cost cement-mixing machine except under conditions which made the use of such machines financially impossible;[12] building trade unions were permitted to boycott materials because they were produced by companies for which rival unions were bargaining agents or because they were prefabricated instead of being put together on the job;[13] unions were allowed to picket or boycott a company solely on the grounds that it dealt with a rival union and despite the fact that if the employer recognized the picketing or boycotting union, he would violate the National Labor Relations (Wagner) Act;[14] and finally, a union could with immunity have its members refuse to work for an employer ready and willing to deal with the union, because of a grudge against the employer, even though the effect was to force the employer out of business.[15]

11 *U.S* v *American Federation of Musicians,* 318 U.S. 741 (1943).

12. *U.S.* v. *International Hod Carriers' Union,* 313 U.S. 539, (1941).

13. *U.S.* v. *Building & Construction Trade Council,* 313 U.S. 539 (1941).

14. *National Labor Relations Board* v. *Star Publishing Co.,* 97 F. 2d 465 (1938).

15. *Hunt* v. *Crumback,* 325 U.S. 821 (1945).

While there are still many gray areas in application of the antitrust laws to labor, these cases – and in particular the *Apex*, *Hutcheson*, and *Allen-Bradley* decisions – broadly define the permissible limits of concerted union activity, and suggest that unions are subject to the antitrust laws under existing legislation only:[16]

1. Where the union intends to achieve some commercial restraint primarily and not as a by-product of its essential intent to advance its own cause (*Apex* case).
2. Where union activity is not in the course of a labor dispute as broadly defined by the Norris-La Guardia Act (*Hutcheson* case).
3. Where a union combines with some nonlabor group to achieve some direct commercial restraint (*Allen-Bradley* case).[17]

The *Apex* case, at first glance, appears to establish a workable criterion for distinguishing lawful and unlawful union action, but closer inspection reveals that the distinction is illusory. Just what is a "commercial restraint"? Can unions picket retail establishments without producing a "commercial restraint"? Is a secondary boycott of retail outlets in order to secure organization of a manufacturing business violative of this standard?

The *Hutcheson* decision, in practical effect, made the antitrust laws inapplicable to unions regardless of their

16. See "Should Labor Unions Be Subject to Antitrust Laws?" *Congressional Digest*, vol. 61 (October, 1961), p. 231.

17. In *Los Angeles Meat and Provision Drivers Union, Local 626* v. *U.S.*, 9 L. Ed. 2d 150 (November, 1962), the United States Supreme Court held that the Norris – La Guardia Act did not bar a federal court from ordering a union to terminate the union membership of self-employed grease peddlers who, the court found, conspired with the union to fix the purchase and sale price of grease, allocate territories, and otherwise violate the antitrust laws.

objective as long as they did not conspire with non-labor elements. There was no need to make such a sweeping pronouncement on the subject, and there are undoubtedly members of the Court today who regret the Court's largesse in granting such a broad exemption to labor. It should be remembered, however, that the Court in 1941 was dealing with a labor movement which during the thirties had never numbered more than 8.5 million members. Perhaps a different decision would have resulted had the Court first been presented with the *Hutcheson* case today, when union members number 19 million. In any case, it is difficult to see why labor should have a right to fix prices or allocate markets even without direct employer conspiracy. These are objectives which the antitrust laws and public policy generally condemn and should be unlawful when carried out by any group in the community.

The *Allen-Bradley* case amplifies the loophole in existing antitrust law. Unions cannot fix prices in combination with employers, but presumably they can do it alone. Courts and commentators have interpreted this case to mean that negotiation of parallel collective bargaining agreements effecting market control, when sponsored by the union, do not violate the Sherman Act.[18] For example, in one large city the contract between the painters' union and painting contractors required all contractors to adhere to a minimum price scale. Should such union-induced price-fixing be lawful?

18. Archibald Cox, "Labor and the Antitrust Laws – A Preliminary Analysis," *University of Pennsylvania Law Review*, vol. 100 (1955), pp. 252, 271. But see the discussion below of *Pennington v. United Mine Workers*, 325 F. 2d 804 (6th Cir. 1963), which upheld a finding of conspiracy between a union and major coal producers to eliminate smaller companies based on, among other things, the union's insistence that all employers pay the same wages.

Northrup-Bloom

Unions and Monopoly Power

We have seen how the Norris–La Guardia Act passed at a time when organized labor was relatively weak and impotent, has today clothed organized labor with power that is denied to other groups in the market place. The contention is frequently urged that a union monopoly is no better than a business monopoly and that both should be subject to the restrictions contained in our antitrust laws, which were enacted to deal with monopolies and restraints on trade. Are unions monopolies? Do unions restrain trade? Consideration of the conflicting arguments relative to proposals to extend the antitrust laws to unions can best be analyzed by enumerating the various kinds of alleged union monopoly power.

Exclusive Jurisdiction. Every union can be said to be a monopolist, for the purpose of a union is to eliminate competition in the labor market. This would be true even if union organization did not have statutory support. In addition, a union is like a monopoly because, once certified by the National Labor Relations Board (and unless decertified), a union has, by law, an area of operation in representing workers in the bargaining unit in which competition from other unions is prohibited. Under the Taft-Hartley Act, employees bargain through unions of their own choosing which the employer must recognize as the exclusive bargaining agent. A majority of persons voting in the election determine the bargaining agent for all of the workers in the bargaining unit. As long as a union remains the certified bargaining agent, it has the exclusive right to represent workers in their relations with the employer. When this power is combined with a union shop, which requires new workers to join the union after 30 days as a prerequisite to holding their jobs, the union has in effect obtained a monopoly over job opportunities with the particular employer. Nonunion workers or members of other unions cannot work for the employer after expiration of the 30-day period.

Many of the staunchest friends of labor – including the late President Franklin D. Roosevelt – have publicly expressed doubts concerning the merits of such "compulsory unionism." There is no doubt that the compulsory aspect of the union shop strengthens the power of union leaders and creates circumstances which may be used by labor bosses to enrich themselves at the expense of the rank-and-file employees. Justice Brandeis, certainly a friend of labor, felt that the ideal condition for strong unionism was to have an appreciable number of men outside the union. As he put it: "Such a nucleus of unorganized labor will check oppression by the unions as the unions check oppression by the employer."[19]

Many supporters of the extension of antitrust laws to unions earnestly believe that such legislation is meaningless unless the "source of union monopoly power" is eliminated, namely, the principle of exclusive representation and the union shop. They concur with the language of the Taft-Hartley Act, which states that "employees shall have the right to self-organization . . . for the purpose of collective bargaining or other mutual aid or protection, *and shall also have the right to refrain from any or all of such activities,*" but they would add as a basic tenet of public policy that employees shall have the right to join – *or not to join* – unions. Advocates of this position have actively promoted the adoption of so-called right-to-work laws banning the union shop. Because of a provision in the Taft-Hartley Act giving state law precedence in such matters, the union shop can be outlawed within state boundaries

19. Quoted in Donald R. Richberg, *Labor Union Monopoly* (Chicago, (1957), p. 118.

even though it is lawful under federal law. As of March 1, 1963, right-to-work laws of general application had been adopted in twenty states.

The importance of the right to work issue in the control of union power will be discussed in the concluding section of this paper.

Industry-wide Bargaining. The practice of so-called industry-wide bargaining has seemed to many people to be a major source of union monopoly power. Actually, the term is a misnomer, for cases of actual industry-wide bargaining are rare. The coal industry is often pointed to as an example of industry-wide bargaining, but it is not. For example, in the bituminous coal industry, bargaining is conducted partly with the Bituminous Coal Operators' Association, partly with the Southern Coal Producers' Association, partly with some smaller groups, and partly with individual operators who do not bargain through the associations. Even in steel, bargaining is normally carried on with individual employers, although the pattern bargaining which has resulted in recent years gives the appearance of industry-wide bargaining. Closer examination of legislative proposals aimed at this type of bargaining indicates they are really concerned with multi-unit bargaining—that is, collective bargaining arrangements covering more than one plant—particularly where the effect of a breakdown in bargaining can substantially curtail production and employment in an industry.

A typical example often cited to support the need for such legislation is the 1959 breakdown in negotiations between the United Steelworkers and the major steel companies, which resulted in idleness for 500,000 steelworkers and enforced layoffs for 100,000 other persons in related industries such as mining and railway transportation.[20] To many people, the struggle between the

20. *Economic Report of the President,* January 1960 (Washington, 1960), p. 14.

United Steelworkers and the major steel companies—and similar conflicts in other key industries—seems like a battle between Goliaths from which the public is bound to emerge the loser.

It is wrong to assume, however, that multiunit bargaining is a device foisted on industry by strong unions. On the contrary, the development of different types of multi-unit bargaining varies from industry to industry, depending upon the basic characteristics of the particular industry. While industry-wide bargaining frequently develops in oligopolistic industries where there are a few relatively large producers, it has also become established in highly competitive industries with many producers, such as the garment industries and bituminous coal.

Frequently, multi-unit bargaining evolves because of employer preference for this kind of bargaining. One of the most important reasons why employers have defended or initiated multi-unit bargaining is the protection it gives them against loss from strikes. In industries such as transportation, building construction, amusements, services, or occasionally retail trade, a strike can result in a loss of business which is never regained because the company deals in a perishable good or service. If a union can pick off employers one by one, employers are, more often than not, helpless to prevent the union from achieving even the most outrageous demands. On the other hand, when the companies form a common front, the union power is blunted because a strike means a strike of the entire industry.

Unions frequently prefer multi-unit bargaining because it enables them to equalize wage costs in industries in which wages are an important cost factor. This is the case, for example, in the men's clothing industry. If wage rates were not equalized on a national basis, employers who compete with one another in the national market would have cost advantages or disadvantages attributable to a diversity of settlements in wage rates.

In industries in which an employee typically works for more than one employer, multi-unit collective bargaining is virtually essential for both employer and union. These trades include the maritime trades, the building trades, and the needle trades. In such industries, failure to equalize wages and working conditions would have the effect of permitting some employers to pay lower wages to employees who also work for other employers paying higher wages. From the union and employer points of view, this is a chaotic situation. For example, in the building industry the low-wage employer would be able to outbid high-wage competitors solely because the union allowed him a favorable rate. Employers prefer that wage competition be neutralized and that competition rest upon efficiency, service, and similar considerations.

It is impossible to explore the rationale and full complexities of multi-unit bargaining in this limited review. Nevertheless, it should be apparent that such bargaining practices cannot be eliminated by legislative fiat without seriously affecting industrial competitive structure and practices. The national bargaining in certain industries was created by the national character of the market for the industry. The real question is not "Shall we have national bargaining?" but rather "Shall it be national bargaining with a strong union or without a strong union?" It is difficult to imagine effective collective bargaining between General Motors and a union if, on the union side, all negotiations had to be conducted on a plant basis between the local union and the company. Furthermore, proposals to atomize labor unions are completely unrealistic.

Nevertheless, this type of remedy is embodied in several of the bills now pending in Congress. Labor contracts, with certain exceptions, would be required by law to be negotiated only between individual employers and local unions. International union officials could no longer negotiate contracts for their locals; the international union would be put in the position of a trade association giving advice to its locals but taking no active role in labor-management negotiations. Obviously, such legislation, if enacted, would disrupt long-standing relationships in many industries and would also prohibit bargaining through employer associations, which many employers feel has done much to stabilize labor-management relations.

Industry-wide bargaining has produced two problems which require solution. The first is the industry-wide strike which may imperil the national health or safety. A discussion of this question is beyond the limits of this article.[21] It should, nevertheless, be pointed out that if a solution is found necessary for this problem, a better approach would be the partial injunction technique. Even if industry-wide bargaining is prohibited, strikes could be called concurrently by several local unions, and still shut an industry down.

The second is the wage-price spiral resulting from industry-wide settlements negotiated by a few men representing industry and labor which produce an industry-wide adjustment of both wages and prices. While the requirement of local bargaining would disrupt pattern wage and price adjustments, it might in the end produce even more inflationary results. As inflationary as steel settlements have been over the years, it is possible that the results would have been worse if there had been a series of local settlements with union vying with union to win the largest wage adjustment for its membership.

Proponents of legislation aimed at prohibiting indus-

21. See Northrup and Bloom, *op.cit.*, Chapters 13-15.

try-wide bargaining maintain that they are trying to protect our free collective bargaining institutions and that unless action is taken to bring back competition in the labor market, the government will be forced to intervene in nationwide strikes, with the result that compulsory arbitration or government dictation of the terms of settlement will result. This is a possibility that must be reckoned with. Nevertheless, there is a strong suspicion that supporters of this type of legislation are more interested in weakening labor than in restoring competition. None of these proposals have contained provisions which would require the breaking-up of industrial giants such as the United States Steel Corporation, for example. The requirement that all collective bargaining be carried out through local unions would generate widespread disorganization in industrial relations and raise problems of enforcement that stagger the imagination. It is unlikely that we can by legislative fiat establish a competitive labor market in our economy, and there is considerable doubt whether such objective, if it could be accomplished, would be desirable.

A case which if upheld may significantly affect the future of industry-wide bargain was recently decided by the Sixth Circuit Court of Appeals. *Pennington v. United Mine Workers*[22] is one of a number of actions brought by small mine operators against the United Mine Worker Union alleging a violation of the Sherman Act on the ground that the 1950 coal agreement between the UMW and the Bituminous Coal Operators' Association was an unlawful conspiracy to force high contract rates on all mines in the industry, large and small alike, and thus freeze out many small operators. A United States district court jury in Tennessee found the union guilty, and the lower court fined the union

22. 325 F. 2d 804 (6th Cir. 1963).

$325,000. The Circuit Court upheld this part of the district court's decision. The case will undoubtedly be further appealed to the United States Supreme Court because of its importance not only to the coal industry but also to all industries in which multiunit bargaining exists. The United Steelworkers of America and the AFL-CIO Industrial Union Department have joined the UMW in defending the coal agreement. Union lawyers state that if UMW practices are held to constitute an antitrust violation, then other unions may be subject to possible antitrust liability when they engage in activities which heretofore have been considered legitimate union conduct.[23]

Market Control. While the viewpoints of organized labor and management frequently clash, nevertheless there are many situations in which their objectives may coincide. In an industry where a strong union continually seeks and obtains large wage increases, the normal pattern of adjustment is in price increases sufficient to offset the increases in cost resulting from the wage increases. Employers look with disfavor on those firms in the industry which do not go along with this trend, and union leaders are likely to be concerned at price-cutting efforts or aggressive attempts to move into territory of other firms on the ground that this will "upset" the industry and endanger the union's wage program. It is easy to visualize, therefore, a situation in which a union will become, in effect, a policeman in an industry and will be able to achieve, through the various pressures on management that only unions can use, maintenance of price policy, market sharing, and other policies affecting the market for the product which the employers themselves could not accomplish without be-

23. *Business Week* (November 3, 1962), p. 49. See also the brief comments by Nat Goldfinger and Theodore St. Antoine in Chapter 16, below.

ing in violation of the antitrust laws. As the Supreme Court intimated in the *Allen-Bradley* case, a union can lawfully accomplish such results so long as it does not actually conspire with management to achieve such objectives.

As a consequence, there are many situations in which unions have been able to exert pressure on marketing policies which, in effect, restrain competition. In some industries – the building trades especially – it has been alleged that the very right to do business is openly controlled by unions; the unions decide who can operate, what wages are to be paid and hours worked, and who may be hired.[24] Numerous examples have been reported of unions in the laundry and dry-cleaning industry preventing "unfair competition" by eliminating price-cutting independents. In the clothing industry the unions have established so-called industry stabilization programs, which impose controls on manufacturers' prices and also place limits on the companies with which the manufacturer may do business. In other industries, unions have refused to work for companies which are not members of a trade association and do not abide by the commercial practices decreed by the union.

A similar type of market control is exerted by unions through geographical restrictions on the permissible area of an employer's business. For example, in Chicago, Illinois, a roofing contractor was told by a union business agent that he was not to solicit or accept any jobs north of 47th Street. When he disobeyed this instruction and sought to extend his area of operations, he found that he could not get supplies or labor to

24. Statement of National Association of Manufacturers in *Congressional Digest,* vol. 61 (October, 1961), p. 244.

operate his business.[25] The union had established a market-sharing arrangement to prevent price-cutting and to make it possible for it to maintain high wages. No single employer had the power to upset this union-maintained monopolistic arrangement.

Unions have also been involved in direct price-fixing activities. For example, the labor agreement between painters and painting contractors in Peoria, Illinois, provided that all contractors must adhere to minimum prices approved by a local board and granted to such board the right to prevent the execution of any work obtained at prices below this minimum.[26]

Union interest in the product market and in the prices received by an employer for his product is, of course, understandable. Price-cutting, declining profits, a disorganized market, too many competitors – all of these threaten the union's objective of maintaining high wage rates. It is difficult to see, however, how union efforts to control prices, market share, or other aspect of the product market can be sanctioned when such action is forbidden to businessmen.

Most knowledgeable students of this problem who seek a limited application of the antitrust laws to unions have centered their attention upon market control or commercial restraint as the critical factor requiring governmental action. For example, after a long study of the problem, the Attorney General's National Committee to Study the Antitrust Laws concluded:

> . . . we believe that where the concession demanded from an employer as prerequisite to ceasing coercive action against him is participation in or submission to such

25. *Hearings before the Committee on Education and Labor*, House of Representatives, 83d Congress, 1st Sess., vol. 8 (Washington, 1953), p. 2809.

26. Cox, *op.cit.*, p. 266.

a scheme for market control or commercial restraints, this union conduct should be prohibited by statute.

Regarding such legislation this Committee recommends: a) It should cover only specific union activities which have as their direct object direct control of the market, such as fixing the kind or amount of products which may be used, produced or sold, their market price, the geographical area in which they may be sold, or the number of firms which may engage in their production or distribution. . . .[27]

Union Featherbedding Practices. Union featherbedding practices involving make-work rules and restrictions on output have increasingly become a matter of public concern in recent years. At a time when we are in a production battle with the Soviet Union and our overseas markets are threatened by new, efficient plants in West Germany, Japan, and other nations, the question is being raised whether we can any longer afford the luxury of featherbedding, which has as its objective inefficiency rather than efficiency in production. This issue has been injected in the antitrust debate on the ground that featherbedding rules constitute an unreasonable restraint of trade beyond the legitimate scope of union activity.

Examples of featherbedding practices are legion. The railroad brotherhoods have carried make-work rules to the extreme, as a result of their position that every item of work *belongs* to a particular employee. If that employee is deprived of the opportunity to work, he is entitled to be paid, and so of course is the man performing the job. The result in many cases is that two days' pay must be given as compensation for a trivial amount of work. Because of retention of archaic rules going back to a time when trains were not as speedy as

27. *Report of the Attorney General's National Committee to Study the Antitrust Laws* (Washington, 1955), p. 304.

today, five different crews may have to be used on a train between New York and Chicago. The building trades are also strong proponents of featherbedding rules. Local 3 of the International Brotherhood of Electrical Workers in New York has insisted that its members rewire apparatus that has come already wired from the manufacturer, even though the employees of the manufacturer are members of the same international union.[28] It is standard practice for the plumbers' union to require that pipes be threaded on the job, even though it is far more economical to do threading in the shop. Similar policies are frequently followed by the plasterers, electricians, and carpenters in the building trades and the stagehands in the amusement industry. In the printing industry, certain advertisers prefer to supply their copy in the form of a mat or cut, with the type already set. The International Typographical Union requires that an exact duplicate of these forms be set up by its members in the plant, proofread, and corrected. This so-called "bogus" type is then junked and melted down.

Union make-work rules have been particularly burdensome where they have excluded improved products, services, or inventions from the market. For example, in the Joliet, Illinois, area, the Glaziers' Local Union No. 27 undertook a comprehensive campaign to eliminate the use of preglazed window sash and doors on building work. Since it completely controlled the labor supply in this area for glazier work, it was able to cut off the supply of this skilled labor until use of preglazed sash was discontinued. Similarly, the plumbers' union in many areas has been able to prevent use of plastic pipe. This new product is superior to metal pip-

28. Sumner H. Slichter, J. Healy, and E. Robert Livernash, *The Impact of Collective Bargaining on Management* (Washington, 1960), p. 320.

ing for some uses, is cheaper, and involves considerably less labor and skill in installation, but the union control of installation has kept it off the market. The painters' union in Chicago has applied restrictions on the use of roller coaters as well as spray guns. These rules not only prevent the use of certain improved paint products but have been estimated to add as much as $100 per house in Federal Housing projects.[29]

The employment of unneeded personnel is most closely associated with the activities of James Caesar Petrillo, former president of the American Federation of Musicians. The contracts of this organization have required the employment of musicians in radio stations, theaters, and elsewhere when no artistic commercial need existed. These practices led to the passage of the Lea Act in 1946, making it unlawful to compel a licensee under the Federation Communications Act (1) to employ or pay for more employees than are needed, (2) to refrain from carrying educational programs with unpaid performers on a noncommercial basis, and (3) to interfere with the production or use of records. According to one recent study, this legislation has been effective, so that "the employment of unwanted staff musicians is no longer a problem in broadcasting."[30]

On the other hand, the attempt to deal with this problem in industry at large in the Taft-Hartley Act has not been particularly successful. Section 8 b (6) of that Act makes it an unfair labor practice for a union "to cause or attempt to cause an employer to pay or deliver or agree to pay or deliver any money or other thing of value in the nature of an exaction for services which are not performed or not to be performed." While this provision was aimed at "featherbedding practices" gen-

29. *Hearings before the Committee on Education and Labor, op.cit.*, vol. 6, p. 2225.

30. Slichter, Healy, and Livernash, *op.cit.*, p. 329.

erally, the Supreme Court has greatly narrowed its scope and has, in effect, ruled that employers can be forced to pay for services that are not wanted or needed. Similar state laws have also been ineffective.[31]

Make-work practices represent an extreme complicated problem in industrial relations. They are essentially an expression of employees' insecurity relative to their jobs. For this reason, they are most frequently found in industries faced by shrinking employment, either because of contracting markets or because of technological change, and in industries such as construction, entertainment, and stevedoring where employment is intermittent. Although featherbedding practices are wasteful and costly to the public, there is a real question whether they can be dealt with effectively by legislation. What agency, for example, is to pass judgment on how fast a man should work or how many men should be required to operate a given machine? Moreover, if a union is barred from actually prohibiting use of an improved device, it can still achieve the same objective by charging a prohibitory rate for employees who use it. To be sure, extreme cases are easy to detect, and it is possible that some form of legislation may be enacted to prohibit such practices. But where is the line to be drawn between practices which clearly make work and those which retard the speed of work in order to prolong the employees' working life, or as a health measure, etc.? Should a union be liable for treble dangers under an antitrust statute because it forbids members to use spray guns, which it contends are injurious to health? It is extremely doubtful whether the courts could cope with this kind of a problem. Yet the complicated and diverse patterns of work practices in industry at large would be dumped in their laps if such practices were brought under the antitrust laws.

31. Northrup and Bloom, *op.cit.,* Chapter 9.

If, on the other hand, the job of policing a new anti-featherbedding law is given to an administrative agency, it will have to pass judgment on a variety of labor relations matters that are intimately related to management production policies. The great danger, therefore, is that such legislation will result in further injection of government into industrial relations to a degree which neither labor, business, nor the public would find desirable.

There is, furthermore, a basic question of public policy which must be considered. Restriction of output is a characteristic of our economy which is not limited to labor organizations. Many businessmen restrict output in order to keep prices high. Numerous professional societies have obtained enactment of legislation which would permit only licensed personnel to pursue certain professions, with the objective of limiting the supply of workers. In New Jersey, the State Bar Association attempted unsuccessfully to have the negotiation of labor-management contracts declared the practice of law. Farmers continually restrict production, plow under crops, and ask to be paid for crops not marketed. How different is all this from union make-work policies? Is it fair to single out labor alone for remedial legislation?

Proposals for Application of Antitrust Laws to Labor

At this writing, four separate bills are pending before Congress aimed at restricting alleged union monopolistic activities (Table 1). Management spokesmen, having achieved some success through the Landrum-Griffin Act in eliminating abuses in the internal administration of unions, are now determined to make an all-out fight to curb union abuses which they contend amount to the uncontrolled use of monopoly power. Supporters of this viewpoint include union haters who see in such legislation a means of weakening

TABLE 1
Comparison of Antimonopoly Bills

	Martin (H.R. 9271)	McClellan (S. 2573)
General purpose	To ban union restrictive practices, multiemployer monopolistic bargaining, and national strikes.	To outlaw strikes in the transportation industry.
Scope of bargaining	Union agents can only bargain for employees of a single company, except in metropolitan areas where city-wide negotiations are allowed.	A union may not combine with another in a strike or plan to substantially restrain transportation.
Effect on union practices	It would be unlawful for a union to (1) interfere with production, (2) restrict the number of persons entering a trade, or (3) control prices or impose featherbedding practices. Featherbedding practices are specifically defined.	It would be unlawful to strike, picket, black-list, or commit any act against an employer which substantially restrains transportation of people or property. "Hot cargo" secondary boycott clauses, whereby a union reserves the right to refuse to handle products, would be illegal.
Effect on employer practices	It would be illegal for any employer to join with another in bargaining, except in metropolitan areas where city-wide negotiations are permitted.	An employer would be prohibited from making an agreement which would require him to cease doing business with another employer.
Coverage	All unions and employers except those subject to the National Railway Labor Act.	Applies only to employers and unions involved in transporting persons or goods in interstate commerce.

(table continues)

TABLE 1 — *Comparison of Antimonopoly Bills (cont.)*

	Thurmond-Alger (S. 2292 H.R. 8407)	Hiestand-Alger (H.R. 228 H.R. 4573)
General purpose	To prevent restraints of trade or actions tending to create a monopoly.	To prevent industry-wide bargaining and national strikes.
Scope of bargaining	A union may not combine with another where it would constitute a restraint of trade or tend to create a monopoly.	A union may not combine with another, whether an international or a local, to plot concessions to be won from employers.
Effect on union practices	It would be unlawful for a union to strike or seek contract provisions which constitute a combination in restraint of trade.	It would be unlawful for a union to strike or seek contract provisions that will substantially or materially affect the production, use, cost, handling, or sales of a product or service.
Effect on employer practices	It would be unlawful for an employer to make a labor agreement in restraint of trade.	It would be unlawful for an employer, in concert tiwh a union, to engage in any conduct to restrain trade or tend to create a monopoly.
Coverage	Applies to all employers and unions.	Applies to all employers and unions.

SOURCE: Chamber of Commerce of the United States, *Labor Relations Letter*, Extra Issue (Washington, D.C., January 1962) p. 4.

organized labor. They also include many thoughtful *public-minded individuals who are friends of organized* labor, but who are also seriously concerned about any uncontrolled aggregation of power, whether it be labor or capital, which can be used to the detriment of the public interest. As a matter of fact, there is evidence of considerable public support for some legislation to curb excesses of unrestricted union power. The Opinion Research Corporation of Princeton, New Jersey, recently conducted a poll which found that 62 percent of the public favored bringing unions under the antitrust laws. Nine percent were opposed, and 29 percent were undecided. According to the same survey, 57 percent of union members support such legislation, 20 percent oppose it, and 23 percent have no opinion.[32]

The idea of free competition economy is still very much a part of the American ideal and strongly affects our national economic policy. While this principle has been compromised many times – in subsidies to industries, support prices in agriculture, tariffs for favored industries, and regulated monopolies in the case of utilities – nevertheless a politician is assured of a favorable audience if he enunciates today the same doctrine embodied in the Sherman Act over seventy years ago, namely, that "*Every* contact, combination in the form of trust, or otherwise, or conspiracy in restraint of trade or commerce" (emphasis supplied) is unlawful. Our national labor policy, therefore, is inconsistent with our general views on economic policy, for in the area of labor relations, we have adopted as our public objective the encouragement and strengthening of monopoly.

The Wagner Act (and its successor, the Taft-Hartley Act), in purpose and application, runs counter to the

32. Chamber of Commerce of the United States, *Labor Relations Letter* (Washington, January, 1962), p. 1.

objectives expressed in the antitrust laws. The Wagner Act fostered the growth of industry-wide unionism and encouraged the organization of 100 percent of an industry without concern for the impact which such extensive organization would have upon prices and the product market. As a consequence, a dual standard in antitrust policy has developed: A union can probably negotiate separate but parallel labor agreements with all employers in an industry and thus effectively police the product market, yet the employers cannot take this action among themselves, nor can the union make such an agreement with all employers as part of one master contract.

Legitimate union action designed to stabilize wage rates in organized companies often necessarily involves an impact on the product market. A union cannot permit low-wage, low-price firms to enlarge their share of the market, for this will endanger the competitive position of the unionized firms and ultimately weaken union control in the industry. Furthermore, union efforts to organize, raise wages, and improve working conditions, when supported by strikes, picketing, boycotts, and similar tactics, all have the tendency to restrain trade. How can we permit legitimate union activity and still bar restraints which are so monopolistic in nature as to run counter to our basic ideas of what is allowable economic strife in a free economy?

This is the problem, and it seems clear that there is no easy solution. Probably the worst thing that could be done would be enactment of a general amendment to the antitrust laws making some distinction between "legitimate" and "illegitimate" labor activities, and then leaving to the courts the amplification of policy through case-by-case decisions. Our existing antitrust laws have not been particularly successful in preventing monopoly in industry, and court decisions have in fact been notably unsuccessful in classifying in businessmen's minds what is lawful and unlawful in this complicated field of law. To inject the courts into the labor monopoly issue would simply add confusion rather than solve the problem.

A Positive Program to Control Excessive Union Power

Because the emphasis in this volume is on monopoly and antitrust, the analysis has concentrated on activities and proposals relating union power to the antitrust approach. The conclusion that the antitrust laws are not appropriate vehicles to handle the question of union power should not be deemed also a conclusion that union power as now bolstered by legislative enactment, judicial decision, and administrative rulings and assistance is in satisfactory adjustment with the public interest. The facts appear to be quite the contrary. But the approach to the problem herein advocated is not primarily through more legislation, but through the appeal of certain aspects of law which now unrealistically favor unions and, to this observer, act contrary to the public interest. The following program is, therefore, proposed.

I. *Repeal or Major Revision of the Norris-La Guardia Act.* Any workable approach to the problems raised by union monopoly and other restrictive practices of organized labor must include a thorough revision of the Norris-La Guardia Act. Some labor experts question whether the reason for its being any longer exists. In the words of Charles O. Gregory, distinguished professor of labor law: "Its original purpose – enabling unions to organize by recourse to economic pressures – has long since been fulfilled; and in many ways the statute has become obsolete."[33] When the Norris-La Guardia Act was passed, there was no Wagner Act nor

33. Gregory, *op. cit.,* p. 551.

Taft-Hartley Act, no procedure for peacefully determining representation disputes, no government agency whose job it was to enable employees freely and without coercion to choose their bargaining representatives. All this has now been changed. Furthermore, the Norris-La Guardia Act actually conflicts with certain provisions of statutes enacted in later years, notably Section 301 of the Taft-Hartley Act. Today, employers cannot, for example, obtain a court order forcing a union to honor its obligation to arbitrate grievances disputes because of the Norris–La Guardia-Taft-Hartley conflict.

After a careful review of this problem, another distinguished law professor, Benjamin Aaron, concluded that the Norris-LaGuardia Act is "urgently in need of amendment."[34] In view, however, of the momentous changes which have occurred since adoption of the Norris–La Guardia Act, both in the economic power of organized labor and in the statutory regulation of labor relations, it is apparent that Norris–La Guardia has no place on the current scene. What is needed is not revision, but repeal, and such repeal should cancel with it the immunity of unions, under the *Allen-Bradley* decision, to commit price fixing or other acts illegal for employers, or employers and unions acting in concert, as recommended by the above-quoted Attorney General's Committee.

II. *Repeal of Sections 8(a)(5) and (b)(3) of the Taft-Hartley Act.* The worst governmental intrusion into the bargaining process and the most consistent restraints on employer ability to control union power result from the "bargaining in good faith" criteria developed by the National Labor Relations Board pursuant to the Act's requirement that employers refrain from

34. Benjamin Aaron, "The Labor Injunction Reappraised," *Labor Law Journal,* vol. 14 (January, 1963), pp. 41-81.

"refusing to bargain." This 8(a)(5) provision, originally a part of the Wagner Act, was supplemented by the Hartley Act.

The effect of these provisions has been "a flood of litigation and an increasingly complex set of regulations stemming . . . from interpretations of the NLRB and the courts."[35] Particularly under the aegis of the present NLRB majority, which has gone to great lengths to further union bargaining power, the NLRB has utilized especially Section 8(a)(5) to control bargaining content, force employers to bargain over matters to such an extent that, as Professor Gregory has noted, it is close to a command that certain things be included in a contract,[36] and otherwise to dilute management's right to manage beyond what seemed possible a few years ago.[37]

Moreover, as Professor William Gomberg, a veteran of twenty-two years in the labor movement, expressed it, the "good faith bargaining clause has made the NLRA an extension of the tactics of the parties. It provides a whipping bag for the frustration of a party to the bargain who refuses to face the consequences of overplaying his hand and then goes running to papa government."[38] Declaring that it is not "the function of the government or the National Labor Relations Board

35. Independent Study Group, *The Public Interest in National Labor Policy* (New York: Committee for Economic Development, 1961), pp. 81-82.

36. Gregory, *op.cit.*, p. 413.

37. In this regard, see, Northrup and Bloom, *op. cit.*, pp. 111-124; L. M. Dispres and S. D. Golden, "The Duty to Bargain," *University of Illinois Law Forum* (Spring, 1955), p. 15; and R. W. Fleming, "The Obligation to Bargain in Good Faith," in J. Shister, *et al*, (eds.), *Public Policy and Collective Bargaining*, Industrial Relations Research Association Publication No. 27 (New York, 1962), pp. 60-87.

38. William Gomberg; "Government Participation in Union Regulation and Collective Bargaining," *Labor Law Journal*, vol. 13 (November, 1962), p. 944.

to provide a miasma of busy work so that the weaker party is spared the pain of looking squarely at his problem," Dr. Gomberg recommends that we stop "saddling the Board with adjudging an amorphous concept of 'good faith' bargaining" and confine its activities to "1. The promulgation of rules and procedures for holding representative elections, 2. Formulating adequate remedies for those workers who are the victims of discriminatory discharge or layoff prompted either by union or employer."[39]

An increasing consensus among authorities in the field is being achieved in favor of Dr. Gomberg's thesis that Sections 8(a)(5) and (b)(3) are violative of the maintenance of collective bargaining.[40] As administered by the present National Labor Relations Board majority, Section 8(a)(5) is being increasingly utilized to advanced union power and to dilute management's right to manage. This is strikingly notable in recent NLRB decisions designed to preclude in most circumstances, the right of employers to lock out. The NLRB's hostile view of the lockout is a throwback to the earlier days of union organization when unrestricted use of the lockout would have seriously weakened

39. *Ibid.*, pp. 945-947.

40. The best example is the already cited report of the Independent Study Group of the Committee for Economic Development, pp. 81-82. Among those subscribing to this report were such well-know students of labor relations as Professors George W. Taylor, John T. Dunlop, Philip Taft, Dr. Clark Kerr, and Mr. David L. Cole — all of whom are liberally oriented insofar as union relations are concerned. Dr. Taylor has long held the opinion that Sections 8(a)(5) and (b)(3) should apply, if at all, only to the first contract negotiated by the parties. This would preclude such biased and arrant nonsense as the attempt to charge the General Electric Company with "bargaining in bad faith" almost two years after it signed an agreement with the charging unions and 100 others.

unions which were then in their infancy.[41] Today, most unions have fat treasuries and strike insurance for members out on strike. To deny a company the right to contract out its work, to lock out its employees, or to shut down its business to the same extent that similar tactics are permissible and protected on the part of unions is as unfair as it is unwarranted. The repeal of Sections 8(a)(5) and (b)(3) would return these rights to employers, would destroy the NLRB's artificial doctrine, and would return the law to what Congress obviously intended, as enuniciated by the Fifth Court of Appeals in overturning the NLRB in the *Dalten Brick and Tile* case, that "a lockout may not be made a violation simply on the ground that this gives advantage to the employer or takes advantage away from the employees, or tips the scales one way or the other."[42]

III. *Maintain Section 14(b) of the Taft-Hartley Act.* Many of the most vigorous proponents of curbing union power believe, as already noted, that limits on the principle of exclusive jurisdiction and on compulsory union membership provisions are the best means of accomplishing their objective. It should be noted forthrightly, that collective bargaining requires exclusive jurisdiction to exist. Employers who advocate the end of exclusive jurisdiction might well look to the newspaper and printing, railroad, and building industries. If they desire the type of union rivalry which now exists in these craft union-dominated industries, plus a continuous open season for one union to solicit another's

41. See Northrup and Bloom, *op.cit.*, pp. 202-210; and Bernard D. Meltzer, "Lockouts Under the LMRA – New Shadows on an Old Terrain," *University of Chicago Law Review*, vol. 28 (Summer, 1961), pp. 614-428.

42. *NLRB* v. *Dalten Brick and Tile Corp.*, 301 F 2d 886 (1962).

members by demonstrating superior truculence toward the management, then they should continue to advocate the abolition of exclusive jurisdiction!

On the other hand, there can be no doubt that compulsory unionism adds to union power by increasing the income of unions, and therefore their ability to pay strike benefits, employ organizers, engage in political lobbying, and conduct other programs favorable to unions. The existence of union security provisions in this regard is more important now than a decade ago because union membership is declining in the face of automation, the shift from blue collar to white collar in the labor market, and other factors well known to students of labor markets and labor unions. The amount of money which can be involved is illustrated by Table 2 which summarizes the facts of the aerospace cases of 1962-1963, where the International Association of Machinists and the United Automobile Workers failed to achieve their aims, except in the case of Douglas Aircraft, despite strong New Frontier Administration political and extralegal support.[43]

The union failure in the aerospace cases, the passage in 1963 by Wyoming of the twentieth state right-to-work law, and the prospect that the aerospace cases will bolster employers who have not yielded on this union goal, indicate that the union security issue will still be a controversial one for years to come. The present law leaves the matter to the states. In view of the diversity of our country, and the need to accommodate various group pressures therein, this seems to be a sound approach. Union power is being restrained in twenty states by this method, and the outlook is for some additions thereto within the decade.

IV. *Allowing Collective Bargaining to Work.* Experi-

43. A discussion of the union security issue, and the Aerospace cases is found in Northrup and Bloom, *op.cit.*, Chapter 8.

TABLE 2

*The Unions' Stake in the Union Shop**

	UAW and IAM Membership	Potential Union Shop Additions	Added Income From Forced Members
Boeing	23,500	9,700	$ 582,000
Douglas	17,400	4,900	294,000
Gen. Dynamics	11,000	11,100	666,000
Lockheed	17,300	13,700	822,000
No. American	22,100	12,900	774,000
Ryan	1,200	250	15,000
Totals	92,500	52,550	$3,153,000

NOTE:

*As the above figures show, UAW and IAM would have added more than $3 million a year to their treasuries by forcing membership on over 50,000 nonunion employees in the aerospace industry.

ence has demonstrated that collective bargaining is the best method of settling conflicts between management and labor with respect to wage levels, method of payment, hours of work, and conditions of employment. Settlements in these areas can be properly left to the private parties because to a large extent the means for working out solutions arising from such settlements are within the power of such parties. For example, if a wage increase is agreed upon, the employer can raise the wages, and he is also in a position to adjust prices, utilization of machinery, and other variables of production and sales.

Suppose, however, that the issue between management and labor is manpower utilization, job security, or guaranteed employment. Can the parties really solve it? Can management and union really deal with these problems? Unfortunately, an increasingly large number of major disputes in recent years have pertained to these issues. In noting this to be true, and citing the strikes then in process, or recently concluded, involving flight engineers of air lines, longshoremen, newspaper printers, steel workers, and railroad employees, Mr. W. Willard Wirtz, Secretary of Labor, declared:

> It is one thing to bargain about terms and conditions of employment, and quite another to bargain about terms of unemployment, about the conditions on which men are to yield their jobs to machines. To the extent that these problems of employee displacement can be met at all in private bargaining, it can be only by a process of accommodation which is almost impossible in the countdown atmosphere of the 30 days before a strike deadline.[44]

Perhaps government or other outside or expert help is needed for labor and management to solve these complex problems. But one may well note that most bargaining is not confined to a 30-day "countdown" period. The parties prepare long in advance and usually know the direction of each other's position and thoughts long before a deadline is reached. Moreover, before turning these issues over to third parties for help or solution, the parties are entitled to ask what magic formula government or third party experts do indeed have to solve these difficult and pressing problems. The fact of the matter is that no solution has been discovered by anyone in many cases, and especially a solution that would please all parties.

Moreover, before we conclude that collective bargaining is not up to the job, perhaps we should give it

44. Address before the National Academy of Arbitrators, Chicago, Illinois, February 1, 1963; reported in 52 LRR 133 *et seq.*

an opportunity to perform its function. It is worthy of note that all the cases cited by Mr. Wirtz as examples of problems too complex for collective bargaining, were complicated by extensive government intervention, which had become, as Mr. Wirtz noted, after failing to settle the New York newspaper strike in early 1963, a "dull instrument."[45] In the flight engineers' case, four airlines – Braniff, Delta, Continental, and United – and the unions involved worked out solutions long before the massive intervention affecting other air carriers was inaugurated. Each airline came up with its own special solution, two peacefully, two after short strikes. The difference between the experiences of these airlines and the others that were subject to 39 boards and intervenors and still had more strikes and difficulties may well be explained by the difference in managerial competences rather than by the difficulty of the problem or the ability of collective bargaining to handle such issues.

Perhaps, in the long run, the best way to contain union power is for management to manage labor relations as it does other functions – and for government to permit management to manage, and to cease not only to bolster union power, but also to stop intervening at every pretext and in a manner which encourages either union or management truculence and discourages the propensity to settle. Collective bargaining will find an equilibrium reasonably satisfactory to the public interest when, and only when, parties are forced to face the consequences of their acts. The avid propensity of politicians to intervene in labor disputes in order to reap political notoriety is, under the present administration, the primary reason why union power is being advanced

45. The Secretary's exact words were: "There can be no doubt that any repeated resort to extraordinary procedures dulls the instrument." See *Daily Labor Report* (January 9, 1963), p. A-3.

at a time when unions are losing both membership and public favor. Those who would reverse this trend must take care not to advocate governmental measures which, like the Taft-Hartley Act, seek to regulate unions, but which in the hands of prolabor administrators can, and do, regulate the bargaining process in a manner favorable to the growth of union power.

CHAPTER 14

The Influence of International Factors

BY KINGMAN BREWSTER, JR.

Introduction

I should like to establish and clarify the limits within which I shall confine my remarks. Some are thrust upon me; others are of my own design. In the former category lie matters of personal qualification and disqualification. Both antitrust policy and the context of international transactions evolve so rapidly that no one can aspire to timeless validity of his analysis, and no academic observer can claim to be wholly up to date. Furthermore, both areas invite a free play of ideological, economic, and political convictions, if not prejudices and biases. I count it a qualification to have convictions in this or any other field, but they had better be made explicit. Mine is a strong bias in favor of the legal enforcement of competition borne of a distrust of the private power which laissez-faire would sanction and of the political power which regulatory substitutes for competition entail.

Now a word about the self-imposed limits on my discourse. For the most part I shall focus attention on the *legal* complications and implications of antitrust policy in foreign commerce. I do not mean to imply that the issues of importance of the United States or its free world partners raised by the maintenance of competition in international trade is limited to the reach and grasp of federal penal law. The desirability of cartels or competition is an issue of political economy on which debate has waxed and positions have shifted from time to time, industry to industry, nation to nation, and forum to forum, and is by no means confined by the limited scope of national or international law. Law in the formal sense is not the only instrument of policy. Indeed it is a relatively minor and feeble one in the field of international transactions and relations. Negotiation, persuasion, economic bargaining, political pressure, and even military government have all been instruments of either pro- or anticompetitive policy well beyond the reach of formal law. However, I would like, for the most part, to limit my observations to the realm of formal law—in particular, that law embodied in the statutes of the United States concerned with the prohibition of restraints of and monopolization of commerce with foreign nations. The thrust of my inquiry will be to identify ways in which the law may differ in its application to foreign commerce from its applications to "trade or commerce among the several states."

The Rationale of Applying Antitrust Laws to Foreign Transactions

Some comment might suggest that the application of the United States' antitrust laws to foreign transactions is an unwarranted extension of our law into the affairs of others, at best missionary, at worst offensively officious. Indeed this may, in fact, be its impact in some situations, as we shall see. However, it is impotant at the outset to be quite clear that the reason for and hence the thrust of the law is quite limited to supposed United States domestic economic interests; it might be said that it is quite chauvinistic.

In strictly legal terms the statutes are concerned only with restraints upon exports from or imports into the United States. Thus restraints which involve only trade among other countries are no concern of the antitrust laws even though competition among or within foreign countries may be vital to the concern of our economic foreign policy with free competitive enterprise as a way of life, or the importance of competition among mature countries for the benefit of the developing countries.

The two strictly United States interests which the law seeks to protect are quite familiar to any student of either the economics or the law of competition. The first is the American businessman's interest in free competitive access to world markets. The second is the interest of American consumers in having access to foreign suppliers and in having the benefits of their competitive presence in American markets.

Within a single economy, call it a single "economic jurisdiction" if you will, these two factors – business opportunity and consumer choice – go hand in hand. The greater the barriers to newcomers in the market, the less choice the consumer will have. This is, of course, not always the case when you are dealing with international trade and investment among separate economies and jurisdictions, often at a considerable geographical remove. American consumers may not be affected simply because a foreign market is tied up by one American company to the exclusion of its rivals. Or American consumers may not be affected simply because United States exporters decide to form a cartel which will allow them to charge foreign customers a monopoly price, or because a group of American firms decide to band together to bargain their way into a foreign market which they might not penetrate if each were on his own. So, at the level of the "business opportunity" interest sought to be protected by the Act, it is clear that restraints which might be struck down at home because they are bound to affect American consumers may be permitted if they affect only foreign consumers, provided they are genuinely voluntary restraints on business choice.

This sounds easy, but the difficulty of clarifying this immunity is illustrated by the Webb Pomerene Export Trade Association Act of 1916. That Act makes export cartels legal unless they affect American consumers and unless they affect the export business opportunity of nonmembers, and it has been very difficult to enforce with good results. It is a little easier to see that exclusive dealerships, tying clauses, and other restraints which might be illegal at home may be legal in export trade, simply because no American customers will be adversely affected. Indeed, the provision of the Clayton Act which covers such restraints does not apply to foreign commerce. It must not be assumed, then, that just because export commerce is restrained that all of domestic law applies; it may not, especially if there is no way in which United States consumers would be affected.

The consumer interest sought to be protected by applying our law to commerce with foreign nations is quite the same as that we seek to protect by the enforcement of competition at home. Keeping a foreign supplier from competing freely in the domestic market is, in this sense, no different from excluding or having an anticompetitive agreement with a domestic rival.

Antitrust Doctrines and Foreign Transactions

If, then, business opportunity and consumer choice are the familiar twin interests which describe the scope and also the limits on the application of antitrust law to foreign commerce, what doctrines have evolved? Do they differ in either concept or incidence from the doctrines which apply to the domestic economy?

Answering these questions is a tall order, tall enough

to reach the high level of abstraction which characterizes discussion of domestic antitrust doctrine. This, it should be recognized, is a matter of almost theological intricacy which, hence, generates the passion of theological dispute. The best I can hope to do is state my assumptions about domestic law and to indicate whether I think they apply in foreign commerce.

Take first the doctrine called *"per se* illegality." I think this stands for the proposition that any restrictive agreement which is not associated with any other useful undertaking is *ipso facto* illegal even if it cannot be proved to do anyone any actual harm. The fact that it was designed to serve no purpose other than the elimination of competition carries the day against arguments that it really did not succeed in eliminating competition. The classic case in foreign commerce is the old fashioned cartel agreement whereby the American agrees to stay out of Europe if his European partner will stay out of the United States. When prosecuted they typically argue and try to prove that the European could not have sold anything in the United States even if he had tried, because of transportation costs, tariffs, consumer acceptance, or the like. But the restraint which kept the foreigner from trying to reach American customers is enough; it is illegal *per se.*

Now for the reasons I mentioned this does not mean that it is *per se* illegal for an American firm to enter a foreign cartel which eliminates competition in foreign markets. If it does not affect United States customers, if it does not restrain the business opportunity of other Americans – even though it is an old-fashioned, naked cartel – *it is not in my mind illegal. But this is not because* the *per se* doctrine is altered in foreign commerce, it is because the restraint does not affect trade to or from the United States.

What, then, of the "rule of reason"? How does it apply to foreign commerce? Is its application different there than it is at home? Again, this requires some assumption about what the "rule of reason" is. Since this is also a vague subject, we will work for the moment with my assumptions about what it is and what it is not, although probably no two people will agree on the meaning of this masterpiece of federal ambiguity. I can do this best by breaking the question down into three considerations: (1), the relevance of the fact that the restraint is incidental to some underlying lawful and useful commercial or capital transaction — the so-called ancillary doctrine; (2), the relevance of the ability of the parties or the arrangement to affect substantially the behavior of output or quality or prices — the so-called market power test; and (3), the relevance of factors or policy considerations which might make the arrangement desirable even though it does restrain competition — the so-called business justification defense.

The "ancillary doctrine" says that if the restraint is coupled with a sale of a business or other transaction and is limited to the protection of the interest transferred or retained then it may be upheld unless it looks as though the elimination of competition was the primary purpose of the whole transaction. Outside the area of patent licensing, the truly ancillary restraint may have become a rare business phenomenon within a single national competitive market. However, it may be quite lively in connection with international capital and licensing transactions among firms which may need to join forces in order to sell in or invest in each others' home areas. The promise not to compete may be essential if an American firm is to find a willing foreign partner to handle his goods abroad. The covenant not to compete in the American market may be essential for the American to be willing to license a foreign firm to use its trade secrets and unpatented "know-how." The logical argument is that but for the restraint the competition restrained would never have existed. The policy argument is that if such ancillary restraints were forbidden many economically useful transactions would never be undertaken. If the restraint is limited in scope and time to the interests created by the underlying license agreement or investment, than I think it is defensible. The doctrine does not change in foreign commerce, but its application is far more prevalent simply because "know-how" is licensed to potential competitors abroad in order to cultivate foreign markets, whereas in the domestic market the firm would normally exploit it through its own internal expansion.

What then of "market power"? It is surely no less relevant in foreign commerce than it is at home. Where the illegality turns on how serious the foreclosure of the market is, or how complete the elimination of competition is, then the market power of the parties to the arrangement becomes relevant. Simple monopolization is the most obvious case, but exclusive arrangements, acquisitions, and joint ventures may also stand or fall depending upon the power to affect the market. Again, the doctrine does not differ conceptually in foreign commerce, but there are difficult problems of market definition posed by the fact first mentioned—namely, that the law is not concerned with foreign consumers. Thus, the entire output of gismos produced in Brazil could be tied up by ownership or agreement, but it might not matter if it turned out that Brazilian gismos played an insubstantial part in the domestic American gismo market. Likewise, the entire Brazilian market for American gismos might be foreclosed by agreement, but it would not be an illegal restraint on the competitive opportunity of the American gismo industry unless it turned out that Brazil loomed large as a competitive factor in the industry after taking into account all domestic and other foreign customers.

What I have referred to as the "business justification defense" is closely related to the "ancillary doctrine" and is not unrelated to considerations of "market power." The essence of the defendant's argument is that it was necessary to enter into the restrictive arrangement in order to do business. There are, however, many variations. In its most modest form it asserts simply that but for the restraint it would have been impossible to sell, license, or invest abroad. Borrowing from Judge Hand's language in the *Alcoa* case, the restraint is alleged to have been "thrust upon" the defendant. Exclusive distributorships, restricted and exclusive licenses, and joint ventures all may, under some circumstances, give rise to this type of justification. This is more likely to be plausible in foreign commerce than in domestic commerce. The distributor, the licensee, and the local partner in his own country each has an indispensibility to the foreign manufacturer which he would not have if the transaction were taking place within a single national market. This is simply because local knowledge, local acceptability, local political and economic influence gives the local distributor, the local licensee, and the local partner tremendous bargaining power. If these parties cannot be protected against competition they may not be willing to handle, or make, or invest in the foreigners goods; and unless he can work through a local partner the foreigner may in fact if not in law be excluded. When to this is added the fact that most foreign countries do not effectively seek to enforce competition, acquiescence in local cartel expectations may be a practical necessity.

Does our law leave room for this defense? The ambiguous answer must be "some, but not much." Loose arguments and generalized proof that cartels are a way of life abroad will not prevail as an excuse for entering into global allocation of territories and division of markets.[1] Simple assertion that a foreign partner desired to have a joint venture buttressed by a world-wide agreement not to compete will not meet the "thrust upon" standard.[2] And even the demonstration that watch movements and watch-making machinery could be obtained only by going along with restrictive requirements sanctioned by the Swiss government will not necessarily justify acquiescance in restraints upon United States manufacture and sales.[3]

However, I am one of those who feel that as a matter of both counseling and advocacy, a restraint can be vindicated if it is demonstrated to be no more restrictive than was necessary in order to do business. The easiest case, of course, is where a local host government requires the restrictive arrangement by a clear cut legal order. The tougher case is where the requirement turns on the bargaining power of local enterprise, or upon the *de facto* pressures which may influence export and import permits, exchange controls, or permits to do business. Here the problem is one of proof. I still believe that in concept the restraint which is thrust upon the defendant is defensible, and that international trade and investment offers many more plausible cases which would qualify for this defense than does doing business at home.

There is one line of so-called business justification which I think is not comprehended by the "rule of reason" and that is that host of arguments which one way or another assert: "Yes, competition has been re-

1. U.S. v. *National Lead Co.*, 332 U.S. 319 (1947).

2. U.S. v. *Imperial Chemical Industries, Ltd.*, 100 F. Supp. 504 (S.D. N.Y., 1951); U.S. v. *Timken Roller Bearing Co.*, 341 U.S. 593 (1951).

3. See Kingman Brewster, Jr., *Antitrust and American Business Abroad* (New York, 1958), pp. 48-49, 483.

strained, but in my particular industry under these particular circumstances competition is not in the public interest." That line of defense was used in domestic cases during the Great Depression. It undoubtedly had a great influence on the outcome in *Appalachian Coals*.[4] However, I feel that it is wholly inadmissible under the law as it stands. In short, the "rule of reason" does not admit the argument that competition itself is unreasonable as a public policy.

Feeling as I do, I reject the appropriateness of asking a court to make exception to the Sherman Act in foreign commerce on the ground that the particular investment or license is in the public interest even though it unreasonably restricts competition. The courts seem to say this in the *National Lead* and *Timken Roller Bearing* case cited above. So, although the occasions for saying that the application of the antitrust laws may be against the public interest are undoubtedly more various and frequent in foreign commerce than in domestic commerce, I do not think that they are any more persuasive as far as the outcome of cases are concerned.

Are there, then, any defenses in foreign commerce cases which are not available in a domestic case. Yes, I think there are. They derive from the jurisdictional limitations on the power of one country's legal system to govern matters within the jurisdiction of another country. This matter of jurisdictional obstacles to effective enforcement of competition in foreign commerce can be thought of on three levels, or, more properly, at three stages of any legal proceeding involving parties or facts or conduct outside the jurisdiction in which the suit is brought. First is the power of the court to bring the alleged defendant before it. Second is the power of the court to compel the disclosure of facts which happened or which have been embodied in rec-

4. *Appalachian Coals, Inc.* v. *U.S.*, 288 U.S. 344 (1933).

ords abroad. Third is the power of the court to prohibit or compel conduct abroad.

Precise pin-pointing of the scope and limits of such powers is a very technical undertaking and there is a wide latitude for reasonable difference of legal opinion. It will suffice here to say that doing business abroad through a foreign corporation which keeps its records abroad does make it more difficult for the Department of Justice to detect, and having detected, to prove the violation. Finally, it is evident that an American court will be loath to compel conduct which is prohibited abroad or to prevent conduct which foreign law requires. This reluctance to invite a showdown of conflicting legal requirements is mirrored in those clauses of consent judgments in which our government has left it open to the defendant to come in and show that compliance would require violation of foreign law.[5] However, general argument that there may be a conflict of policy, or that perhaps foreign legal rights would be upset by the American decree is not itself persuasive.[6] In short, it is not enough to say that the foreign government may not be sympathetic to competition, or that foreign courts might uphold the expectations of the foreign licensee or joint venturer who felt deprived of his protection by the decree of an American Court.

Concluding Comments

From this brief, cryptic, and somewhat abstract run down of the scope and limits of American law as I see it, it might well be asked whether the law makes sense in its application to foreign transactions. Even if the

5. *U.S.* v. *United Fruit Co.*, Civil No. 4560 (E.D. La., 1954) (consent decree, February 4, 1958).

6. *U.S.* v. *Imperial Chemical Industries, Ltd.*, 105 F. Supp. 215 (S.D. N.Y., 1952); *U.S.* v. *Holophane Co.*, 119 F. Supp. 114 (S.D. Ohio, 1954), *aff'd. per cur.* 352 U.S. 903 (1956)

policy underlying it makes some sense, is it too rigid and too inflexible to accommodate the variety of political and economic realities which describe international transactions and relations?

At the level of policy objectives, my impression is that the enforcement of competition makes abundant sense in those areas and in those industries and in relation to those countries where our commercial policy is one of free competitive trade. In short, in manufactured goods traded with our industrial allies, Japan and the Common Market, prohibition of private barriers to trade is essential if we are to have the benefit of progressive removal of public barriers to trade.

When one turns to the high priority national interest in the rapid development of less mature economies outside the Soviet sphere, there is a more complicated question. On the one hand it is clear that our interest in economic development urges that developing countries have the benefits of competition among their capital and commodity suppliers, to cut the cost of capital imports and improve the terms of trade enjoyed by their exports. This alone would find antitrust law in line with development policy. On the other hand, it is also clear that few markets in developing countries are broad enough to support more than one firm. Capital is too scarce to make redundant capacity palatable. Political as well as economic risk is such that the chance to share it with a partner may be essential to the willingness to invest. Generally, I would say that joint ventures are not deterred by the antitrust laws unless they bring together major competitors in a facility which is big enough to have an impact on American import prices. Such cases may well exist, however. They may be important to economic development. If they are deterred by antitrust considerations there is a serious policy conflict. This policy is not readily and reliably resolved by present antitrust standards and procedures.

At the next level of discourse — the intangible costs and drain on productive international enterprise caused by having to take antitrust considerations into account — we face the general antitrust problem posed by the ambiguity and uncertainty of present doctrine. The rule of reason may be welcome to the advocate trying to salvage a situation under attack; it defies confident counseling. I have the impression, however, that worthy business arrangements are not often deterred by inconclusive legal advice.

At the final level of this analysis — the jurisdictional — there is the much mooted question of the impact of our antitrust laws upon international law and international relations. The most I can say is that while I think that the outrage to foreign powers and sensibilities has been real, it is grossly exaggerated by some commentators. Our effort to regulate matters affecting our exports and imports is not as much of a legal aberration from the practice of nations as it has been painted. The political impact of such matters may be great upon the circle of those whose immediate interests are affected, but can scarcely be said to be a matter of profound popular concern. Nonetheless, in a sensitive world in which collective serenity is so crucial, any gratuitous friction among allies is to be opposed. It is my opinion that the sources of friction can be cured by interpretation and administration of the law well short of its withdrawal to the waters' edge.

Even as the law changes in the hands of the courts, the context of international economic, political, and strategic affairs changes much more rapidly and even less predictably. So I end with a reminder that conviction and opinion in these matters can be made obsolete not only by better analysis and judicial development but also by shifts in our national interest and its circumstances.

CHAPTER 15

Antitrust Policy: a View from Corporate Counsel

BY LAURENCE I. WOOD*

Introduction

The prior chapters have surveyed many of the overriding antitrust policy questions which are being, have been or should be considered. An eminent group of experts, drawn largely from the ranks of the academic world and government, have made contributions focused on these issues. The concluding chapters are designed to furnish leavening examples of mere human reaction to the policy issues and currently popular prescriptions by those most directly affected by the prescribed medicine – corporate counsel, labor, and management.

J. Robert Oppenheimer once said that there are two ways of looking at the world of arts and sciences. His description of these two kinds of "views" seems to me equally applicable to the world of law and the corporation.

> "One is the view of the traveler, going by horse or foot, from village to village to town, staying in each to talk with those who live there and to gather something of the quality of its life. This is the intimate view, partial, somewhat accidental, limited by the limited life and strength and curiosity of the traveler, but intimate and human, in a human compass. The other is the vast view, showing the earth

*The author wishes to express his sincere gratitude to Walter A. Schlotterbeck of the New York Bar who was of invaluable assistance in the preparation of this chapter.

with its fields and towns and valleys as they appear to a camera carried in a high altitude rocket. In one sense this prospect will be more complete; one will see all branches of knowledge, one will see all the arts, one will see them as part of the vastness and complication of the whole of human life on earth. But one will miss a great deal; the beauty and warmth of human life will largely be gone from that prospect."[1]

Since we cannot reproduce truly intimate pictures, we must confine ourselves to "bird's-eye" views of the world of antitrust. However, I ask you to keep in mind that what we are looking at from our overflight are people — items that come only in packages of one — who have rights and duties with respect to each other. No university, political party, government, corporation, or other institution ever performed any physical or mental act. Temporal laws and violations of temporal laws have meaning and consequences only as they affect people and their relations to one another.

Corporate counsel sees on a day to day basis the application of the antitrust laws to hundreds of human beings. At corporate headquarters, a sales office, a manufacturing plant, the luncheon table, the car pool, or in his office, corporate counsel is in intimate and informal contact with the many businessmen who in total devise and carry out a particular corporation's competitive business programs. These people cover the range from the recent business school graduate, through the seasoned marketing manager, to the highest policy makers of the corporation or some subdivision of the corporation. Counsel can never forget that the advice he gives affects not only the corporation as an institution but these people as well. The penalties and business con-

1. J. Robert Oppenheimer, *Prospects in the Arts & Sciences*. One of a series of radio broadcasts delivered in 1954 during the celebration of Columbia University's 200th anniversary.

sequences which follow from law violations will be visited not merely upon an abstraction known as a corporation but upon individuals. These people are presumed by the law to know its requirements. They look to corporate counsel almost daily to fulfill this presumption.

Civil Rights and Antitrust

A frank recognition of the primacy of the rights of individual people lies at the heart of our governmental and legal systems. Fundamental legal rights belong equally to the rich and the poor, to the conservative and the liberal, to the religious and the irreligious. They even apply to those who because of their radical views or antisocial acts are hated by most of the other people in the community, or who by their acts have done most to derogate from those rights.

There always has been, however, a large segment of opinion which expresses impatience with some of the "time consuming" and "inefficient" legal processes which have been developed to protect individual rights. This kind of viewpoint draws comfort today from the enormous technical and social problems of modern life and perhaps more basically from the fact that there often seem to be just too many human beings whose rights have to be considered and interwoven.

This impatience with traditional forms of legal procedure is evident in the antitrust field. It sometimes takes the form of forgetting that human rights are involved at all. Since major economic activity today is carried on through large institutions — corporations, labor unions, and governmental bodies — it is tempting to regard only the institutional forest and lose sight of the human trees. A few quotations will illustrate my point:

"It seems to me broadly speaking, that as dear to us as is due process and in the end the protection of private rights, we are going pretty far in this country when these corporations are clothing themselves with all these rights."[2]

and

"We should remain mindful of what is involved here. In this matter The Mead Corporation is under investigation by the Federal Trade Commission. It is a large, complex, corporate entity. No natural person is under investigation. . . .

"From the foregoing it is clear that here we are not concerned with the usual type of situation where the civil rights of a natural person are brought into focus. Instead, the real question is whether we shall become so enmeshed in arguments regarding inapplicable legal theories that our time and efforts will be so taken up and spent that we shall become unable to gather and study factual data relating to the structure and inter-relationships of large interstate corporations."[3]

Corporations and forests are remote and comfortable abstractions. People and trees are uncomfortable realities which exist today as they have in the past.

To my mind, some of the most critical antitrust policy questions lie in this area of the recognition and protection of individual rights. These policy issues are presently being debated in such categories as: (1), the right to be represented by counsel before administrative agencies;[4] (2), the right to a trial of issues of fact

2. Chairman Paul Rand Dixon of the Federal Trade Commission, testifying before the Antitrust and Monopoly Subcommittee of the Senate Judiciary Committee, 87th Cong., 1st Sess. (June 7, 1961), on S. 167.

3. Commissioner MacIntyre dissenting the *The Mead Corp.* investigation, CCH Trade Reg. Rep., Paragraph 16,241 (opinion issued January 3, 1963).

4. *The Mead Corp.*, see fn. 3; *FCC* v. *Schrieber*, 201 F. Supp. 421 (D.C. Cal. 1962); *Wanderer* v. *Kaplan*, 1962 Trade Cases Paragraph 70,535 (D. D.C.).

and law before the issuance of an injunctive order;[5] and (3), the necessity for explicitness in criminal antitrust statutes[6] and in administrative orders[7] which contain penalities in the nature of criminal sanctions. I am optimistic that these policy questions will be rightly resolved, provided only that people in the legal profession, government, our private economic institutions, and universities recognize that they exist (sensitivity to the existence of civil rights issues is half the battle) and that they should take precedence over other policy issues concerning the substance of the laws – a subject to which I turn next.

Antitrust Objectives

There is broad national consensus supporting the objectives of antitrust as is clearly demonstrated by the consistent support they have received from both political parties, a subject which Mr. Austern has reviewed in the first chapter. In a political sense the antitrust laws reflect one aspect of the traditional American distrust of concentration of power. Our governmental structure as established by the Constitution clearly reflects this distrust. In the political area this distrust is reflected in the balance of power between the legislative, executive, and judicial branches of the federal government and in the guarantees of specific individual rights against governmental restraint provided by the Bill of Rights.

The basic antitrust laws embody this same distrust of

5. Temporary cease and desist order bill. See, e.g., HR. 594, 87th Cong., 2d Sess.

6. *U.S.* v. *National Dairy Products Corp.*, 372 U.S. 29 (1963).

7. Note, Permissible Scope of Cease & Desist Orders: Legislation & Adjudication by the FTC, *University of Chicago Law Review*, vol. 29 (1962), p. 706; *F.T.C.* v *Broch*, 363 U.S. 166 (1959); Rehearing denied 364 U.S. 854 (1960); *Korber Hats, Inc.* v. *F.T.C.*, 311 F. 2d 358 (1962).

concentration of power in the sphere of our economic life. The general terms in which the Sherman Act is couched have been likened to the provisions of a constitution. In a large sense such generality reflects a reluctance to impose upon a competitive enterprise system the fetters of particularized regulations while at the same time making it clear that there are broad principles within which commerce and trade must be conducted. In this sense it is the objective of our basic antitrust law to foster commerce and trade free from the bureaucratic domination of government which, experience teaches, accompanies detailed regulations, while at the same time securing such commerce and trade from the domination of unregulated private enterprise. The concept of antitrust is thus a cornerstone of our economic system both as a matter of political philosophy and as a matter of practical politics.

Despite general agreement with such antitrust objectives, it would be misleading to give the impression that all is harmony in the world of antitrust. Perhaps the businessman's most frequent complaint about the antitrust laws is that their scope is uncertain. He is concerned that he must act in the face of the risk that his actions may later be declared illegal. He is troubled that in some instances there appears to be a "double standard"—one rule of law for the large concern and another for the small.[8] Some are deeply troubled by the fact that actions which seem to them honestly competitive may be viewed by others as manifesting antisocial behavior when judged under such awe-inspiring terms as "conscious parallelism," "administered prices," or "predatory practices."

A considerable measure of predictability is certainly a necessary component of any body of law, and anti-

8. For an explicit recommendation for a "double standard," see Chapter 6, above, by Louis B. Schwartz.

trust is no exception to this principle. However, I believe that in general most businessmen recognize that the enormous variety and complexity of economic life, as well as the dynamic nature of the economy, makes the development of a fully definitive set of rules not only impossible but probably undesirable. They appreciate that the essential difference between a regulated economy and a free economy is that, in the latter, individuals and companies retain the decision-making initiative. The Sherman Act is expressed in a few basic "thou shalt nots." This means that the business community is free to choose among many alternatives which do not violate the prohibitions. In the final analysis, there is a real parallel between the Sherman Act and our democratic system, of which it has become such an integral part. Both are capable of improvement, but not of ultimate perfection and, most important, both are, in their basic concepts, preferable to any known practical alternative.

My personal observation is that most businessmen are keenly aware of the fact that they have a greater stake in preserving basic antitrust principles than any other group in our society, and that they would concur in Judge Loevinger's comments when he said:

> "The great issue of this age is whether this nation, or any nation, can achieve full economic development, the satisfaction of all material needs, and the provision of adequate economic opportunities for all, together with political and civil liberty."[9]

Perhaps the greatest concern of businessmen today arises from the fact that they are caught in a moment of uncertainty as to just what the law or the government will or should do in the day-to-day workings of

9. *Recent Developments in Antitrust Enforcement,* address by Lee Loevinger to Antitrust Section, American Bar Association April 7, 1961.

the economy. They would be less than human if they were not conscious of the manner in which antitrust investigations, whether by Grand Juries or by Congressional Committees, become the subject of newspaper publicity and not infrequently follow upon the making of significant business decisions. They would be less than human if they liked those particular applications of certain laws which subject them to penalties for refusing to testify in a public hearing without full representation by counsel; or which subject them to criminal sanctions under a 25-year-old statute the precise meaning of which the Supreme Court postpones ruling on until after a detailed trial and which three members of the Court believe to be unconstitutionally vague; or which expose them to substantial monetary penalties for violation of orders couched in the vague, general, and sweeping language of a statute.

But, in general, American businessmen are fully in accord with the basic objectives of the antitrust laws. The most important present problem lies in the area of the interpretation, application, and sound administration of those laws. I believe that there can be no quarrel with the proposition that enforcement of these laws must avoid any semblance of being capricious, politically inspired, or completely unpredictable. Such a state of affairs can lead only to a state of fear and paralysis. Fear arising out of uncertainty does not move men to action – and businessmen who are not moved to action can do little to promote an expanding rate of economic growth.[10]

10. See *U.S.* v. *Philadelphia National Bank*, 83 S. Ct. 1715 (1963), at 1741, for tacit recognition of this view. "... unless businessmen can assess the legal consequences of a merger with some confidence sound business planning is retarded.... And so in any case in which it is possible, without doing violence to the Congressional objective embodied in §7, to simplify the test of illegality, the courts ought to do so in the interest of sound and practical judicial administration."

I am not, on the other hand, among those who criticize some flexibility in the antitrust laws. Nor do I have any strong dedication to the idea that more specific antitrust statutes are generally preferable. Nevertheless, I do wonder whether "American antitrust law really [has] developed its categories . . . or has it retrogressed to the point where its categories are so imprecise that the antitrust lawyer becomes a purveyor of impressionism?"[11]

To the layman, the antitrust laws frequently appear to require the making of vast and critical economic value judgments in the inhospitable framework of legal jargon. From what I read, they often appear in the same light to the expert. Nevertheless, the business manager must be able to make his business decisions with speed. As John Kenneth Galbraith has said:

> "Modern industrial processes are closely interdependent; delay in one place will ordinarily cause delay with cumulative effect elsewhere. There is, accordingly, a high premium on timely decision. Perhaps the most distinctive requirement of the industrial establishment, as compared with the traditional government agency, is its dependence on timely decision. In the industrial firm a bad decision made on time will not usually be as costly as a good decision made too late. The bad decision can often be reversed at low cost. The time lost waiting for the good decision can never be retrieved."[12]

The sanctions available for application in antitrust cases are truly impressive. All antitrust litigation involves enormous expenditures of money, time, and energy which are exacted from the businessman and

11. Joseph Taubman, "Pools, Combinations, Conspiracies & Joint Ventures," *Antitrust Bulletin,* vol. 4 (May-June, 1959).
12. John Kenneth Galbraith, *Economic Development in Perspective* (Cambridge, Mass., 1962), p. 64.

the business. The effect of such litigation (which is inherently protracted) on normal commercial operations can hardly be overemphasized. Unsuccessful antitrust litigation brings painful consequences. At a minimum the court will order comprehensive governmental and judicial regulation which will affect business planning for what the lawyers – with unworldly perspective – call perpetuity. Drastic limitations on property rights or forced divestiture can mean the sudden end of a business or part of a business.

For individuals, convictions of antitrust offenses can and do result in the kinds of punishments reserved for those called "criminals" by society – fines and imprisonment. Loss of an antitrust case also calls forth the treble damage claimant. He will seek to prove a causal relationship between the failures or shortcomings of his own business and some established transgression of the law.

In these circumstances it is incumbent upon all of us who are interested in antitrust and the formulation of policy to strive to clarify the enforcement and to refine the categories of antitrust as precisely as is practicable.

The Enforcement and Refinement of Antitrust

Agreements Among Competitors. As a general rule, agreements among competitors which have the purpose of eliminating, restraining, or even moderating the vigor of competition are absolutely prohibited by Section 1 of the Sherman Act. This rule against the elimination of competition requires that each businessman exercise independent judgment and act independently in the market place, except where the legislature has changed the rules after a resolution of the basic policy issues – as it has in some regulated industries.

The most difficult aspect of this branch of the antitrust law is not the determination of which agreements are lawful and which are unlawful, but a resolution of the crucial question of whether there was an agreement. Businessmen know that the existence or absence of an agreement is a matter for a judge and jury to decide on the basis of the evidence presented to them. In reaching their conclusion, they frequently must decide on the basis of surrounding circumstances or so-called circumstantial evidence.

It is also true, however, that as a result of many competitive factors, the actions of the competitors in the market place may be similar or even uniform despite the fact that no agreements have been made. Obviously, competing businessmen are no more capable of proving a negative than anyone else and they can no more establish conclusively that a particular pricing or other marketing decision was made *without* agreement with a competitor than they can prove conclusively that ghosts do not exist. The utmost that the businessman can invariably be expected to do is to make his decision unilaterally and upon the basis of his independent assessment of competitive situations, trusting that should he ever be challenged this pattern of conduct will permit him to rebut circumstantial evidence which might otherwise point in the direction of agreement.

These are areas in which the world of judicial theory and the world of daily business can be widely separated. In the theoretical world it is not difficult to believe that significant business decisions will be documented by extensive economic analyses and written confirmation of action to be taken. While it is true that the more important business decision may be preceeded by lengthy discussion of alternatives, such study and discussion all too often takes place in formal meetings. And once a decision is reached, the reasons underlying it and the alternatives which have been weighed and debated almost immediately evaporate in the absence of a written contemporaneous record. Lawyers have great difficulty persuading their clients of the importance of preserving a record of the many factors which were considered. Businessmen are no different from doctors and housewives in their aversion to spending precious time on record keeping. Nevertheless, the courts have made clear their conviction that such con*temporaneous documents carry much greater weight* than statements of good intentions or denials of illegal purpose in the trial of an antitrust case – a trial which may take place ten years after the fact when recollections are dim or even wholly nonexistent.

The businessman must bear in mind that a clean conscience will not necessarily be determinative in the face of charges brought against him. He must learn that one of the prices he pays for operating in a competitive society – for being free to meet his competitors' offers – is, to some extent, the diminution of the pleasures of innocence. The problems of persuading a jury may all too often, and sometimes unfairly, thrust upon him, as a matter of necessity, the burden of being able to prove the innocence of his conduct.

On the other hand, a corollary of much of what I have said about the problem of proof of agreements among competitors is that antitrust enforcement agencies and Congressional committees must also realize the equivocal nature of similar or even identical practices. Since similarity of practices can often be the result of the forces of the market, such similarities should not indiscriminately be presumed to be inherently collusive.

Agreements with Customers and Suppliers. While agreements with competitors (in their capacities as competitors) should not exist at all, there is no way of avoiding the making of agreements with suppliers or customers. Most of the regular relationships which business concerns have with others are governed by contracts, either written or oral, such as purchase and sale contracts, franchise agreements or leases. Clearly, not all such agreements are illegal restraints of trade. However, the line between lawful contracts and agreements in unreasonable restraint of trade is not always easy to draw.

While distribution intermediaries frequently play an important role in taking a product from the manufacturer to the consumer, in some important respects the relationship between the manufacturer and the consumer of a product is direct. The producer cannot entirely delegate to others his responsibilities to the consumer. Nor would he necessarily want to do so, since his trade reputation, reflected in part in his trademarks and trade names, are valuable assets. The antitrust laws place narrow but important limitations on the degree to which a manufacturer can participate in the distribution process after he has made his first sale.

Neither Congress nor the courts have always been convinced that agreements between suppliers and consumers to make the distribution process more orderly are totally without redeeming features. This ambivalent attitude applies even with respect to resale price maintenance agreements as evidenced by the state fair trade laws and the federal exemptions contained in the Miller-Tydings and McGuire Acts.

Policy questions concerning the validity of other types of partially restrictive agreements between suppliers and customers continue to be debated. Contracts requiring a seller to deal exclusively with a buyer, or so-called exclusive distribution agreements are, absent aggravating circumstances, apparently proper in many circumstances.[13] Restraints upon a buyer confining him

13. Stanley D. Robinson, "Providing for Orderly Marketing of Goods," *Section of Antitrust Law*, American Bar Association, vol. 15 (1959).

to a specific territory or to a specific class of customers stand on a less certain footing. The policy implications of such contracts have been considered a number of times by Congress, as in connection with the so-called antibootlegging bills.[14] The legal issues only recently came before the Supreme Court in the *White Motor* case.[15]

The trial court had held that territorial and customer restraints were separate *per se* violations of the Sherman Act.[16] While three Justices of the Supreme Court agreed with the trial court's holding, a majority was unwilling to reach this conclusion at this stage of the proceedings. Justice Douglas, writing for the majority, pointed out this was the first case involving vertical territorial restraints and that the Court "[knew] too little of the actual impact both of that restriction and the one respecting customers to reach a conclusion on the bare bones of the documentary evidence." The majority of the Court concluded, therefore, "The applicable rule of law should be designed after a trial."

This decision may not provide much comfort for the idea that vertical agreements among sellers and buyers should be individually judged to determine whether they are undue restraints on competition. On the other hand, the reluctance of the majority of the Court simply to create new *per se* categories at this time holds forth some hope that the development of antitrust policy in this area may be a more discriminating and scientific process in keeping with the flexible nature of fundamental antitrust law.

In addressing these questions it may be helpful to consider that competition may be viewed in at least two

14. See e.g. HR. 9769, 83d Cong., 2d Sess. (1959).
15. *White Motor Co.* v. *U.S.*, 372 U.S. 253 (1963).
16. *U.S.* v. *White Motor Co.*, 194 F. Supp. 562 (N.D. Ohio, 1962).

ways; namely, the competition between those handling the products of the same supplier and competition between manufacturers and sellers of different brands. It is possible that competition in the market as a whole may be enhanced more by fostering interbrand rivalries even if this means some lessening of competition with respect to the same brand.

In practical human terms, however, the key issue in the field of vertical agreements is the same as that which exists with respect to agreements among competitors—namely, when does an "agreement" exist. One of the most difficult tasks confronting corporate counsel is to explain clearly and completely to a salesman—be he a young cub or a mature veteran—how he must act in his relationships with intermediate wholesalers, distributors, or dealers. In many instances the good customer may be viewed by the salesman as having a community of interest with the manufacturer in the promotion of the manufacturer's product. Yet in legal contemplation he is viewed solely as in the position of a buyer of goods. The salesman needs to be constantly reminded that while it is his job to sell the customer as much as the customer will buy, he must stop short of committing the customer to deal with him exclusively. Moreover, while the manufacturer's representative can expect a distributor or dealer to expend effort in covering an assigned customer group or territorial area of "primary responsibility,"[17] the salesman cannot safely limit the reseller's right to sell to other customers or in other territories.

No matter how much a small businessman may solicit or welcome advice concerning how the products should be priced, the salesman must scrupulously avoid

17. See *U.S.* v. *Bostitch, Inc.*, 1958 Trade Cases Paragraph 69,-207 (D. R.I.); *Matter of Sandura Co.*, FTC Docket 7042, Trade Reg. Rep. Paragraph 15,945 and Paragraph 16,095.

any comments which might be construed as part of an improper agreement concerning resale prices or other competitive practices. While he must be courteous in listening to complaints concerning the unfair pricing, advertising, or marketing practices of other distributors or dealers handling the manufacturer's product, he must make it clear to all concerned that all dealers or distributors have a clear field in the marketing of products they have purchased.

How well each salesman draws these lines can determine the legality of his company's practices. The complexity of these problems and the possibilities of isolated examples of human error creeping into the process cry for a close scrutiny of the total corporate policy and purpose rather than the application of a ritualistic *per se* factual as well as legal approach.

Section 2 of the Sherman Act. For people working in a large corporation, the ultimate problem of category refinement is presented by Section 2 of the Sherman Act. However appropriate it may have been to the decision of that particular case, Judge Wyzanski's eclectic approach to Section 2 in *United Shoe Machinery* creates many perplexing problems for legal advisers to substantial business concerns as well as for the formulation of antitrust policy on other than a case-by-case legislative basis. Judge Wyzanski found that the business practices utilized by United Shoe Machinery Corp. were in one sense natural and normal and,

> "honestly industrial . . . the sort of activities which would be engaged in by other honorable firms. . . . Yet, they are not . . . the inevitable consequences of ability, natural forces, or law. They represent something more than the use of accessible resources . . . they are contracts, arrangements, and policies which, instead of encouraging competition based on pure merit, further the dominance of a particular firm. In this sense, they are unnatural barriers;

they unnecessarily exclude actual and potential competition; they restrict a free market. While the law allows many enterprises to use such practices, the Sherman Act is now construed . . . to forbid the continuance of effective market control based in part upon such practices. . . . Market control is inherently evil and constitutes a violation of Section 2 unless economically inevitable, or specifically authorized and regulated by law."[18]

This is a candid and graphic description of how the court reached its decision in the case. How can it be transplanted to other industries, other times, and other people? The businessman is faced with the need for timely action as well as with the desire to avoid the designation "monopolist." I assure you he does not take kindly to the kind of advice which says: "I can't tell you exactly what it is, but I know it when I see it."

Clayton Act. Let me illustrate the problem of category refining further by looking at one method of proceeding—in my opinion an unsatisfactory one. The Clayton Act was designed to supplement the Sherman Act by explicitly prohibiting in their "incipiency" certain types of practices which if permitted to continue, would probably conflict with basic antitrust policies. Unfortunately, the cases have not demonstrated that more specific antitrust statutes necessarily are better techniques of policy formulation or even that they lead to greater certainty or understanding of the law.

A number of the provisions of the Clayton Act (e.g. Section 3 concerning exclusive dealing contracts and Section 7 on mergers and acquisitions) present similar key issues of application. They concern: (1), the market area in which competitive effect is to be tested and (2), the standards to be followed in determining whether the effect of the contract, acquisition, or merg-

18. *U.S.* v. *United Shoe Machinery Corp.*, 110 F. Supp. 295, 344-345 (1953); *aff'd. per cur.* 347 U.S. 521 (1954).

er "may be substantially to lessen competition, or to tend to create a monopoly" in any line of commerce. The trend in both the exclusive dealing cases and the merger cases has been to define the market in such a way as to make the particular agreement unlawful. In fact, the effects of a merger or acquisition have frequently been tested with respect to a whole array of markets and submarkets in an apparent effort to delineate one or more in which the prohibited effect might be found. Moreover, once the market has been defined there has been a regrettable tendency to duck any policy issues based upon a careful study of the actual or predictable competitive effect and to substitute instead what some have called a rule of "quantitative substantiality" – in short, "how much is involved in the transaction?" Consequently – while the decisions have not gone to the ultimate so far – the feeling has grown that the statute could become a prosecutor's dream tool which could be invoked at his discretion to strike down the use of any such contracts or acqusitions by substantial companies.

Many mergers or acquisitions – as well as exclusive dealing or requirements contracts – are not challenged. The many cases which are brought are, like most other lawsuits, examples of unhappy backgrounds. Many of them contain aggravating or attention-getting subsidiary facets. The mere fact that there are many cases belies the idea that there is clear understanding of the scope of the law. The truth of the matter is that the key to illegality may well rest in the imaginative use of discretion in deciding whether to bring cases.

How then is a businessman to judge *in advance* whether a requirements contract, merger, or acquisition will be attacked and, if attacked, stricken down? Although there has been much discussion of so-called advisory or clearance programs established by the enforcement agencies, most antitrust practitioners will agree, I am sure, that they present only illusory comfort. I believe that there is a large opportunity here for the academic world as well as government enforcement officials to search for a means to provide more general and reliable guidance for businessmen in this area without the great waste and name calling which are concomitants of litigation.

As an aside, one of the most disturbing aspects of this area of law is the absence of any real statute of limitations providing a period in which the legality of a merger or acquisition may be tested. As you know, the *General Motors du Pont* decision struck down in 1957 an acquisition of stock which was consummated in the period 1917-1919.[19]

Justice Brennan, writing for the majority, treated the long time lapse between acquisition and challenge in incendiary language:

> "The fire that was kindled in 1917 continues to smolder. It burned briskly to forge the ties that bind the General Motors market to du Pont, and if it has quieted down, it remains hot, and, from past performance, is likely at any time to blaze and make the fusion complete."

Perhaps these expressions apply only to the unique situation before the court. However, there is no equivocation in his conclusion that "the test of a violation of Section 7 is whether at the time of suit there is a reasonable probability that the acquisition is likely to result in the condemned restraints."

Certainly a more helpful determination of the initial propriety of merger or acquisition should be available. This does not mean that future consequences of the merger or use of the acquired property would be be-

19. *U.S.* v. *E. I. du Pont de Nemours & Co., et al.*, 353 U.S. 586 (1957).

yond challenge. The broader provisions of the Sherman Act seem however, to be more appropriate vehicles for resolving the kinds of antitrust policy issues which are presented long after the particular business transaction has been completed.

Robinson-Patman Act. What can be said with respect to the Robinson-Patman Act? Congressman Celler of Brooklyn, a strong supporter of vigorous antitrust enforcement, stated at the time of the enactment of this law:

> "[T]he courts will have the devil's own job to unravel the tangle. . . . You have the herculean task to make it *yield sense*."[20]

His predictions have been largely borne out. Candor impels the admission that any analysis of the Robinson-Patman Act is primarily an analysis of the unsuccessful efforts of the Federal Trade Commission to breath into it a viable meaning. In its headlong efforts to make the statute easy to enforce, the Commission seems to have all but foreclosed itself from using the statute in a flexible manner designed to achieve its broad policies in harmony with the basic antitrust philosophy of the Sherman Act.

Price differences in the chain of distribution have assumed the position of *per se* illegality. The cost justification defense, which was regarded as a primary means of reconciling the statutory provisions with basic antitrust policy, has proved to be a promise broken to the hope. The Commission's position with respect to the "meeting competition" defense has produced a maze of legal technicalities which have served to make the defense almost totally unavailable. Whether students of this area of the law in the schools, in government,

20. *Congressional Record,* vol. 80 (1936), p. 9419.

or in the courts can arrest this trend and reverse it so as to permit more intelligent policy formulation is a question which I cannot answer. The greatest opportunity for taking a fresh look rests with the Commission itself. Here again, the application of the law and therefore its practical scope are determined today by the selection of the cases which the Commission decides to try. Once a complaint is filed, it is odds-on that the body of experts will find the practice which it has challenged is an "unfair method of competition" or that a promotional payment was not made available to all competing customers on "proportionally equal terms."

The worst feature of this kind of law-making is that once the experts have classified a practice as improper (after lengthy trial and consideration of the intricacies of the law) the tendency is to adopt a cease and desist order which parrots the ambiguous statutory language. This device turns a broad civil statute into a criminal law. Further transgressions of any kind are punishable by penalties of up to $5,000 for each violation, or day of violation. Many people are then subject to this new imprecise penal rule. The consequences of drawing an inaccurate line are extremely serious to these people or their lawyers. This is a civil rights issue of major importance. While the courts are beginning to recognize and focus on this issue,[21] the element of righteous indignation is somehow lacking in most of the learned commentary on the Commission's work.

Government-Business Relationships

Future resolution of antitrust policy will, of course, depend principally upon specific cases. However, the general tenor of government-business relationships will set the framework within which decisions will be

21. *F.T.C.* v. Broch, 368 U.S. 360 (1962); *Korber Hats, Inc.* v. *F.T.C.*, 311 F. 2d. 358 (1962).

made as to which cases should be brought and the manner in which policy directions should be pushed.

The problem is not one that business managers can nor should solve alone, much, of course, as they would like to. In making the decision as to who best has the clear, unbiased understanding of the economic system there is little question as to whom those in the business world would choose — they would choose themselves. And the government employee would select the government employee. It is reminiscent of that wonderful song, "I Believe in You," from Frank Loesser's "How To Succeed In Business," in which Robert Morse sings, while looking at himself in the mirror and acknowledging that he sees a face that somehow he can trust:

> "You have the cool, clear eyes of a seeker of
> wisdom and truth
> Yet there's that upturned chin and that grin of
> impetuous youth
> Oh, I believe in you,
> I believe in you."[22]

Certainly the recent phase of quasi-hostility between government and business does not advance us toward a solution as to a proper relationship between the two. Economic growth and freedom of enterprise are both objectives which government and business hold in common, and should pursue in cooperation rather than in conflict.

The elements of antibusiness and antigovernment bias should disappear as there develop a full and intelligent study, discussion and exploration of the relative roles of government and business in our extremely complex economy — and there is broad public understanding of such concepts as business competition, the role

22. Copyright 1960 Frank Loesser. All rights throughout the entire world controlled by Frank Music Corp., 119 West 57th Street, N.Y. 19, N.Y. Used by permission.

of the profit incentive, and the importance of investment for growth. Without contact on these issues ignorance and self-righteousness increase. Differences of opinion there will always be on these issues, but these should be a wholesome, vital kind of difference, supported by the best traditions of a lively democracy. To paraphrase Edmund Burke, I feel that it is our business "rather to run the risk of falling into faults in a course which leads us to act with effect and energy, than to loiter out our days without blame and without use" by merely talking to those who share broadly our own outlook and views.

I should like to see this continuing exchange of views conducted on a more sophisticated level. Belaboring the obvious or preoccupation with slogans will not move us more rapidly toward a workable relationship. The resolution of economic problems requires a deft hand and mature and perceptive minds. The responsibility for finding such a relationship is not only heavy but even a little frightening. That is the kind of age in which we live.

CHAPTER 16

A View from Labor

BY NAT GOLDFINGER AND
THEODORE J. ST. ANTOINE

Introduction

It will come as no surprise that our attitude, as union spokesmen, toward further extension of the antitrust laws over the activities of American labor organizations is much like the attitude of Calvin Coolidge's minister toward sin: we're against it. We feel our attitude is justified. But in contributing to a volume graced by so distinguished a company of scholars, it may be best that we do not confine ourselves merely to developing our own case in support of a conclusion which some might accuse us of having harbored all along.

We therefore shall take two different approaches. First, we believe there has been enough discussion of labor and antitrust over the past decade to enable us now to state flatly that, except among certain popular publicists and certain ax-grinders, a large part of the argument has come to an end. A growing consensus exists among disinterested legal experts and labor economists on one simple but fundamental proposition. The antitrust laws as they now stand are not the appropriate vehicle for dealing generally with union economic power, and at least in the absence of much more proof of practical need they are probably not even the appropriate vehicle for dealing with certain alleged specific "abuses" of union economic power. The first portion of this paper will show why that proposition has properly come to command the assent of most nonpartisan labor specialists.

As our second contribution we shall submit data indicating that, whatever theoretical avenues for union economic abuses have been left open by current interpretations of the antitrust laws, in actual practice such abuses simply have not occurred on a scale sufficient to justify further legislative regulation. This does not necessarily mean that unions have a more sensitive social conscience than corporations, much as we might like to persuade ourselves that this was the fact. It may just mean that some old economic laws are proving even harder to repeal or amend than the laws of Congress. But in any event we take it that no sensible person will insist on tinkering with such complex mechanisms as the antitrust laws or established labor relations procedures merely to satisfy a passion for eliminating some theoretical possibility of wrongdoing. If real, substantial, unremedied abuses cannot be pinpointed, proposals for altering the status quo should be rejected.

In the course of our discussion we will also make a few passing remarks regarding labor's attitude toward the antitrust laws in their application outside the labor field.

The Appropriateness of Antitrust Regulation of Organized Labor

Present Status of the Law. Herbert Northrup and Gordon Bloom have supplied an excellent historical outline of how the doctrine of restraint of trade, backed up by the antitrust arsenal of injunctions, treble damages, and criminal penalties, was formerly applied to organized labor, and of how Congress and the Supreme Court eventually repudiated a broad antitrust approach in this area.[1] The temptation to take advantage of their hard work and to avoid a restatement of that history is entirely too much for us. We shall content ourselves with a couple of brief comments. First, no one can fully appreciate organized labor's deep hostility toward any suggestion of regulation via the antitrust route without recalling this painful demonstration of judicial ineptitude, as the courts' performance in dealing with unions under antitrust procedures has been characterized by numerous observers.[2] Secondly, we have some reservations about the Northrup and Bloom interpretation of current Supreme Court doctrine on the status of union activity under the antitrust laws, and so we shall say a few words setting forth our own understanding of the present state of the law.

The landmark decision is *United States* v. *Hutcheson*.[3] The Supreme Court there held that labor union boycotting activity which was immunized against injunctions by the Clayton and Norris–La Guardia Acts was likewise to be immunized against prosecution under the Sherman Act. In effect, this meant that peaceful conduct by a labor organization in the course of a labor dispute is generally no longer subject to regulation through the antitrust laws. There are some impor-

1. See Chapter 13, above, by Herbert R. Northrup and Gordon F. Bloom. See also Felix Frankfurter and Nathan Greene, *The Labor Injunction* (New York, 1930); Edwin E. Witte, *The Government in Labor Disputes* (New York, 1932); Charles O. Gregory, *Labor and the Law*, 2d rev. ed. (New York, 1961), especially pp. 95-104, 205-209.

2. In addition to references in fn. 1, see also Archibald Cox, "Labor and the Antitrust Laws – A Preliminary Analysis," *University of Pennsylvania Law Review*, vol. 104 (1955), pp. 252, 265; M. I. Sovern, "Some Ruminations on Labor, the Antitrust Laws and *Allen-Bradley*," *Labor Law Journal*, vol. 13 (November, 1962), p. 958.

3. 312 U.S. 219 (1941).

tant qualifications to this principle. In *Allen-Bradley*[4] the Supreme Court held that unions could not "aid non-labor groups to create business monopolies and to control the marketing of goods and services" without running afoul of the Sherman Act. This exception in situations where unions join in the unlawful combinations or conspiracies of employers is a highly significant one, as we shall see later. In addition, since fraud and violence are not absolutely protected against injunctions by the Clayton and Norris–La Guardia Acts, to the extent a labor organization engages in such conduct it may lose its antitrust immunity. It might thus become subject to the earlier *Apex Hosiery*[5] rule that a union violates the antitrust laws if its concerted activity has the object of restraining "commercial competition."

So long as a genuine labor organization is acting in its capacity as a representative of employees,[6] and is acting peaceably, we do not think there is any less of a "labor dispute" involved or any less insulation from antitrust coverage merely because the union is said to be aiming at "direct commercial restraints." Nor do we think that antitrust immunity may be lost by a union's negotiation of a typical "restrictive" contract with a single employer, or even necessarily by its negotiation of parallel restrictive contracts with several employers. But both these conclusions are subject to dispute under existing law.[7] We shall discuss the practical implica-

4. *Allen-Bradley Co.* v. *International Brotherhood of Electrical Workers, Local 3*, 325 U.S. 797, 808 (1945).

5. *Apex Hosiery Co.* v. *Leader*, 310 U.S. 469, 495-501 (1940).

6. Persons who are essentially independent contractors or entrepreneurs cannot cloak themselves with immunity from the antitrust laws by banding together and calling themselves a "union." *Columbia River Packers Assn.* v. *Hinton*, 315 U.S. 143 (1942); cf. *Teamsters Local 626* v. *U.S.*, 371 U.S. 94 (1962).

7. Our positions are supported by former Professor Cox, *op.cit.*, pp. 267, 271, but the Attorney General's National Committee to Study the Antitrust Laws leaned the other way. See *Report of*

tions of these fine points when we consider proposals to outlaw union activities supposedly aimed at direct market control.

Proposals to Extend Antitrust Regulation of Organized Labor. What is meant by proposals to subject unions to further regulation under the antitrust laws? Assuming that the proponent knows what he is talking about — and commentators less partisan than ourselves have suggested that this may often be too charitable an assumption[8] — the proposal at least means that whatever conduct is substantively proscribed shall be liable to the stiff antitrust sanctions of injunctions, treble damages, and criminal penalties. The critical question is what conduct shall be substantively proscribed. Here the proposals span the horizon, from the vague but emotionally charged outpourings of the congenital antiunionist to the precise prescriptions of those sincerely concerned about maintaining a proper power balance among the various competing interests in the economy. We shall try to deal with the most prominent among these diverse proposals.

Union Monopoly Over Labor. We feel we beat a dead horse when we take up the argument that unions should be subject to the antitrust laws because they maintain a monopoly over the supply of labor. Of

the Attorney General's National Committee to Study the Antitrust Laws (Washington, 1955), pp. 297-299. On the question of "labor dispute," compare *Allen-Bradley Co.* v. *IBEW Local 3*, 325 U.S. 797, 807, n. 12 (1945), with *Hawaiian Tuna Packers* v. *Longshoremen*, 72 F. Supp. 562 (D.C. Hawaii, 1947). On the negotiation of restrictive contracts with one or more employers, see Roberts, J., concurring in *Allen-Bradley*, 325 U.S. at 814-815; Sovern, *op.cit.*, p. 961. As to the need for the participation of more than one employer, might it not make a difference whether the violation charged was a monopoly rather than a combination in restraint of trade?

8. See, e.g., Sovern, *op.cit.*, pp. 957-958.

course they do, whenever they can, which happens to be far less often than they would like. That is the very nature of labor organizations. The whole question of exclusive bargaining authority, of the union shop, and of all the other accoutrements of union "monopoly" is properly regarded as a problem in labor relations, not antitrust, policy. As Justice Stone said in *Apex Hosiery:* "A combination of employees necessarily restrains competition among themselves in the sale of their services to the employer; yet such a combination was not considered an illegal restraint of trade at common law when the Sherman Act was adopted."[9] Sar Levitan put the matter in economists' terms when he said: "While labor may be a commodity, it is definitely a most heterogeneous product, and the concepts of monopoly cannot be rightly applied to unions, who perform a vital function in reconciling the differences of the pluralistic labor interests."[10]

We know of no responsible student of labor relations who suggests that antitrust concepts should have anything to do with union control over the supply of labor *per se,* and we know of numerous writers who have said any such notion was unworthy of serious consideration.[11] The proper domain of antitrust law is the product market, and the labor market is something entirely different. True, union monopoly in the labor market might indirectly, with employer connivance, affect the product market. That is a separate question, and we shall deal with it later. But so long as the labor market is considered by itself, anyone who argues the appropriateness of antitrust regulation is doing no more

9. *Apex Hosiery Co.* v. *Leader,* 310 U.S. 469, 502 (1940).

10. Sar Levitan, "An Appraisal of the Antitrust Approach," *Annals of the American Academy of Political and Social Science,* vol. 333 (1961), p. 114.

11. See, e.g., Chapter 13 above, by Northrup and Bloom; Cox, *op.cit.,* p. 254; Gregory, *op.cit.,* pp. 525-526; Sovern, *op.cit.,* p. 963.

than revealing his own misconceptions about both the fields of labor and of antitrust.

Perhaps much of the rather inarticulate feeling in the United States against union "monopoly" power is attributable to what has previously been described by Thomas Austern and Donald Dewey as a sentimental bias toward rugged individualism, carried over from the days of the Old Frontier.[12] If so, this is one provincialism which we in the labor movement like to think we have transcended. But ill-founded or not, that sort of thinking is often decisive when legislation is enacted. It is one of the great merits of a book such as the present one that it can call to account such undisciplined feelings parading in the guise of thought.

Boycotts, Featherbedding, and Jurisdictional Disputes. Three specific types of union activities often became the target of attack in the heyday of antitrust regulation, and they remain today among the examples of union conduct most often cited as justifying a restoration of antitrust control. Those activities are boycotts, featherbedding, and jurisdictional disputes. A short answer can be made covering all three of them: they are already subject to as much regulation under the National Labor Relations Act as is possible without an intolerable intrusion of governmental authority into the processes of free collective bargaining.

Boycotts are regulated in great detail by sections 8(b)(4) and 8(e) of the NLRA,[13] which make most

12. See above Chapter 1, by H. Thomas Austern, and Chapter 4, by Donald J. Dewey.

13. 61 Stat. 141 (1947), as amended by 73 Stat. 542-44 (1959), 29 U.S.C. Section 158 (b)(4) and (e) (Supp. III, 1962). In our view federal labor legislation has already deprived labor unions of much-needed economic weapons. But that is a theme for another day. See, e.g., Theodore J. St. Antoine, "Secondary Boycotts and Hot Cargo: A Study in Balance of Power," *University of Detroit Law Journal,* vol. 40 (1962), p. 189.

traditional employee boycott activities and "hot cargo" arrangements unfair labor practices, and by section 303 of the Taft-Hartley Act, which provides a damage remedy for anyone suffering a business or property loss as a result of a prohibited boycott.[14] Jurisdictional strikes are declared an unfair labor practice by section 8(b)(4)(D) of the NLRA, and section 10(k) of the Act prescribes a special procedure whereby the National Labor Relations Board is in effect required to arbitrate unresolved jurisdictional disputes.[15] In these areas, at least, the superimposing of antitrust remedies is unnecessary, and would undoubtedly be the source of much administrative confusion.[16]

Featherbedding is a somewhat knottier issue. Section 8(b)(6) of the NLRA[17] makes it an unfair labor practice for a union to require an employer to pay for services which are not performed. The Supreme Court, however, has interpreted this to mean that there is no violation if the services are actually performed, even though they are unwanted by the employer, as in the setting of "bogus" type in the printing industry.[18]

On the face of it this situation may call for further relief. But what relief? If a statute is written to forbid a union to demand work "unnecessary" to an employer, who is to judge what is necessary? Is the employer to have unfettered say, regardless of the employees' in-

14. 61 Stat. 158 (1947), as amended, 29 U. S. C. Section 187 (Supp. III, 1962).

15. 61 Stat. 149 (1947), 29 U.S.C. Section 160(k) (1958); *NLRB* v. *IBEW Local 1212*, 364 U.S. 573 (1961).

16. See Sovern, *op.cit.*, pp. 958-959; Cox, *op.cit.*, pp. 263-265; Levitan, *op.cit.*, p. 112. Senator McClellan's antitrust proposal, S. 287, 88th Cong., 1st Sess., would make "hot cargo" agreements in the transportation industry violations of the Sherman Act, even though they are already outlawed by the amended NLRA.

17. 61 Stat. 142 (1947), 29 U.S.C. Section 158 (b)(6) (1958).

18. *American Newspaper Publishers Assn.* v. *NLRB*, 345 U.S. 100 (1953).

terest in health and safety? And even if the employer is enabled to eliminate half his jobs, what is to be done when the remaining employees then ask for double their previous wages? Are the employees bilking their employer, or merely demanding their fair share of the increased productivity of the enterprise? The only way to answer these questions would seem to be by an unprecedented interjection of some governmental agency into the process of determining the substantive terms of union contracts. The practical objections to this undermining of collective barganing as we know it have led impartial observers to shy away from advocating any further effort to regulate featherbedding through legislation.[19]

Furthermore, featherbedding is only a symptom, not the disease. The root problem is the displacement of workers' skills by advancing technology, and the threatened consignment of more employees to the growing ranks of the unemployed. In the end society always gets the new techniques, usually with the unions' "willing acceptance."[20] In the meantime there would seem small economic loss and much humane gain in leaving unions free to negotiate, within the relatively narrow limits allowed them by competitive pressures, on such measures as layoff schedules, severance pay, retraining allowances, and similar methods for cushioning the blow on the employees affected.

Industry-wide Bargaining. A common proposal is to outlaw practices often lumped together under the term "industry-wide bargaining."[21] This is actually a mis-

19. See Chapter 13 above, by Northrup and Bloom; Cox, *op. cit.*, pp. 274-275; Gregory, *op. cit.*, pp. 529-530; Levitan, *op. cit.*, p. 116.
20. Sumner H. Slichter, James J. Healy, and E. Robert Livernash, *The Impact of Collective Bargaining on Management* (Washington, 1960), pp. 348-349, 371.
21. See, e.g., H.R. 333, 88th Cong., 1st Sess., introduced by Representative Martin of Nebraska.

leading phrase because it is used to cover quite different types of activities. One type can more accurately be labeled "area-wide" or "market-wide" bargaining. In the construction industry, for example, it is customary for all or most of the contractors in a city or similar geographical area to join together in an association and to bargain jointly with the union representing the employees of a particular craft. The keynote of this kind of bargaining is voluntariness on the part of the employers. Employers do not have to join these associations or engage in joint bargaining, and the National Labor Relations Board stands ready to enforce their right to refrain. Contractors combine because it is in their best economic interest.[22] By securing uniform union contracts they eliminate wage differentials as a source of price competition among themselves. At the same time they assure themselves of a supply of labor at a known rate prior to the time when they must estimate costs in preparing bids on a job. This kind of "industry-wide" bargaining concededly serves so valuable a function in volatile industries like construction that it seldom comes under serious attack.

More often the object of criticism is a situation best described as "industry-wide unionization." This refers to the fact that in certain industries, such as steel, automobiles, rubber, clothing, and coal-mining, a single large international union has organized practically all the employees of the major producers. The unions in several of these industries bargain separately rather than jointly with employers, but there tends to be a pattern in the settlements. The opponents of industry-wide unionization would in effect confine a union to representing the employees of a single employer, and would minimize the role of the international union.

22. See Chapter 13 above, by Northrup and Bloom; Cox, *op.cit.*, p. 275ff.

This is the kind of proposal which smacks of armchair reasoning, not analysis of the real world. Theoretically, it might be supposed that a union "monopolizing" the employees of all the employers in an industry could withhold employee services until the employers succumbed to whatever terms the union demanded. This of course overlooks the fact that the "commodity" withheld is not inanimate, but a highly perishable product having limited means for surviving without current earnings. Apart from that, the effects of industry-wide unionization in actual practice do not bear out the apprehensions of *a priori* speculation.

Two widely varying classes of industries have been the subject of most single-union organization. One class, embracing steel, automobiles, and rubber, is oligopolistic, with little classical competition in basic prices. Scholars have found no evidence that the presence of a single union produces a markedly different pattern of wage determinations and price levels from that in other oligopolistic industries, like meat-packing, where rival unions exist.[23] We shall return for a closer look at the impact of unionization on wage levels when we deal with the statistical material in the second part of our study.

On the other hand, another class of industry characteristically organized by one union is at the opposite end of the spectrum, and is intensely competitive. The garment industry is representative of this type. Here numerous commentators have applauded the stabilizing effect of a strong union policing the industry to prevent cutthroat competition based on wage-slashing,

23. See Cox, *op. cit.*, p. 278; Richard A. Lester, "Reflections on the 'Labor Monopoly' Issue," *Journal of Political Economy*, vol. 55 (November, 1947), p. 529; cf. Sam Peltzman, "The Relative Importance of Unionization and Productivity in Increasing Wages," *Labor Law Journal*, vol. 12 (August, 1961), p. 725.

which would be injurious to employers and employees alike.[24]

Symptomatic of the unrealistic attitude of the foes of industry-wide bargaining is their obsession with that bogeyman, the international union. Somehow they feel that individual employees would all be reasonable men if it weren't for the union, and that even local unions wouldn't be so bad if it weren't for the international. This is really just another manifestation of parochial prejudice against bigness. Seasoned observers of the labor scene have consistently noted that in a labor dispute where feeling runs high, it is almost invariably the more mature, experienced officials of the international union who can be counted on to exercise a moderate, restraining influence on the local union officers and members.[25] For this and other reasons the whole notion of breaking up large unions is dismissed by knowledgeable critics.[26]

Price-Fixing and Market Controls. There is one area of union conduct which some well-informed, sober thinkers consider may be suitable for the application of antitrust concepts. Broadly speaking it may be summed up in the phrase Justice Stone popularized in *Apex Hosiery,* namely, restraints on "commercial competition." More precisely, it consists of union activity aimed at preventing competition in the marketing of goods and services through restraints on the kind or

24. See, e.g., Chapter 13 above, by Northrup and Bloom; Richard Lester and Edward A. Robie, *Wages Under National and Regional Collective Bargaining* (Princeton, 1946), pp. 93-95; Levitan, *op.cit.,* p. 115; Malcolm Cohen, "Unions and the Antitrust Strawman," *Labor Law Journal,* vol. 14 (February, 1963), pp. 211-212.

25. Lester, "Reflections. . . ," *op. cit.,* p. 533; Carroll R. Daugherty and John B. Parrish, *The Labor Problems of American Society* (Boston, 1952), p. 307; Cox, *op.cit.,* p. 279.

26. See Chapter 13 above, by Northrup and Bloom; Gregory, *op.cit.,* p. 527; Levitan, *op.cit.,* p. 115.

quantity which may be used or sold, the prices at which they may be offered, and the firms which may have access to the market. In the past there has been some sentiment supporting Justice Stone's broadly worded test,[27] but serious students now tend to regard it as too vague and indefinite for practical use.[28] Attention has therefore shifted to the possible proscription of specific union practices having as their object price-fixing and market controls.

This approach has been suggested by the Attorney General's National Committee to Study the Antitrust Laws, by former Professor Cox of Harvard Law School, by Virginia's Professor Gregory, and by a study group of labor specialists headed by Clark Kerr of California.[29] But several comments are in order. First of all, not one of these experts affirmatively recommended that regulation of organized labor's activities should be effected by amendment of the antitrust laws as such. Professor Gregory and Clark Kerr's panel took the tack that the regulation should be accomplished through changes in existing laws governing labor-management relations. Laws developed to deal with business behavior simply do not provide the right framework for dealing with union behavior. Furthermore, Professor Cox cautioned that because of the

27. The House of Delegates of the American Bar Association once voted in favor of a return to the *Apex* test. *American Bar Association Reporter*, vol. 77 (1952), p. 479.

28. "Restraining commercial competition" is not a term of art. It could easily be construed as covering all secondary boycotts. See Chapter 13, above, by Northrup and Bloom; Cox, *op.cit.*, p. 263.

29. *Report of the Attorney General's National Committee to Study the Antitrust Laws*, *loc.cit.*, discussed in Russell A. Smith, "Antitrust and Labor," *Michigan Law Review*, vol. 53 (June, 1955), p. 1119; Cox, *op. cit.*, pp. 272ff.; Gregory, *op. cit.*, p. 527; Independent Study Group, *The Public Interest in National Labor Policy* (Committee for Economic Development, 1961), pp. 138-139.

grave danger of interference with free collective bargaining, any reduction of labor's immunity from antitrust policies should be considered only "if the theoretical abuses have practical importance," and he emphasized that "there is no reliable information on the extent or economic importance of union efforts to shelter employers from competition in the product market."[30] The "practical importance" of any "theoretical abuses" still remains to be demonstrated. Indeed, mounting evidence indicates that it is nil.

One reason is that the tightening up of the secondary boycott and hot cargo provisions of the National Labor Relations Act, as previously discussed, has effectively eliminated some of the principal weapons which unions would have to rely on in any effort to enforce controls over the product market. Another reason flows from the practical implications of the *Allen-Bradley* exception to the general doctrine of union immunity from the antitrust laws.

Unions are subject to the antitrust laws, according to *Allen-Bradley,* if they join a combination of nonlabor groups to restrain trade. How would a union in a competitive industry go about arranging to fix prices or otherwise institute market controls? Obviously by getting employer agreement, and hardly by getting the agreement of only a single employer. So parallel restrictive agreements with numerous employers are ordinarily required. Now we have said earlier that we do not think such parallel arrangements with individual employers necessarily constitute an antitrust violation. But it is hard to deny that employer knowledge that all the other employers in the market are signing identical restrictive agreements with a union may be strong evidence of an illegal combination among the employers, adherence to which would constitute a violation by the union as well.

30. Cox, *op.cit.,* pp. 272, 280.

When there is added the factor that joint bargaining through employer associations is the rule in most industries in which unions have been accused of market-rigging, one can see how little room is actually left even today for union immunity in situations where the so-called "theoretical abuses" might otherwise occur. Professor Sovern of Columbia Law School, in disputing the need for further antitrust regulation of organized labor, underscored this particular point when he said: "Indeed, no reported decision since *Allen-Bradley* has upheld a clear sheltered market arrangement on the ground that the union brought the scheme off by itself and without employer connivance."[31] The practical case for added antitrust prohibitions thus collapses.

Still and all, some persons' sense of symmetry will be disturbed by the notion that a particular arrangement will violate the antitrust laws if effectuated by two or more employers acting in combination, but not necessarily if the selfsame arrangement is effectuated at the instigation of a labor organization. To this we have two answers.

The first is highly pragmatic. Sorting out the licit from the illicit among union activities has long proved a formidable task for the courts, and the results have not been happy ones. At least if a court can concentrate first on determining whether a restrictive agreement is union-inspired rather than employer-inspired, this gives it something more solid on which to fasten its evidentiary apparatus. In this sense the conclusion that a particular arrangement has resulted from union importuning of employers, rather than from an employ-

31. Sovern, *op.cit.*, p. 962. See also Cox, *op.cit.*, p. 271. Examples of the cases are *U.S.* v. *Employing Plasterers Assn.*, 347 U.S. 186 (1954); *U.S.* v. *Employing Lathers Assn.*, 347 U.S. 198 (1954); *IBEW Local 175* v. *U.S.*, 219 F. 2d 431 (6th Cir. 1955), *cert. den.* 349 U.S. 917 (1955); *Westlab, Inc.* v. *Freedomland, Inc.*, 198 F. Supp. 701 (S.D. N.Y., 1961) (no employer association involved).

er combination in which a union has joined, provides a sort of "badge of authenticity" that the object of the arrangement is to improve employees' working conditions rather than to restrain trade. Surely Justice Black had something like this is mind when he said in *Allen-Bradley:*

> "The difficulty of drawing legislation primarily aimed at trusts and monopolies so that it could also be applied to labor organizations without impairing the collective bargaining and related rights of those organizations has been emphasized both by congressional and judicial attempts to draw lines between permissible and prohibited union activities. There is, however, one line which we can draw with assurance that we follow the congressional purpose. . . . A business monopoly is no less such because a union participates, and such participation is a violation of the Act."[32]

32. *Allen-Bradley Co.* v. *IBEW Local 3,* 325 U.S. 797, 811 (1945). Where joint bargaining is carried on between a union and an employer association, the element of employer combination may automatically be supplied. In such circumstances the courts would still face the vexing problem of sifting out agreements lawfully concerned with the employees' working conditions from agreements unlawfully concerned with restricting competition among the employers. For an illustration of a judicial assay, see *Jewel Tea Co.* v. limitation on hours for sale of fresh meat), *rev'd.,* 331 F. 2d 547 (7th Cir. 1964), *cert. filed* July 2, 1964, U.S. Sup. Ct. No. 240, Oct. Term, 1964. See also Sovern, *op. cit.,* pp. 961-962, fn. 40, and cases cited.

In *Pennington* v. *United Mine Workers,* 325 F. 2d (6th Cir. 1963), *cert. granted* May 18, 1964, U.S. Sup. Ct. No. 48, Oct. Term, 1964 a court took the extreme position that a jury could infer a conspiracy on the part of a union and the major coal producers to eliminate smaller and weaker companies from such evidence as the union's insistence that all employers meet the same standards of employee compensation. Possibly this holding is of limited applicability, turning on the peculiar history and economics of the coal industry. But if upheld and extended broadly, the decision could have a shattering impact on activities at the very core of the labor movement. Union antitrust violations might be found, not on the basis of agreements dealing with prices or other elements of the product market, but on the basis of agreements, dealing with that most central of union concerns — wages.

Our second answer raises larger questions. Throughout this book has run an undercurrent of discontent with the whole mechanism of antitrust as it currently operates. Donald Dewey, for example, wound up suggesting that the traditional economic case for antitrust was no longer persuasive, and that the major virtue of antitrust was its preservation of consumer choice and its dispersal of decision-making.[33] American labor probably shares an instinctive attachment for, but no vested interest in, the antitrust concept as applied to business. If antitrust cannot withstand analysis in the light of present day knowledge, adjustments may be in order. In view of the political realities, however, legislative adjustments may not readily be forthcoming. This being so, existing exemptions, such as those for labor organizations, provide us all with at least a certain measure of relief in a less than ideal situation. As long as this particular exemption is beneficial rather than harmful to society, therefore, it should not be eliminated merely to satisfy a vague yearning on the part of business that labor be made to share the same bed of misery. This naturally invites a closer inquiry into the role of organized labor in our society, and its actual impact on the American economy. Before accepting that invitation, let us pause briefly to see just where we have arrived.

We set out to demonstrate that a consensus has been reached among objective experts that the antitrust laws are not the proper instrument for dealing with supposed abuses of economic power by organized labor. We have shown that only in the area of union-imposed

33. See Chapter 4 above, by Donald J. Dewey. Certainly if the justification for antitrust is reduced to the preservation of consumer choice this reinforces the view that antitrust tools are unsuited for the labor market. Consumer choice has meaning when it comes to buying a Chevrolet or a Studebaker, but not when it comes to hiring one fully qualified building tradesman or another.

market controls does the concept of restraint of trade have significant appeal to serious students. Even there the remedy ordinarily proposed is not amendment of the antitrust laws. The current trend, of which Messrs. Northrup and Bloom seem to be the latest exponents,[34] is to suggest amendments to existing labor laws. Yet, as we have indicated, the whole notion that unions can impose effective controls over the product market, as such, without facing antitrust sanctions now appears to be a theoretical possibility having no practical importance. Especially when the subject is something as sticky as labor legislation, prudence dictates that if no action is necessary as a practical matter, no action should be taken.

The Role and Effect of Organized Labor in the American Economy

Even scholars as careful as Professor Northrup, Mr. Bloom and Professor Gregory are sometimes carried away in their contemplation of union economic "power."[35] A look at the actual structure, function, and effect of labor organizations in this country will readily refute any suggestion that union power must be curbed lest it inflict grave injury upon the economy.

Structure and Function of Unions. Organized labor in the United States is an aggregation of diverse institutions, structures, and collective bargaining systems—far different from the monolith that antilabor propagandists attempt to paint. To obtain an adequate view of trade unionism in America, we must attempt to place organized labor in proper perspective.

34. See Chapter 13, above, by Northrup and Bloom.
35. *Ibid.;* Gregory, *op. cit.,* pp. 228, 526-527.

A View from Labor

According to the Department of Labor,[36] there were, in 1960, 14 million members of AFL-CIO affiliated unions within the United States, and 2.9 million members of nonaffiliated organizations. Reported union membership represented 23.3 percent of the total labor force and 32.1 percent of the number of employees in nonfarm establishments, or an estimated 35 percent to 40 percent of all persons eligible for union membership. In some types of economic activities, such as railroading, contract construction, and transportation equipment, union membership represents approximately 75 percent or more of total employment. In others, union membership represents smaller, and in some instances infinitesimal, percentages of the total number of employees in the industry.

There are 131 national and international unions affiliated with the AFL-CIO, and in addition about 50 unaffiliated organizations. The AFL-CIO itself is a voluntary association of independent affiliates. Each AFL-CIO affiliated national or international union is an autonomous institution, with its own rules and regulations, its own structure, and its own collective bargaining policies and practices.

Unlike the organized labor structures of some other countries, such as Sweden, the labor federation in the United States has only very limited authority and power. The locus of power in organized labor in the United States resides mainly in the diverse national and inter-

36. Figures in this section are drawn from *Directory of National and International Labor Unions in the United States, 1961*, Department of Labor Bulletin No. 1320, Bureau of Labor Statistics (Washington, 1962), esp. pp. 46-47 (1962). Over the past decade union growth has not been keeping pace with the growth of the labor force. Indeed, proportionate union membership is now less than the 23.9 percent of the work force where it stood in 1947, the year the Taft-Hartley Act was passed.

national unions and, to some extent, in the even more diverse local unions.

In 1960 there were 71,210 local unions in the United States, about 57,000 in AFL-CIO affiliated national and international unions. These local organizations are semi-autonomous bodies, with their own rules, regulations, and structures. Traditionally, the local union has been the foundation on which organized labor in this country is based. Despite the tendency in the postwar period for the locus of authority to shift from the local union to the national or international organization – a tendency which has been fostered by economic changes, as well as by the adoption of the Taft-Hartley and Landrum-Griffin Acts – the local unions remain the base of American organized labor. In this regard, too, trade unionism in the United States differs significantly from the much more centralized organized labor movements of Western Europe and most other parts of the world.

The diversity of trade union institutions and structures is a reflection, in large part, of the diversity of collective bargaining policies and practices. In contrast with the undustry-wide type of bargaining that prevails in many other countries, there is very little genuine industry-wise bargaining in this country. The men's outer garment industry and the Pacific Northwest pulp and paper industry are among the few exceptions to the general pattern. All told, the Labor Department estimates that there were approximately 150,000 separate collective bargaining agreements between unions and employers in 1960.

Typically, the collective bargaining relationship in the United States is between a local union, assisted by its national or international union, and a single firm or plant, or between a local union and a group of employers within a local labor market, or between several locals and their national or international union, on the one hand, and a multi-plant firm, on the other hand.

The diversity of collective bargaining policies and practices is in turn a mirror of the diversity of industrial structures in the nation. In each case, the union obviously has developed after the establishment of the industry and it has adapted its structure and collective bargaining methods to the facts of life within the particular economic environment in which it functions. In addition to industrial and regional differences, variables in the conditioning forces include diverse traditions of union evolution that range from 100 years of development, in the case of some crafts, to a mere three decades, in the case of some of the unions in mass production industries.

The old unions of skilled craftsmen in the building and printing trades follow bargaining patterns that are in contrast to the unions in the mass production industries. The construction industry operates essentially in local markets. Employment is usually seasonal and the employment relationship between a worker and a particular employer is frequently casual. Labor is mobile within the market and tends to be based on craft skills. A large number of firms, including contractors and subcontractors, exist in the market. Products of the industry are usually sold in the same local market in which they are produced.

Collective bargaining relations in the building and construction industry, as a result, are typically between local unions and local employers' associations. In the same local market, each particular trade is usually covered by a separate agreement with the corresponding employers' association and there may be as many as 20 or more collective bargaining agreements in the market's industry; there also may be a market-wide agreement between the local council of building trades unions and the local employers' association covering general industrial relations for all crafts.

In the mass production industries, such as basic steel and automobiles, collective bargaining takes a form that is considerably different from the general pattern of the building and construction industry. These mass production industries are generally oligopolistic and are dominated by giant multi-plant firms that produce in various parts of the country and sell in the national market. The dominant companies employ tens of thousands of wage and salary earners. Business investment in plant and equipment is great in these industries and the total number of firms is relatively small. Price leadership by the dominant firm or firms is usual and administered prices predominate. The presence of competition arises mainly from other industries — as in the competition between aluminum and steel for construction purposes — and from quality, style, and trade-in value, as in the auto industry.

The unions in the mass production industry generally emphasize standard wage movements throughout the industry, in contrast to the emphasis on local market standard wage scales in the building and construction industry. The typical bargaining in the basic steel and auto industries is between the international union and its locals, on the one hand, and one of the dominant companies on the other hand. This wage movement becomes the standard that the union seeks to apply to the other companies in the industry.

In the steel industry, an oligopoly with an undifferentiated product, the union has tended to follow the policy of bargaining simultaneously with all the major companies in the industry. A settlement, however, is usually made first with only one of them, the dominant United States Steel Corporation. That settlement then sets the pattern for agreements with the other companies, with the possibility of some slight variation in terms. This procedure in the steel industry follows the traditional pattern of wage and price setting in the industry, with U.S. Steel in the leadership position. The tendency toward rather uniform wage and price movements in the steel industry goes back to the early years of this century, long before the birth of the union, when U.S. Steel was created and the present structure of the industry was established.[37]

In the auto industry, an oligopoly with a differentiated product, the union bargains with one company at a time. When settlement is reached with the "leader," the attempt to conclude similar agreements with the other companies in the industry begins. Some variations above and below the first settlement occur in the agreements with the other companies.

Actually, the diversity in collective bargaining policies and practices is even more pronounced than what is briefly indicated above. On the union side, the details of the collective bargaining agreement in a multiplant company—such details as work rules and wage incentives—are usually negotiated by the local unions and plant managements, as supplements to the company-wide master agreements. Moreover, on the union side, the agreements are administered on a day-to-day basis by the local unions, with great variations in procedures and practices, even within a single international union.

Through collective bargaining, unions seek to influence the economic environment in which they operate, and union pressures constitute a prodding force on management to maintain efficient operations. Union

37. George Seltzer, "Pattern Bargaining and the United Steelworkers," *Journal of Political Economy*, vol. 59 (April, 1951) George W. Taylor, "Introduction," in Robert Tilove, *Collective Bargaining in the Steel Industry* (Philadelphia, 1948).

practices in collective bargaining, however, are not based on any rigid mechanical formulas. The union seeks to obtain the best possible agreement, within the confines of its economic environment, and to maintain and expand employment opportunities in the labor market or industry in which it functions.

Within the organized labor movement in the United States there is thus no uniform collective bargaining pattern or even a closely similar institutional structure. Variations in economic climate, institutional development, and personal leadership have given rise to considerable differences in collective bargaining approaches. An almost infinite variety of strategies, tactics, and attitudes can be found in the collective bargaining behavior of American unions, with their multitude of decision-making centers in international unions, regional bodies, joint boards, and local unions.

What does all this teach us about the exercise of union power? American unions do not dominate the institutional structures or employment practices of American industry; they adjust to them. American unions are not so organized as to enable them to exert massive and coordinated pressure on management; their authority is widely diffused and their interests are atomized and sometimes conflicting. It only remains to consider that most critical of all issues: the impact of unionism on wage and price levels in the economy.

The Effect of Unions on Wages. Most management officials and classical economists emphasize wages as a cost of production, with rather clear-cut implications for employment and prices. Wage-setting, as the pricing of labor, is considered in this view to be comparable to the pricing of commodities. To the trade unionist, ideas about wage determination proceed from somewhat different considerations.

It is generally agreed that labor differs from commodities. Labor cannot be separated from the personality of the human worker. The employment of labor implies a continuing relationship, while the purchase of a commodity is a much simpler transaction that takes place at a given time.

Wages are determined unilaterally by the employer in an unorganized firm and by collective bargaining where union organization is recognized. In the commodity markets, the seller commonly determines the price. In most cases, the seller in the commodity market has greater influence upon the price of a product through his influence on production than employees have upon wages, even when collective bargaining prevails. Under collective bargaining the setting of wages and employment conditions is not made unilaterally by the union, but jointly by the union and employer.

From their earliest days, trade unions have maintained that labor is not a commodity and that wage determination should be viewed differently from the pricing of commodities. The Clayton Act of 1914 – with its declaration that "the labor of a human being is not a commodity or article of commerce"[38] – has had some influence on the legality of union conduct, but it seems to have had little influence on public thinking about collective bargaining and wage determination. To the trade unionist, wages are not only a cost item for the employer, but essential sustenance for employees and their families. Ethical and social considerations, as well as economic considerations, properly belong in the area of wage determination.

The results of collective bargaining in recent years fail to reveal the presence or the exercise of monopoly power by organized labor. Indeed, they indicate rather clearly the relative weakness of trade unions during a

38. 38 Stat. 731, Section 6 (1914), 15 U.S.C. Section 17 (1958).

period of rising unemployment and spreading part-time work schedules. In most markets, the slow growth of the economy, along with a generally unfriendly political climate that has accompanied rapid and radical technological change, has substantially increased the economic power of employers, relative to the strength of trade unions.

Let us examine the relationship of real hourly earnings of employee groups to the rise of output per manhour in the total private economy. When real hourly earnings are in parallel movement with productivity, the distribution among the factors of production in the economy remains stable. But when real hourly earnings lag behind the nation's output per manhour, it means that the employee group is receiving a smaller share of the economy's gains in productive efficiency.

An examination of the trends of recent years indicates that most groups of workers, represented by unions, have been receiving a smaller share of the benefits of rising productivity, while a larger share has been going to other income recipients. This shift in income distribution among the factors of production is the reverse of what would be expected from the existence and exercise of trade union monopoly power. Indeed, the recent trend is generally reminiscent of the 1920's, when trade unions were admittedly weak, although the magnitude of the gap between the movements of real hourly earnings and the nation's productivity is smaller than it was in those years, when this economic imbalance was setting the stage for the Great Depression.

The years 1955 and 1956 were the last which saw substantial and widespread wage and fringe benefit gains by most unions. Since then, the pace of improvements in wages and fringe benefits has tended to slow down. In the period from 1956 to 1962, output per manhour in the total private economy increased 17.8 percent, using one set of data, and 20.8 percent, using another statistical concept, according to the most recent studies of the Department of Labor.[39] As compared with this 17.8 percent to 20.8 percent rise in productivity in the total private economy between 1956 and 1962, real hourly compensation, including fringe benefits, of all employees in the private economy increased only an estimated 15.2 percent.[40]

Since hourly compensation of all employees in the private economy includes the salaries and fringe benefits of executives and supervisory employees, as well as all others, the small lag behind productivity indicates a shift in income distribution away from employees in private enterprises to other income recipients – such as the cash flow to business and the salaries of government employees. The small lag of aggregate real compensation per employee manhour in the private economy behind the nation's productivity also indicates the probability that there are more substantial lags for many specific groups of employees. Examination of available data reveals that this reasonable probability proves to be the case. The real hourly compensation of many groups of employees has lagged significantly – sometimes substantially – behind advances in the private economy's productivity, indicating important shifts in income distribution, with smaller shares going to certain groups of employees and increased shares to other income recipients.

In the six years between 1956 and 1962, for example, real hourly earnings of production and maintenance

39. See *Economic Report of the President* (January, 1963), p. 209.

40. Estimate by the AFL-CIO for 1962, based on Department of Labor estimates for 1956-1961 and on data of the Department of Commerce and Department of Labor for 1962.

workers in manufacturing industries increased only 10.1 percent.[41] Since real hourly earnings include payroll fringes, such as paid holidays and shift premiums, but exclude nonpayroll fringes, such as pension plans, the 10.1 percent figure would have to be increased somewhat to arrive at a full measure of the advance in real hourly compensation. The addition of two or three percentage points would bring the advance in real hourly compensation of factory production and maintenance workers up to an estimated 12 or 13 percent between 1956 and 1962. In contrast, as we have noted, output per manhour of the total private economy rose 17.8 or 20.8 percent in that period of time. The share of factory production and maintenance workers in the gains of the economy's productivity has thus markedly declined since 1956.

Similar trends prevail for nonsupervisory employees in wholesale trade, where real hourly earnings increased only 10.2 percent between 1956 and 1962, and in retail trade, where the real hourly earnings of nonsupervisory employees increased 12.2 percent. Bituminous coal miners, whose real hourly earnings rose only 3.3 percent in the six years years from 1956 to 1962, have received but a small share of the benefits of the economy's rising productive efficiency.

Real hourly earnings of nonsupervisory employees on Class I railroads went up 14.4 percent in 1956-1962, indicating the probability of a small decline in their share of the economy's gains in output per manhour of work. For construction workers, whose real hourly earnings increased 15 percent in those six years, the trend was roughly similar to that of railroad employees. The income share in the nation's advancing productivity of nonsupervisory employees in electric utilities, whose real hourly earnings rose 17.1 percent in 1956-1962,

41. This and the following data have been derived from Department of Labor sources.

probably remained relatively stable, as did the income share of nonsupervisory employees in telephone companies, whose real hourly earnings increased 19.3 percent.

These figures reveal a general trend of lagging real hourly earnings behind the nation's productivity advances for many key groups of employees in the economy – union-organized employees, as well as nonunion. If the arguments of the labor monopoly advocates were valid, however, there would be no such lag for unionized sectors of the economy. Indeed, the labor monopoly advocates would have us believe that highly unionized groups of employees would actually increase their income shares by pushing up their real hourly earnings, over long periods of time, beyond the advances in the nation's productivity. Such has clearly not been the case in 1956-1962. Moreover, since the pioneering studies of Paul Douglas it has become a much-debated point among labor economists whether the spread of unionism has brought about any substantial long-term shift in the distribution of income in favor of the wage-earning class.[42]

42. See, e.g., Paul H. Douglas, *Real Wages in the United States, 1890-1926* (Boston, 1930); Clark Kerr, "Labor's Income Share and the Labor Movement," in George W. Taylor and Frank C. Pierson, eds. *New Concepts in Wage Determination* (New York, 1957), pp. 260, 280-287; Lloyd G. Reynolds, *Labor Economics and Labor Relations,* 3d ed. (New York, 1959), pp. 467-475; Peltzman, *op.cit.,* p. 725. It has also been noted that "even within the framework of price theory and assuming unions to be monopolies, it is not necessarily true that under unionism wages are higher but employment is less." Frederick Meyers, "Price Theory and Union Monopoly," *Industrial and Labor Relations Review,* vol. 12 (April, 1959), p. 445. Unemployment, in the view of organized labor, is a problem for the whole of society to wrestle with. Consequently, unlike Donald Dewey, unions see no inconsistency in supporting minimum wage legislation or seeking modest wage increases through collective bargaining, even in periods of unemployment. Labor should not have to bear the full brunt of curing depressed employment ills by the process of spreading available work at substantard wage levels. But cf. Chapter 4, above, by Donald J. Dewey.

The power of organized labor in the process of collective bargaining and wage determination has been grossly distorted and exaggerated by the opponents of unionism. The facts reveal that economic and political forces, in recent years, have tended to reduce the relative power of unions, while the power of employers has generally increased. The actual imbalance in the American economy is not one of excessive union power, but, in most cases, of relative weakness.

The Effect of Unions on Prices. It is often claimed that evidence of the monopoly power of trade unions can be found in the inflationary impact of wage increases that emanate from the supposedly powerful union monopolies. The focus of this charge has been on industrial wages and prices, where wage increases, it is claimed, have created serious price pressures. Such assertions are rarely backed by any set of supporting evidence. When facts are presented, they are usually irrelevant or simply distortions.

Facts, however, are available on industrial costs and prices. They do not reveal any general wage pressures on the industrial price level in recent years. They fail to indicate the operation of wide-spread union monopolies that exercise overwhelming power in the economy's industrial sector.

The price pressures of the early postwar years, 1947-1953, are generally interpreted to have been war-related—pressures resulting from shortages and demand-pull connected with the aftermath of World War II and the outbreak of the Korean War. The current charges about union wage pressures usually center on the period since 1953. Actually, the government's Wholesale Price Index for industrial goods rose about 12 percent between 1953 and 1962, a slow increase at an average annual rate of approximately 1.3 percent. Almost all of this price rise, however, occurred before the end of 1958. The level of industrial prices has been relatively stable in the more than four years since the final months of 1958.[43]

The wages of factory production and maintenance workers are, of course, only one of the many business costs in industry. There are other costs, such as salaries, depreciation of plants and machines, raw materials, advertising, and various overhead costs, in addition to profits. Total direct employment costs of the average company in the United States – wages, salaries, and fringe benefits of all employees – are about 25 percent of the sales dollar, according to Standard and Poor's financial reporting service. In examining the validity of the charge about union wage pressures, it is the wages and fringe benefits of factory production and maintenance workers, alone, that are relevant, since it is this group that is generally represented by trade unions in collective bargaining with industrial employers. In the average industrial company, the wages and fringe benefits of factory production and maintenance workers, alone, are about two-thirds of total employment costs. Factory workers' wages and fringe benefits in the average industrial firm, therefore, are only about 15 percent to 20 percent of the sales price – certainly not the only cost or the major cost, as is sometimes implied.

Furthermore, the wage cost of an item is not the hourly wages and fringe benefits of factory workers. Industrial companies do not produce hours. They produce and sell goods. As far as wage costs go, the issue is: How much wages and fringe benefits are there in a particular item? The relevant issue is the wage and fringe benefit cost per unit, which is related not only to the hourly earnings and fringe benefits of production and maintenance workers, but also to output

43. Based on data from the Department of Labor.

per manhour of work and to the rate of capacity utilization. The relevant question in examining actual wage pressures is: Have the unit costs of factory workers risen substantially enough, in recent years, to provide significant upward pressures on the level of industrial prices?

The record shows that the unit wage cost of factory production and maintenance workers, including payroll fringe benefits, in 1962, was actually 6.6 percent less than in 1953. With the addition of non-payroll fringe benefits, such as pension plans, the estimated unit cost of factory production and maintenance workers dropped about 3 to 4 percent in the nine years between 1953 and 1962.[44] The unit costs of factory workers, who are largely represented by unions, declined from 1953 to 1955. They rose from the summer of 1955 to the early months of 1958. Since early 1958, unit wage costs have dropped substantially and almost continuously, and by 1962 they had reached the level we just mentioned, approximately 3 to 4 percent below 1953.

The hourly wages and fringe benefits of factory workers increased, of course, in the years between 1953 and 1962. But output per manhour rose more rapidly than the increases in wages and fringe benefits. The result was a decline in wage costs per unit of output. This decline of wage costs, between 1953 and 1962, cannot rationally be claimed as the cause of the 12 percent rise in the level of industrial prices in that period of time. The facts on the unit costs of factory workers are the reverse of what the labor monopoly advocates claim. The actual causes of the rise in industrial prices have to be sought elsewhere.

There is no room here for a detailed study of the

44. Based on data from the Federal Reserve Board, the Department of Labor, and the Department of Commerce.

structure of industrial costs and prices since 1953. But examination of the facts discloses that the actual causes of the pressures on the level of industrial prices since 1953 have been mainly the sharp increases in salary and other overhead costs and depreciation costs per unit, as well as the pricing policies of several key oligopolistic industries in a period when industrial output has increased only slowly and substantial amounts of industrial capacity have been idle.

In any case the actual record of unit wage costs in American industry in recent years does not reveal evidence of any formidable power being wielded by trade unions. As we have shown, the unit costs of factory production and maintenance workers have actually declined, which is hardly the result one would expect from union monopolies in the industrial sector of the economy. This decline of unit wage costs, accompanied by a lag of real hourly compensation of factory production and maintenance workers behind the nation's rising productivity, demonstrates relative weakness rather than the existence and exercise of any overwhelming power on the part of labor unions generally in American industry.

The Value of Unions in Society. At this point we may have succeeded so well in deflating the notion of unions' overwhelming power that we may also have succeeded in raising some questions about their ability to be of much use to their members. This is not the place to embark on an extended survey of the value of labor organizations in our society. But a few words may be appropriate, especially since they will suggest still another reason why antitrust regulation is incompatible with the nature of trade unions.

To say that unions may have done less than is sometimes thought about redistributing national income is certainly not to say that they have been without significant economic effect. By pressing for pensions, supplemental unemployment benefits, and similar nonwage forms of compensation, for example, they have obviously played a major and beneficial role in determining the *shape* of the labor slice of the economic pie. Furthermore, union pressures have tended to bring about a greater uniformity in wage levels from firm to firm, from region to region, and from business cycle to business cycle. Richard Lester has thus observed that "the wage structure in American industry now is probably less 'distorted' than it was in all nonunion industry during the 1920's."[45] In addition, the hiking of rates in former low-wage areas has been cited as a frequent spur to increased labor productivity.[46]

The value of the labor movement, however, cannot be assessed solely in economic terms. It is a truism, but one which can easily be overlooked, that unions are not profit-making endeavors, and that they serve their members not only as economic instrumentalities, but also as political, social, and industrial conciliation institutions.[47] They give the laboring class a niche in the power structure of modern society; they assure the individual workingman protection against arbitrary action by management; they provide a quasi-judicial system for the orderly and peaceful disposition of grievances in the work place. In the exercise of these functions unions of course must wield a certain kind of power. But it is incongruous to try to regulate that kind of power under the antitrust laws. One might

45. Lester, "Reflections . . . ," *op.cit.*, p. 523.

46. Sumner H. Slichter, *The Challenge of Industrial Relations: Trade Unions, Management, and the Public Interest* (Ithaca, 1947), pp. 34, 69, 72-73.

47. For development of these points, and of their implications for proposed antitrust regulation, see Lester, "Reflections . . . ," *op.-cit.*, p. 517; Levitan, *op.cit.*, pp. 114-115. See also Albert Rees, *The Economics of Trade Unions* (Chicago, 1962).

just as well try to use the antitrust laws to regulate the power of the League of Women Voters, or the Civil Liberties Union, or the American Arbitration Association.

In any event we would all stand to lose if drastic restrictions were imposed on organized labor because, as Sar Levitan says, such restrictions would "be accompanied by sacrificing the positive contributions which unions have made to their members and society."[48] Unions are a natural development in a free society. They are the best means yet devised for bringing democracy into industrial life, and for giving the voice of the individual worker a chance to be heard. Labor organizations should be fostered, not fettered, and especially they should not be fettered by the application of laws wholly at odds with their nature and purposes.

Conclusion

We have talked too much about a subject which has probably come to bore most labor scholars. We should have liked to say more about antitrust policy as it applies to business in the 1960's. We should have liked to say a great deal—if it would not be out of place in a volume on Antitrust—about Professor Northrup's proposals for amending the labor relations laws to strip organized labor of many of its present protections. But we have skirted these areas in order to take advantage of that most rare of opportunities: the chance to signal the end of an intellectual debate. Among serious, knowledgeable thinkers, a consensus has been reached. Whatever may, or may not, be the place of antitrust in the field of business, it has little, if any, place in the field of labor. We have enough serious problems in the separate worlds of antitrust and labor without compounding our tasks by combining them.

48. Levitan, *op.cit.*, p. 115.

CHAPTER 17

The Impact of Antitrust Law on Corporate Management

BY JOHN J. CORSON

Introduction

Whatever one's views on the role of antitrust legislation in preserving competition and ensuring the continued vigor of a private-enterprise economy, one fact is clear: For the large company seeking to advance the interests of its stockholders, the antitrust statutes are most often a vexation—fettering at worst, frustrating at best. An account of their impact on top management, therefore, is very apt to sound like a catalogue of complaints. At least inferentially, it is likely to suggest a rather petulant critique of prevailing antitrust policy.

To offer such a critique is no part of the objective of this paper. It does not question the premise that the maintenance of free enterprise requires the enforcement of the Sherman Act, the Clayton Act, the Federal Trade Commission Act, and the Robinson-Patman Act; nor does it attempt to evaluate the legal or economic implications of antitrust law. This paper is concerned with the impact of antitrust and trade regulation statutes on the functioning of the corporate enterprise. It considers how these laws affect the corporation's market behavior, its internal functioning, and particularly the manner in which top management responds to the competitive challenges of the market place.

The questions with which this paper is concerned are two: First, what is the *practical* impact of antitrust law – the Sherman Act, the Clayton Act, the Federal Trade Commission Act, and the Robinson-Patman Act – *on corporate behavior*? Second, how can corporate management, within the limits imposed by antitrust policy, best act to preserve maximum competitive and innovative vigor in the enterprises for which they are responsible?

Dimensions of the Problems

Let us first examine two sets of quantitive data that suggest the overall dimensions of the problem. Table 1 shows that the aggregate number of antitrust suits filed has increased eightfold each year from 1945 to 1961. In addition, a large number of antitrust investigations initiated each year do not materialize as suits, though they often have an equal effect on corporate behavior. These investigations are not included in Table 1, but it is fair to assume that they have increased at least proportionately.

Table 2 shows that more than 34 percent of the companies on Fortune's list of the top 500 corporations, have been involved in some formal antitrust or trade regulation proceeding in the five years ended December 31, 1962, two-thirds of these on price-fixing charges. The proportion of large corporations feeling the impact of enforcement through informal investigations is, of course, larger. Indeed, it is probable that the influence of antitrust law enforcement and trade regulation influence the competitive *strategy* of every company which has won a dominant role in its industry.

Impact on Corporate Action

The full significance of antitrust in the corporate scheme of things, however, cannot be appreciated in quantitative terms alone. Far more revealing is an examination of its qualitative effects – in particular, of

TABLE 1

Antitrust Suits Commenced, 1945-1961

Fiscal Year	Total Govern-mental	Civil Govern-mental	Criminal Govern-mental	Total Private
1945	29	20	9	27
1946	33	18	15	68
1947	44	33	11	64
1948	37	19	18	78
1949	66	39	27	162
1950	76	42	34	157
1951	53	37	16	209
1952	32	20	12	261
1953	32	16	16	212
1954	31	21	10	163
1955	49	33	16	209
1956	54	30	24	227
1957	56	38	18	188
1958	55	33	22	270
1959	65	23	42	250
1960	87	60	27	228
1961	63	42	21	378
Totals	862	524	338	3,151

SOURCE: Compiled from Annual Reports of the Administrative Office of the United States Courts for the Fiscal Years ended June 30, by Richard A. Whiting for articles in the *Virginia Law Review,* 1961, 1962.

the ways in which it influences management behavior, and of the resulting problems of internal corporate functioning.

Antitrust law is designed to interfere with collusive agreements between competitors, with the growth of monopoly, and with the exercise of monopoly power in predatory competition. In the process of preventing such ends, does the enforcement of antitrust law have other effects on the behavior of corporate managements which may neither be as apparent or socially desirable? Do the enforcement and prospect of enforcement of the antitrust laws tend to stultify initiative and sap the competitive vigor of corporate managements? As a basis for considering these and related questions, let us examine some of the key areas where the enforcement of antitrust laws may infringe on normal corporate competitive strategy.

TABLE 2

Number and Proportion of Largest U.S. Corporations Involved in Antitrust and Trade Regulation Suits

Charged with:	Total	As Percent of Fortune 500*
Acquisitions	45	9
Illegal brokerage payments	2	.04
Exclusive dealing	15	3
Price fixing	108	22
Price discrimination	36	7
Clayton Act damage suits	14	3
Licensing — patents	19	4
Market allocation	16	3

NOTES:

*Of the companies included in the Fortune 500:

24 percent have been involved in antitrust cases in the Federal court system over the last five years.

An additional 10 percent have been involved in complaints and hearings before the FTC relating to antitrust matters.

A total of 34 percent have been involved in some sort of antitrust difficulties that can be tabulated.

This does not include investigations, both corporate or industry-wide, conducted by FTC or Congressional committees that have not reached the formal complaint stage. These investigations by the FTC appear to be numerous. Nor does this count include companies whose operations are limited because of previous consent decrees or court orders.

John J. Corson

Limiting Management's Market Knowledge. It was Adam Smith, the patron saint of free-enterprise economists, who wrote almost two centuries ago that: "People of the same trade seldom meet together, even for merriment and diversion, but the conversations ends in a conspiracy against the public, or in some contrivance to raise prices." For prices – Adam Smith might have added – constitute knowledge of the market that businessmen seek to guide their production and marketing actions. The electrical equipment cases and a succession of others[1] reemphasized the necessity of ensuring that salesmen do not discuss prices with competitors. The consequence of these cases varies markedly from industry to industry as prevailing practices of publicizing price information varies. But two consequences for corporate managements warrant consideration.

Walter Hoadley, Jr., Vice President and Treasurer of the Armstrong Cork Company, has claimed that, as a consequence of the drying-up of this conventional source of price information, price levels in several industries are depressed abnormally. Purchasers have been able to force prices down by claiming that they have received offers of lower prices and that the corporation must meet such lower prices or lose the business. Fearful that even to inquire what prices a competitor may have quoted is to risk violation of the law, the seller meets a price never actually quoted.

Whether Mr. Hoadley's observation be generally valid, the limitation of price information available to marketing executives does affect their ability to compete. Sellers and buyers, the economists reason, are best able to compete when they are informed of the nature of the market, including prices prevailing. Such

1. Eg., current actions involve aluminum conductor cable, asbestos pipe, and other materials.

knowledge of the market best enables individual sellers (and buyers) to respond to market conditions and to make informed decisions as to prices. A principal source of such market intelligence has been the salesman. A part of his skill is that of being informed as to prevailing prices that he may act responsively, or may petition his superiors for the approval of his offering lower prices. The constraints that grow out of the convictions in the electrical equipment case markedly limit the salesman's utility as a source of price intelligence, despite the fact that the mere exchange of price information is not in itself illegal.[2]

An illustration of such constraints (of minor importance by itself) is seen in the abandonment by a number of companies of the practice of having salesmen submit "Lost-Business Reports." Typically, salesmen have been required to submit such reports explaining why they failed to make a sale, what competitor may have offered a lower price, and to cite evidence of that lower price. Corporate officials are increasingly loath to require such written statements from salesmen fearing that they would induce consultation with competitors that might be interpreted as involving action to influence price competition rather than merely the exchange of price information.

Limiting Opportunities for Growth. Aggressiveness and self-seeking, including aggressive expansionism, are usually regarded as virtues in the free enterprise system. But consider the impact of requirements arising out of antitrust law enforcement on the executives of a corporation already grown large in its industry, or a corporation that seeks growth through the introduction of new products.

2. John J. Galgay, "Antitrust Considerations in the Exchange of Price Information Among Competitors," an address before the Society of Business Advisory Professions, March 14, 1963.

Consider first, for example, that impact of the consent decree requiring International Business Machines Corporation[3] to limit its sales of tabulating cards to not more than one-half of the total of all such sales. Consider the belief of this company not only in the superior quality of the cards it offers, but in the desirability that the users of IBM machines use cards fashioned particularly and skillfully for these machines and then consider how the sales manager simultaneously instructs his salesmen to sell these cards vigorously —but not to sell too many.

Consider next the impact of a consent decree[4] upon the experience of the Owens-Corning Fiberglas Corporation in striving to grow through the introduction of a succession of new products. The decree required that Owens-Corning Fiberglass license manufacturers, under appropriate royalty agreements, to produce under certain patents it holds for a period of years, and to distribute products derived from this basic material. The central problem posed for corporate officials is that of selecting licensees while conforming with the constraints established by the decree. To make and distribute new products from this distinctive and relatively novel basic material requires that the licensee be capable of such efficient manufacture and imaginative and aggressive distribution as will ensure the dislodging of long-established products from the market. For example, Fiberglass screening requires carefully controlled manufacture and effective promotion if it is to compete with conventional galvanized and aluminum window screening.

3. A similar problem confronts other companies in varying forms, e.g., the General Motors Corporation (diesel engines) and the Aluminim Company of America.

4. *U.S.* v. *Owens-Corning Fiberglas Corporation et al.*, Civil Action No. 5778 (W.D., N.D. Ohio, 1949), filed June 23, 1949.

But the "selection" of licensees suggests discrimination to any processor who is not selected—as many corporations (in addition to those operating under consent decrees) have learned. OCF, hence, has found it difficult to comply with the law and to select licensees who by OCF's standards will do a satisfactory job of processing and a job of distribution equal to the task of establishing this product in the market. In one Midwestern city a distributor protested to the U.S. Attorney that OCF was discriminating against him by refusing to sell one of Fiberglas' new products. Upon the advice of counsel, the corporation decided to sell raw material to this distributor, despite the protests of the sales staff that this distributor would put an inferior product on the market, that he was incapable of adequately advertising and promoting the sale of the product, and that he had proved his financial irresponsibility in previous dealings with the company. The distributor subseqoently failed.[5]

Limiting Pricing Action. In the ideal competitive world, corporate officials use the pricing of the products they offer for sale as a major means of competing. But the application of the antitrust laws in three types of cases raises questions as to the extent to which, and under what circumstances, corporate executives can use price as a competitive tool. Let me cite three examples:

United Shoe Machinery Corporation: Take, for example, the incidence of Judge Wyzanki's decision in the *United Shoe Machinery Corporation* case.[6] The Court adjudged the defendant to have violated the

5. An interesting analysis of this problem is provided by Vernon A. Mund, "The Right to Buy — and Its Denial to Small Business," a staff report prepared for the Select Committee on Small Business, U.S. Senate, 86th Cong., 1st Sess. (July 9, 1959).

6. *U.S.* v. *United Shoe Machinery Corporation*, 110 F. Supp. 295, 303 (D. Mass., 1953) *aff'd. per cur.* 347 U.S. 521 (1954).

Clayton Act in that it had not offered shoe machines for *sale*, as well as for *lease*. The Court directed United Shoe to offer the machines for sale at a price that would be as attractive to the average buyer as the rental at which the machines are offered for lease. In short, the defendant was ordered to make its machines available to shoe manufacturers at sales prices and rentals that are "economically equivalent."

I do not suggest that the Court's decision was either poor law or poor economics. Indeed, it is difficult to see what alternative the Court had, once it concluded that United Shoe should be required to offer machines for sale as well as for lease. I cite this case to illustrate another kind of problem, posed by this decision, for the executives of a number of companies. The concept of "economic equivalency" of sales prices and rentals was the subject of extended debate and negotiation between the defendant and shoe manufacturers, and the monitorship of the Court when the first sales prices were set. Yet the concept is and has always been complex and unclear. Indeed, compliance with the Court's order has, in some measure, taken the pricing function from corporate executives and placed it in the hands of the corporation's lawyers and a consulting economist. The decision, while restricted in its application to United Shoe Machinery, obviously has repercussions on the behavior of other large companies which have sale-lease alternatives.

U.S. Rubber Company: A similar experience followed the judgment of the Court in 1954 in the *U.S. Rubber Company* case.[7] Here the Court directed the defendant to price tires sold under its own brand name at prices to yield profits no greater than the profits derived from the sale of tires manufactured for oth-

7. *U.S.* v. *United States Rubber Company, Consolidated Rubber Manufacturers, Ltd., and Dunlop Rubber Co., Ltd.*, Civil Action No. 50-564 (S.D. N.Y., 1954).

er distributors to be sold under their private brand names.[8] The net consequence of this decision is that every time U.S. Rubber, by staff action, lowers costs, increases prices, or otherwise raises profits, it must pass back the additional profit to its dealers in rebates. Corporate executives, hence, face the problem of stimulating the zeal of the staff when their company is substantially denied the incentive of increased profits, and are limited to their use of price as a tool in building the sales of their own brand of tires.

The Sun Oil - Jacksonville Case:[9] This case provides still another illustration of the limit to which corporate executives can use pricing as a competitive tool. In this case the Supreme Court decided that Sun's sales management had violated the Robinson-Patman Act in granting lower prices to a dealer who was confronted by markedly lower retail gasoline prices offered by a nonbrand dealer located immediately across the street. The Court ruled, in effect, that Sun either should have lowered its wholesale price for gasoline to all dealers in the Jacksonville area, or should have made no reduction in prices. In other words, the Court rejected Sun's plea that its executives were meeting competition by the reduction of prices and that it was thus justified in the action it took. Presuming this decision is good law and is good economics, it still poses for corporate executives a difficult problem of dealer relations and limits their ability to use price as a competitive tool.

Each of these cases illustrates problems that confront

8. A similar constraint on a corporation's freedom to utilize pricing as a competitive tool is the consequence of a consent decree in *U.S.* v. *Libby-Owens-Ford Glass Company* (N.D. Ohio, 1948).

9. *F.T.C.* v. *Sun Oil Co.*, 371 U.S. 505 (1963). For discussion of issues in this proceeding, see Howard R. Lurie, "Trade Regulation – Robinson-Patman Act – Price Discrimination in the Marketing of Gasoline," *Michigan Law Review*, vol. 61 (March, 1963), pp. 962-969.

other corporate officials than those who manage the three corporations that have been cited. Most corporate officials must find ways of acting promptly as sales opportunities arise and the use of price as a competitive tool is a customary response; for an increasing minority, compliance with such constraints as have been pictured limits their freedom to use price as a tool with which to compete.

Limiting Corporate Acquisitions. Another tool with which corporate executives compete in the modern business world is acquisition.[10] Yet for an increasing number of firms this means of waging competition is either explicitly forbidden or is denied by the fear that the next acquisition will be the one that attracts the action of the Department of Justice.

Recently, for example, a division of the Continental Can Company was subject to two divestiture suits, is a party in industry investigations—each covering a number of companies—before three antitrust grand juries, and is involved by virtue of similar industry-wide actions in several Federal Trade Commission investigations. Most of these actions involve only its operations in the paper industry, as distinguished from the metal, glass, plastic, or other operations. In the face of this number of actions, Company policy requires that any possible future acquisition be studied most carefully for its antitrust defects and, in certain fields related directly to some of the challenged areas, acquisitions are not being considered at all.

Problems for Management. Put yourself in the position of the chief executive of any large corporation whose obligation it is to see that his staff complies

10. For an elaboration of the view stated in this paragraph, see Jesse W. Markham, "Antitrust Trends and New Constraints," *Harvard Business Review* (May-June, 1963), p. 85, and, by the same author, Chapter 8, above.

with the antitrust laws *and* is continuingly agressive in expanding the business. What does the executive do to educate his staff as to what actions are prohibited by law or by consent decrees under which the company operates, *and* to maintain the staff's aggressiveness and initiative?

The Problem of Staff Education: The complexity of antitrust legislation, with its numerous and often subtle implications for a wide range of operating situations, requires a continuous, well-organized, and thoroughgoing effort to alert every responsible individual in the organization to the pitfalls that surround him in the performance of his assigned functions. To appreciate the scope of the organizational response required to avoid conflict with antitrust and trade regulation statutes, consider the report submitted to the Westinghouse Electric Corporation in 1962 by a Board of Advice. This report by four distinguished scholars[11] retained by the Corporation pictures the magnitude and complexity of the problems faced by the Corporation in ensuring compliance with antitrust law, and evaluates the adequacy of the measures Westinghouse had adopted to meet these problems.

These scholars noted the dimensions of the task faced by Westinghouse. Westinghouse manufactures approximately 8,000 products, many of which are constantly changing as a result of research and innovation. It sells these products in many different markets, which vary markedly in their competitive character. Approximately 1,650 of its more than 100,000 employ-

11. Dean Erwin N. Griswold of Harvard Law School; Dean Eugene V. Rostow of Yale Law School; Professor S. Chesterfield Oppenheim of Michigan Law School; and Dr. A.D.H. Kaplan of the Brookings Institution. The report was published by Westinghouse in August 1962. See also Richard A. Whiting, "Antitrust and the Corporate Executive, I and II," *Virgina Law Review*, vol. 47 (1961 p. 929, and vol. 48 (1962), p. 1.

ees located at numerous plants and sales offices throughout the United States bear pricing and marketing responsibility.

To acquaint all employees with the Corporation's policy of antitrust compliance, Westinghouse employs, in the Board's words, "policy directives, letters, memoranda, and a continuing series of personal conferences on all levels" as well as a comprehensive educational program. In addition, it has established as a part of its Law Department an Antitrust Section to review regularly the activities of all "management persons who have pricing and marketing responsibility."

All this, in the Board's opinion, still did not fully meet the demands of the problem. It recommended that, in addition, Westinghouse retain a competent economic staff to plan, organize, and carry out an even more sustained program of continuing economic and legal education for its managerial and sales personnel.[12]

The Problem of Controlling the Sales Staff: Such educational efforts, of course, meet only part of the problem.[13] At least equal in importance, where a company's sales force is concerned, is the question of control. No salesman, corporate executives like to say, ever lost a sale through any fault of his own; the trouble was that he was obliged to quote a price higher than that offered by the competitor who got the order. The danger that salesmen may be tempted to overstep the bounds of safety and propriety in attempting to as-

12. The resultant program is described by Thomas M. Kerr, Jr. in "The Westinghouse Experience: One Companpy Reviews Its Antitrust Program," *The Climate of Antitrust,* Transcript of Special Conference, National Industrial Conference Board (New York, March 7, 1963).

13. Their utility is confirmed, however, by a comment from the bench in one Federal district court regarding the corporation's efforts to educate its staff in evaluating an alleged violation.

certain and meet competitors' prices is often acute. A Milwaukee lawyer, invited to talk to a client's sales force on the meaning of the Robinson-Patman Act, was given his assignment in these words:

> "I want you to scare the socks off these salesmen. I'm fed up with the way they've been cutting our prices and then justifying themselves by saying they had to meet prices set by competing salesman – whom they never did or never should have talked to."

Improving necessary controls on salesmen, however, may have unwanted effects on the direction of their efforts. One sales manager reports:

> "Our house counsel, our local law firms, and our New York counsel repeatedly question our salesmen about particular transactions and warn them about illegal or compromising actions. The salesmen, hence, have become preoccupied with questions of legality rather than of account strategy."

This executive's comment opens up a much larger question: How can management simultaneously stimulate sales initiative and curb the salesmen's customary freedom to maneuver? And, beyond the sales organization proper, how can it prevent timidity and inertia from replacing aggressiveness as the dominant temper of corporate innovators, marketers, and policymakers?

Positive Management Response

To meet these challenges, a positive management response is clearly required – a response which is at once informed, responsible, prudent, and intelligently aggressive. Few chief executives, even with legal training, can possess an intimate, sophisticated knowledge of the ramifications of antitrust law and enforcement policy. Yet many corporate executives find antitrust problems an integral and, for some, substantial[14] part of their day-to-day job. To fulfill their responsibilities in this area, hence, an increasing number of executives in major companies must be aware of the location and stringency of the antitrust limits which the corporation is obliged to function. Without fairly precise knowledge of this kind, management risks overstepping legal boundaries, or unnecessarily restricting its competitive strategies in conformance with imagined prohibitions.

It would, of course, be simpler for top management to leave the whole problem in the lap of the legal department where it has traditionally rested. As long as the impact of antitrust enforcement was limited to the prospect that a pricing action or merger might sometime be challenged, antitrust problems could be regarded as the exclusive responsibility of the lawyer. As the frequency of action has increased, this has become less and less possible. Compliance with the law has come to affect day-by-day pricing, marketing, advertising, and product decisions — decisions for which, in large organizations, responsibility is often decentralized. Such decisions require understanding possessed by few lawyers. More important, they entail risks. They cannot be left to lawyers because they involve the very warp and woof of management.

This is not to say that line management can do without counsel. It is the sales manager who knows best what reactions must be expected from customers, competitors, and salesmen if prices are raised or lowered. It is the comptroller who knows best what costs are involved. It is the economist who can best assemble

14. A cursory inquiry of several executives suggests that for this very limited sample approximately 15 to 20 percent of their time is consumed in the handling of antitrust problems.

the facts on which judgments are based (by lawyers and judges as well as executives) as to the dimensions of the relevant market[15] and whether a particular merger will substantially lessen competition. But it is only the chief executive who can properly compound the several viewpoints, assess the risk involved, and commit the corporation to the right course of action.

The wise executive will consult his counsel frequently and fully. He will see to it that his lawyers keep staff members throughout the organization alert to the legal implications of various actions they may take. But if he lets the lawyers make the decisions directly or indirectly, he puts the dynamics of the enterprise into partially informed hands guided by minds that must be expected to be little venturesome or negative.[16] Worse, he abdicates his responsibility.

The advice the top executive can expect from his legal staff cannot, as it happens, be completely authoritative. The meaning of the antitrust laws is continually evolving. New decisions give new meaning to the words of the statutes.[17] Amendments extend their applications. New economic developments (e.g., the use of joint ventures) pose new problems of application. In consequence, counsel cannot advise management

15. The size and nature of the market is usually a central question in antitrust legislation. The determination of the relevant market (and its size and nature) is surrounded by an increasing volume of legal precedent but is still an economic decision to be resolved on the basis of facts which the economist is best equipped to assemble and analyze. See *Report of the Attorney General's National Committee to Study the Antitrust Laws* (Washington, 1955), Chapter VII.

16. For other points of view, see H. Thomas Austern, "Corporate Counsel Communication: Is Anybody Listening?" *The Business Lawyer* (July, 1962), pp. 869-875; and Jos. R. Creighton, "Corporate Counsel and Antitrust," *American Bar Association Journal* (July, 1962), pp. 654-655.

17. This is certainly true of *Brown Shoe Co.* v. *U.S.*, 370 U.S. 294 (1962), and *F.T.C.* v. *Sun Oil Co.*, 371 U.S. 505 (1963).

in these areas with as much assurance as they may interpret many other statutes.

Frequently, corporate executives find themselves confronted with trying choices in weighing a contemplated action that might bring on a legal challenge. Are the potential rewards worth the risk of expensive litigation? The lawyers cannot say. They can only, sometimes with little confidence, provide an estimate of the risk. The decision is, and should be, management's. Illustrations of these alternative courses are legion. The United Shoe Machinery Corporation, bound by the comprehensive and complex decision of Judge Wyzanski in 1955 (and subsequent treble damage suits) was forced into a posture of risk avoidance. The U.S. Rubber Company seems to have been forced into a similar position by the 1954 consent order that governs its action.

An aggressive and enterprising company president of my acquaintance well exemplifies an opposite response. Though he gives weight to the advice of legal counsel, he persists in aggressively taking calculated risks whenever antitrust problems arise. A similar attitude is evident in the cement industry, where major producers appear to have decided that, since economic forces favor merger, they will drive ahead and risk the possible consequence of divestiture actions.

Even where no specific legal bonds have been imposed on the company, the temptation is often present to avoid provoking a legal challenge by keeping corporate strategy well within the known limits of the law. Yielding to this temptation may seem in the interests of the corporation in the short run, but over the long term its cost to the company may be great. The plain fact is that, short of abandoning basic and legitimate corporate aspirations, management cannot avoid risk in this area of changing law and shifting patterns of enforcement. To attempt it is to submit to a tyranny far worse than any imposed by existing law—the tyranny of self-wrought shackles.

Conclusion

The problem I have tried to depict will not be met by any amendment of the antitrust laws or modification of enforcement practices. It is essentially a management problem. For the executive of the large corporation, coping with its manifold aspects—education of staff, choice of distributors, pricing, acquisitions, even public relations—requires new understanding, new skills, perhaps new and additional organization. But above all, it requires courage.

For the corporation itself, the rewards of a positive, considered, and aggressive policy toward compliance with the antitrust laws are frequently substantial. For the economy as a whole, such aggressiveness on the part of thousands of individual companies is a powerful stimulating force. It is, in fact, an important guarantee of the continued strength and vitality of our competitive private-enterprise system.

Index

Aaron, B., 346
Adams, W., 85, 279, 280, 284
Adelman, M. A., 34, 38
administered prices, 16, 38-44, 89-116, 373. *See also* collusion, conscious parallelism, conspiracy, oligopoly, price-fixing, quasi-agreement
agreements, 377-83. *See also* collusion, conspiracy, price-fixing
agriculture, 48-49, 71, 304-5
Agricultural Adjustment Act, 304
Agricultural Marketing Agreement Act, 304
Alhadeff, C. P., 235
Alhadeff, D. A., 228, 229, 230, 235, 239
antitrust, origins of, 3-16; and common law, 72-73; and national goals, 62-87; and politics, 5-6, 15; number of suits, 428-29. *See also* specific laws and topics
Arnold, T., 312
Austern, H. T., 441
Austin, J., 297

Bain, J. S., 110, 118, 201
Bank Holding Company Act of 1956, 239, 305
Bank Merger Act of 1960, 239, 282
Barber, R. J., 285
basing point system, 40
Beard, C., 4, 5, 9
Beard, M., 5
Bergson, A., 67
Bernstein, M. H., 278
bilateral monopoly, 54
Black, H., Justice, 24, 406
Block, H., 300
Bloch, M., 48
Bock, B., 170
Bonini, C. P., 118
Bowman, M. J., 103
Bowman, W. S., 118
boycotts, 18, 19, 313, 314, 323, 324, 397-98, 404
Brennan, S. W., Judge, 186
Brennan, W. J., Justice, 23, 386
Burke, E., 390

Capper Volstead Act, 304
Cassidy, R., Jr., 201, 210
Celler, E., Representative, 124, 387
Celler-Kefauver Act, *see* mergers
Chamberlin, E. H., 134, 146
Chambers, D., 233
Charnes, A., 233
Childe, C. E., 268
Civil Aeronautics Act, 309
Civil Aeronautics Board, 280, 281, 303
civil rights, 370-72
Clark, J. B., 78, 80
Clark, J. M., 92, 135-43, 147
Clayton Act, *see* price discrimination, exclusive dealing, labor unions, mergers, Robinson-Patman Act, tying agreements
Coase, R., 55
Cohen, M., 402
Cole, D. L., 348
Collins, N. R., 192, 193
collusion, 39-40, 189, 428; in gasoline retailing, 210-16; in regulated industries, 279. *See also* administered prices, conspiracy, price-fixing, quasi-agreements
commercial bank mergers, 225-43, 282

Conant, M., 112
concentration, 161, 191-93; of inland water carriers, 254; and mergers, 166; in petroleum refining, 215; of reresearch and development, 286-88, 297-98; in trucking, 254. *See also* market shares
conjectural interdependence, 90-91, 107, 109, 110, 112, 113, 114, 116
conscious parallelism, 16, 89-116, 373. *See also* administered prices, conspiracy, price-fixing, quasi-agreements
consignment selling, 219
conspiracy, 20, 189; between employers and employees, 322-25, 332-34, 393-94, 402-6. *See also* collusion, conscious parallelism, price-fixing
Controller of the Currency, 282
Cook, P. L., 101
Coolidge, C., President, 391
Cooperative Marketing Act, 304
Cox, A., 325, 335, 393, 394, 401, 404, 405
Creighton, J. R., 441
cross-elasticity of demand, 133, 151-52, 154

Daugherty, C. R., 402
Day, R. E., 178
de Chazeau, M. G., 208
"deep pocket" effect, 181, 184-85, 188
defense industries, 284-97
Defense Production Act, 310-11
De Gaulle, C., 48, 49
Denison, E., 244
deregulation, 298-99
differential competition, 135-37
Dispres, L. M., 347
dissolution, 150, 169-72
divestiture, 150, 169-72, 184-85, 436
divorcement, 150
Dixon, P. R., Chairman, 371
Doerfer, Commissioner, 281
dominant firms, 124-28. *See also,* concentration, market shares, monopolization
Douglas, P. H., Senator, 298, 419
Douglas, W. O., Justice, 23, 220, 381
Duncan, D. J., 189
Dunlop, J. T., 348

economies of scale, 32, 55, 118, 155, 190, 229-30, 299
Edwards, C. D., 156, 180
effective competition, 140-43, 147
Eisenhower Administration, 44, 58
Eisenhower, D. D., President, 284
Elman, Commissioner, 28
entry, 137, 155, 238-39; by large corporations, 188; in regulated industries, 279-84, 299
European Common Market, 44-49, *See also* Treaty of Rome
excess capacity in steel, 43; in gasoline retailing, 206-10
exclusive buying contracts, 220
exclusive dealing, 126, 219-20, 358, 380-83, 384
exemptions from antitrust laws, 15, 50-61, 261, 273-311; and regulation, 277-84; and administrative preemption, 284-97. *See also* fair trade, labor unions, McGuire Act, Miller-Tydings Act, Reed-Bulwinkle Act, Robinson-Patman Act

fair trade, 15, 24, 52, 212. *See also* McGuire Act, Miller-Tydings Act, resale price maintenance
featherbedding, 336-40, 397-99

Index

Federal Communications Act, 338
Federal Communications Commission, 281, 303
Federal Maritime Board, 281
Federal Power Commission, 303
Federal Trade Commission Act, 14, 301, 426, 427
Fellner, W., 90, 153
Fetter, F. A., 73
Fleming, R. W., 347
Ford, H., II, 274
foreign transactions, 355-67. *See also* Webb-Pomerene Export Trade Association Act
Frank, Judge, 278
Frankfurter, F., Justice, 276, 322, 393
Friedman, M., 64
Friendly, H. J., 249, 250
Frisch, R., 90

Galbraith, J. K., 74, 83, 89, 183, 274, 376
Galgay, J. J., 431
Gellhorn, W., 283
Goldberg, A., Justice, 25, 30
Golden, S. D., 347
Gomberg, W., 347-48
good faith defence, *see* price discrimination
Gramley, L. E., 229
Gray, H. M., 85, 284, 290
Greene, N., 393
Gregory, C. O., 317, 345, 347, 393, 396, 402, 403, 408
Griswold, E. N., 437
Groeber, H. v.d., 46
Grove, M. A., 225
Grunfeld, Y., 45
Guzzo, C. J., 213

Hand, L., Judge, 86, 362
Harberger, A. C., 77
Hart, P., 118
Healy, J., 337, 338, 399
Heflebower, R. B., 39, 94
Hendry, J. B., 280
Hitler, A., 68
Hoadley, W., Jr., 431
Holmes, Justice, 31
Homestead Act of 1862, 4
Hoover, H., President, 315
Horvitz, P., 229
Houssiaux, J., 46
Hughes, Chief Justice, 8
Hurter, A. P., 260

Ignatius, P. R., 296
industry-wide bargaining, 328-33, 399-404
injunctions, *see* labor unions, Norris-La Guardia Act
interchangeability, 132-33, 139
interfirm organization, 103, 116
interindustry competition, 138, 139, 227. *See also* intermodal competition
intermodal competition, in transportation, 248-50, 263-69
international trade, 355-67. *See also* European Common Market, Webb-Pomerene Export Trade Association Act
intramodal competition, in transportation, 259-61

Jaffe, L. L., 277
Johnson, D. G., 101
Jones, W. L., 201, 210
jurisdictional disputes, 397-99

Kahn, A. E., 208
Kaplan, A. D. H., 437
Kaysen, C., 90, 96, 121, 123, 143-46
Kefauver, E., Senator, 21, 260
Kennedy Administration, 246
Kennedy, J. F., President, 245
Kerr, C., 348, 419
Kerr, T. M., Jr., 438
Keynes, J. M., 69
Khrushchev, N. S., 42
kinked demand curve, 111
labor unions, 50-51, 53-54, 312-54, 391-425; and anti-

trust laws, 340-45, 391-425; and prices, 420-23; and social values, 423-25; and wage rates, 414-20. *See also* boycott, conspiracy, National Labor Relations Act, Norris-La Guardia Act, Taft-Hartley Act

Landis, J. B., 277
Landrum-Griffin Act, 410
Langdon, J., 261
Lanzillotti, R. F., 285, 291
Lea Act of 1946, 338
Leeman, W., 78
Leontief, W. W., 289
Lester, R. A., 401, 402, 424
Levitan, S., 396, 402, 425
Levitt, T., 203
Liebling, H. I., 228
Livernash, E. R., 337, 338, 399
Livingston, S. M., 203
Locklin, D. P., 247
Loesser, F., 389
Loevinger, L., 266, 374
Long, R. B., Senator, 285
Lurie, H. R., 435

MacIntyre, E., Commissioner, 30, 371
Mack, R. P., 103
Maloney Act, 308
Mansfield, E., 118, 119
market shares, in merger cases, 36-37, 160-62, 171-74, 176-77, 183, 186-87; and monopolizing, 121-25, 149, 151
Markham, J. W., 34, 436
Marshall, A., 98, 297
Martin, Representative, 399
Mason, E. S., 96
McAllister, H. E., 202
McCarran-Walter Act, 307
McClellan, J., Senator, 295, 398
McGee, J. S., 78
McGuire Act, 380. *See also* fair trade, resale price maintenance
McKee, T. H., 6
Means, G. C., 92
Meiklejohn, H. E., 103
Meltzer, B. D., 349
mergers, 26, 32-38, 73, 81-82, 110, 126, 156, 157-63, 164-88, 384-87, 436-37; number of cases, 167-74; of commercial banks, 178, 225-43, 282; conglomerate, 156, 179-182; horizontal, 171-79; and market shares, 171-74, 176-77, 184, 186-87; of railroads, 59-60; in regulated industries, 279-84; and small business, 181-82, 185, 187-88, 191-94; vertical, 26, 157, 161, 179
Meyer, J. R., 246, 254, 256, 264
Meyers, F., 419
Meyner, R., Governor, 209
Miller-Tydings Act, 301, 380. *See also* fair trade, resale price maintenance
Minow, N. N., 279
Monopolies and Restrictive Practices Act, 45
monopolizing, 117-23, 129-63, 383-84; in foreign commerce, 361-62; by labor unions, 395-97, 401, 406
Moore, F. T., 294
Moss, R. R., 228
Motor Carrier Act of 1935, 57, 253
Mund, V. A., 433
Murcier, A., 46

National Labor Relations (Wagner) Act, 323, 343-44, 346, 404
Neale, A. D., 85, 94, 122
Nelson, J. C., 250, 253, 262
Nelson, R. L., 34, 169
Nicholls, W. H., 40
Norris-La Guardia Act, 303, 313, 315-20, 326, 345, 393, 394

oligopoly, 26, 83, 90, 110; and collective bargaining, 401, collective bargaining, 401, 412-13. *See also* administered prices, conscious parallelism, concentration, market shares
Oppenheim, S. C., 437
Oppenheimer, J. R., 368-69
Osborn, R. C., 118
"overbanking," 225, 226, 237, 239

Paige, D. C., 67
Parrish, J. B., 402
patents, 288-90
Patinkin, D., 81
Patman, W., Representative, 192
Peck, M. J., 74
Peckman, J., 244
Peltzman, S., 401, 419
Penrose, E., 231
per se rules, 17, 23-26, 39, 126-28, 162, 359
Petrillo, J. C., 338
Phillips, A., 74, 103-4
Pierson, F. C., 419
Plowman, E. G., 250
Prais, S., 118
Preston, L., 192, 193
price-cutting, 78-82
price discrimination, 9, 10, 26-31, 126, 387-88, 435-36; in gasoline, 216; geographic, 256-59, 269; in railroad rates, 56, 247-48, 269. *See also* Robinson-Patman Act
price-fixing, 15, 16, 18, 19, 50, 84; and labor unions, 335-36, 402-6. *See also* administered prices, collusion, conspiracy
price wars, gasoline, 200-221
procurement, Department of Defense, 285-97
Public Utility Holding Company Act, 123, 304
Quality Stabilization Act, 52. *See also* fair trade, resale price maintenance
quasi-agreement, 107, 112, 153, 154
quasi-integration, gasoline, 217-24

racketeering, 19
railroads, 5-6, 55-58, 59-61, 244-72
rate bureaus, 261. *See also* Reed-Bulwinkle Act
rate simplification, railroads, 271
reciprocity, 185-86
Reed, Justice, 132-33
Reed-Bulwinkle Act, 58, 309
Rees, A., 424
resale price maintenance, 52-53, 217, 219. *See also* fair trade, Quality Stabilization Act, Miller-Tydings Act, McGuire Act
research and development, 285-97
retailing, 196-200; of gasoline, 199-221
Reynolds, L. G., 419
Richardson, G. B., 92
Richberg, D. R., 327
right-to-work laws, 327-28
Rigley, R., Judge, 281, 282
Roberts, Justice,
Robertson, A. W., Senator, 240
Robie, E. A., 402
Robinson, J., 67
Robinson, S. D., 380
Robinson-Patman Act, 12-13, 17, 24, 26-31, 40, 75, 189, 301, 302, 387-88, 426, 427, 435. *See also* price discrimination
Roosevelt, F. D., President, 68, 319
Roosevelt, T. R., President, 7
Rostow, E. V., 437
Rottenberg, I., 34
Rowe, F. M., 29

Index

Ruggles, R., 75
rule of reason, 8, 9, 114, 224, 359-60, 363

Scharfman, J. L., 5
Schlotterbeck, W. A., 368
Schmookler, J., 74
Scholl, R. H., 207
Schumpeter, J. A., 65, 66, 74
Schwartz, B., 279, 282
Schwartz, L. B., 278
Schwartzman, D., 77
Seltzer, G., 413
Sherman Act, *see* administered prices, boycotts, collusion, conspiracy, labor unions, mergers, monopolizing, price-fixing
Sherman, J., Senator, 6
Shipping Act, 308
Shister, J., 347
Simon, H. S., 118
Simons, H., 63, 73
Slichter, S., 337, 338, 399, 424
small business, 11, 20, 36-37, 86, 118, 127-28, 189-224, 373; and mergers, 181-82, 185, 187-88, 191-94; and technological progress, 73-75
Smith, A., 76, 273, 430
Smith, C., 229
Smith, R. A., 403
Sovern, M. I., 393, 395, 396, 405
Steed, A. B., 216
steel prices, 41-44, 88-89, 113
Stenason, J., 246
Stigler, G. J., 74, 96-97, 99, 118, 231, 252
Stone, H., Justice, 396, 402
substitutability, 134, 136, 154, 227

Taft, P., 348
Taft-Hartley Act, 303, 326, 327, 338, 343, 346-50, 410
Taubman, J., 376
Taylor, G. W., 348, 413, 419
technological progress, 73-75
Texas Railroad Commission, 51
Tilove, R., 413
transportation, 244-72
Transportation Act of 1920, 57
Transportation Act of 1940, 57, 253
Transportation Message, April 5, 1962, 245-46
Treaty of Rome, 45, 123-24. *See also* European Common Market
Troxel, E., 260-61
Truman Administration, 44
Turner, D. F., 90, 96, 111, 121, 123, 143-46
tying agreements, 358

unemployment, 68-70, 71
unfair competition, 14, 77-81

vertical agreements, 379-83
vertical integration, 120. *See also* mergers

wages and prices, 41, 69-70
Wallich, H. C., 63-64
Warren, Chief Justice, 143, 158
Watkins, M., 140
Webb-Pomerene Export Trade Association Act, 307, 358
Weeks, S., 59
Weinfeld, Judge, 159
Wheeler-Lea Act of 1938, 13, 301
White, Chief Justice, 8
White, L. D., 74
Whiting, R. A., 428, 437
Wilcox, C., 90
Williams, E. W., Jr., 251
Wirtz, W. W., 352-53
Witte, E., 393
Wood, H. R., 95
Wright, W. W., 209
Wyzanski, Judge, 150, 383, 433

Yamey, B. S., 45

Zwick, C., 246

Table of Cases

Allen Bradley Company v. Local Union No. 3, I.B.E.W., 325 U.S. 797 (1945), 53, 303, 322, 324, 334, 346, 394, 395, 404, 406
American-Eastern Merger, C.A.B. Docket 13355 (1962), 179
American Newspaper Publishers Association v. N.L.R.B., 345 U.S. 100 (1953), 398
American Tobacco Company v. U.S., 328 U.S. 802 (1946), 100
Apex Hosiery Company v. Leader, 310 U.S. 469 (1940), 320, 324, 394, 396, 402
Appalachian Coals, Inc. v. U.S., 228 U.S. 344 (1933), 8, 364
Atlantic Refining Company, F.T.C. Docket 7471 (1963), 220

Brown Shoe Company v. U.S., 370 U.S. 294 (1962), 33, 35-37, 60, 83, 120, 158, 160-62, 172, 181-83, 194, 441

Chicago Board of Trade v. U.S., 246 U.S. 231 (1918), 25
Chicago R. I. & P. Ry. v. Commissioner, 47 F. 2d 990 (7th Cir. 1931), 21
Columbia River Packing Assn. v. Hinton, 315 U.S. 143 (1942), 53, 394
Consolidated Foods, Inc., F.T.C. Docket 7000 (1962), 119, 184-185
Continental Baking Company, F.T.C. Docket 7630 (1963), 30
Corn Products Company v. F.T.C., 324 U.S. 726 (1945), 10
County of Marin v. U.S., 356 U.S. 412 (1958), 57

Duplex Printing Company v. Deering, 254 U.S. 433 (1921), 314, 321

F.C.C. v. RCA Communications, Inc., 346 U.S. 86 (1953), 276
F.C.C. v. Schrieber, 201 F. Supp. 421 (D.C. Calif, 1962), 371
F.T.C v. A. E Staley Mfg. Company, 324 U.S. 746 (1945), 28
FT.C v. Borch, 363 U.S. 166 (1959), 372
F.T.C. v. Broch, 368 U.S. 360 (1962), 388
F.T.C. v. Morton Salt Company, 334 U.S. 37 (1948), 10
F.T.C. v. Cement Institute, 334 U.S. 839 (1948), 40
F.T.C. v. Sun Oil Company, 371 U.S. 505 (1963), 10, 25, 29, 30, 31, 435, 441
Foremost Dairies, Inc., F.T.C. Docket 6495 (1962), 174, 185
Forster Manufacturing Company, Inc., F.T.C. Docket 7207 (1963), 10

George Van Camp & Sons Company v. American Can Company, 278 U.S. 245 (1929), 10

Great Northern Ry. v. *Commissioner*, 40 F. 2d 372 (8th Cir. 1930), 21

Hawaiian Tuna Packers v. Longshoremen, 72 F. Supp. 562 (D.C. Hawaii, 1947), 395
Hunt v. Crumback, 325 U.S. 821 (1945), 323

International Boxing Club v. U.S., 358 U.S. 242 (1959), 122
I.B.E.W. Local 175 v. U.S., 319 F. 2d 431 (6th Cir. 1955), 405

Jewel Tea Company v. Meat Cutters Locals, 215 F. Supp. 839 (N.D. Ill., 1963), 406

Korber Hats, Inc. v. F.T.C., 311 F. 2d 358 (1962), 372, 388

Lockner v. New York, 198 U.S. 45 (1905), 31
Loewe v. Lawlor, 208 U.S. 274 (1908), 313, 321
Los Angeles Meat and Provision Drivers Union, Local 626, v. U.S., 371 U.S. 94 (1962), 53, 324, 394

Mead Corporation, CCH Trade Reg. Rep., Para. 16,241 (1963), 371
Mennan Company v. F.T.C., 228 Fed. 774 (2d Cir. 1929), 10
Mogul Steamship Company v. McGregor, Gow & Company, 21 Q.B.D. 544 (1888), 23 Q.B.D. 598 (1889), (1892) A.C. 25, 72

National Biscuit Company v. F.T.C., 229 Fed. 733 (2d Cir. 1924), 10
N.L.R.B. v. Dalton Brick & Tile Corporation, 301 F. 2d 886 (1962), 349
N.L.R.B. v. I.B.E.W Local 1212, 364 U.S. 573 (1961), 398
N.L.R.B. v. Star Publishing Company, 97 F. 2d 465 (1938), 323
Northern Pac. Ry. v. U.S., 356 U.S. 1 (1958), 24
Northern Securities Company v. U.S., 193 U.S. 197 (1903), 7, 56

Old Colony Bondholders v. New York, New Haven and Hartford R.R., 161 F. 2d (1947), 279

Pevely Dairy Company v. U.S., 178 F. 2d 363 (1949), 113, 115
Pennington v. United Mine Workers, 325 F. 2d 804 (6th Cir. 1963), 325, 332-33, 406

Reynolds Metals Company v. F.T.C., 309 F. 2d 223 (C.A.D.C., 1962), 184

Sandura Company, F.T.C. Docket 7042, Trade Reg. Rep., Para. 15,945 & 16,095, 382
Standard Oil Company v. F.T.C., 355 U.S. 396 (1958), 28

Standard Oil Company of New Jersey v. U.S., 221 U.S. 1 (1911), 8, 132
Sun Oil Company, F.T.C. Docket 6934 (1963), 220
Sunshine Biscuit, Inc. v. F.T.C., 306 F. 2d 48 (7th Cir. 1962), 10

Tri-Valley Packing Association, F.T.C. Docket 7496 (1959), 28

Union Leader Corporation v. Newspapers of New England, Inc., 284 F. 2d 582 (1st Cir. 1960), 121
United Brotherhood of Carpenters and Joiners v. U.S., 330 U.S. 395 (1947), 303
U.S. v. Aluminum Company of America, 148 F. 2d 416 (2d Cir. 1945), 86, 121, 362
U.S. v. Aluminum Company of America (N.D.N.Y., 1963), 186-87
U.S. v. American Federation of Musicians, 318 U.S. 741 (1943), 323
U.S. v. American Tobacco Company, 221 U.S. 106 (1911), 8
U.S. v. Bakersfield Association Plumbing Contractors, Inc., 1959 Trade Cases, Para. 69,266, 25
U.S. v. Bethlehem Steel Corporation, 168 F. Supp. 576 (1958), 159, 162-63, 172, 174, 175, 176-77, 194
U.S. v. Bostitch, Inc., 1958 Trade Cases, Para. 69,207 (D.R.I.), 382
U.S. v. Building and Construction Trade Council, 313 U.S. 539 (1941), 323
U.S. v. Columbia Steel Company, 334 U.S. 495 (1948), 120, 175, 177
U.S. v. Continental Illinois National Bank (D.C.N.D. Ill., 1961), 282
U.S. v. E. C. Knight Company, 156 U.S. 1 (1895), 7
U.S. v. E. I. duPont de Nemours & Company, 351 U.S. 377 (1956), 122, 131-47
U.S. v. E. I. duPont de Nemours & Company et al., 353 U.S. 586 (1957), 156-59, 386
U.S. v. Employing Plasterers Association, 347 U.S. 186 (1954), 405
U.S. v. General Electric et al. (E.D. Pa., 1961), 17, 18, 21, 41
U.S. v. Holophane Company, 119 F. Supp. 114 (S.D.Ohio,1954), 365
U.S. v. Hutcheson, 312 U.S. 219 (1941), 321, 324
U.S. v. Imperial Chemical Industries, Ltd., 100 F. Supp. 504 (S.D.N.Y., 1951), 363
U.S. v. Imperial Chemical Industries, Ltd., 105 F. Sup. 215 (S.D.N.Y., 1952), 365
U.S. v. International Hod Carrier's Union, 313 U.S. 539 (1941), 323
U.S. v. Joint-Traffic Association, 171 U.S. 505 (1898), 56

U.S. v. Libby-Owens-Ford Glass Company (N.D. Ohio, 1948), 435
U.S. v. Lowden, 308 U.S. 225 (1939), 57
U.S. v. McKesson & Robbins, Inc., 351 U.S. 305 (1956), 52
U.S. v. Morgan, 118 F. Supp. 621 (S.D.N.Y., 1953), 25
U.S. v. National Dairy Products Corporation, 372 U.S. 29 (1963), 17, 372
U.S. v. National Lead Company, 332 U.S. 319 (1947), 363
U.S. v. Owens-Corning Fiberglass Corporation (W.D.N.D. Ohio, 1949), 432-33
U.S. v. Philadelphia National Bank, 374 U.S. 321 (1963), 178, 239, 282, 375
U.S. v. Reading Company, 226 U.S. 224 (1912), 57
U.S. v. Socony-Vacuum Oil Company, 310 U.S. 150 (1940), 24
U.S. v. Southeastern Underwriters Association, 332 U.S. 533 (1944), 308
U.S. v. Standard Oil Company of California, 337 U.S. 293 (1949), 210
U.S. v. Terminal Railroad Association, 224 U.S. 383 (1912), 57
U.S. v. Timken Roller Bearing Company, 341 U.S. 593 (1951), 363
U.S. v. Trans-Missouri Freight Association, 166 U.S. 290 (1897), 56
U.S. v. Trenton Potteries Company, 273 U.S. 392 (1927), 24-25, 165
U.S. v. Union Pacific Railroad Company, 226 U.S. 61 (1912), 56
U.S. v. United Fruit Company (E.D.La., 1954) (consent decree, Feb. 4, 1958), 365
U.S. v. United Mine Workers, 330 U.S. 258 (1947), 320
U.S. v. United Shoe Machinery Corporation, 110 F. Supp. 295 (1953), 129-31, 383-84, 433-34
U.S. v. United States Rubber Company (S.D.N.Y., 1954) 434-35

Wanderer v. Kaplan, 1962 Trade Cases, Para. 70,535 (D.D.C), 371
Westlab, Inc. v. Freedomland, Inc., 198 F. Supp. 701 (S.D.N.Y., 1961), 405
White Motor Company v. U.S., 372 U.S. 253 (1963), 22, 25, 220, 224, 381
Willers, Inc.-Purchase (Portion)-Everson, 10 Fed. Carr. Cas. 222 (1953), 280

Lightning Source UK Ltd.
Milton Keynes UK
UKHW020019140522
403009UK00008B/996

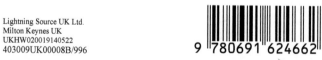

9 780691 624662